New Interpretations in
Naval History

U.S. GOVERNMENT OFFICIAL EDITION NOTICE

Use of ISBN Prefix

This is the Official U.S. Government edition of this publication and is herein identified to certify its authenticity. ISBN 978-1-935352-36-5 is for this U.S. Government Publishing Office Official Edition only. The Superintendent of Documents of the U.S. Government Publishing Office requests that any reprinted edition clearly be labeled as a copy of the authentic work with a new ISBN.

Legal Status and Use of Seals and Logos

The logo of the U.S. Naval War College (NWC), Newport, Rhode Island, authenticates *New Interpretations in Naval History: Selected Papers from the Eighteenth McMullen Naval History Symposium Held at the U.S. Naval Academy 19–20 September 2013,* edited by Lori Lyn Bogle and James C. Rentfrow, as an official publication of the College. It is prohibited to use NWC's logo on any republication of this book without the express, written permission of the Editor, Naval War College Press, or the editor's designee.

For Sale by the Superintendent of Documents, U.S. Government Publishing Office
Internet: bookstore.gpo.gov Phone: toll free (866) 512-1800; DC area (202) 512-1800
Fax: (202) 512-2104 Mail: Stop IDCC, Washington, DC 20402-00001

ISBN: 978-1-935352-36-5

NAVAL WAR COLLEGE HISTORICAL MONOGRAPH SERIES NO. 25

The historical monographs in this series are book-length studies of the history of naval warfare, edited historical documents, conference proceedings, and bibliographies that are based wholly or in part on source materials in the Historical Collection of the Naval War College.

The editors of the Naval War College Press express their gratitude to the U.S. Naval Academy Foundation, whose generous financial support made possible the publication of this historical monograph.

New Interpretations in Naval History:
Selected Papers from the Eighteenth
McMullen Naval History Symposium
Held at the U.S. Naval Academy
19–20 September 2013

Edited by Lori Lyn Bogle and
James C. Rentfrow

NAVAL WAR COLLEGE PRESS
NEWPORT, RHODE ISLAND
2018

The contents of this volume represent the views of the authors. Their opinions are not necessarily endorsed by the Naval War College or by any other agency, organization, or command of the U.S. government.

Printed in the United States of America

Historical Monograph Series

NAVAL WAR COLLEGE PRESS
Code 32
Naval War College
686 Cushing Road
Newport, R.I. 02841-1207

TABLE OF CONTENTS

FOREWORD

The U.S. Naval Academy's naval history symposium, named the McMullen Naval History Symposium since 2006, has been held regularly in Annapolis, Maryland, since its first meeting in 1971. Initially, it was a small event for a limited group of invited speakers, but in 1973 it began to take on its present form. Today, this symposium continues to be one of the most important events for the scholarly and professional exchange of ideas and interpretations in the field of naval history. It serves this purpose not only in the United States for American naval history but in the world at large for global naval history. It has certainly become the largest regular meeting of naval historians in the world. Its meeting location in Annapolis, on the historic grounds of the Naval Academy, with its large and active history department, fine museum, rich historical collections, and numerous naval memorials, is an ideal place to bring together such a large group of highly informed experts, including naval professionals and civilian academics, to exchange research information and ideas on a scholarly level.

More than a dozen published volumes of selected papers have captured the essence and growth of the Naval Academy's symposium over the decades. Like this volume, most have carried the now well-established title of *New Interpretations in Naval History.* Typically, each volume in the series has been a selection from the many papers presented at each symposium and has ranged widely across all periods of naval history and the histories of many navies. Not limited to any particular theme, other than presenting a new interpretation of whatever subject on which the researcher is working, each symposium and its resulting volume present very useful samplings of current thinking, new themes, and new approaches in naval history. Collectively, the series has been a great stimulus to advancing and to encouraging naval history. The volumes that these symposia generate continue to chart the state of naval history as a field of research and inquiry.

The eighteenth symposium in the series took place at the Naval Academy in Mahan and Sampson Halls on 19–20 September 2013. It was directed by Dr. Lori

xii NEW INTERPRETATIONS IN NAVAL HISTORY

Bogle, with Dr. James C. Rentfrow, deputy director. The 2013 McMullen Naval History Symposium was generously funded by the Bill Daniels and Dr. John McMullen families. For the two-day period, the program of events listed seven sessions, with a total of forty-four panels and 212 participants serving as session chairs, presenters, or commentators. From that large number, the editors have selected for this volume twenty-two papers that range from studies in late antiquity to the Vietnam War era. In between, the topics vary in focus from the naval education of a Siamese prince in Britain to eighteenth-century medicine, environmental history, international law, amphibious operations, and personnel issues.

Two major events occurred during the course of the symposium. The first was a banquet luncheon during which the Director of Naval History, Naval History and Heritage Command, Capt. Henry "Jerry" Hendrix, delivered remarks entitled "The Influence of History upon Seapower," and the Naval Historical Foundation presented its newly established Commodore Dudley W. Knox Naval History Life Achievement Award to its first recipients: Dr. James C. Bradford, Dr. William N. Still, Jr., and Dr. Philip K. Lundeberg. In the second event, Dr. Gene A. Smith, as the occupant of the Naval Academy's Class of 1957 Chair of Naval History and Heritage, gave the Class of 1957 Keynote Address on the 1815 "Navy and the battle of New Orleans" (included in this volume). In addition, symposium participants were able to enjoy the Naval Academy Museum's special exhibition, displayed in Mahan Hall, *The Naval War of 1812*, featuring a selection of materials from the private collection of William I. Koch and the Naval Academy Museum's collection.*

In publishing this selection of papers from the McMullen Naval History Symposium, the Naval War College, as a graduate-level educational and research institution, and the Naval Academy, at the undergraduate level, join together in the mutual interest of helping to promote a better and deeper understanding of navies and naval history.

JOHN B. HATTENDORF, D.PHIL.
Ernest J. King Professor of Maritime History
Chairman, Maritime History Department

---

* A catalog of the exhibit was published as William S. Dudley, with J. Scott Harmon and maps by Helen Riegle, *The Naval War of 1812: "America's Second War of Independence"; Collections of William I. Koch and the U.S. Naval Academy Museum* (Virginia Beach, Va.: Donning, [2013]).

I *The Education and Experience of a Siamese Prince in the British Royal Navy*

RICHARD A. RUTH

In 1894, following the worst year in Siam's modern history, King Chulalongkorn the Great (r. 1868–1910) sent two of his young sons to Britain as part of a plan to save his embattled kingdom. He dispatched Prince Abhakara and Prince Vajiravudh to acquire the education and skills that would allow Siam to defend itself against encroachment and subjugation by the Western powers threatening to consume that rapidly shrinking Southeast Asian kingdom. His plan for the two boys, it appears, was that they would return home with the right combination of technical expertise, global savvy, and martial confidence to ensure Siam's survival during that perilous age. In the case of Abhakara, the young prince did acquire all of those attributes while abroad. But he also got something more. He gained the right elements of youthful biography that later enabled his devotees to transform him into a legendary savior figure and even a demigod.

Chulalongkorn's dispatch of his sons to Europe was driven by desperation. In 1893, France, on the flimsiest of pretexts, had laid claim to all of Siam's Lao territories east of the Maekong River. Paris had demanded the territories as reparations for the death of a French army officer shot by Siamese troops. The Frenchman had been killed while leading a unit of soldiers into Siamese territory. The conflict had been set in motion by commercially minded French colonial officials eager to gain a "back door" into southwest China through the upper reaches of the Maekong. As a response to the killing, French gunboats rushed past Siam's barricades on the Gulf of Siam and blasted their way up to Bangkok. Their guns leveled at the capital—and its many royal palaces—the French warships forced Siam to cede roughly a third of its territory and pay a huge indemnity. The Siamese looked to Great Britain, its de facto protector, to force France to return the territories. But London did nothing. Chulalongkorn was devastated by the loss and remained out of public sight for most of the following year. He was said to have suffered a physical and psychological collapse from the ordeal. The potential loss of further territory—and even Siam's sovereignty—weighed heavily on his psyche throughout that stressful period. His dispatch of two of his most gifted sons to study Western military sciences came in the midst of this period of extreme crisis for the last independent kingdom in Southeast Asia.

The policy of sending Siamese princes to elite English secondary schools and universities for advanced study was not new.[1] But in response to the events of 1893, the focus of the palace's foreign-education policy had changed. Previously, Chulalongkorn had sent princes to the United Kingdom to study law, politics, and economics as part of a broad and gradual program of modernization. His plan had been not so much to transform Siam into a Western-style democracy as to help the Southeast Asian kingdom acquire the governing institutions that would make it a civilized nation in the eyes of Western imperialists. But in light of the events of 1893, his foreign education policy took on the qualities of an urgent rescue. France's aggression had taught Siam's leaders that diplomacy was much more effective when it had gunboats attached to it.

This paper is a study of the earliest phase of Abhakara's education in naval sciences. It examines his admission to the Royal Naval College at Greenwich, within the scope of geopolitical circumstances that framed the relationship between Siam and the Western colonial powers. It focuses primarily on the experiential aspects of his studies while afloat with Britain's Mediterranean forces. Principally, it argues that while a key episode of Abhakara's youthful military experience with the British navy appears to be more a matter of hearsay than confirmable fact, its veracity is immaterial to its importance in the creation of his legendary status. This paper provides cultural context for this apocryphal story and explains its value in the cult of worship that has grown up around Abhakara within the Royal Thai Navy and beyond. Specifically, it argues that Thai biographers writing in the late twentieth century distorted this episode to make it serve the narrative of Abhakara's later life as a mystic. This paper uses original research in British archival sources along with an analysis of material published in official Thai histories. It is the first product of my continuing research on this illustrious historical figure, and it represents my initial efforts at reconciling apparent conflicts between the British records—scant as they are—and the oft-told Thai tales of the prince's British naval escapades. These efforts were presented at the symposium on 19 September 2013 for the purpose of discussion, refinement, and improvement ahead of their publication in a full-length English-language study.

Prince Abhakara Kiartiwongse (Aphakon Kietwong) is a unique figure in Thailand's modern history. He is the only historical figure of the modern era—the period of the Chakri dynasty, which spans roughly the last two centuries—who is revered as a demigod without ever having reigned as king. He is celebrated by devotees who regard him as both an important historical figure and a quasi-mystical figure. There are more than a hundred official shrines dedicated to him throughout the kingdom. Yet unlike other celebrated Thai royal or political figures of the past two hundred years, he is almost unknown outside Thailand. Even within Thailand his veneration is relatively muted in the broad national context. He does not appear on the currency. There are no major roads named for him. Also, as I will argue in a forthcoming book, his popularity is likely a source of discomfort for Thailand's political and military leaders.

Born 19 December 1880 in Bangkok's Grand Palace, Abhakara was the twenty-eighth child of King Chulalongkorn. (Chulalongkorn fathered seventy-seven children with his ninety-two consorts.) Abhakara's mother was Chao Chom Manda Mode.[2] She was of a prominent aristocratic family, but her relatively low royal status hindered Abhakara's potential to become a future king of Siam. But it did not rule that out entirely, which made him a suspect in various royal plots throughout his adulthood.[3] While Abhakara never held the title of crown prince, as his closest princely half-brother did, he was one of Siam's most important leaders of the early twentieth century. His official service within the Royal Siamese Navy was a crucial part of the kingdom's modernization drive in the years around World War I. Among the positions he held during his forty-two years were director of the Naval Education Department, deputy commander in chief of the Royal Siamese Navy, inspector general of the navy, chief of the Naval General Staff, member of the Privy Council, and minister of the navy.[4] He also bore the official title Prince of Chumphon. But he is equally well known by his unofficial titles "Satet Tia" (Royal Father) and "Mo Phon" (Blessed Doctor). He is most closely identified with an epithet commonly applied to him, "Father of the Royal Thai Navy."

He is revered as the Father of the Royal Thai Navy because of his role in creating a modern naval force and for founding its naval academy.[5] During the first decades of the twentieth century he taught naval sciences to several classes of naval officers in Bangkok and Thonburi, and later he helped Siam acquire its first modern warships.[6] Shrines dedicated to him, authorized and unofficial alike, appear throughout every region of the country, even far inland. Likewise, vendors hawk portraits, statues, amulets, and other likenesses of him everywhere, but especially in coastal areas around Thailand's naval bases. In recent years, his biography has been the subject of several laudatory volumes and television documentaries created by researchers affiliated with the Royal Thai Navy.[7]

At the heart of this hagiographic veneration of Prince Abhakara is the story of his naval education in the United Kingdom and on British warships during the final years of the nineteenth century. Education is the first of the two important foundation stones on which the mythology of Prince Abhakara rests. The narrative of his formative years as student abroad fits into universal model in the myth of the "returned hero." It contains the adventurous stories of "Departure, Initiation, and Return."[8] The young Abhakara journeyed abroad during a period of great peril for his homeland. He endured and was strengthened by trials that would have humbled lesser men. He tempered his soul in war's ghastly crucible. He returned home to serve his people. And in the specifically Thai cultural context of this narrative, he returned home bearing enhanced soul-stuff, wrought from an elite education and uncommon experiences, that was to help his kingdom maintain its independence from the Western colonial powers.

Prince Abhakara and Prince Vajiravudh were the first Siamese of any status to study military sciences in Great Britain. Abhakara was the first Siamese admitted to the Royal Naval College at Greenwich. He was the first non-British member of a royal house to study there since the United Kingdom had implemented the system of naval officer education in place at the time. These firsts were not easily arranged. Owing to political sensitivities regarding British colonial interests in Southeast Asia, his admittance into the naval college was not a simple affair. It took extraordinary diplomatic maneuvering to secure official permission from British authorities to allow him to study there.

Abhakara's admittance to the United Kingdom's naval academy carried specific dangers for Britain. In a broad sense, the Siamese military-modernization effort that it symbolized posed a distant but definite threat to the Pax Britannica that British interests had sought to maintain throughout Southeast Asia. Specifically, it had the potential to upend the delicate diplomatic relationship that Britain had worked to foster with its rival France. Abhakara's enrollment would have to be handled with utmost care if London was to avoid potentially explosive conflicts with Paris over their respective colonial ambitions on the other side of the world. To admit a Siamese prince might not only rankle the feelings of long-standing allies seeking similar privileges but also pull Britain into an explosive and costly conflict, one that would have repercussions for its imperial domains all over the globe. Abhakara would be admitted to Britain's top naval sciences college, but because of these diplomatic concerns, the courses he would be able to take were limited.

In a letter dated 16 May 1899, Evan MacGregor, writing on behalf of the Admiralty to the president of the Royal Naval College, Adm. Richard E. Tracy, laid out the case for admitting the Siamese prince:

> My Lords, whilst they maintain unimpaired their objections to according to Foreign Officers the privilege of study at the College, are of the opinion that the application of the Siamese minister may be regarded as standing on a different footing inasmuch as the course at Greenwich may fittingly be considered as the termination of the course Educational Training which the Prince has already been allowed to undergo, and which commenced in the "Britannia."
>
> They have therefore decided to concede as a special case the request for His Royal Highness to join.[9]

The Admiralty gave Abhakara permission to study only navigation and piloting. It did not grant the prince entry into courses that would further his knowledge of the more specifically military aspects of naval sciences. In fact, the orders to grant Abhakara a seat at the college came with a specific instruction to bar him from attending courses on military tactics at sea: "The permission thus granted, however, is not to extend to the Gunnery and Torpedo Courses," the orders warned, "which are of a confidential character."[10]

The British effort to keep Abhakara away from torpedoes is another important element of the overseas-education portion of his biography. Nearly every book about Abhakara emphasizes both British anxiety about allowing Siam access to advanced torpedo technology and the prince's efforts to circumvent those prohibitions. The stories reflect long-standing Thai ambivalence about Britain's intentions toward Siam during the colonial era. They also reinforce the accusations of betrayal leveled at Britain after it failed to stop French aggression. The letter hints at the British anxiety regarding Siam's potential to become a regional naval power capable of not only defending itself against future European encroachment but possibly asserting its interests in the region.

Abhakara was well prepared for an English education. He had studied English with British tutors in Bangkok and then spent a year and a half at Ascot improving his language skills and pursuing other subjects with tutors. In 1897, when Abhakara left his basic studies with his English tutor, it was British policy to give future officers experience on board training ships as midshipmen before returning them to the classroom for advanced academic study at the Royal Naval College. Most British midshipmen acquired experience on board the training vessel HMS *Britannia*. Abhakara, however, acquired a similar initiation during a six-week voyage on board his father's yacht, HMS *Maha Chakri*. He trained under the captain as the vessel carried Chulalongkorn from Siam to Europe for his first state visit to the West. An oft-told story goes that Chulalongkorn prohibited the yacht's captain from giving Abhakara any special privileges while he learned as a midshipman.[11] In November 1897, Abhakara left the Siamese vessel and began his British training in the Mediterranean Sea on board the battleship HMS *Revenge,* under the command of Commodore Reginald Prothero. Thai biographers note with pride that Prothero was a commander of fierce temperament and imposing physical attributes who bore the epithet "Prothero the Bad." As one Thai biographer describes him, Prothero was "tall and large bodied, with eyes like a hawk's, a hooked nose, and a black beard that stretched to his waist." He is said to have been notorious for terrorizing "flunkies" and for "talking with his fists."[12] Abhakara endured 335 days on board Prothero's *Revenge*. His biographies stress that Abhakara passed his trials under the fearsome British commander with a mark of "very good."[13]

Abhakara continued shipboard training in the Mediterranean for another nine months on board other British warships. He spent time on the battleship *Ramillies,* the sloop *Cruiser,* and the reconnaissance vessel *Hawk*. By the conclusion of this apprenticeship Abhakara had earned a diploma certifying "character and ability" in the subjects of navigation, guns, and steam. From there he was allowed to proceed to Greenwich to further his studies in navigation and piloting. There he would continue to make his kingdom proud by passing his demanding courses with satisfactory marks. But notwithstanding his success on ships and in classrooms, it was an episode that occurred ashore on foreign soil during this phase of his education that would most bolster his reputation in matters military and metaphysical.

This most important experience on his European sojourn occurred on the Mediterranean island of Crete. The island was still a territory of the Ottoman Empire, although most other Greek-majority areas in the region had won their independence and had coalesced into an independent Greece five decades earlier. Ethnic Greek insurgents seeking political union with Greece repeatedly attacked better-armed Ottoman troops throughout 1897–98. The fighting engulfed towns and villages throughout the island. As the casualties mounted and press accounts of the bloodshed spread throughout Europe, popular sentiment in the West grew strongly in favor of the island's scrappy Greek insurgents. Greece tried to land troops to aid the Cretan uprising but was blocked by ships of Britain, France, Italy, and Russia, who feared an escalated conflict. These "big four" nations dispatched naval forces and worked in concert to end the violence. Throughout the fighting the British sent several battleships to various points on the island to protect the Greek rebels. Ultimately, the great powers expelled the Ottoman troops and put the island's administration under the joint control of four of their admirals.

The most costly fighting for the British, however, occurred after Ottoman/Greek clashes had died down. Following the appointment of a Greek Christian as the head of the Cretan Revenue Service, rural ethnic Turks and irregular Ottoman forces rampaged in the city of Heraklion. On 25 August 1898 they massacred hundreds of the city's Greek Christians. Frenzied mobs attacked the British forces escorting the new revenue chief to the customhouse, killing seventeen soldiers and ransacking the consulate. Britain responded with naval might. The Admiralty sent a flotilla to Crete. Royal Marines landed at Heraklion and fought armed Turks throughout the city. Within months, the British marines had put down the Turkish rebels and expelled all remaining Ottoman forces. The operation marked the end of Ottoman rule over Crete that had lasted more than 250 years.

Allusions to Abhakara's time with the British during the Cretan uprisings and massacres are numerous in recent biographies but are scant on details. Abhakara's biographies contain descriptions of the massacre and British response alongside descriptions of the earlier uprising and fighting. They highlight the bloodshed and suggest that Abhakara had spent time near the British soldiers and the casualties they left. An often-cited part of this narrative is the deprivation that Abhakara endured while ashore with the British. According to Phra Yahanaklangsamut (Bunmi Phanthumanawin):

> The prince used to tell a story of when he was a student in the Royal British Navy and how he had the opportunity to put down the rioting on the island of Crete. For three months he had to eat and sleep outdoors in the cold. On the battlefield, he had to sleep among the corpses of the recently killed. And sometimes he went without food. He had to eat snails that he had caught and fried with onions. The corpses of those who had been shot in their guts smelled terrible, even the ones who had just died.[14]

The quotation is a critical component in the many later biographies of Prince Abhakara. It is evidence that he was more than a student of naval military campaigns. He witnessed brutal fighting close-up. He endured the privations of cold and hunger that combat soldiers experience on campaign in foreign lands. He lived, slept, and ate among the dead, and even more importantly, among the recently killed. On the basis of this experience on Crete with the British marines, his biographers have declared him a "war veteran" before the end of his teens.[15] The study in foreign classrooms proved him a worthy intellect, while his training on board British ships demonstrated his adaptability and resourcefulness. But it was the fighting in Crete that made him a warrior. But well known as the Crete story is to Abhakara's devotees, it may fit more easily in the category of legend than of fact.

First, it is difficult to determine when Abhakara could have spent three months on Crete. He was on several ships involved in the Cretan incident, but there is no record of his being in any of the landing parties put ashore during this period. In fact, the only mention of him in any of the ships' logs records his being transferred off HMS *Revenge* just before the ship set sail for Crete following the killing of the British soldiers in August 1898. Second, there appears to be no mention of this story in any biography of Abhakara published before 1970. From my research to date, the most likely source of this story is a history of the Royal Thai Navy that was included in a funeral volume distributed in 1974 to commemorate the death and cremation of Bunmi Phanthumanawin.[16]

The framing of the Crete battle story is important. None of the official biographies attests to its veracity. Instead, all present the episode as narrated by Phra Yahanaklangsamut. Even he does not claim that the story is true, nor does he say that Abhakara was the original source. Instead, he starts this tale of youthful adventure with the mild disclaimer "I heard that." I am not interested in the veracity of the story, however, as much as in the reasons why it would be included repeatedly in biographies published in recent decades. Why include an unconfirmed story? Why repeat hearsay that cannot be authenticated by ships' logs or documentary evidence? Beyond the veteran status conferred on Abhakara by his proximity to combat, there are other reasons why the story is a crucial element in his biography. They concern Abhakara's later stature as a mystical figure.

Much of the middle part of his biography concerns his encounters with the metaphysical. He is described as capable of performing acts beyond the ability of other people, such as instantly curing diseases that were incurable in his day. He is famous for eradicating the fear of ghosts and spirits that plagued many of his naval cadets. He is rumored to have had the power to disappear into thin air.[17] If Abhakara's first "life" was as the modernizer of the Siamese navy, his second was lived as a mystical healer reputed to possess extraordinary skills, knowledge, and healing powers. Abhakara turned to mystical medicine after being fired in early 1911 by his brother Vajiravudh, now king, from his job as deputy commander of the Royal Siamese Navy. Abhakara had fallen under his brother's suspicion for several reasons. He was rumored to be part of a planned revolt against Vajiravudh. Court suspicions of Abhakara intensified shortly after these rumors arose when a group of naval officers he had trained brawled with the king's pages at a Bangkok restaurant. In another incident from this period, a naval officer—drunk on duty— lost a gun overboard from one of Siam's ships. These episodes prompted Vajiravudh to remove his brother from his position.[18]

With this abrupt change of careers, Abhakara set about reinventing himself. His new incarnation would be the near opposite of all he had worked to become in the previous three decades. With his beloved and long-reigning father now gone from the world and his increasingly suspicious and erratic brother calling the shots from the Chakri throne, Prince Abhakara appears to have sought exit from the hothouse of Siamese court politics and bureaucratic competition. He seems to have sought a kind of invisibility from the seeing world, a state that would become both symbolic and, as some adherents believe, genuine. No longer would he dedicate himself so publicly to modernizing and defending the nation through the strengthening of its arms. Instead, he would immerse himself in the metaphysics and esoterica of traditional folklore, in the hazy ontological area where religion, science, and superstition overlap. With his new mastery of traditional knowledge he would labor incognito to revive fading folk wisdom in the service of the poor and marginalized. Gone would be the grand uniforms, foreign weapons, and lofty titles he had borne as a public official and princely symbol of the Chakri dynasty's vitality. In their place would be a simple costume and modest possessions, even a new and kindly visage. Having spent years laying the groundwork for the first epithet he would carry into history, that of the Father of the Royal Thai Navy, he abandoned his quest for power, prestige, and accomplishment and became a humble healer known to his patients as Mo Phon, "Blessed Doctor."

Prince Abhakara's transformation was as magical and beguiling as any alchemic feat of his day. In nearly six years out of government service, he threw himself into the study of traditional medicine, Buddhism, and what is known in Thai as *saiwet*. The term translates roughly as "incantations" or "spells," but broadly speaking it is a body of esoteric knowledge to which Westerners would commonly refer as the occult or black magic. In Thailand, *saiwet* does not necessarily have the often negative connotation attached to those English terms in the Christianized and scientifically minded West. His study of these subjects would have appeared odd at the time when compared with the system of naval-science education he had undergone in Britain, and it would have been at odds with the program of modernization that had spanned the previous six decades. But for many of his present devotees, the immersion in *saiwet* enhances the mystical aura that permeates their veneration of him as a magical being. Once out of government Abhakara tracked down a renowned doctor of traditional medicine and entered into study that was more like an apprenticeship than a college course. He studied the folk cures that had survived into the modern era despite increasing competition from imported patent medicines and Western scientific methods. Later, Abhakara set up his own laboratory, using the best imported scientific equipment of his day to test the results of the treatments about which he had learned. He tested them on animals he had brought into the lab for experimentation. He tested the efficacy of these traditional cures alongside similar tests on the best-known foreign cures of his time, including those of the Chinese, Japanese, and Europeans. While engaged in these scientific experiments, he continued his study of *saiwet* as a mystical complement to the folk medicine and Western cures he explored.[19]

During his half-decade as a healer Prince Abhakara drove himself to improve his techniques and to expand his knowledge. At the same time, he was allegedly pursued by the police and their informants throughout the capital and kingdom because of lingering court suspicions over the true purpose of his movements. After he had mastered the body of medical knowledge that he deemed the most efficacious, he set out to treat the sick and neglected among Siam's indigent populations. He is remembered in naval histories for his care of sailors, both enlisted men and officers. His reputation for what Thai Buddhists call *mettha,* or loving-kindness, grew as he brought his healing skills to communities traditionally spurned by Siam's nobility. He laid the groundwork for an enduring and devoted following among Thailand's ethnic Chinese by caring for their sick. Accounts of miraculous cures among the Chinese coolie population contributed to his nickname Mo Phon. Equally legendary are the stories of wealthy Chinese offering great sums in appreciation for his miraculous cures, all of them turned down or redirected toward Buddhist charities. This willingness to treat Chinese as equals was a sharp contrast to his kingly brother's reputation for anti-Chinese sentiment.[20] All this time he was followed by members of the police who—presumably acting on orders from the palace—monitored his actions and noted his contacts. His reputation for miracles was enhanced by his supposed ability to shake off his police pursuers. Later his devotees would exchange stories of Abhakara's power to disappear, tales that may owe their origins to this period of his life.[21] He was helped in his pursuit of anonymity by a change in his appearance. He donned simple tunics and trousers. He grew an impressive mustache that curled at the ends. He carried his tools, medicines, and papers in a *yam*, a simple flat bag of sewn cloth often associated with Buddhist monks and rural peasants—although his was fine silk. He looked more like a spirit medium than a prince.

The stories of his miraculous feats in the realm of the mystical are buttressed by the tale of his youthful adventure on Crete. A key component of this legend is his proximity to corpses. Why does it matter that he lived among the dead? The circumstances have a bearing on popular Thai beliefs about ghosts. Thai culture recognizes numerous kinds of ghosts, each with its own habits, qualities, and appearance. The spirit known as a *phi tai hong*, or ghost of the violently killed, is the most feared. The *phi tai hong* are said to congregate at the sites of their deaths. They are feared because the suddenness and horrific circumstances of their deaths have left them confused and desperate. They will try to attach themselves to living passersby. Worse, they sometimes try to kill people in the same violent manners in which they lost their own lives. Even today many Thais go to great lengths to avoid places where people have recently suffered violent deaths. Thai believers will bypass road intersections where fatal car crashes have taken place, because of their fear of the *phi tai hong*.

Abhakara's supposed time among battlefield corpses provides a biographical component to which his adherents can point when explaining his later reputation—in life and death—for extraordinary spiritual powers. In a sense, he comes of age on two powerful planes. One is a battlefield created by British military forces possessing the most modern homicidal technology available at the time. The other is a mystical zone populated by restless and powerful souls. The description of his eating is particularly significant. The consumption of creatures—the snails on which he subsisted while moving across Crete—that may have crawled among these human corpses suggests an image of Abhakara as literally sustaining himself on creatures from among the dead. Snails are not carnivores or scavengers; they do not thrive on carrion, and their consumption in Siam is not considered particularly exotic. But the account of Abhakara eating these somewhat loathsome creatures following the description of the corpses suggests both physical toughness and metaphysical fearlessness. It marks his character as extraordinarily strong and represents a transformative experience from adolescence into adulthood.

The British education portion of Abhakara's biography provides the professional basis for his later emergence as Father of the Royal Thai Navy. As important as the educational and experiential aspects of his foreign journey were in facilitating the creation of the Royal Thai Navy, I would argue that the spiritual aspects of his European sojourn are equally important for the creation of the legend that has grown up around Abhakara in recent times. The story of experience in combat on Crete gives him veteran status as a warrior. Also, as I have suggested, it implies spiritual prowess, presenting him as a teenager who lived among the corpses of battlefield casualties. True to his father's hopes, Prince Abhakara acquired a great deal during his adolescence abroad. He got education and experience with the imperial age's best navy. In the contemporary era, biographers and devotees have invoked the somewhat imprecise record of his youthful exploits to find sources of his life's achievements and of the mystical aura he has acquired in death.

NOTES   I am grateful to the McMullen Foundation for supporting the research in this paper. I want to thank Lori Bogle for organizing this symposium. Also, I owe a debt of gratitude to my colleagues Ernest Tucker, Donald Wallace, and Sharika Crawford for their inputs on the initial draft. Likewise, I want to thank the Danish historian Hans Christian Bjerg for his suggestions regarding the role of European naval officers in the Siamese navy.

1 David K. Wyatt, *The Politics of Reform in Thailand: Education in the Reign of King Chulalongkorn* (New Haven, Conn.: Yale Univ. Press, 1969), p. 89.

2 Jeffrey Finestone, *The Royal Family of Thailand: The Descendants of King Chulalongkorn* (Bangkok: Phitsanulok, 1989), p. 62.

3 Walter F. Vella, *Chaiyo! King Vajiravudh and the Development of Thai Nationalism* (Honolulu: Univ. of Hawaii Press, 1978), p. 265.

4 Chaimongkhon Udomsap, *Phraprawat phon rua ek phrachao borommawongthoe kromluang chumphon udomsak* [History of Admiral Prince Chumphon] (Bangkok: Santi Tham, 1961), p. 12.

5 Khon Muang Chumphon, *Rueang khuan ru kieukap Satet Tia* [Stories You Should Know about Our Royal Father] (Nonthaburi City, Thailand: Chalongbun, 2008), pp. 18–19.

6 Vella, *Chaiyo!*, p. 120.

7 *Satet tia . . . phua chat lae nawai* [Royal Father . . . for the Nation and the Navy] (Nonthaburi City, Thailand: Nai Wit, [2011?]).

8 For the best-known explanation in English, see Joseph Campbell, *Mythos: The Shaping of Our Mythic Tradition* (Shaftesbury, U.K.: Element Books, 1999).

9 Letter from Evan MacGregor (Admiralty) to Adm. President Richard E. Tracy, N. 5569/1899, The National Archives (United Kingdom).

10 Ibid.

11 Dr. M. R. Aphidet Aphakon, *Luang pusuk kap kromluang chumphon* [Luang Pusuk and the Prince of Chumphon] (Bangkok: Comma, 2009), p. 37.

12 Ibid., p. 38.

13 Ibid.

14 Ibid., p. 39.

15 Ibid.

16 *Anuson Nai Ngan Phra Rachathan phloeng sop phonruatri phra yahanklangsamut (bunmi phanthumnawin)* [Cremation Memorial for Admiral Phra Yahanaklangsamut (Bunmi Phanthumanawin)] (Bangkok: Department of the Navy, 1974).

17 Khon Muang Chumphon, *Rueang khuan ru*, pp. 53–54.

18 Chenchop Yingsumon, *130 pi mai mi wan dai, Phonruaaekphrabaromwongthoe Kromluang Chumphon Khetudomsak* [130 Years and Still No Day of Death: The Admiral Prince of Chumphon] (Nonthaburi City, Thailand: DK, 2010), pp. 35–36.

19 Ibid., pp. 36, 38–40.

20 Vella, *Chaiyo!*, pp. 193–94.

21 Khon Muang Chumphon, *Rueang khuan ru*, p. 53.

II *Continuity or Change?*
Late Roman Naval Forces

JORIT WINTJES

The battle was the key to eventual victory on another continent—as the civil war had finally broken out, two fleets opposed each other, one trying to force access to foreign shores, the other trying to prevent it. The latter had larger ships and more of them, while the former was inferior in numbers, though its ships, while smaller, were faster and more agile. In the end, the smaller force turned out to be victorious, and victory at sea opened the door for an eventual victory on land, resulting in the empire finally falling, once again, into the hands of one man, a man who was well aware of the important role sea power had played in his campaign—so aware, in fact, that the first coins of a new city he founded as a result of the battle depicted Victory standing on the prow of a ship. This Victory appeared frequently on the coins of the newly founded city, making it obvious that the city itself was the main monument to the successful conclusion of the civil war.

A "Naval Century"

What sounds like a very brief sketch of the battle of Actium and its consequences in 31 BC in reality refers to events more than 350 years later—in the year AD 324, when Constantine defeated Licinius, finally to become the sole ruler over the undivided empire.[1] In Constantine's campaign of AD 324, sea power played a prominent part. While the victory over Licinius's admiral, Amandus, was not the decisive action of the war, it was of key importance, inasmuch as it made possible the transfer into Asia Minor of Constantine's army, which finally defeated Licinius at the battle of Chrysopolis.[2] The city Constantine eventually founded as a symbol of his newly won control over the undivided empire—Constantinople—was at the same time a symbol of a victory that was specifically a naval one, as the examples from its coinage mentioned above show.[3] It may come as a surprise that Constantine associated himself so strongly with a naval victory, as his impact on the late Roman military is usually seen in the completion of army reforms that had originated during the latter decades of the third century. Yet the military history of the fourth century, usually associated with an array of famous yet often poorly understood land battles (ranging from the engagement at the Milvian Bridge in AD 312 to the catastrophe at Adrianople in AD 378), also saw the heaviest fighting at sea since the end of the civil wars in 31/30 BC. The fourth century was—in more than only one way, as the foundation of Constantinople shows—a century in which naval power mattered. Or to put it pointedly, it was a naval century, one in which the Roman military machine displayed outstanding naval capabilities.

The purpose of the present paper is to shed some light on Roman naval activity in the fourth century, as it has long been in the shadow of both what happened on land at the same time and general political developments, developments that would eventually, at the beginning of the fifth century, see Roman rule in Western Europe begin to crumble. As a review of all Roman naval history of the fourth century would be impossible within the confines of this paper, the main focus will be on northwestern Europe, in particular the waters around Britain. It is instructive to look at the level of naval activity in these waters, as, although one would instinctively assume them to have been backwaters in the world of Roman naval power, even there the level of naval activity was considerable.

Sources

It is useful to take a brief look, before proceeding to what happened off the shores of the Atlantic and the North Sea in the fourth century, at the available sources for naval activity during that period. One of the often-repeated truisms about the late Roman military is that the reorganizations instigated by Diocletian, which decreased the size of army units considerably, must have had some effect on the way the Romans organized their naval forces as well. Indeed, it often has been suggested that naval units were remodeled in a similar way, with larger units—"fleets"— being broken up and their subunits—"squadrons"—turned into independent units.[4] While this model at first appears to be quite convincing, as it mirrors developments in the army, the actual evidence is far from conclusive, not only because there is precious little evidence available in the first place, but also because the nature of what is available changes quite dramatically—something that is quite often overlooked in the discussion of late Roman naval forces.

If one compares the Roman military (including naval forces) of the first three centuries AD with that of the fourth, this change in the nature of the available evidence becomes instantly obvious. Perhaps the single most important source of information on the "old" army is the considerable amount of surviving inscriptional evidence. It yields valuable information on force organization, unit structure, the occupations of soldiers, their names, families, etc., information that does not surface in, for example, the literary or archaeological record. In addition, coins and documentary evidence from wooden tablets and papyri allow insights into everyday matters, where again other sources are mostly silent. Literary sources gain importance when it comes to the operational history of the Roman army, reconstructing which from inscriptions, coins, or documents alone is highly problematic, if possible at all. Conversely, if the inscriptional evidence were absent, the operational history could still be reconstructed, but much of the information on the structure of the army, its unit names, career structures, etc., would simply be lost. Simply put, while literary evidence can tell the observer *what* the army *did,* inscriptions are a key to understanding *how* the army was *organized.*

Unfortunately, when it comes to the "new," post-Diocletian army, inscriptional evidence largely dries up. Literary evidence is still available, allowing insights into the operational history of the army; also, for questions of everyday history, coins and papyri are still available. But inscriptions, particularly private inscriptions, by and large are not. This loss of a whole segment of evidence is due to a general change in the so-called epigraphic habit, a change that while evident enough is still poorly understood. In other words, the Romans by the end of the third century largely stopped putting up inscriptions in stone, and it is not known why. It may be that instead of cutting inscriptions into stone they now started painting them or using perishable materials.[5] Whatever the reason, and save for a few examples, inscriptions set up by individuals disappear almost completely, and official inscriptions are hard to find outside the military and the imperial court.

Instead, perhaps the single most important piece of evidence for the "new" army is a document—the *notitia dignitatum*—that allows insight into the structure of the Roman army in a way unavailable for the early and high principate. However, while it undeniably provides a fascinating insight into how the Roman state and its military were organized in the late fourth and early fifth centuries—or were *supposed* to be organized, or even were *thought* to be organized by someone not directly involved—its interpretation is fraught with difficulties. There is still no agreement on what the document's actual purpose was, though it does not seem to have been official. This is not the place for a detailed discussion of the *notitia;* it is sufficient to note that whoever wrote it, for whatever purpose, did not create a snapshot of the organizational structure of the Roman state at any one time. Instead, the document has sections with information older than that in others.[6]

Despite these severe limitations, however, the influence of the *notitia* on Roman army studies has been enormous, and understandably so, as it preserves at least some of the information—like unit names—that for the early and high principate is available in the epigraphic evidence. As a consequence, the Roman army of the fourth century is still mainly seen from the perspective of the *notitia*—and if one looks at Roman naval forces as well through the eyes of the *notitia,* the result is very different indeed from what is generally accepted about Roman naval forces of earlier times.

Comparing the "old" Roman naval forces with the "new," post-Diocletian ones, the first thing that immediately catches attention is the fact that most of the units known from early and high imperial times seem to have vanished, while a good many other units seem to have sprung up from nowhere.[7] This would fit quite nicely with the reforms of Diocletian, with many new units populating the Roman army order of battle, many of them remnants of larger units known from earlier times. Yet such an interpretation of the evidence is, methodologically speaking, unsound, as it fails to take into account the specific nature of the *notitia dignitatum,* which yields information that simply does not exist for earlier centuries.

In other words, the existing model of the way Roman naval forces were organized during the early and high principate is basically the result of an analytical approach to the inscriptional evidence available, which in turn means, given that some of the units are attested in fewer than a dozen inscriptions, that one may well miss important pieces of the overall picture simply because of the lack of evidence. Conversely, for the fourth and early fifth centuries the *notitia dignitatum* presents an organizational chart telling the reader which units were supposed to exist and what their (presumably) official names were at the time of the composition of the relevant section of the document. It is known neither whether the nomenclature used in this document reflected that used in the units nor whether the units listed in the *notitia* existed at all in the first place. For the purpose of the present paper, however, the question of how far the depiction of Roman naval forces in the *notitia* actually matches reality is not of key importance, as information about the role of Roman naval forces and their capabilities—something on which the *notitia* is silent—can be gained from the literary record.

Operational History: The Waters around Britain

Join the navy, see the world, and live a life of adventure—but not so, according to a still widely accepted concept of Roman naval history, for the Roman sailor. On that view, during the early and high empire Roman naval forces basically had not a lot to do; the sailors of the units in Misenum were famously working the awnings in the Coliseum;[8] and Roman naval history had pretty much come to an end, and not a few studies on Roman naval history end with the battle of Actium.[9]

In reality, nothing could be farther from the truth. From the amphibious operations of Drusus in Germany in 12 BC right down to Septimius Severus's campaign in Scotland in AD 208–11, Roman military history is full of large-scale naval operations that differed from those of the late Republic only in that engagements between two fleets of warships had become uncommon, as Rome had no enemies left willing to build warships (or capable of doing so) with which to contest sea control. Yet operations such as Aelius Gallus's expedition to Arabia in 25 BC, Germanicus's campaigns in Germany in AD 16, the invasion of Britain under Claudius in AD 43, Claudian operations in Mauretania between AD 41 and AD 44, or the civil wars of AD 69 and AD 193 regularly involved hundreds of ships and tens of thousands of men, proving that the Roman military machine was able to muster considerable naval capabilities.

So there *was* a Roman naval history after Actium, and for much of the early and high principate its study is, to a greater or lesser degree, depending on the region and the unit at which one looks, supported by inscriptional evidence—evidence that, as stated above, peters out in the latter half of the third century. In the case of northwestern Europe, on which this paper will focus, the epigraphic material breaks off with an inscription dated to the late 240s, a stone set by a certain Saturninus of the *classis Britannica*.[10] As this is the last mention of that particular *classis* in the epigraphic record, and as there is no *classis Britannica* in the *notitia dignitatum,* it has been suggested in the past that the unit "disappeared" (whatever that may have meant in reality) afterward. Yet even if that was the case—and apart from the absence of the unit's name on inscriptions there is neither a single piece of evidence nor any sound reason for it—Roman naval forces in general did not "disappear" at all. To the contrary, the literary record shows that the post-244 period was full of naval activity in the waters around Britain.

Generally one has to assume that events on the continent regularly made the transfer of troops necessary, as the frontier in Britain at the time was apparently quiet and units from there were used to support forces on the Rhine and the Danube.[11] After the fall of the Gallic empire in AD 274, the relocation of Burgundians and Vandals to Britain (apparently a result of Emperor Probus's Raetian campaign in AD 278) must have involved a large-scale transport operation, and Emperor Carinus may then have instigated another round of campaigning in Britain in the early 280s, as he used the title "Britannicus maximus"—though attempts to identify the scope and nature of either of these operations have so far been unsuccessful.[12] Diocletian may have completed this latter campaign, as he made use of the title as well;[13] in any case, the presence of the emperor meant the transfer of a considerable number of personnel from the continent to Britain and back. Only a few months later, events in northwestern Europe again warranted Diocletian's attention, and he sent to Gaul his newly appointed caesar, Maximian, who prepared for a campaign to commence in northern Gaul in spring 286.[14] Among Maximian's staff served Carausius, who immediately after the successful conclusion of the campaign in Gaul was tasked with securing the northern shores of the Gallic provinces, which at the time were apparently suffering from barbarian incursions.[15] Again, very little is known about the nature of this campaign, though, as it was directed against Franks and Saxons, it must have included amphibious operations in the Rhine estuary.

In fall 286, Carausius then fell from favor, was accused of various wrongdoings, was found guilty in absentia, and received a death sentence.[16] His reaction was quite dramatic, if understandable—he had himself elected emperor by his soldiers and gained control over northern Gaul and the British provinces, thereby establishing what came to be known as the "Britannic empire." Maximian managed to wrest control over parts of northern Gaul from Carausius during his first attempt to crush the Britannic empire but ultimately failed, when in 289 his invasion force (of significant size) was shattered by autumn storms.[17] While no details about the composition of Maximian's force have survived, it is obvious that it must have been considerable, as Maximian had to match a sizeable part of the army of the British provinces in strength, if not in numbers. As not only the British legions but also several units from the continent feature on Carausius's coinage, one would assume that—even taking into account that these units may have been severely understrength—together with the auxiliaries available, Carausius could muster a force of at least twenty thousand men.[18] Assuming Maximian had gathered an invasion force of about that size, he would probably have required five hundred ships or more to get this force to Britain.

During the following years there seems to have been an uneasy truce between Carausius and Rome;[19] only in 293 did Maximian undertake another attempt at bringing the Britannic empire under central control again. In the course of a campaign led by Maximian's caesar, Constantius, Carausius first lost Boulogne-sur-Mer, a key harbor in northern Gaul, before eventually falling victim to usurpation by Allectus, the commander of his guards.[20] It took Constantius another two years to prepare for a new invasion, which eventually came about in 296. Although the landing itself was unopposed, it must have been an undertaking of enormous dimensions, as Constantius had two fleets, one sailing from the Seine estuary for the Isle of Wight, the other leaving from the Boulogne-sur-Mer area.[21] The overall total in numbers of ships and manpower may well have considerably exceeded Maximian's first attempt in 286.

Within a decade, Constantius was back in Britain, accompanied by his son Constantine. A campaign in summer 305 led him far into Scotland;[22] while no details have survived, it was apparently successful enough to earn for Constantius the title "Britannicus Maximus II" and for his son the loyalty of his father's soldiers—when Constantius died at York in July 306, his son was hailed as the new augustus.[23] Constantius's campaign in Scotland followed the example set by Septimius Severus, whose campaign of 208–11 was logistically supported largely by sea; it is likely that Constantius also made extensive use of ships to support his operations.

Constantine returned to Britain at least two times during the following years;[24] in 313/314, major military operations must have been under way, as Constantine again won the title "Britannicus maximus."[25] While nothing is known about the nature of this campaign, every time the emperor went to Britain taking elements of his army with him a major transport operation was necessary, involving thousands of men and possibly hundreds of ships. During the following decade the focus of Constantine's attention shifted toward the Mediterranean and the civil wars against Maxentius and Licinius. One would assume that during these conflicts Constantine regularly transferred troops from Britain to the continent and back again, as the British *exercitus* was, at least initially, his key power base, though no evidence for such shifts survives.

After the death of Constantine in 337, the northwestern provinces of the empire fell to his son Constantine II, who in 340 was killed in a civil war against his brother Constans. Constans in turn visited Britain late in January 343 and during the same year fought the Franks in the Rhine estuary, a campaign that must have seen a significant amount of amphibious warfare.[26]

The rule of Constans came to an end in January 350, when his guard commander, Flavius Magnus Magnentius, was elected emperor in Autun.[27] He seems to have been held in special favor by the units stationed in Britain, and although he suffered a defeat against Constantius II in the battle of Mursa in September 351, he still managed to control much of the western provinces for another two years, his power mainly based on the control over the units stationed in Britain. Magnus Magnentius was finally defeated in the battle of Mons Seleucus in 353, after which he committed suicide. The aftermath of the usurpation of Magnus Magnentius must again have seen a considerable shuffling of troops to and from Britain, as contingents transferred to the continent were sent back and units of questionable loyalty moved to other provinces.

Northwestern Europe soon demanded imperial attention again. When Julian was sent to Gaul to defend the provinces from Germanic incursions in AD 356, he first campaigned against Alamanni and Franks on the middle Rhine, before turning in the late 350s to the lower Rhine, where Germanic attacks had closed the Rhine delta to merchant traffic, interrupting the supply of grain, which to a large extent was shipped from Britain, to Lower Germany. The situation necessitated a major military response, and Julian spent much of AD 358 preparing for a large-scale amphibious operation, drawing together two hundred ships and having another four hundred built;[28] all this proves that the Roman military administration of the mid-fourth century still had the capability to get off the ground an operation that was comparable in dimension to earlier large-scale undertakings.

Only a few years later, another large-scale military action was necessary in northwestern Europe. Barbarian incursions had wreaked havoc in the British provinces; a significant part of the army, together with two high officials, had been lost.[29] Emperor Valentinian quickly dispatched Severus, a *comes domesticorum*, to Britain, followed after a few months by the *magister equitum*, Flavius Iovinus.[30] Both had little success, so in the autumn of 367 Valentinian ordered the *comes rei militaris*, Theodosius, the father of the later emperor Theodosius, to take command of operations in Britain.[31] Theodosius took four core units of the western field army with him and over the course of the campaigning season of 368 managed to defeat the barbarians and restore the provinces.[32] While only a few pieces of information survive about Theodosius's operations, it is clear that these extended to the continent. In fact, rare inscriptional evidence suggests that the most important part of Theodosius's operations was a campaign against the Saxons living in the northern parts of the Rhine estuary.[33] As Theodosius himself apparently was in Britain for the whole duration of the campaign, probably using London as his main base, his only way to strike against the Saxons was by means of amphibious operations—again of significant size, perhaps involving forces similar in scale to those employed by Julian eighteen years earlier.[34]

The last decades of the fourth century and the early years of the fifth saw two usurpations that again resulted in the transfer of troops to the continent in, presumably, large numbers. Magnus Maximus, who had been elevated by his troops in summer 383, probably took some of the troops stationed in Britain to the continent, units that after his defeat in 388 in the battle of the Save might have been transferred back to Britain again.[35] In the winter of 406/407, the collapse of the Rhine frontier triggered events in Britain that eventually led to the usurpation of Constantine III, who again took to the continent a large part of the British army, most of which never saw its bases again.[36] While Constantine's removal of a large part of the garrison of Roman Britain is usually seen as a key step toward the eventual demise of Roman rule in Britain, it also shows clearly that even at such a late stage Roman military administration was still capable of organizing the orderly transfer of thousands of troops, for which hundreds of ships were necessary. The infrastructure that made the easy exchange of troops and equipment on a large scale possible must still have been in place to a large extent even as late as the early 400s.

Conclusion

When Constantine had the Victory coins struck in memory of his victory at sea over Licinius, he was emulating Augustus in several ways, one of which was styling himself as a victor in a civil war that to a large extent had been fought at sea. However, the battle of the Dardanelles in AD 324 was not an isolated incident in a period otherwise known for naval inactivity, nor was the struggle for power between Constantine and Licinius one between two generals who did not know exactly what they were doing with the naval forces at hand. Instead, the events in AD 324 provided an early climax for a century that as a whole was characterized by intense naval activity—and that therefore should be put right beside the last decades of the Roman Republic in terms of general importance for Roman naval history.

At the same time, analysis of the operational history of Roman naval forces in northwestern Europe—a closer look at other theaters such as the Rhine, Danube, or Euphrates frontiers would yield similar results—shows clearly that despite any possible decline of Roman land forces, and despite any political setbacks during a period still commonly known as the "Crisis of Empire," Roman naval forces had an unbroken history of activity. Far too little is known about organizational and equipment changes that may have happened during the ca. AD 250–400 period; probably there were some, as one would expect over the course of a century and a half.

Yet whatever these changes may have been, far from reducing Roman naval capabilities or diminishing the importance of Roman naval forces, they allowed a pace of operations unchanged as compared with those of earlier centuries. Right up to the end of Roman rule in northwestern Europe, Roman naval forces were obviously capable of organizing and undertaking large-scale operations. That means that even for the latter half of the fourth century not only was the knowledge how to do so still available but also a considerable infrastructure must still have been in place. It also raises the question how both the knowledge base and the infrastructure vanished, apparently rather suddenly, at the beginning of the fifth century. But that would be the topic of another paper.

NOTES 1 On Constantine's civil war with Licinius see Averil
Cameron, "The Reign of Constantine," in *The
Cambridge Ancient History*, vol. 12, *The Crisis of
Empire, AD 193–337*, ed. Alan K. Bowman et al.
(Cambridge, U.K.: Cambridge Univ. Press, 2005),
pp. 93–95. For the naval part see Dietmar Kienast,
*Untersuchungen zu den Kriegsflotten der römischen
Kaiserzeit* (Bonn: Habelt, 1966), pp. 138–41.

2 On Amandus see Arnold H. M. Jones et al., *Proso-
pography of the Later Roman Empire* (Cambridge,
U.K.: Cambridge Univ. Press, 1971), vol. 1 [hereafter
PLRE 1], p. 50 (Amandus 2).

3 On this coinage see Francesco Gnecchi, *I Medaglioni
Romani* (Milan: Hoepli, 1912), vol. 2, pp. 136–37,
141 (bronze medallions); and Henry Cohen,
*Description historique des monnaies frappées sous
l'Empire romain, communément appelées médailles
impériales* (Paris: Rollin et Feuardent, 1859–68), vol.
7, p. 326 (coins minted in 330).

4 For the *classis Britannica* see, for example, David J. P.
Mason, *Roman Britain and the Roman Navy* (Stroud,
U.K.: Tempus, 2003), pp. 170–71, and Marek Żyrom-
ski, *Praefectus Classis: The Commanders of Roman
Imperial Navy during the Principate* (Poznań, Pol.:
Wydawn. Naukowe Inst. Nauk Politycznych i Dzien-
nikarstwa Uniw. Im. Adama Mickiewicza, 2001), p.
14.

5 On this important change in the epigraphical habit
see Ramsay MacMullen, "The Epigraphical Habit in
the Roman Empire," *American Journal of Philology*
103 (1982), p. 245f., and Elizabeth A. Meyer, "Explaining the Epigraphic Habit in the Roman Empire:
The Evidence of Epitaphs," *Journal of Roman Studies*
80 (1990), pp. 81–94.

6 On the *notitia dignitatum* see, in particular, Arnold
H. M. Jones, *The Later Roman Empire, 284–602: A
Social, Economic and Administrative Survey* (Oxford,
U.K.: Basil Blackwell, 1964), vol. 3, pp. 347–80; Gui-
do Clemente, *La "Notitia Dignitatum"* (Cagliari, It.:
Sarda Fossarato, 1968); the essays collected in Roger
Goodburn and Philip Bartholomew, eds., *Aspects of
the Notitia Dignitatum* (Oxford, U.K.: Archaeopress,
1976); Peter Brennan, "The User's Guide to the
Notitia Dignitatum," *Antichthon* 32 (1998), pp.

34–49; and Michael Kulikowski, "The *Notitia Dignitatum* as a Historical Source," *Historia* 49 (2000),
pp. 358–77. For a detailed but controversial analysis
of the entries on the Roman army see Dietrich
Hoffmann, *Das spätrömische Bewegungsheer und die
Notitia Dignitatum* (Düsseldorf, F.R.G.: Rheinland-
Verlag, 1970).

7 The best example is the two *classes* stationed on the
Danube frontier *(cl. Pannonica* and *cl. Moesica),*
which do not appear in the *notitia dignitatum;* instead, the *notitia* locates no fewer than twelve units
along the river. For a general overview of Roman
naval units in the late third, fourth, and fifth centuries see Robert Grosse, *Römische Militärgeschichte
von Gallienus bis zum Beginn der byzantinischen
Themenverfassung* (Berlin: Weidmann, 1920), pp.
70–79.

8 Ernst Hohl, ed., *Scriptores Historiae Augustae*
(Leipzig, G.D.R.: Teubner, 1965), vols. 1, 2, Comm.
15.6.

9 See, for example, William L. Rogers, *Greek and
Roman Naval Warfare* (Annapolis, Md.: Naval
Institute Press, 1937), p. 538: "After many centuries
of naval warfare, the battle of Actium established
the economic unity of the Mediterranean basin
and thereafter, for over three centuries the peace of
Rome prevailed over those waters, during which period the Roman navy shrank to a mere coast guard
for the protection of the public against pirates."

10 Otto Hirschfeld, ed., *Inscriptiones Galliae Narbonen-
sis Latinae = Corpus Inscriptionum Latinarum 12*
(Berlin: G. Reimer, 1888), p. 686.

11 See, e.g., Theodor Mommsen, ed., *Inscriptiones
Aegypti et Asiae. Inscriptiones provinciarum Europae
Graecarum. Inscriptionum Illyrici partes I–V =
Corpus Inscriptionum Latinarum 3* (Berlin: G.
Reimer, 1873), p. 3228 (dating from the mid-250s),
where legionary vexillations are mentioned that
had been transferred to the Danube together with
auxiliary units assigned to them.

12 For the relocation under Probus see Ludwig
Mendelssohn, ed., *Zosimi comitis et exadvocati fisci
Historia nova* (Leipzig, Ger.: B. G. Teubner, 1887)
[hereafter Zos.], 1.68.3. For Carinus see Hermann

Dessau, ed., *Inscriptiones Latinae Selectae* (Berlin: Weidmann, 1892–1916), vols. 1–3 [hereafter ILS], p. 608; for the relocation, Zos., 1.68.3.

13 ILS, p. 615. See Patrick J. Casey, *The British Usurpers Carausius and Allectus* (London: Batsford, 1994), pp. 93–94.

14 On the *bagaudae* see Ralf Urban, *Gallia rebellis: Erhebungen in Gallien im Spiegel antiker Zeugnisse* (Stuttgart, Ger.: Franz Steiner, 1999), pp. 94–96; and Philippe Badot and Daniel De Decker, "La naissance du mouvement Bagaude," *Klio* 74 (1992), pp. 324–70.

15 Carlo Santini, ed., *Eutropii Breviarium ab urbe condita* (Leipzig, G.D.R., B. G. Teubner, 1979), 9.21.

16 Ibid. See Casey, *British Usurpers Carausius and Allectus*, pp. 39–41, and Anthony R. Birley, *The Roman Government of Britain* (Oxford, U.K.: Oxford Univ. Press, 2005), p. 375.

17 Roger Aubrey Baskerville Mynors, ed., *XII Panegyrici Latini* (Oxford, U.K.: Clarendon, 1964) [hereafter Paneg.], 8.12.2.

18 For Carausius's coinage see Hugh P. G. Williams, *Carausius: A Consideration of the Historical, Archaeological and Numismatic Aspects of His Reign* (Oxford, U.K.: Archaeopress, 2004), pp. 68–71.

19 Pierre Dufraigne, ed., *Aurelius Victor: Livre des Césars* (Paris: Les Belles Lettres, 1975), 39.38. See Casey, *British Usurpers Carausius and Allectus*, p. 110f., and Birley, *Roman Government of Britain*, p. 381f.

20 Allectus has been identified as some sort of financial official in the past (by, e.g., Casey, *British Usurpers Carausius and Allectus*, pp. 127–29). See, however, Birley, *Roman Government of Britain*, p. 375f. For Boulogne-sur-Mer see Paneg. 8.6.1–7.3.

21 For the invasion, Paneg. 8.15.1.

22 Ibid., 6.7.2.

23 For the title *Britannicus Maximus II* see Margaret Roxan, *Roman Military Diplomas 1954–1977* (London: Univ. of London, Institute of Archaeology, 1978), p. 78.

24 The main source for these visits comprises the ADVENTUS AUG coins (Carol H. V. Sutherland, ed., *The Roman Imperial Coinage*, vol. 6, *The Diocletian Reform: Maximinus II [294–313]* [London: Spink, 1967], pp. 133–45; Patrick M. Bruun, ed., *The Roman Imperial Coinage*, vol. 7, *Constantine I: Licinius [313–337]* [London: Spink, 1966], 1.2.21) minted on the occasion of Constantine's visits. See Birley, *Roman Government of Britain*, p. 411f.; see also Casey, *British Usurpers Carausius and Allectus*, pp. 184–86.

25 ILS, p. 8942, ILS, p. 696. See also Timothy D. Barnes, *The New Empire of Diocletian and Constantine* (Cambridge, Mass.: Harvard Univ. Press, 1982), p. 81.

26 For the engagement with the Franks see Richard Förster, ed., *Libanii opera* (Leipzig, Ger.: B. G. Teubner, 1903–27), vols. 1–12 [hereafter Lib.], *or.* 59.126–35, and Günther Christian Hansen, ed., *Sokrates: Kirchengeschichte* (Berlin: Akademie

Verlag, 1995), 2.13.4. On the dating of his visit see Theodor Mommsen and Paulus Meyer, eds., *Theodosiani libri XVI cum constitutionibus Sirmondianis et leges novellae ad Theodosianum pertinentes* (Berlin: Weidmann, 1905), 11.16.5, and Pierre-Louis Malosse, "Qu'est donc allé faire Constant 1er en Bretagne pendant l'hiver 343?," *Historia* 48 (1999), p. 466f.

27 On Magnentius see PLRE 1.532 (Magnentius). See also Urban, *Gallia rebellis*, pp. 101–103, and John Drinkwater, "The Revolt and Ethnic Origin of the Usurper Magnentius (350–53), and the Rebellion of Vetranio (350)," *Chiron* 30 (2000), pp. 131–45.

28 Joseph Bidez and Franz-Valéry-Marie Cumont, eds., *Imperatoris Caesaris Flavii Claudii Iuliani Epistulae, leges, poematia, fragmenta varia* (Paris: Les Belles Lettres, 1922), *Ep. Ad. Ath.* 279d–80c. See also Lib. *or.* 18.82–87, and Wolfgang Seyfarth, ed., *Rerum gestarum libri qui supersunt* (Leipzig, G.D.R.: B. G. Teubner, 1978), vols. 1–2 [hereafter Amm. Marc.], 18.2.3–4.

29 Amm. Marc. 27.8.1–9.1, 28.3.1–8, 30.7.9–11. For an overview of all the available sources see Birley, *Roman Government of Britain*, pp. 431–39.

30 On Flavius Iovinus see PLRE 1.462–63 (Iovinus 6); and Birley, *Roman Government of Britain*, p. 430. On Severus see PLRE 1.832 (Severus 8); and Birley, *Roman Government of Britain*, p. 429.

31 On Theodosius see PLRE 1.902–904 (Theodosius 3); and Birley, *Roman Government of Britain*, pp. 430–40.

32 Amm. Marc. 28.3.7.

33 Denis Feissel, *Recueil des inscriptions chrétiennes de Macédoine du IIIe au VIe siècle* (Paris: De Boccard, 1983), n. 273. See also Paneg. 2.5.4, and Karl Friedrich Weber and Julius Caesar, eds., *Hegesippus de bello judaico* (Marburg, Hesse-Cassel: Elwert'sche Universitätsbuchhandlung, 1864), 5.15.1.

34 For Theodosius in Britain see Amm. Marc. 28.3.7.

35 Continental units may have been sent to Britain as well; see Mark W. C. Hassall, "Britain in the Notitia," in *Aspects of the Notitia Dignitatum*, ed. Goodburn and Bartholomew, pp. 103–41. For taking troops from Britain see Günther Christian Hansen, ed., *Sozomenos. Historia Ecclesiastica: Kirchengeschichte* (Turnhout, Belg.: Brepols, 2004), vols. 1–4, *h.e.* 7.13.10. Some units attested on the continent according to the *notitia dignitatum* appear to have been transferred from British garrisons, though whether that was done under Maximus is unclear; see, e.g., the *pedites Seguntienses* (Otto Seeck, *Notitia dignitatum. Accedunt notitia urbis Constantinopolitanae et laterculi provinciarum* [Berlin: Weidmann, 1876], Occ. 5.65), which may have come from Caernarvon. On Maximus see Patrick J. Casey, "Magnus Maximus in Britain: A Reappraisal," in *The End of Roman Britain: Papers Arising from a Conference, Durham 1978*, ed. P. J. Casey (Oxford, U.K.: Archaeopress, 1979), pp. 66–79; and Birley, *Roman Government of Britain*, pp. 443–50.

36 For removing troops from Britain see Zos. 6.2.1, 6.5.2. On the usurpation see Birley, *Roman Government of Britain*, pp. 455–60.

III *Captain Vancouver and the Coast Salish*
Contact History as Naval History in the Pacific Northwest, 1792

MADELEINE PECKHAM

On 21 May 1792, in a remote inlet in the Pacific Northwest, Lt. Peter Puget found himself in "a most awkward predicament."[1] Two days before, he had been dispatched by the captain of HMS *Discovery*, George Vancouver, with a week's worth of provisions and two boats to survey the inland waters surrounding what would later be called Puget Sound.[2] Approaching a native village at the end of Carr Inlet, Puget's men spotted several canoes. He was initially unconcerned, but the encounter soon became tense. The Native Americans did not understand his attempts to communicate in the Nootka language. They were unmoved by offers of gifts. They soon made it clear, in Puget's words, that "our Departure would be more agreeable than our Visit." Puget obliged, and the canoes left them alone.[3]

Later in the day, when half of Puget's party was ashore, the canoes returned. This time they were armed. Puget ordered his men to eat their noontime meal ashore as planned, but he could not ignore the signs that an attack was imminent. He was in a difficult position, "for unwilling to fire on these poor People, who might have been unacquainted with the advantage we had over them, & not wishing to run the Risk of having the People [that is, his men] wounded by the first discharge of their Arrows, I absolutely felt at a Loss how to Act."[4] To demonstrate his superior firepower, Puget ordered a swivel gun fired into the water at a safe distance. He expected the natives to be astonished and afraid. They were unperturbed. To Puget's total astonishment, they responded by offering to trade their bows and arrows.[5] Reflecting on this incident, Puget complained of the natives' initial "Ingratitude" to "our Liberality and Kindness." He would not have hesitated to use force if necessary. Yet his breathless run-on sentences speak to the enormous relief he felt at, as he put it, "not having carried Matters to an Extremity."[6]

Puget's encounter with Native Americans in Carr Inlet calls into question conventional historical interpretations of eighteenth-century "first contact" events. Puget was not an incurious exploiter of the local population. Instead, he was concerned with cultivating goodwill, avoiding violence, and understanding indigenous behavior. The journals of Puget's *Discovery* colleagues are full of similar observations. Unfortunately, this delicacy did not extend to most Europeans who later used Vancouver's charts to colonize the Pacific Northwest. If *Discovery*'s involvement with Native Americans was uncharacteristically peaceful compared with later colonial activity, that suggests a question: What factors specific to *Discovery*'s mission influenced how its officers interpreted Native Americans? And, if Vancouver and his officers did not violently oppress the native population, as we might have expected, why did they not?

Beyond "Native/Newcomer" Relations

George Vancouver, captain of HMS *Discovery,* had been dispatched by the Admiralty in 1791, with HMS *Chatham* also under him, to settle the remaining details of the Nootka controversy, a territorial dispute between Spain and Britain over the Pacific coast of North America. He was ordered to oversee the repatriation of British property on what is now Vancouver Island and to survey the coastline from California to Alaska. *Discovery* and *Chatham* arrived on the Pacific coast in the spring of 1792.[7] Though Capt. James Cook had made first contact with the Nootka people in 1778 on Vancouver Island, inland Washington waters—home to the Coast Salish peoples—remained uncharted by Europeans until Vancouver's arrival in 1792.[8] For this reason, the so-called Salish Coast offers an ideal opportunity to examine a first contact between British naval personnel and Native Americans. Although Vancouver's 1792 summer survey continued north of the forty-ninth parallel into what is now Canada, this study focuses on events in the present-day United States, where most of the first contacts occurred and initial impressions were formed.

But what made *Discovery*'s first contact with the Coast Salish unique? On one hand, historians have rightly been encouraged to recognize diverse indigenous perspectives, but more work is needed to turn an equally critical eye to their European "discoverers." Broad historical approaches that depersonalize the individuals involved into faceless projections of imperialism are insufficient. Vancouver's voyage was a naval operation. *Discovery*'s peaceful approach to Native Americans was strongly shaped by the service culture of the Royal Navy and the professional experiences of Vancouver and his officers. It is important to note that European naval personnel initiated many, if not most, formal first contacts with Pacific indigenous peoples during the eighteenth century.[9] In light of this, it is possible to offer a new, naval-history interpretation of meetings between Pacific indigenous peoples and their European "discoverers," one that transcends the oversimplified "native/newcomer" formulation. As this investigation of Captain Vancouver and the Coast Salish demonstrates, a critical rethinking of eighteenth-century contact history must consider that it is a *naval* history.

Rediscovering *Discovery*

The 1992 bicentennial of Captain Vancouver's arrival on the Salish Coast was, to many historians, no cause for celebration. Commemorating Vancouver's achievements seemed inappropriate in light of the brutal treatment of indigenous peoples that resulted from later use of his charts and surveys.[10] That Vancouver's bicentennial coincided with the five hundredth anniversary of Christopher Columbus's "discovery" of America seemed only to confirm his place in a long history of brutal colonial oppressors. It is true that works such as Thomas R. Berger's *A Long and Terrible Shadow* and Ronald Wright's *Stolen Continents* are necessary correctives to previous historiography that now seems too congratulatory of European expansion.[11] Yet it is also essential to make distinctions between the goals and actions of different European explorers and to situate them in their diverse historical and geographical contexts. The "oppressor/victim" framework is of little help when trying to understand what motivated explorers such as Vancouver, who did not participate directly in colonial settlement, or to explain why he and his men did not engage in the violent, exploitative behavior that Berger and Wright insist was globally manifested by Europeans in the early modern period.

Moreover, one does not have to accept uncritically the "oppressor/victim" paradigm to see the importance of indigenous perspectives in the history of European expansion. As historical interest has shifted away from a celebratory view of European exploration and colonization, new attention to the study of "native/newcomer relations" has offered valuable insight into previously unheard indigenous voices. Peoples of the Pacific Northwest, including the Coast Salish, Nuu-chah-nulth (Nootka), Tlingit, and Squamish, have been the focus of much of this research.[12] Though this approach is essential to understanding the indigenous side of the native/newcomer exchange, most ethnohistorical scholarship is inherently local, or "community based," and either uninterested in probing the motivations of many different "newcomer" groups or poorly positioned to do so.

Strangely, Vancouver's expedition to the Pacific Northwest has rarely featured prominently in traditional naval history. Faced as they are with the more obvious glamour of the French Revolutionary and Napoleonic Wars, it is little wonder that historians immersed in the naval tumult of Europe in the 1790s often overlook Vancouver's voyage. The home to which Vancouver and his men returned in 1795 must indeed have felt unfamiliar to them, isolated as they had been from news of the rapidly changing European political landscape. Perhaps modern naval historians continue to treat Vancouver with similar uncertainty, unsure exactly where he belongs. While much work has been done to consider Britain's empire as a seaborne one, few historians have directly associated this fact with the naval personnel who actually realized it.[13] The naval dimension of first-contact situations during the eighteenth century has likewise seldom, if ever, been considered.

Discussion of first contact between British naval personnel and indigenous peoples in the Pacific has usually focused on Cook's three Pacific voyages. Glyndwr Williams's work on Cook's interpretations of indigenous peoples is particularly relevant to this study. Williams argues that Cook displayed an impressive ability to assess Pacific peoples within their own contexts, rather than in relation to European expectations of indigenous behavior.[14] If this interpretation was not widely adopted by the general public, Williams argues, it is because Cook's observations never appeared in the original published accounts of the voyages and were supplanted by Sir Joseph Banks's decidedly less sympathetic portrayals.[15] However, there is good reason to believe that Cook's crewmates, Vancouver among them, incorporated their captain's knowledge and perspective into their later Pacific service. While serving under Cook, Vancouver developed a particularly strong reputation for dealing skillfully with native peoples. Lieutenant King described in his journal of the third voyage the key role that Vancouver played in negotiations to recover Cook's remains after he was killed by Hawaiians at Kealakekua Bay. King noted that amid extreme tensions, Hawaiian leaders coming on board *Resolution* "seemd rejoiced to see Mr Vancouver . . . who best understood them."[16]

As Vancouver knew, establishing good relations with indigenous communities was crucial to naval success abroad. Making first contact with "undiscovered" peoples also afforded an opportunity for experienced naval officers to apply their knowledge of other cultures. It is within this interpretive framework—of professional necessity and professional experience—that *Discovery*'s experiences with indigenous peoples need to be viewed. Unfortunately, this value-neutral approach has largely been overlooked in favor of assessing whether Vancouver was culturally sensitive—"ahead of his time," according to a present-day standard—or whether his observations are too polluted by his own cultural bias to be of any use. In an effort to reconsider European observations of native peoples, some historians have concluded that we cannot glean any reliable information from explorer/colonizer accounts, because they reflect nothing more than preconceived European notions. Others have suggested that contact events result by their very nature in failure to communicate and in inevitable conflict.[17] A close reading of *Discovery*'s officers' own accounts, however, suggests that they were neither incurious nor quick to violence.

Native/Naval Relations?

Rather than a "native/newcomer" history, we need a "native/naval" history. The social history of the late-eighteenth-century Royal Navy is the key to understanding the behavior of *Discovery*'s officers on the Salish Coast. This historical orientation allows us to glimpse some of the shared assumptions and motivations that guided Vancouver and his officers. In this, my work relies heavily on N. A. M. Rodger's *The Wooden World*. Rodger ultimately concludes that "the wooden world [of the eighteenth-century Royal Navy] was built of the same materials as the wider world," but it is impossible to dismiss the unique service culture that his study elucidates.[18] Though much of Rodger's analysis should be reassessed relative to the changing historical and social circumstances after 1775, it remains an appropriate and necessary basis for this study. Because of the nature of the available source material, this study focuses primarily on commissioned officers. There are several surviving accounts by officers—published journals, official logs, and private diaries—that make it possible to examine different aspects of native/naval first contacts.

The distinctive naval experience that shaped *Discovery*'s approach to native peoples was foundational; it was shared throughout the officer corps of the Royal Navy. Naval officers formed a distinct class within the eighteenth-century "better sort." The typical naval officer chose the service because he lacked an inheritance or the political connections or academic ability that might have afforded him other respectable options.[19] Those not from landed families were considered gentlemen in name only.[20] The work was unglamorous, uncomfortable, dangerous, and low paying. Unlike in the army, the purchase of commissions was forbidden, though officers with strong patronage networks were more likely to succeed. Promotion was open, in theory, to all those who acquired the necessary skills.[21] The skills-based nature of naval advancement is particularly evident in the humble backgrounds of officers chosen for exploratory voyages in which technical ability was especially critical—George Anson was the second son of a Stafford lawyer, William Bligh's father was a Plymouth customs officer, and James Cook, son of a Yorkshire farm laborer, began his seafaring career in the merchant service.[22] What the naval officer often lacked in book learning he made up for in technical expertise and raw experiences of survival. Moreover, officers' informal education in commanding what Rodger has shown to be ethnically, socially, and racially diverse naval crews had a far greater impact on their interactions with indigenous peoples than has been previously considered.[23]

Discovery's officers reflected many of these trends. Vancouver was the youngest son of a customs official, beginning his naval career in 1772 at age fourteen. Vancouver's first experience of naval life was service under Captain Cook on board *Resolution,* in Cook's second and third Pacific voyages. Vancouver was among the first to benefit from Cook's early support for naval chronometers, and he became skilled at mathematics and lunar calculations.[24] John Naish, author of the only recent biographical study of Vancouver and his officers, attributes Vancouver's perfectionism and famously short temper to the early loss of both his parents, but it seems just as likely that his rigid personality developed under the intense strain of service in the Pacific.[25] Vancouver's experiences with Cook brought him into contact with diverse indigenous cultures, and his proficiency in dealing with native peoples of the South Seas made him a qualified candidate for future missions in the Pacific.

Vancouver's proven skill at hydrography was also a major asset in peacetime, when most naval officers struggled to find positions. It was in this capacity, while surveying the Caribbean from 1786 to 1789, that he first met several of the men who were to become his officers on the 1791 voyage, including Joseph Whidbey, who would be *Discovery*'s sailing master, and Peter Puget, its third lieutenant.[26] Puget—like many other naval officers the younger son, of a family of bankers—went to sea at age twelve. He too benefited from a thorough mathematical education on board ship and saw action against French Caribbean colonies during the American Revolutionary War. After peace was declared, Puget, age nineteen, began his surveying work with Vancouver in Jamaica.[27]

Unlike many of his colleagues, Thomas Manby, master's mate, came from a prominent family in Norfolk and had little naval experience abroad. Nonetheless, Manby must have demonstrated a level of competence and bravery that made him tolerable to Vancouver, who had a famously short temper for unskilled young aristocrats wished on him by well-connected parents. This was most clearly demonstrated by Vancouver's drastic response to the insolent conduct of Midshipman Thomas Pitt, second Baron Camelford and a cousin of the prime minister. Vancouver, after administering public rebukes, demotion, and even flogging, eventually despaired of compelling young Pitt's obedience and in 1793, sent him home from Hawaii under arrest on board the supply ship *Daedalus*.[28] Vancouver surely understood that doing so was political suicide. His treatment of Pitt dogged him for the final years of his life after his return to England in 1795, permanently damaging his reputation.[29] As Naish observes, Vancouver treated indigenous leaders much more carefully than he did members of the British aristocracy.[30] Far from home, Vancouver evidently felt that competence and experience outranked noble birth.

Discovery's officers were members of a service that demanded lifelong commitment, practical skills, and the ability to work with different races, classes, and cultures. These irreducible factors of the naval profession were the defining elements of first contact on the Salish Coast.

Interpreting Native/Naval Contact on the Salish Coast

The shared Royal Navy culture of *Discovery*'s officers is the central element of their writings about the Coast Salish. Vancouver and his officers' remarkably cautious, curious treatment of Native Americans is not necessarily proof of their personal magnanimity or racial sensitivity. However, the surprisingly peaceful coexistence of *Discovery* and the Coast Salish shows convincingly that it was specifically as naval officers that Vancouver and his officers developed their objectives and expectations for first contact. The three texts on which this study relies—Vancouver's published account of the voyage, Puget's official log, and Manby's private diary—offer many possible avenues for assessing the native/naval contact. Though we can be certain that Manby confined his more salacious observations of indigenous women to his private diary and that Puget may have been more ethnologically curious than some of his colleagues, the diversity of perspectives from men on the same ship is extremely valuable.

In reading these accounts, it is important to remember that *Discovery*'s primary activity in the Pacific Northwest was coastal surveying. Most of the surveying of inland Washington waters had to be conducted in small boats with limited supplies, making peaceful interaction with Native American communities critical to success. We should be cautious not to conflate conciliation with respect or to suggest that engaging in trade meant that *Discovery*'s officers considered the Coast Salish to be their "equals." However, Vancouver repeatedly advocated a peaceful approach to the area's native residents, because he knew that maintaining good relations was essential to his mission. Vancouver was not uniquely sensitive in this regard. This approach was specifically enumerated in the orders he received from the Admiralty in 1791: "In the execution of every part of this service," the orders concluded, Vancouver was "strictly charged to use every possible care to avoid disputes with the natives" and to "conciliate their friendship and confidence."[31] The Admiralty, concerned with future operations in the Pacific Northwest, knew that a peaceful relationship with local indigenous peoples would enable naval operations, bolster Britain's territorial claims, and facilitate future colonial development.

Vancouver took seriously his orders to avoid conflict with native peoples. Before arriving in Tahiti in December 1791, he issued an extensive list of "Rules and Orders" outlining proper conduct for his crew in dealing with "the natives of the several South-Sea islands." Like the orders Cook promulgated when he first visited Tahiti in 1769, Vancouver's rules set expectations for fair and honest trading supervised by officers, restitution for stolen or damaged property, and a system of barter that set trade values of specific British items relative to native goods. Vancouver understood that poor treatment of the native population would hinder trading relationships and make it difficult to maintain a safe winter anchorage in Tahiti. Vancouver stressed this point when he ordered that "every fair means be used to cultivate a friendship with the different Indians, and on all occasions to treat them with every degree of kindness and humanity."[32]

While examples abound of poor communication and misinterpretation of Salish behavior and customs, officers' claims of pursuing a "reciprocal friendship" with those they encountered seem credible, in light of their frequent repetition and the total absence of bloodshed during the exploration of the Salish Coast.[33] Vancouver and his officers viewed conflict and threats of violence as noteworthy; they appeared to be the exception rather than the rule of indigenous behavior. Vancouver characterized Puget's previously described encounter in Carr Inlet as displaying on the Coast Salish side "a character so diametrically opposite to that which, in every other instance, seemed to govern [their] general conduct. . . . [It was] an extraordinary circumstance, for which it is difficult to account."[34] Although confusion and misunderstanding were often inevitable, Vancouver and his officers were adamant that violence must be avoided.

But a practical peacekeeping mandate does not fully explain the naval diarists' interest in Coast Salish culture. Again, the naval perspective suggests the answer. Vancouver and his officers came equipped with personally acquired knowledge of diverse indigenous peoples throughout the Pacific, the Caribbean, and other far-flung locales. As a result of career experiences, they had a context for establishing and interpreting first contact, even though they lacked specific knowledge of the local culture. Though Vancouver and his colleagues may have borne many of the usual biases of eighteenth-century Britons, they also displayed a remarkable ability to weigh prevailing assumptions against their own observations.

Because the naval outlook strongly influenced what *Discovery*'s diarists considered noteworthy, it is unsurprising that much of what the officers noticed related to maritime activity, such as boats, weapons, and coastal settlements. These observations were by no means as demeaning or self-congratulatory as one might expect. On the contrary, the naval diarists often showed appreciation for Coast Salish ingenuity and design. Manby and Puget credited the native canoes as being "well adapted for going fast" and ideally suited to inland waters.[35] Vancouver described Coast Salish bows and arrows as being "of superior construction"; echoing many of his fellow officers, Manby found them "well calculated for the purpose, and manifest[ing] a degree of genius in their formation."[36]

Discovery's officers were less impressed with Coast Salish settlements. Puget and Manby described native villages as extremely dirty, frequently referring to "the horrid Stench which came from all parts of these Habitations."[37] Manby considered the first Coast Salish people he encountered as "in person filthy and stinking" and characterized them as "the nastiest race of people under the sun."[38] While cultural standards of hygiene certainly varied, repeated observations from *Discovery*'s officers of "filth" are understandable in light of the eighteenth-century Royal Navy's unusually high standards of cleanliness. In eighteenth-century Europe, dirty or foul-smelling air was thought to spread disease.[39] This belief significantly influenced Royal Navy shipboard communities. While eighteenth-century science could not explain the causes of infectious disease, the correlation of unsanitary conditions with illness was evident, and it was well understood that proper hygiene in the close quarters of a ship was essential to good health. Eighteenth-century naval officers' obsessive efforts to keep their ships smelling sweet, including daily washing of the decks and weekly laundry when possible, had a demonstrably positive effect on crew health, though not for the reasons they believed.[40] *Discovery* was no exception. Manby described how "the utmost precaution is therefore daily taken to prevent any infection taking place . . . and the greatest attention is paid to dryness and cleanliness."[41] Though cultural chauvinism undoubtedly played a role, it is clear that naval notions of hygiene strongly shaped the officers' reactions to Coast Salish villages.

Despite their initially negative impressions of Coast Salish communities, *Discovery*'s officers displayed an impressively thoughtful eighteenth-century view of other cultural differences. The frequent use of face and hair paint excited much comment from *Discovery*'s officers, and even Manby, who regarded Coast Salish fashions as particularly "odious," understood that the Salish applied paint to "make themselves more beautiful, in their own opinion."[42] Puget observed, with regard to face paint, that

> every Person had a fashion of his own, & to us who were Strangers to Indians, this Sight conveyed a Stronger Force of the Savageness of the Native Inhabitants, than any other Circumstance we had hitherto met with; not but their Conduct, friendly and inoffensive, had already merited our warmest Approbation, but their Appearance was absolutely terrific [that is, terrifying] & it will frequently occur, that the Imagination receives a much greater Shock by such unusual Objects, than it would otherwise would, was that Object divested of its Exterior Ornaments or Dress, or the Sight was more familiarized to People in a State of Nature & Though we could not behold these Ornaments with the same satisfactory Eye as themselves, yet in receiving the looking Glasses, each appeared well Satisfied with his own Fashion.[43]

Puget also suggested a surprising comparison to the Coast Salish use of face paint, describing how "the Paint only differed in the Colours & not the Quantity used by our own Fair Country women—In these two Instances we meet with some Resemblance to our Customs."[44] Though he still felt that the Coast Salish style was "absolutely terrific," he knew it was simply a matter of taste.

Vancouver and his officers also rejected prevailing European beliefs about Native Americans when they found them to be unsupported by evidence. Foremost among these was an assumed native propensity for violence. John Meares, a central figure in the 1790 Nootka controversy, related wild tales of indigenous aggression in the account of his adventures, but Vancouver's officers remarked in contrast on the "present pacific Dispositions" of the Coast Salish they encountered in the same area.[45] Puget likewise became skeptical of the claims of American merchant captain Robert Gray that "he lost an Officer and 2 or 3 Men who were barbarously murdered by the Natives" in the Strait of Juan de Fuca.[46] An anonymous diarist on *Chatham*, thought to be either its clerk or surgeon, related a story from late April 1792 in which Captain Gray "gave no very favourable account of the Northern Indians whose daring and insolent spirit had carried them to very unwarrantable lengths. . . . Several people of different Ships had been treacherously murdered"—yet the diarist found that his own ship's first encounter with indigenous visitors was peaceful.[47]

It is impossible to determine whether Meares and Gray did something to provoke a violent reaction from the area's Salish inhabitants before *Discovery* arrived. However, considering the friendly response that Vancouver's trading overtures received, it is clear that either Meares and Gray greatly exaggerated the belligerence of the coast's inhabitants or Vancouver's efforts to avoid conflict and trade fairly contributed directly to keeping the peace. It is possible to imagine that private merchants might have had less incentive to cultivate peaceful relations with the indigenous locals, who controlled the supply of their valuable furs, than did naval officers, whose primary concern was the safety of their surveying teams. From the sources available, one can only speculate. However, Manby suggested that the mercantile rivalry between Meares and Gray—and more broadly, Britain and the United States—may have motivated the spread of false information, "which is believed with greedy avidity and given to the deluded public factum factorum, dressed up in the language with a chart annexed to it." [48] It is likely that outlandish tales of hostile natives and other subterfuge were deployed to discourage trade competition in the area. Manby himself retreated to the old explanation of "savage fury" to explain why so many Coast Salish individuals displayed nasty scars and missing teeth, but it is clear that aside from his involvement in the tense situation involving Peter Puget's surveying team in Carr Inlet, Manby had little personally acquired evidence to support this explanation. [49]

Vancouver and his officers were also keenly interested in whether the Coast Salish practiced cannibalism. Many eighteenth-century Europeans associated cannibalism with "primitive" cultures, and it remained a stomach-turning subject of curiosity on exploratory voyages throughout the period. [50] Vancouver's account contains a puzzling incident that occurred while sharing a meal with about a dozen Native American guests. After asking permission to cross the literal line in the sand that Vancouver had drawn between his men and the Salish party, the indigenous visitors sat alongside the British crew, exchanging food. However, when Vancouver offered to share some venison with them, "they could not be induced to taste it. They received it from us with great disgust." This strong negative response to venison "left no doubt in our minds that they believed it to be human flesh." Before Vancouver had convinced them of their mistake, they "threw [the meat] down on the dirt, with gestures of great aversion and displeasure." [51]

This proof was enough to dispel any lingering doubts—Vancouver concluded that although "these people have been represented . . . as accustomed inhumanly to devour the flesh of their conquered enemies, . . . this instance must necessarily exonerate this particular tribe from so barbarous a practice." [52] Manby also surmised that the scorched human bones he sometimes encountered while walking in the woods represented a kind of Coast Salish burial practice rather than mealtime propensities, indicating that in light of this, "I think it ungenerous in those navigators that pronounce the inhabitants of this part of America cannibals." [53] Puget forcefully seconded this, declaring, "I cannot think any Person authorized to fix such an indelible Stain on the Character of any Tribe, & much more so on the Numerous inhabitants of NW America whose Manners Customs Religion Laws & Government we are yet perfect Strangers to." [54] While we can only speculate about why Vancouver's Coast Salish dinner guests really recoiled from the venison, it is clear that Vancouver and his officers were happy to dispel the myth that the Coast Salish practiced cannibalism. Vancouver had, after all, actually encountered a culture that practiced ritual cannibalism, when he was with Cook in New Zealand in 1773.[55]

Trading was another fruitful ground for cultural speculation. Manby assumed that "the introduction of European manufactures occasioned a material alteration in the economy of the inhabitants by exciting them to industry in hunting for valuable furs," though on some level he understood that the Coast Salish did not share a European notion of property.[56] Yet a trade motivation, regardless of cultural meaning, certainly existed on both sides; *Discovery*'s officers for their part judged bartering encounters on the basis of their own cultural expectations of fairness. *Discovery*'s trade relations with Coast Salish communities were positive and appeared, at least to the British officers, to be advantageous to both sides. It is noteworthy that the word most frequently used by *Discovery*'s officers to describe their native/naval dealings is "honest." Vancouver repeatedly described that trade was conducted "in a very fair and honest manner";[57] Puget made so bold as to speculate after a particularly successful trade encounter, "If these People behave with such Confidence to Strangers, may we not infer, that Innate Principles of Honesty actuated their Conduct on this Occasion?"[58] What Puget interpreted as "Innate Principles of Honesty" was probably an experience of the Coast Salish custom of ritual gift giving and reciprocity called the *potlatch*.[59] However, celebratory descriptions of Coast Salish honesty in trading are revealing with respect to Euro-naval commercial expectations formed at home. Measured against the nightmarish experiences that naval officers often had dealing with rapacious Britons throughout the global empire, this enthusiastic response to Coast Salish "honesty" is perhaps unsurprising.[60]

If the distinctively naval perspective of *Discovery*'s officer diaries sometimes seems unclear, the published account of Archibald Menzies, the voyage's supernumerary botanist, provides a useful contrast.[61] Menzies was not a naval officer but a civilian surgeon by trade and an enthusiastic amateur naturalist. His powerful patron Sir Joseph Banks, president of the Royal Society, secured Menzies a place on *Discovery*, in spite of Vancouver's vigorous objections to civilian passengers. As might be expected, Menzies's account focuses far more on flora and fauna and the potential for land cultivation than on many of the subjects that interested the naval officers. However, the Coast Salish are relatively absent from his account. This may be because, being a passenger and not an officer on *Discovery*, he probably had less direct contact with indigenous people than did his shipmates who supervised trading and other formal encounters. Yet it is also clear that Menzies was less ethnologically curious than his naval colleagues. His descriptions of the Coast Salish are notably sparse, and he excludes from his journal encounters with Native Americans at which we know he was present.

It might be tempting to expect a certain learned sensitivity in Menzies's account because of his scientific education, but compared with the naval officer accounts, just the opposite seems to be true. A particularly illustrative circumstance occurred when Vancouver, Puget, and Menzies, on a walk, came on human skeletons buried in "a very singular manner," placed in canoes suspended from trees.[62] Vancouver initially speculated that this may have been the final resting place of dead warriors and felt "particularly solicitous to prevent any indignity from being wantonly offered."[63] Puget considered that "the Natives I have Reason to believe do not much frequent this Place but on the most Solemn Occasions" and expressed discomfort at forming "conjectural ideas" about their religious traditions. He insisted on the need to gain "sufficient acquaintance with the Native Inhabitants [in order to] assume any Knowledge of their Manners or Customs."[64] In recording this extraordinary sight, Menzies coolly remarked only that it was "probably the remains of some superstitious ceremony" and returned to his lengthy discourse on local plants.[65]

Conclusion

Vancouver, Puget, Manby, and the rest of *Discovery*'s officers formed part of a naval profession that was culturally and socially distinct from other eighteenth-century imperial actors. Naval officers' professional experiences and career histories strongly influenced how they responded to indigenous peoples and how they described them. When *Discovery*'s officers encountered the Coast Salish, a previously "undiscovered" people, the naval perspective they shared was paramount in shaping their behavior toward and interpretations of the native people. Vancouver and his officers cooperated peacefully with the Coast Salish because their surveying and diplomatic mission demanded it but also because they were eager to learn more about the inhabitants of the Pacific Northwest. *Discovery*'s officers displayed an ethnological curiosity and openness to positive impressions of the Coast Salish that far exceeded the demands of their mission. Where Meares and other Europeans familiar with the area characterized its inhabitants as savage, violent, and unpredictable, *Discovery*'s officers came to different conclusions. They encountered the Coast Salish as naval officers—professionally focused, experienced in dealing with indigenous people on their own terms, and intensely curious.

In this paper I have presented a new framework for understanding a specific kind of early modern European/indigenous contact. Further work is necessary to test the extent to which the native/naval paradigm also applies to similar historical examples. Though comparisons with other first contacts, including Vancouver's other indigenous encounters on the *Discovery* voyage, are outside the scope of this study, there is abundant European source material available that can be used to probe how naval service cultures affected accounts of native/newcomer interaction. A native/naval rethinking of Cook's three voyages or a comparative study of French or Spanish naval exploration and first contact would be particularly instructive.

Indigenous oral traditions may also offer important insights into native interpretations of naval contact.

In undertaking a critical rethinking of imperial expansion that explores diverse European perspectives and goals, it is often tempting to wonder whether one's subjects were "ahead of their time" or uniquely accepting of difference. However, as this paper has sought to demonstrate, probing the multitude of ways social background, career, or personal history influenced European "discoverers" frees us from becoming partisans in the "oppressor/victim" debate. It is beyond question that Vancouver and his officers did not share our present-day beliefs about the equal value of diverse cultures. But it is also worth considering that if Vancouver and his men did not descend to the standard of destruction and cultural violence that we have come to expect of eighteenth-century Europeans, perhaps the answer lies with them, not with us. By integrating scholarship on the social and personal histories of *Discovery*'s officers with a close reading of their accounts of first contact with the Coast Salish, it is clear that the distinctive Royal Navy experience was the primary lens through which Vancouver and his officers interpreted this "undiscovered" people. It is enough to say that when *Discovery* left the Strait of Juan de Fuca in July 1792, Vancouver remembered the Coast Salish as "those who we had been so happy, on former occasions, to call our friends."[66]

N O T E S   I would like to acknowledge gratefully the support
of my thesis supervisor, Dr. Matthew Neufeld, whose
encouragement, criticism, and example have been
indispensable to my work. Thanks also to Dr. Keith
Carlson, who piqued my interest in the Salish Coast
and provided me with many sources for this paper
that I might otherwise have been unable to obtain.

1 Peter Puget, journal, in *With Vancouver in Inland
Washington Waters: Journals of 12 Crewmen, April–
June 1792,* ed. Richard Blumenthal (Jefferson, N.C.:
McFarland, 2007), p. 34. For the sake of convenience, I have chosen to cite from Blumenthal's
transcription of Peter Puget, which I have verified
against facsimiles of the handwritten original: *A Log
of the Proceedings of His Majesty's Sloop Discovery,
George Vancouver Esq., Commander, kept by Lieutenant Peter Puget from the 4th day of January 1791, to
the 14th day of January 1793,* ADM 55/27.99, The
National Archives, Kew, United Kingdom.

2 George Vancouver, *A Voyage of Discovery to the
North Pacific Ocean and round the World, 1791–
1795,* ed. W. Kaye Lamb (London: Hakluyt Society,
1984), vol. 2, p. 544.

3 Puget, journal, p. 33.

4 Ibid., pp. 34–35.

5 Ibid., p. 35.

6 Ibid., p. 46.

7 For a more detailed treatment of the Nootka con-
troversy, see Derek Pethick, *The Nootka Connec-
tion: Europe and the Northwest Coast, 1790–1795*
(Vancouver, B.C.: Douglas & McIntyre, 1980); N.
A. M. Rodger, *The Command of the Ocean: A Naval
History of Britain, 1649–1815* (New York: W. W.
Norton, 2005), pp. 364–65; and Vancouver, intro-
duction to *Voyage of Discovery,* vol. 1.

8 For the purposes of this study, "Coast Salish" refers
to indigenous people who lived in the area surrounding the inland waters of Washington and the
Strait of Juan de Fuca. Coast Salish is one of several
cultures in the Pacific Northwest, and the term
denotes inclusion in the Salish linguistic group. Because of Cook's experience with the Nootka people,
Vancouver was able to differentiate between these
two neighboring cultures on the basis of language
differences. I have chosen to refer to the people Vancouver encountered in summer 1792 as Coast Salish

rather than using modern or officially recognized
First Nation / tribal designations, because late-
eighteenth-century indigenous communities are not
interchangeable with the territorially discrete gov-
ernance units of the present day. Precontact Coast
Salish people migrated frequently and did not share
the Western understanding of land ownership. For
this reason, isolating a particular indigenous group
in the precolonial period is extremely difficult,
especially when working from European sources. I
have chosen to include only examples that I believe
with a high degree of certainty to involve Coast
Salish peoples. For further discussion of these issues,
see Wayne Suttles, *Coast Salish Essays* (Seattle: Univ.
of Washington Press, 1987), and Keith Carlson, *The
Power of Place, the Problem of Time: Aboriginal Identity and Historical Consciousness in the Cauldron of
Colonialism* (Toronto: Univ. of Toronto Press, 2010).

9 For a thorough overview of the many varieties of
Pacific exploration in the eighteenth century, see
Nicholas Thomas, *Islanders: The Pacific in the Age of
Empire* (New Haven, Conn.: Yale Univ. Press, 2010).

10 A more comprehensive discussion of this can be
found in Robin Fisher and Hugh Johnston, introduction to *From Maps to Metaphors: The Pacific
World of George Vancouver,* ed. Robin Fisher and
Hugh Johnston (Vancouver: Univ. of British Columbia [hereafter UBC] Press, 1993), pp. 17–29.

11 Thomas R. Berger, *A Long and Terrible Shadow:
White Values, Native Rights in the Americas,
1492–1992* (Vancouver, B.C.: Douglas & McIntyre,
1991); Ronald Wright, *Stolen Continents: The New
World through Indian Eyes* (Toronto: Penguin Books,
1993).

12 Notable titles include Robin Fisher, *Contact and
Conflict: Indian-European Relations in British Co-
lumbia, 1774–1890* (Vancouver: UBC Press, 1980),
and Suttles, *Coast Salish Essays.* Important recent
examples are Carlson, *Power of Place;* Noel Elizabeth
Currie, *Constructing Colonial Discourse: Captain
Cook at Nootka Sound* (Montreal, Que.: McGill-
Queen's Univ. Press, 2005); and Yvonne Marshall,
"Dangerous Liaisons: Maquinna, Quadra, and
Vancouver in Nootka Sound, 1790–5," in *From Maps
to Metaphors,* ed. Fisher and Johnston, pp. 160–75.

13 Jeremy Black, *The British Seaborne Empire* (New
Haven, Conn.: Yale Univ. Press, 2004); David

Cannadine, ed., *Empire, the Sea and Global History: Britain's Maritime World, c. 1760–c. 1840* (New York: Palgrave Macmillan, 2007); Rodger, *Command of the Ocean.*

14 Glyndwr Williams, "'Far Happier than We Europeans': Reactions to the Australian Aborigines on Cook's Voyage," in *Buccaneers, Explorers and Settlers: British Enterprise and Encounters in the Pacific, 1670–1800* (Burlington, Vt.: Ashgate, 2005), p. 508, previously published as "'Far Happier than We Europeans': Reactions to the Australian Aborigines on Cook's Voyage," *Historical Studies* 19, no. 77 (1981), pp. 499–512; Williams, "The English and Aborigines: First Contacts," in *Buccaneers, Explorers and Settlers,* p. 3, previously published as "The English and Aborigines: First Contacts," *History Today* 38 (1988), pp. 1–9.

15 Williams, "'Far Happier than We Europeans,'" p. 509.

16 Lt. James King, quoted in Vancouver, *Voyage of Discovery,* vol. 1, p. 9.

17 For discussion of these perspectives, see Robin Fisher, "Vancouver's Vision of Native Peoples: The Northwest Coast and Hawai'i," in *Pacific Empires: Essays in Honour of Glyndwr Williams,* ed. Alan Frost (Vancouver: UBC Press, 1993), pp. 147–63.

18 N. A. M. Rodger, *The Wooden World: An Anatomy of the Georgian Navy* (Annapolis, Md.: Naval Institute Press, 1986), p. 346.

19 Ibid., p. 253.

20 Ibid., p. 259.

21 Ibid., p. 262.

22 Sir John Barrow, *The Life of George Lord Anson* (London: John Murray, 1839), p. 1; Gavin Kennedy, *Bligh* (London: Duckworth, 1978), p. 1; Richard Hough, *Captain James Cook* (New York: W. W. Norton, 1994), pp. 1–5.

23 Rodger, *Wooden World,* pp. 158–59.

24 John Naish, *The Interwoven Lives of George Vancouver, Archibald Menzies, Joseph Whidbey, and Peter Puget: Exploring the Pacific Northwest Coast* (Lewiston, N.Y.: Edwin Mellen, 1996), pp. 27–34.

25 Ibid., p. 28.

26 Ibid., pp. 36–37.

27 Ibid., p. 70.

28 Ibid., p. 132.

29 Ibid., pp. 351–73.

30 Ibid., p. 86.

31 Vancouver, *Voyage of Discovery,* vol. 1, p. 286.

32 Ibid., p. 377.

33 Puget, journal, p. 33.

34 Vancouver, *Voyage of Discovery,* vol. 2, p. 560.

35 Thomas Manby, *Journal of the Voyages of the H.M.S. Discovery and Chatham* (Fairfield, Wash.: Ye Galleon, 1992), p. 152. While the purely speculative remarks in this edition's introduction might lead some to think that the unnamed editors of this, the only published edition of Manby's "letter journal," have taken liberties with the transcription, I have verified its accuracy against photocopies of the original, in the Beineke Rare Book and Manuscript Library (Yale University). I have chosen, for the sake of convenience, to cite from the 1992 print edition. See also Puget, journal, p. 23.

36 Vancouver, *Voyage of Discovery,* vol. 2, p. 537; Manby, *Journal,* p. 182.

37 Puget, journal, p. 40.

38 Manby, *Journal,* p. 148.

39 For more on the underpinnings of early modern beliefs about infectious gases, see Roy Porter, *Disease, Medicine and Society in England, 1550–1860,* 2nd ed. (Cambridge, U.K.: Cambridge Univ. Press, 1993), pp. 17–26.

40 Geoffrey L. Hudson, ed., *British Military and Naval Medicine, 1600–1830* (New York: Editions Rodopi B.V., 2007); Rodger, *Wooden World,* pp. 105–109.

41 Manby, *Journal,* p. 71.

42 Ibid., p. 148.

43 Puget, journal, p. 40.

44 Ibid., p. 41.

45 Ibid., p. 16.

46 Ibid., p. 25.

47 Unsigned journal from HMS *Chatham* in *With Vancouver in Inland Washington Waters,* ed. Blumenthal, pp. 206–207.

48 Manby, *Journal,* p. 151.

49 Ibid., p. 183.

50 Coll Thrush, "Vancouver the Cannibal: Cuisine, Encounter, and the Dilemma of Difference on the Northwest Coast, 1774–1808," *Ethnohistory* 58, no. 1 (Winter 2011), pp. 1–35, esp. 20.

51 Vancouver, *Voyage of Discovery,* vol. 2, pp. 551–52.

52 Ibid., p. 552.

53 Manby, *Journal,* p. 165.

54 Puget, journal, p. 27.

55 Anne Salmond, *The Trial of the Cannibal Dog: The Remarkable Story of Captain Cook's Encounters in the South Seas* (New Haven, Conn.: Yale Univ. Press, 2003), p. 125.

56 Manby, *Journal,* pp. 181–82.

57 Vancouver, *Voyage of Discovery,* vol. 2, p. 525.

58 Puget, journal, p. 23.

59 For a detailed discussion of the Coast Salish potlatch, see Suttles, *Coast Salish Essays.*

60 See J. M. Haas, *A Management Odyssey: The Royal Dockyards, 1714–1914* (New York: Univ. Press of America, 1994).

61 Archibald Menzies, *Menzies' Journal of Vancouver's Voyage: April to October 1792,* ed. C. F. Newcombe (Victoria, B.C.: Legislative Assembly, 1923).

62 Vancouver, *Voyage of Discovery,* vol. 2, p. 539.

63 Ibid.

64 Puget, journal, pp. 26–27.

65 Menzies, *Menzies' Journal,* p. 20.

66 Vancouver, *Voyage of Discovery,* vol. 2, p. 575.

IV *British Naval Administration and the Manpower Problem in the Georgian Navy*

SAMANTHA A. CAVELL, J. ROSS DANCY, and EVAN WILSON

For Britain's Royal Navy in the eighteenth and early nineteenth centuries, there was no aspect of naval warfare that caused as much difficulty and anguish as manning the fleet. Finding the necessary skilled seamen to man warships was the alpha and omega of the navy's problems. Naval administrators' success in solving this problem laid the foundation for the navy's remarkable performance in the two decades of war with revolutionary and Napoleonic France. Administrators failed, however, to solve the problem of officer recruitment, a failure that had significant human cost. These two contrasting perspectives provide a useful framework for analyzing the navy's labor market. The controversial system of impressment largely succeeded in providing skilled seamen for the navy, while the chaotic pattern of officer entry failed to control the number of officers competing to command its ships. The argument presented here relies on large data sets to demonstrate how naval administrators grappled with the contrasting imbalances in the labor markets for both officers and men in the late Georgian navy. Their greatest success—the Impress Service—has been misused and misunderstood by both naval reformers and historians, while their greatest failure—controlling officer entry—has been largely ignored.

The historiography of British naval manpower, and in particular the extensive literature on impressment, has suffered from a noticeable lack of data. At the heart of this chapter's section on the "lower deck" (that is, what would now be called "enlisted personnel," so named for where their berthing spaces were found) is the first substantial and statistically significant study of the recruitment of over twenty-seven thousand sailors during the French Revolutionary Wars.[1] Its analysis suggests that most of the assumptions underpinning the current scholarship on impressment are inaccurate: impressment was in fact comparatively rare and targeted a select group of experienced sailors. There are far fewer assumptions about the labor market for officers, because there is little existing scholarship on the subject. This paper attempts to rectify this oversight by, again, relying on large databases: one of 556 officers who passed examinations for lieutenant from 1775 to 1805, and another of 3,417 officer recruits between 1771 and 1821.[2] Utilizing recently digitized sources and extensive archival records, the data sets describe the full range of commissioned officers' career patterns at the end of the long eighteenth century. Taken together, this research revises two significant aspects of British naval historiography, while at the same time providing the first comprehensive picture of the manpower problem of the Georgian navy.

The Lower Deck

During the second half of the seventeenth century, Charles II's navy relied mainly on ships' officers to man the fleet. With little in the way of organization and facing a constant shortage of volunteer skilled manpower, the navy had to rely on impressment, a medieval prerogative of the Crown.[3] Often these efforts were not enough, and naval manning had to be supplemented by placing embargoes on outward-bound shipping until merchants provided enough sailors.[4] But the seventeenth-century navy was usually employed only seasonally, to fight in the local waters of the North Sea. Not until the ascension of William III in 1689 and the beginning of more than a century of wars with France did the equation change. Warfare with France was waged throughout the year, in distant waters, with substantial fleets, and over long periods.[5] Manning the navy haphazardly was no longer an option. The Admiralty made many unsuccessful attempts to change naval manning policy over the first half of the eighteenth century; it was not until it took the manning issue out of the hands of ships' officers and organized a dedicated recruiting service that it made any major progress toward supplying its vastly expanding naval force with the necessary manpower.

The Impress Service, an administrative branch of the navy, was the primary means by which the navy recruited men ashore and in coastal waters. Its origins can be found in the War of the Austrian Succession, when the navy introduced two "regulating captains" in London to inspect men taken by press-gangs before sending them to ships. The captains streamlined the process of impressment on land and ensured that the men being pressed were actually mariners and not simply vagrants or criminals. During the Seven Years' War, regulating captains were posted in several coastal cities, including Bristol, Liverpool, Whitehaven, Newcastle, Yarmouth, and Edinburgh. Further expansions in 1756, 1759, and 1762 saw many other cities receive regulating captains to supervise press-gangs, including Gloucester, Winchester, Reading, Southampton, Aberdeen, Exeter, and Cork.[6] Regulating captains supervised press-gangs, which were themselves generally recruited from local "tough men" and commanded by lieutenants. The lieutenants of the gangs were issued press warrants that gave them the legal right to take men for service in the navy. Press tenders (that is, craft) at sea were armed with undated warrants and ready to collect men from incoming merchant ships once war broke out. The creation of an administrative branch of the navy specifically dedicated to impressment made the process of naval manning and mobilization significantly more efficient.[7]

But what percentage of sailors was conscripted? The historiography of impressment has been filled with misconceptions. The first detailed statistical study of British naval manpower between 1793 and 1801, the height of the manpower issue in the age of sail, demonstrates that only 16 percent of seamen in the Royal Navy were actually impressed, while 73 percent volunteered.[8] This finding undermines the majority of the historiography of impressment, since even the most conservative estimates have placed the number of impressed seamen at one in three. Some historians have even claimed that three in four sailors were pressed.[9] The high percentage of volunteers challenges the existing interpretation of how press-gangs functioned. Together, the database's analysis of the proportions of pressed and volunteer seamen turns the historiography of impressment on its head.

If the majority of sailors volunteered, the stereotypical picture of the press-gang lurking in dark corners to surprise ordinary men and drag them off to sea needs serious revision. A press-gang's base of operations, called a "rendezvous," was usually in a local inn or somewhere else where sailors typically congregated.[10] The purpose of the rendezvous was to recruit skilled seamen to volunteer, not to impress men against their will. Thus the rendezvous was highly visible and marked with flags, recruiting posters, and patriotic symbols: it was important that these places not look ominous, as such places would have little chance of attracting volunteers. Press-gangs conducted recruiting drives, which included speeches glorifying naval life and improvised bands marching up and down the street playing patriotic tunes.[11] The chance to win glory and prize money was a common theme. A good example is a recruiting poster for the frigate *Pallas,* under the command of Lord Cochrane from 1804; it is filled with references to prize money.[12] Admittedly, Cochrane had a reputation as a daring and lucky officer, but recent research has shown prize money was much more abundant for all members of the Royal Navy than previously thought.[13]

Another important element of Cochrane's poster is its admonition that "none need apply but Seamen or Stout Hands." Lieutenants of the Impress Service and others sent ashore with press-gangs from warships were under unequivocal instructions from the Admiralty "not to impress any Landmen, but only such as are Seafaring Men, or such others as are described in the Press-Warrant, and those only as are able and fit for His Majesty's Service, and not to take up Boys or infirm Persons, in order to magnify the Numbers upon your Accounts, and to bring an unnecessary charge upon His Majesty."[14]

Clearly, the Admiralty did not want press-gangs to bring in additional unskilled landsmen. In such a large operation mistakes were unavoidable, especially as sailors not wanting to be conscripted commonly claimed not to be seamen.[15] But on the whole, press-gangs targeted experienced seamen. Contrary to what some historians have said, the majority of the men on the lower deck of British warships

Volunteer Skill Levels
Total: 8,336 Men

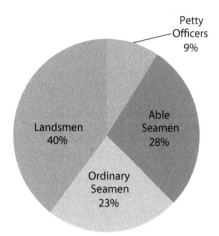

Pressed Seamen Skill Levels
Total: 1,822 Men

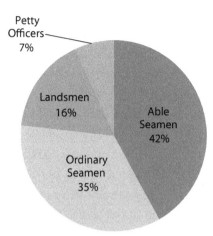

were not strangers to the sea, and indeed many were highly skilled. Petty officers (in effect, junior noncommissioned officers) made up about 12 percent of the crew, and "able seamen" (experienced and versatile deep-ocean sailors) made up a further 36 percent.[16] Together, they formed nearly half of the lower-deck complement of a ship. These men were the navy's lifeblood, without which it could never have functioned to its fullest ability. A further quarter of the lower deck comprised "ordinary seamen," who had experience at sea, often in coasters or fishing boats, but likely had served little in large, square-rigged, blue-water sailing vessels. That left just over a quarter of the men to be rated as landsmen, meaning they had little experience at sea.[17] The figure shows the skill levels of volunteers and pressed men.[18]

Volunteers were more likely than not to be landsmen or ordinary seamen, while the skill levels of pressed men were often high: nearly half were rated as either able seamen or petty officers. Though pressed men made up a minority of the lower decks of British warships, it was a highly qualified minority.

Essentially, impressment sought deep-sea sailors for Royal Navy service.[19] Able seamen were difficult to find, because it took years to learn the required skills. Most had begun working at sea in their early teenage years, likely in coasting or fishing vessels that used light sailing rigs that could be handled by boys.[20] Able seamen needed to be agile enough to work high in the rigging, but they also needed the strength of full-grown men to handle the large, heavy sails of warships. Therefore, the age window in which men could fill this vital position on board naval ships was relatively narrow. The average age of pressed able seamen was twenty-two, while the average age of pressed ordinary seamen and landsmen was twenty.[21] The fact that able seamen were on average two years older than ordinary seamen and landsmen reflects the time it took for a seaman to gain the knowledge and experience necessary to perform at that level of competence.

Impressment was a system meant not only to target specific men for naval service but also to preserve others *from* naval service. Many men had statutory protections by virtue of their positions in merchant ships, such as masters, chief mates, boatswains, and carpenters; so too did essential dockyard personnel.[22] Other seamen too were protected, including men serving on coasters, colliers, and whalers, as well as fishermen, apprentice boys, and foreigners, if they had served less than two years in a British ship.[23] Press-gangs did not simply sweep up everyone who fell into the category of seaman or "person who used the sea." Many such individuals were vital in their present positions to Britain's infrastructure and consequently its ability to wage war. Impressment did not increase the number of seamen in Britain; rather it ensured that the Royal Navy had enough skilled manpower to function at top form without draining other essential maritime services of skilled men. Impressment helped guarantee the success of British sea power by ensuring that the overall skill level of the lower deck remained high enough to give British warships an edge over their adversaries. The maritime labor market could not accomplish this without impressment's intervention.[24]

The Quarterdeck

On the quarterdeck—that part of the ship where command decisions were taken and thus the province of commissioned officers—the manpower problem was reversed. By the start of the Napoleonic Wars, the oversupply of commissioned officers in the Royal Navy posed a significant problem, one for which there was no obvious or easy solution. The difficulty stemmed in large part from the Admiralty's inability to gain control over officer recruitment or the entry of officer candidates—"young gentlemen," as they were commonly known—into the service. The decentralization of appointing officer trainees, left almost entirely in the hands of naval captains, meant that the Admiralty exercised little control over the number of the boys inducted to become commissioned officers.[25] A finite number of positions for lieutenants, commanders, post captains, and admirals was fed by a massive, overpopulated corps of trainees, a situation that led to unemployment among lieutenants and officer aspirants on a scale not seen before. This section attempts to explain the oversupply in the officer corps by examining its source—the lack of centralized control of officer recruitment or advancement in the precommissioned ratings.

Decentralized officer recruitment and Admiralty attempts to wrest control of officer entry can be traced back to the seventeenth century. Traditionally, naval captains used their powers of patronage to select boys who would be trained for command. These boys entered as "captain's servants," a rating that denoted them as protégés under the direct supervision of the captain. The exercise of patronage enabled captains—by obliging colleagues and influential and aristocratic civilians looking to the futures of their sons—to amass both social and professional status. Accordingly, these prerogatives were jealously guarded, and captains were wary of infringements on those powers by the Admiralty and the Crown.

Early attempts at regulating officer recruitment met with limited success. In the wake of the Restoration, Charles II recognized a need to raise a corps of skilled young officers who were also noblemen by birth and therefore inherently loyal to the Crown. In 1661 Charles instituted the "volunteer per order," or "King's Letter Boy," as a means of encouraging the sons of the nobility to enter the service.[26] In 1677 Charles also instituted examinations for lieutenant, which ensured that aspiring officers would be qualified for advancement to commissioned rank.[27] Such centralized programs of recruitment and advancement presented naval captains with the first challenges to their time-honored power to nominate officer candidates and promote them as they saw fit. While the examination proved to be one of the most enduring and successful programs instituted by the Royal Navy, the King's Letter Boy idea did not outlive the turn of the eighteenth century. Between 1677 and 1701 the Admiralty sought to make the appointment as King's Letter Boy the only avenue to commissions. The weight of tradition, however, proved immovable, and the captain's-servant system of entry continued to flourish.[28]

The Admiralty's next attempt to exercise at least a measure of control over officer recruitment was the Naval Academy, founded on the grounds of the Portsmouth Dockyard. The school opened in 1733, yet despite its success and popularity its capacity of only forty students limited the Admiralty's ability to exercise much control thereby over recruitment.[29] In addition, captains generally rejected "collegians" as coddled, overeducated, and underskilled upstarts.[30] Capt. Sir John Phillimore, for example, refused to accept graduates on board his ship, while the future admiral B. J. Sullivan, an academy graduate, was told by the captain of his first ship that "he had never known a collegian worth his salt."[31] Such opinions, however unmerited, reflected resentment toward measures that infringed on captains' powers of nomination. Overall, the Naval Academy achieved little by way of centralizing officer recruitment. Even at its peak, just prior to its closure in 1806 (before its reinvention as the Royal Naval College), the academy was never responsible for more than 2 percent of the Royal Navy's total officer entry.[32]

From 1733 until the outbreak of war with revolutionary France, it appears that the Admiralty made few attempts to further its goal of gaining control of officer entry. The cycles of war and peace that characterized much of the period kept both the quantity and social/professional quality of the officer corps manageable. Surpluses in the trainee officer corps and boys unsuited for command were, in most cases, culled naturally with each demobilization. The Royal Navy did not, throughout the eighteenth century, provide permanent employment for its officers or men, and peace often resulted in mass redundancies.[33]

Ironically, this process of demobilization and retrenchment presented the Admiralty with a considerable problem in 1790 with the onset of the Nootka Sound crisis. The Admiralty's hasty and shortsighted response became the catalyst for the most significant problem of oversupply in the officer corps that the service had ever faced. In May 1790, the Royal Navy prepared for war with Spain over the latter's claims to the British territory of Nootka Sound near Vancouver. A sizeable fleet had been kept in service since the American Revolutionary War, but peacetime manning meant that large numbers of officers and men were "beached."[34] Rapid mobilization for the Nootka crisis now created a shortage of lieutenants. Drawing from the pool of midshipmen and "master's mates" (experienced petty officers or midshipmen appointed by captains as noncommissioned officers) who had passed the examination for lieutenant, the Admiralty created 150 new commissioned officers on a single day, 20 November 1790.[35] These appointments accounted for nearly half of all the commissions awarded for that year.[36] The looming possibility at the same time of war with Russia over the fortress of Ochakov on the Black Sea only emphasized the navy's need to strengthen its officer corps. In the short term, the new promotions solved the shortage of lieutenants. They also opened up vast numbers of positions in the precommissioned ratings, midshipmen and master's mates. These openings were predominantly filled by boys who had served their two years as captain's servants. This upward movement in the precommissioned ratings, in turn, created openings at the entry level for new captain's servants.

The potential long-term consequences of the promotion boom and the subsequent boom in entry-level recruitment were soon recognized by the Admiralty. The actions of the First Lord, Earl Spencer, suggest that he was aware of the need, among other things, to reduce the number of officer aspirants by gaining control of recruitment. The decentralized selection of captain's servants was not the only problem associated with that rating. The role of a captain's servant was also poorly defined, which meant that while some boys so designated were officer trainees, others were destined for the lower deck or even servants in the domestic sense. The rating left much to a captain's imagination and personal preferences, a situation that the Admiralty realized would be untenable in a prolonged state of war. In an Order in Council in 1794, Spencer introduced a new system for inducting boys into the service, replacing the captain's servant rating with three new classes of entrant.[37] "First Class Volunteers," preferably the sons of gentlemen, were to be officers in training; "Second Class Boys" were to be trained as seamen; "Third Class Boys" were actual servants but could become Second Class Boys as they grew older.[38] The order effectively cut the number of places for future officers by 20–25 percent. It was a clear indication of the Admiralty's recognition of the need to gain control over the number of boys entering the service with the intention of becoming com-missioned officers.

Despite the reductions, Admiralty in-letters and correspondence books show little reaction by captains to the new directive.[39] One explanation is that many cap-tains had no intention of complying with the new order. Muster books reveal that a captain would simply enter a young gentleman in whatever classification presented an opening until a First Class Volunteer billet became available.[40] For many cap-tains, it appears, quarterdeck recruitment continued much as it had before the new regulations.

Another factor that contributed to the problem was access to the lieutenant examination. The Admiralty placed no limits on the number of midshipmen or mates who could sit the examination and no quotas on the number who could be passed. Any young gentleman who was at least twenty years old and could prove that he had spent six years at sea and for two of them had been rated midshipman or master's mate was eligible to sit the examination. The result was that many more aspirants to commissioned rank were in the service during the French wars than the Admiralty had anticipated. The navy continued to expand throughout the first decade of the nineteenth century, reaching a peak in terms of ships and manning in 1810–11;[41] nevertheless, the number of lieutenants' positions available on ships was still not enough to absorb all the young hopefuls flowing into the service through this unregulated system of entry.

Evidence from an 1817 Admiralty survey of officers suggests some typical career paths of officers unable to distinguish themselves among the horde of lieutenants.[42] John Smith, for example, received his commission in 1793 but managed to secure employment on only one other ship. His active career ended in 1795, but he was still ready—apparently still hopeful of assignment at sea—to answer the Admiral-ty's survey in 1817, and he lived until 1835.[43] With each passing year his chances for employment grew smaller. William Mercer was similarly unsuccessful. He spent a few weeks as a lieutenant on board the ship of the line *Polyphemus* in May 1794; the remainder of his active service in the navy was served as the commander of, first, *Dolphin* and then *Dover,* both cutters operating in the Channel. With the Peace of Amiens he was put ashore and so remained for the rest of his career.[44]

Unemployment (that is, at sea) was deadly for a naval career, because it was nearly impossible to impress superior officers with one's ability while ashore. The majority of officers who passed examination for lieutenant between 1775 and 1805 never managed to secure promotion from lieutenant to commander.[45] Many, like Smith and Mercer, spent only a few years at sea before languishing ashore, unassigned and on meagre half pay, for the rest of their lives. At least a commis-sion assured them half pay; midshipmen and master's mates, even ones who had passed their examinations, received no pay at all when unassigned, leaving many thousands of officer aspirants to face unemployment and, in many cases, destitution. After a decade or two of service at sea many of these "young gentlemen" were no longer young. Peace meant that many would be left to fend for themselves and face the worst consequences of demobilization. To ameliorate the problem, the Admiralty awarded hundreds of peacetime promotions for "passed midshipmen" and mates to the rank of lieutenant. This was effectively a "promotion out" of the service. The half pay that came with a lieutenant rank was intended as a pension for long service that had not been rewarded with promotion during the war.[46]

In 1804, the Admiralty initiated another round of attempts to ameliorate the unemployment of lieutenants. In 1805, First Lord Barham created the position of "sublieutenant," which was to be filled by a passed midshipman or master's mate.[47] It was an assignment that generally applied to smaller vessels under the command of lieutenants—brigs, "bombs" (vessels armed with single large mortars for shelling fortresses), and fireships, vessels that were considered dead-end appointments, given to the least promising officers. Accordingly, the position of sublieutenant was not popular, especially among ambitious young gentlemen. The next round of attempts to address the problem came after Trafalgar: the Admiralty froze promotions. The primary consequence seems to have been anger among senior officers hoping to advance the careers of their protégés.[48] In 1808, the lords commissioners of the Admiralty tried a different approach, reducing the proportion of prize money awarded to captains.[49] This was intended in part to deter young gentlemen from naval service, dulling the luster of a naval career by reducing their potential earnings if and when they became captains. Such measures were too little, too late. Unemployment was a fact of life for thousands of lieutenants, master's mates, and midshipmen during the Napoleonic Wars.

Not until after the French wars did the Admiralty finally address the problem effectively. Less than two months after Waterloo, Lord Melville's Admiralty introduced new regulations that took away a captain's authority to appoint new entrants without the permission of the lords commissioners. The order also robbed captains of their authority to rerate, disrate, or discharge any young gentleman without the Admiralty's permission, and it demanded that all captains complete quarterly returns stating the names of all the young gentlemen on board, as well as their ratings, ages, and seniority in the service.[50] This order effectively ended more than 150 years of tradition in which captains monopolized the selection and advancement of officer trainees in the precommissioned ratings. The order of 1815 represented the first direct policy decision aimed at centralizing officer entry and marked the first truly effective move on the part of the Admiralty to take control of the number of aspirants, the pace of entry, access to the lieutenant examination, and the social quality of those who would be groomed for commissioned rank. The timing was important. Such an aggressive attack on captains' autonomy and ability to wield patronage might in other circumstances have been met with opposition. Peace, however, had meant a rapid reduction in the size of the fleet and extensive retrenchment. Captains who feared for their own employment prospects and those of their officers were less likely to be concerned with recruits and the loss of traditional prerogatives related to appointing them. Fears of retribution that might have resulted from voicing objections to the Admiralty's new measures may have also gone a long way toward keeping detractors silent. The regulations came too late for the generation of officers who had joined the navy in the last quarter of the eighteenth century.

Conclusion

The contrast between the quarterdeck and lower-deck manpower problems was stark. On the lower deck, the Admiralty succeeded in streamlining naval recruitment by taking the majority of the task of manning warships out of the hands of officers serving on board warships. The Impress Service was responsible for recruiting volunteers as well as pressing skilled seamen. Impressment was a necessary evil, and seamen accepted it as an unavoidable aspect of naval life.[51] In all the grievances of the mutineers at Spithead and the Nore in 1797, impressment was not mentioned.[52] In his memoirs, William Spavens, who was pressed a number of times, showed no resentment toward the press.[53] The British fleets of the French Revolutionary Wars were not manned by impressed men; rather, pressed men formed a supplement within a mainly volunteer force, and they functioned to raise the overall skill level of the lower deck. In the end, seamen were conscripted into the Royal Navy by press-gangs because their skills were one of Britain's most prized military assets.[54]

In contrast, the Admiralty failed to wrest control of officer entry from captains. The half-hearted attempts following the Restoration—the King's Letter Boys and, later, the Naval Academy—failed. The stresses of the navy's conflicts did not threaten a crisis on the quarterdeck. The scale and duration of the French wars, however, pushed the officer recruitment system past the breaking point. The Admiralty's attempts to restore equilibrium to that labor market became increasingly frequent, but they remained generally ineffective. Britain endured two decades of war with an enormous waste of manpower resources, as thousands of lieutenants and lieutenant hopefuls sought, ever more hopelessly, to find employment at sea. Only demobilization at the peace in 1815 provided the lords commissioners with the opportunity to solve the problem.

NOTES 1 See Jeremiah Dancy, "British Naval Manpower during the French Revolutionary Wars, 1793–1802" (unpublished DPhil thesis, Univ. of Oxford, 2012).

2 For lieutenants, Evan Wilson, "The Sea Officers: Gentility and Professionalism in the Royal Navy, 1775–1815" (DPhil thesis, Univ. of Oxford, 2014), published as *A Social History of British Naval Officers, 1775–1815* (Woodbridge, Suffolk, U.K.: Boydell, 2017). For officer recruits, S. A. Cavell, *Midshipmen and Quarterdeck Boys in the British Navy, 1771-1821* (Woodbridge, Suffolk, U.K.: Boydell, 2012), p. 217.

3 Roland G. Usher, Jr., "Royal Navy Impressment during the American Revolution," *Mississippi Valley Historical Review* 37, no. 4 (1951), p. 679.

4 Bernard Capp, *Cromwell's Navy: The Fleet and the English Revolution, 1648-1660* (Oxford, U.K.: Clarendon, 1989), p. 263.

5 Daniel A. Baugh, *British Naval Administration in the Age of Walpole* (Princeton, N.J.: Princeton Univ. Press, 1965), pp. 147–48; N. A. M. Rodger, *The Command of the Ocean: A Naval History of Britain, 1649–1815* (New York: W. W. Norton, 2005), pp. 205–206.

6 Stephen Gradish, *The Manning of the British Navy during the Seven Years' War* (London: Royal Historical Society, 1980), p. 57.

7 Ibid., p. 103; Dancy, "British Naval Manpower," p. 276.

8 Dancy, "British Naval Manpower," p. 68.

9 Michael Lewis, *A Social History of the Navy, 1793–1815* (London: Chatham, 2004), p. 139; Gradish, *Manning of the British Navy,* p. 62; Nicholas Rogers, *The Press Gang: Naval Impressment and Its Opponents in Georgian Britain* (London: Continuum, 2007), pp. 3–5.

10 Nicholas Blake and Richard Russell Lawrence, *The Illustrated Companion to Nelson's Navy* (London: Chatham, 1999), p. 64; Usher, "Royal Navy Impressment during the American Revolution," pp. 675–77.

11 Dancy, "British Naval Manpower," p. 93; Christopher Lloyd, *The British Seaman, 1200–1860* (London: Collins, 1968), p. 130.

12 Recruitment poster for *Pallas,* PBH3190, National Maritime Museum, Greenwich, U.K.

13 Daniel Benjamin and Christopher Thornberg, "Organization and Incentives in the Age of Sail," *Explorations in Economic History* 44 (2007), pp. 317–41.

14 "Instructions to Officers Raising Men, 1807," ADM 7/967, The National Archives, Kew, U.K. [hereafter TNA].

15 Lloyd, *British Seaman,* pp. 161–62.

16 Dancy, "British Naval Manpower," p. 72.

17 Ibid.

18 Ibid., pp. 137, 202.

19 Michael Duffy, *Soldiers, Sugar and Seapower: The Expeditions to the West Indies and the War against Revolutionary France* (Oxford, U.K.: Clarendon, 1987), pp. 20–21; N. A. M. Rodger, "'A Little Navy of Your Own Making': Admiral Boscawen and the Cornish Connection in the Royal Navy," in

Parameters of British Naval Power, 1650–1850, ed. Michael Duffy (Exeter, U.K.: Univ. of Exeter Press, 1998), p. 83; David J. Starkey, "War and the Market for Seafarers in Britain, 1736–1792," in *Shipping and Trade, 1750–1950: Essays in International Maritime Economic History,* ed. Lewis R. Fischer and Helge W. Nordvik (Pontefract, U.K.: Lofthouse, 1990), p. 37.

20 Marcus Rediker, *Between the Devil and the Deep Blue Sea: Merchant Seamen, Pirates and the Anglo-American Maritime World, 1700–1750* (Cambridge, U.K.: Cambridge Univ. Press, 1987), pp. 12–13.

21 Dancy, "British Naval Manpower," p. 225.

22 Lewis, *Social History of the Navy,* p. 106.

23 Denver Alexander Brunsman, "The Evil Necessity: British Naval Impressment in the Eighteenth-Century Atlantic World" (unpublished PhD thesis, Princeton Univ., 2004), p. 11; Tim Clayton, *Tars: The Men Who Made Britain Rule the Waves* (London: Hodder & Stoughton, 2007), p. 170; Dwight E. Robinson, "Secret of British Power in the Age of Sail: Admiralty Records of the Coasting Fleet," *American Neptune* 48, no. 1 (1988), p. 6.

24 Rogers, *Press Gang,* p. 31.

25 Officially, captains were allowed four servants per hundred crew members; House of Commons Sessional Papers, U.K., 1700 VI, p. 9. Such regulations were frequently ignored, and to circumvent them captains often rated protégés as "able" or "ordinary" seamen. Cavell, *Midshipmen and Quarterdeck Boys,* pp. 7–8.

26 Royal proclamation, 8 May 1676, in *British Naval Documents, 1204–1960,* ed. John B. Hattendorf et al. (Farnham, U.K.: Navy Records Society, 1993), p. 283.

27 Order in Council of December 1677, quoted in R. D. Merriman, ed., *Queen Anne's Navy: Documents Concerning the Administration of the Navy of Queen Anne, 1702–1714* (Farnham, U.K.: Navy Records Society, 1961), p. 317.

28 Merriman, *Queen Anne's Navy,* p. 311.

29 H. W. Dickinson, *Educating the Royal Navy: Eighteenth- and Nineteenth-Century Education for Officers* (Abingdon, U.K.: Routledge, 2007), pp. 19–21, 40–44.

30 R. Vesey Hamilton, ed., *The Letters and Papers of Admiral of the Fleet, Sir Thomas Byam Martin* (Farnham, U.K.: Navy Records Society, 1903), vol. 1, p. 24.

31 Quoted in Dickinson, *Educating the Royal Navy,* p. 45.

32 Ibid., p. 39.

33 Rodger, *Command of the Ocean,* p. 380.

34 Between 1785 and 1790 the number of ships of the line in service actually increased, from 137 to 145; Jan Glete, *Navies and Nations: Warships, Navies, and State Building in Europe and America, 1500–1860* (Stockholm: Almqvist & Wiksell, 1993), vol. 2, p. 553. Conversely, manpower dropped from 105,443 in 1782 (the peak manning year, during the American conflict), to 20,396 in 1789, just months before the Nootka armament. Jeremy Black, "Naval Power, Strategy and Foreign Policy: 1775–1791," in *Parameters of British Naval Power,* ed. Duffy, p. 110; Rodger, *Command of the Ocean,* pp. 638–39.

35 Wilson, "Sea Officers."

36 Rodger, *Command of the Ocean,* p. 380.

37 House of Commons Sessional Papers, U.K., 1794 XXXII, p. 537.

38 Ibid.

39 ADM 2/272–3, ADM 2/772–3, TNA.

40 S. A. Cavell, "A Social History of Midshipmen and Quarterdeck Boys in the Royal Navy, 1761–1831" (unpublished PhD thesis, Univ. of Exeter, 2010), p. 260, app. K.

41 Rodger, *Command of the Ocean,* p. 608.

42 Survey Return of Officers' Services, ADM 9/1–7, TNA.

43 ADM 107/9/177, ADM 9/6/1787, TNA; Patrick Marioné, *The Complete Navy List of the Napoleonic Wars, 1793–1815* (Brussels: n.p., 2004), CD-ROM, s.v. "Smith, Commander (Rtd) John (04) (d. 1835)."

44 ADM 9/6/1798, TNA.

45 Career outcomes for a random sample of 556 officers' passing certificates; ADM 107/6–33 and ADM 6/88–103, TNA. See also Wilson, "Sea Officers."

46 Lewis, *Social History of the Navy,* p. 197; idem, *The Navy in Transition: A Social History, 1814–1864* (London: Chatham, 1960), pp. 67–68.

47 ADM 1/5215, TNA. Sublieutenant was a temporary rating, purpose-built to alleviate wartime pressures on the commissioned ranks. It was eliminated with the close of the war in 1815 and was not reinstated as a rank until 1861.

48 Collingwood's post-Trafalgar letters are filled with dire requests for promotion confirmations. See G. L. Newnham Collingwood, ed., *A Selection from the Public and Private Correspondence of Vice-Admiral Lord Collingwood,* 1st American ed. (New York: Carville, 1829), pp. 153, 157–58, 163–64.

49 Daniel Benjamin, "Golden Harvest: The British Naval Prize System, 1793–1815" (unpublished article, Clemson, S.C., 2009), pp. 10–11. Our thanks to Dr. Benjamin for permission to cite his article.

50 ADM 3/185, TNA; "Circular from the Naval History of the Present Year, 1815," *Naval Chronicle* 34 (1815), p. 167.

51 Baugh, *British Naval Administration,* pp. 149, 159–61; J. S. Bromley, "The British Navy and Its Seamen after 1688: Notes for an Unwritten History," in *Charted and Uncharted Waters,* ed. Sarah Williams and David Palmer (London: Trustees of the National Maritime Museum, 1981), p. 159; Lloyd, *British Seaman,* pp. 149–51; N. A. M. Rodger, *The Wooden World: An Anatomy of the Georgian Navy* (Annapolis, Md.: Naval Institute Press, 1986), p. 151; Rodger, *Command of the Ocean,* p. 499.

52 Rodger, *Command of the Ocean,* p. 447.

53 William Spavens, *Memoirs of a Seafaring Life: The Narrative of William Spavens, Pensioner on the Naval Chest at Chatham,* ed. N. A. M. Rodger (Bath, U.K.: Folio Society, 2000), p. 12.

54 Usher, "Royal Navy Impressment during the American Revolution," p. 680.

V   Victuals and Libations in the U.S. Navy during the Time of Sail and Early Steam

DENNIS RINGLE

During the late afternoon of Thanksgiving Day 1996, deployed in the Mediterranean Sea, the men and women serving on board the guided-missile cruiser USS *Vicksburg* (CG 69) feasted on five hundred pounds of twenty-four-pound turkeys, several hundred pounds of prime rib beef and virginia ham, eight hundred pounds of fresh shrimp, corn on the cob, corn-bread stuffing, cranberry sauce, and pumpkin pie.[1] This very high-calorie and nutritious meal, although unique for that special day, illustrates the commitment of the U.S. Navy to providing a high quality of life for its enlisted sailors.

For the Navy, from its inception to today, the forgotten weapon has always been food. In the era of sail and the early years of steam, if a ship was to fight, its sailors had to eat and its hold had to be replete with barrels of food and liquids, which were as vital as its guns. During this period, a commanding officer was responsible not only for manning and equipping his warship but also for the crew's safety and health. The sailor's diet was significant to a warship's ability to fulfill its mission. In an era void of scientific knowledge regarding the merits of nutrition, the commanding officer relied on his years of experience and observation to ensure that his command was healthy enough to endure the rigors of life at sea.

Food, then, played a vital role in the fledgling Navy. Not only did provisions provide nourishment for men through long hours of fatiguing work and watch standing exposed to harsh elements or to the excessive temperatures of engine rooms, but meals also broke the monotony of endless days at sea and contributed to the good morale of the crew. For many sailors the opportunities to eat three times a day became the highlights of the daily routine. As one sailor wrote, "When breakfast is done, the next thing I look forward to is dinner, and when that's done, I look for supper time."[2]

The U.S. Navy, from its beginnings, made a concerted effort to ensure that its men received a balanced diet that included periodic fresh provisions. On 1 July 1797, Congress approved the following daily ration, which incorporated a variety of foods and beverages rich in protein, carbohydrates, and alcohol, if somewhat deficient in vegetables that contained vitamins A and C.

That the ration shall consist of as follows: Sunday, one pound of bread, one pound and a half of beef, and half a pint of rice; Monday, one pound of bread, one pound of pork, half a pint of peas or beans, and four ounces of cheese; Tuesday, one pound of bread, one pound and a half of beef, and one pound of potatoes, or turnips and pudding; Wednesday, one pound of bread, two ounces of butter, or in lieu thereof six ounces of molasses, four ounces of cheese, and half a pint of rice; Thursday, one pound of bread, one pound of pork, and half a pint of peas or beans; Friday, one pound of bread, one pound of salt fish, two ounces of butter, or one gill of oil, and one pound of potatoes; Saturday, one pound of bread, one pound of pork, half a pint of peas or beans, and four ounces of cheese; and there shall also be allowed one half pint of distilled spirits per day, or in lieu thereof one quart of beer per day, to each ration.[3]

It should be noted that a "ration" consisted of not one but all three meals in a day—breakfast, dinner (noon), and supper. The cost of one ration in 1797 was twenty-eight cents.[4]

Table 1 is a nutritional breakdown of the Navy ration. Table 2 is the recommended daily intake for an active twenty-five-year-old male, five feet eight inches tall and weighing 160 pounds. In addition, table 2 lists the nutritional value of a day's ration according to the 1797 law. By the end of one week the sailor's diet exceeded the recommended daily intake for calories, protein, fat, carbohydrates, and salt. Despite the high caloric intake, however, there were no reported cases of obesity during this period. The high sodium intake, however, could pose a problem. The near-term effects of the salty diet could have included excessive thirst and possibly dehydration. A long-term high-sodium diet can cause high blood pressure that may eventually lead to cardiovascular disease. Also, the diet was deficient in vitamins A and C, by approximately 50 percent.

Vitamin A is found in milk products and in yellow and green vegetables. One advantage vitamin A has over other nutrients found in the Navy diet of the time is that its nutritional value is not diminished when cooked. Vitamin A is important in the formation of teeth, bones, the central nervous system, the immune system, and night vision. A person deficient in vitamin A is more susceptible than others to respiratory and digestive-tract infections.[5]

Vitamin C is found in citrus fruits, berries, potatoes, cabbages, and other vegetables. Unlike vitamin A, vitamin C loses its nutritional value when exposed to air (oxidation) or mixed with water. It is important to tooth and bone formation, strengthens the immune system, enhances wound healing, and promotes healthy gums.[6] A person with vitamin C deficiency may show signs of the dreaded disease of scurvy within forty days.

Scurvy, a noncommunicable disease, was once all too familiar to sailors and the scourge of all seafaring men. Fortunately for the American "tar," by his time this formerly deadly disease had been all but eradicated. The symptoms of scurvy, the great nautical disease of the sixteenth through eighteenth centuries, were severe fatigue, pain in the joints and limbs, loss of appetite, bleeding gums, loosening of teeth, and anemia. If left untreated, it ultimately led to a slow and painful death.

Table 1

Nutritive Value of Foods

Food	Weight	Cals.	Protein (gram)	Fat (gram)	Carb. (gram)	Vit. A (µg)	Vit. C (mg)	Na (mg)
Salt pork, taw	1 lb.	3,396	23	366	0	0	0	6,464
Salt beef	1½ lb.	1,758	90	150	0	0	0	9,696
Salted cod	1 lb.	416	100	1.2	0	0	0	6,464
Biscuit, hardtack	1 lb.	1,203	32	0	184	0	0	0
Rice, unenriched	8 oz.	890	15	2	150	0	0	0
Potatoes	1 lb.	336	8	0.4	72	36	40	0
Beans	8 oz.	654	45	2.6	110	0	0	0
Butter, salted	2 oz.	402	0	46	0	405	0	322
Peas, dried	8 oz.	117	0	1	21	1,109	58	0
Turnips, raw	1 lb.	120	4.4	1	24	0	120	0
Cheese, cheddar	4 oz.	452	28	36	0	75	0	696
Molasses	6 oz.	430	3.6	0	103	0	0	0
Rum, 80 proof	8 oz.	512	0	0	0	0	0	0
Whiskey, 80 proof	8 oz.	512	0	0	0	0	0	0
Beer	32 oz.	459	5	0	39	0	0	0
1818, 1842, 1861 Changes to the Sailor's Diet								
Lemon juice	1 oz.	6	0	0	0	1	7.4	0
Dried fruit	4 oz.	104	0.5	0	28	0	2	0
Cranberries	4 oz.	52	0.4	0	88	20	15	0
Pickles	4 oz.	12	0	0	0	63	1.2	0

Sources: Margaret S. Chaney and Margaret Ahlborn, *Nutrition*, 3rd ed. (Boston: Houghton Mifflin, 1943), pp. 390–410; *Self: Nutrition Data*, nutritiondata.self.com/facts/. Na is the chemical symbol for sodium.

Table 2
Recommended Daily Intake (RDI) for a Medium, Active Male, 5 Feet 8 Inches, 160 Pounds

	Cals.	Protein (gram)	Fat (gram)	Carb. (gram)	Vit. A (μg)	Vit. C (mg)	Na (mg)
RDI	3,074	56	90	130	900	90	2,300
Sunday	4,363	137	152	334	0	0	9,696
Sunday % of RDI	142%	245%	169%	257%	0%	0%	422%
Monday	6,244	83	403	205	1,184	58	7,160
Monday % of RDI	203%	148%	448%	158%	132%	64%	311%
Tuesday	3,929	134	151	280	66	160	9,696
Tuesday % of RDI	128%	239%	168%	215%	7%	178%	422%
Wednesday	3,459	75	83	334	480	0	1,018
Wednesday % of RDI	113%	134%	92%	257%	53%	0%	44%
Thursday	5,765	100	369	294	0	0	6,464
Thursday % of RDI	188%	179%	410%	226%	0%	0%	281%
Friday	2,869	140	48	256	441	40	6,786
Friday % of RDI	93%	250%	53%	197%	49%	44%	295%
Saturday	5,168	83	372	205	1,184	58	7,160
Saturday % of RDI	168%	148%	413%	158%	132%	64%	311%
7-day average % of RDI	148%	192%	250%	210%	53%	50%	298%

The medical profession did not discover that the cause of scurvy is vitamin C deficiency until 1911; however, naval officers and surgeons had long since come to the conclusion through observation and from the writings of several prominent British physicians that the consumption of fruits and vegetables not only prevented but cured the disease.[7]

Unfortunately, the Navy experienced isolated cases of scurvy through the end of the American Civil War. But much earlier, during the Quasi-War with France of 1798–1800, USS *Constellation* had reported only a single case of scurvy during a one-year period. In that conflict one other warship, the gunboat USS *Philadelphia,* reported several cases of scurvy; however, there were no recorded deaths due to scurvy during the Quasi-War.[8] Even more remarkable was the favorable health experience of the crew of the frigate USS *Essex* on a voyage to the Far East. The commanding officer, Capt. Edward Preble, recorded in his journal, "The scurvy appears among the people." Within a month, however, Preble could report to the Secretary of the Navy that the crew was "in general good health."

During the Barbary Wars and the War of 1812, in long voyages to the Far East, and in research expeditions such as the Wilkes Exploring Expedition of 1838–42, the sea service maintained an enviable record of good health and was almost completely free of scurvy.[9] But there were, as noted, a few cases, isolated but inexcusable, of scurvy during the Civil War. The side-wheel steamer USS *Mahaska* experienced an outbreak stemming from personal neglect by the commanding officer and the ship's surgeon while enforcing the blockade of the Confederate port of Charleston, South Carolina. In another instance, the surgeon assigned to the sailing patrol vessel USS *Fernandina,* learning of the presence of scurvy on board another Navy warship, immediately directed that ship's paymaster to increase the crew's daily ration of fresh vegetables.[10]

During the transitional period between sail and steam the Navy was successful in preventing scurvy thanks to such astute ship's surgeons, as well as commanding officers. In addition, the Navy diet, established in 1797 and slightly modified throughout the first half of the nineteenth century, contributed greatly; although, as noted, it contained only half the recommended intake of vitamin C, the records indicate that it was sufficient to prevent scurvy. Unfortunately, the diet's deficiency in vitamin A appears to have had a far greater effect on the health of the sailors. During the first fifty years of the Navy's existence, sailors suffered from and in some cases died of a variety of diseases, but the most prevalent were respiratory and digestive-tract disorders and a plethora of fevers.[11]

Many factors can lead to respiratory disease. One relevant potential cause is constant exposure to dampness. The Navy's obsession with cleanliness resulted in decks being frequently washed down. The lower decks, where the sailors ate and berthed, lacked proper ventilation to dry the wet wood. A very damp environment resulted.[12] Additionally, sailors were frequently exposed to cold, rain, and spray, leaving their clothes in a constant state of dampness for extended periods. Meanwhile, their diet's vitamin A deficiency potentially weakened their respiratory immune systems.

A good example of the vitamin A deficiency leading to respiratory problems seems to have occurred during the First Barbary War (1801–1805). Reprovisioning the squadrons blockading the North African coast proved a problem throughout the conflict. This situation caused periodic shortages in provision. The medical log of surgeon Peter St. Medard of the frigate USS *New York* records that 60 percent of the crew's illnesses were respiratory in nature.[13]

The legislation on subsistence for sailors omitted one important item: water. Ships' manifests report the loading of numerous casks of water; the daily water ration was left to individual commanding officers. Capt. Thomas Truxtun, commanding the frigate USS *Constellation,* wrote the service's first known water-ration order to his officers on 29 June 1798; it authorized for each man four and a half pints of water daily. One month later Captain Truxtun increased the ration by half a pint. He also authorized the cook to use an additional ten and a half pints of water per man for cooking. Interestingly, the enlisted water ration exceeded the officers' by half a pint.[14] The Navy regulations of 1814 finally set the daily sailor's water ration at one-half gallon. This would include the water used by the ship's cook in food preparation.[15]

In today's Navy, the ship's senior medical representative and chief engineer are responsible for the quality of the water; they use portable water-quality testing kits and bacteria-killing chemicals to assure the crew of safe, clean water. This was not the case during the age of sail, when the water was only as good as its source. "Foul" water no doubt contributed to a large number of digestive-tract illnesses. During the Quasi-War, *Philadelphia* experienced firsthand the effects of bacteria-laden foul water. The ship ran aground trying to cross the bar at the mouth of the Delaware River. The crew worked incessantly to lighten the ship by moving and throwing overboard tons of stores. The warm temperature, coupled with a low water level in the river, resulted in the thirsty men drinking tainted water. Shortly thereafter the majority of the crew was stricken with diarrhea. The ship's surgeon suspected that "dirty" river water was the culprit.[16]

Diarrhea was not the only disease that could be transmitted by "tainted" water; the dreaded typhoid fever was another. This infectious disease is transmitted by the typhoid bacterium, *Salmonella typhi,* in shellfish, raw fruit, vegetables, unpasteurized milk, and water contaminated by the feces of typhoid victims. Although most typhoid victims eventually recover, about a fifth develop pneumonia (potentially aggravated by vitamin A deficiency) or intestinal hemorrhage that can lead to death.[17]

The only treatment for typhoid fever during this period was a regimen of isolation, rest, and plenty of fluids. Because of how the disease is spread, good personal and food hygiene is critical; in the age of sail the only way the Navy could hope to prevent an outbreak was to obtain clean drinking water and procure provisions free of the bacteria. The Navy fortunately took advantage of a then-new technology that provided some ships with clean water—the freshwater distiller. The ability to distill from saltwater large quantities of freshwater for drinking, food preparation, and washing greatly aided in the war against typhoid fever and digestive-tract illnesses. By the time of the Civil War it was common for ships without steam (used by distillers) to obtain fresh distilled water from steam-powered ships in their squadrons.

Fernandina's surgeon wrote in his diary that the steamship USS *Wamsutta* frequently condensed water for his own ship. For sailors assigned to steamships, water was usually in abundant supply. In a letter to his mother William Clark wrote, "The ship's condensers made so much water that we have twice as much water as the ship requires, this gives us plenty to wash with."[18] But prior to the introduction of steam, ships continued to obtain freshwater as chance allowed and from questionable sources. Only the astute eyes of the commanding officer and surgeon regarding the location and source of freshwater would help prevent these debilitating and sometimes lethal diseases.

In 1802, the Secretary of the Navy informed the chairman of the Committee on Naval Affairs, Samuel L. Mitchill, that as a result of complaints from the sailors he was going to increase the daily enlisted ration. His letter acknowledged that the current diet was lacking in meat and vegetables. He added one pound of pork (but at the same time eliminated the nutritious fish ration). He also increased the pea ration, by a half pint, and for the first time added vinegar. He reduced the bread or biscuit ration by two ounces and added a pound and a half of Indian meal for the week. Overall, the changes added fat, sodium, and carbohydrates to the diet.[19]

The enlisted ration remained constant until 1818, when the Navy made a small but significant addition to the sailor's bill of fare. First, the 1818 regulations authorized commanding officers, when feasible, and at a reasonable price, to purchase fresh meat twice a week. The second, and more important, addition called for the issue of "Lemon Acid" to the crew twice a week for warships "on cruises of unusual duration and particularly in hot climates." The quantity was left up to the ship's surgeon. This change would play a significant role in combating scurvy.[20] A good example of a surgeon's decision to issue lemon juice occurred during Wilkes's voyage. The surgeon assigned to USS *Peacock* ordered two bottles of lemon juice to each enlisted mess (of eight to ten men each). During the same voyage the surgeon on board USS *Porpoise* issued lime juice once a week.[21]

The ration remained unchanged this time until 1842. At that point, in an effort to improve the image of the enlisted sailor and attract quality men to the service, the Navy and Congress not only modified the tar's diet but reduced the spirit ration by half. The 1842 ration added four ounces of either dried apples, raisins, or some other dried fruit to the daily menu. In addition, the new act called for a weekly allowance of eight ounces of cranberries or pickles. Three other items added to the daily ration in 1842 were coffee, tea, and cocoa. Whatever beverage was issued, two ounces of sugar accompanied it.[22] Today, the average person living in the United States consumes four and a half ounces of sugar daily.[23]

The Navy diet underwent one more change during the age of sail and the transition to steam. On 18 July 1861, with the Civil War only three months old, Congress altered the sailor's ration once again. Although the daily staples of salted meat and biscuits prevailed, the 1861 ration added new options offered by the technology of the day. The salted-meat ration could be replaced by twelve ounces of canned meat. In addition, fresh potatoes could be substituted for by desiccated potatoes. These changes illustrate the Navy's commitment to change in order to provide an improved quality of life for the enlisted man.[24] Throughout the transitional period between sail and steam, sailors' diets remained rich in calories, protein, fat, carbohydrates, and, unfortunately, sodium. The addition of lemon acid in 1818, followed by dried fruit in later years, improved the vitamin C quantity. Vitamin A remained the only nutrient lacking in their otherwise nutritious diet.

Navy regulations ensured that enlisted personnel received diets adequate for their demanding daily schedules. It was one thing to require such provisions on paper, but it would be up to the Navy itself, commanders of forces, commanding officers of ships, and their designated subordinates to make sure that allocated provisions were received. From the onset of the Quasi-War the Navy was concerned about the logistical challenges of provisioning its warships.

On Christmas Eve of 1798, the Secretary of the Navy informed the Speaker of the House of the financial requirements for equipping and provisioning a forty-four-gun frigate manned by four hundred men for twelve months. The provisions included 310 barrels of beef, 310 barrels of pork, 1,220 gallons of molasses, 144 hundredweight (cwt, units of one hundred pounds) of rice, 1,930 pounds of butter, 15,000 pounds of cheese, 240 bushels of beans, 8,650 gallons of rum, 53 barrels of flour, 49 barrels of Indian meal, 1,022 cwt of bread (biscuits), 730 bushels of potatoes, and 177 cwt of salt fish. The total cost to the nation would be $28,277.89.[25] It was rare, however, that frigates in that era were outfitted with a year's supply of food at once. A more realistic approach was taken in the summer of 1798: the secretary informed the civilian agent responsible for supplying USS *Constitution* that four months of provisions should suffice for warships deployed to the West Indies (i.e., the Caribbean).[26] Prior to a ship's departure, the vast amount of stores and provisions had to be hoisted on board by block and tackle and "struck below" into the hold of the ship. Care had to be taken that provisions were placed in the order needed—that is, what was needed first on top. In addition, the positioning of the provisions had to be such that the stability of the ship was not impaired, since these items also acted as ballast.

During the Quasi-War, warships operating in the West Indies faced few problems with logistics. The ships were either sufficiently provisioned before leaving the States or resupplied in friendly West Indian islands. In the Far East, however, reprovisioning required long-range planning. The Secretary of the Navy contracted with several merchant ships to meet and supply USS *Congress* and *Essex* when they anchored in Batavia (now Jakarta, Indonesia). The ships carried the usual foodstuffs of salted beef, pork, beans, peas, Indian meal, and biscuits. The supply ships also carried sauerkraut, because of its imperishability. The supply vessels also carried "porter" (port) and wine for the officer's mess.[27]

One of the most remarkable examples of early commitment to resupplying distant ships occurred at sea. What is believed to be the first recorded case of underway replenishment in the U.S. Navy occurred on 13 December 1799, when the frigate USS *General Greene* received two thousand pounds of beef, pork, and twenty-four gallons of beans from another frigate, USS *Boston*.[28] Two weeks later, *Constitution* received provisions from the civilian schooner *Elizabeth* while "lying too." The provisions were transferred by small boats until the winds stiffened to a point where it was unsafe to continue the replenishment. That evening *Constitution* took *Elizabeth* under tow; the evolution was completed the next day.[29] The U.S. Navy is admired worldwide for its underway replenishment techniques; these two incidents established the precedent.

When in the first half of the nineteenth century the Navy could not resupply its warships around the globe, commanding officers were authorized to purchase food from foreign agents. By the Civil War, under the tutelage of Secretary of the Navy Gideon Welles, a remarkable logistical system had been established. Welles expressed the importance of keeping sailors well provisioned: "It is essential that the crews have frequent supplies of fresh provisions and other necessaries conducive to health."[30] The key element of this system was a group designated supply vessels. Their primary mission was to provide fresh meat, vegetables, and ice to the blockade fleet. A typical supply ship assignment originated in New York City; for the next approximately three weeks the supply ship delivered provisions to blockading squadrons along the Atlantic seaboard and in the Gulf of Mexico. As a result, a blockading ship regularly received fresh provisions every two or three weeks—a remarkable achievement, even by today's standards.[31] The Navy, since its humble beginning of the 1790s, had gone to considerable lengths to ensure that the diet of enlisted sailors met the needs of the hardworking men.

To this end, the Navy further gave considerable attention to food preparation. It established early on the importance of food by making ship's cooks warrant officers.[32] Although their duties would not be delineated officially until the 1814 regulations, in 1798 Captain Truxtun summarized the duties of the cook on board *Constellation*. His ship's cook was to soak the provisions prior to cooking, supervise the issuing of the prepared food, and "be vigilant" about the tending of the galley fire. Truxtun expected the cook to be cordial and to prevent waste, such as the discarding of the "slush," or fat, from the day's meal.[33] The Navy regulations of 1814 basically reiterated what Truxtun had written sixteen years earlier.[34] But even then written direction did not go beyond the soaking of meat prior to cooking and the amount of food required for each meal; actual food preparation was left to the imagination and culinary skills of the individual ship's cook.

Navy cooks did not do personally all the work of preparing, cooking, and serving the three daily meals. They received assistance from a handful of men chosen by their "messes." A typical mess consisted of ten to twelve men usually of the same rating or watch rotation. The number of messes varied with the ship's complement. The men shared a large, wooden chest of cups, plates, knives, forks, and spoons. Each mess chose one of its members to serve as the cook's assistant, or "mess cook." The mess cooks spread large pieces of canvas on the deck for the men of their messes to sit on while they ate and drew eating utensils from their assigned chests. Before the meal, they assisted the cook in "breaking out" the daily rations from the storeroom. While the cook prepared the meal, the mess cooks drew pans of hardtack and buckets of boiling water for their messes, adding coffee or tea and sugar. While the men drew their beverage of the day, the mess cooks returned to the galley for the main course. After the meal the mess cooks "policed the area" and returned the eating utensils and canvas. The members of the mess usually rotated every week. The mess cook routinely received a small stipend, approximately seventy-five cents a month, drawn from the pockets of his mess mates.[35]

On the six days of the week when salt beef, pork, or fish was to be served, the mess cooks drew the salted rations from the hold and soaked them for several hours in large copper cauldrons. The cauldrons held between sixty-eight and 120 gallons of water; the soaking removed some of the salt. USS *Columbus,* a seventy-four-gun ship of the line manned by seven hundred sailors, had three such cauldrons. The kettles were six feet deep, four feet wide, and six feet long. One was used to boil coffee or tea, one to soak and cook the meat, and one for rice, beans, or duff (see below).[36]

The preparation of food three times a day required teamwork, foresight, imagination, and hard work. Although the Navy occasionally failed to provide the authorized quantity and variety of food, numerous ship's logs, personal diaries, letters, and journals convey clearly that it was committed to a balanced and nutritious diet. Charles Poole, a quartermaster assigned to a new steam cruiser, described the daily ritual of eating: "We go down to breakfast which consist of a pan of potato scouse [potatoes and hardtack cooked together with butter], a pot of coffee, and plenty of hard bread, and thus passes the most important hour of the day. . . . At 12 PM we have dinner consisting of fresh bread and vegetable soup. . . . At 4 PM we get our supper, which consist of hot tea or coffee and hard bread."[37]

A standard bill of fare on board the monitor USS *Nahant* was scouse for breakfast, hot stew for dinner, and boiled beef and potatoes for supper.[38] A passenger on board the steamer USS *Delaware* referred to breakfast as "a hearty meal, consisting of canned meats, scouse, and good hot coffee."[39] The food on board the sloop of war USS *Portsmouth* received mixed reviews from a twenty-one-year-old carpenter's mate, who described a meal of soup with meat as "tasting good," although he thought a Christmas dinner of bean soup and "salt junk" (salted meat) was inappropriate for the holiday.[40]

Periodically the meat was served raw. One sailor recounted such a meal, his first on board a Navy warship:

> When [it was] called out, "come and get your tea," I got my pot, pan and spoon, and proceeded to the galley, or cooking range, where each individual received a quart of tea, ready sweetened, with which we betook ourselves to the mess, a place on the lower deck where, in a mess chest, are kept the bread and meat and whatever else may constitute the daily allowance of food. Here the individual who was the acting "cook of the mess," had set our supper out on a mess cloth on deck. It consisted of sea-bread, raw salt pork, cold boiled potatoes, and vinegar. We gathered around the cloth, each one bringing his tea, and a seat, although some squatted right down on deck. When all was arranged, an old salt said, "well boys, here's everyone for himself, and the d——l for us all—Jack, pass the pork," and this was grace to the first meal I ate in the service.[41]

This same sailor discovered that eating with his messmates could be hazardous. It was common for tars to settle grievances during mealtime. In addition, a sailor who got to the choice piece of meat first was likely to discover his beverage "accidently" overturned or his bean soup running on the deck.[42]

The other main staple of the sailor's diet was biscuit, or "hardtack." The hardtack cracker, three inches square and approximately an inch thick, consisted of flour and water. The manufacturer baked the dough at a low temperature for several hours, producing a dry cracker that was durable and easy to package and transport to the fleet. Unfortunately, however, over time hardtack acquired an affinity for moisture, which encouraged mold. In addition, maggots and weevils took up residence in the crackers.[43] One sailor likened the worms he found in hardtack to chestnut worms, with white bodies and black heads. His frequent encounters with worms led him to recall in his memoir, "Break open a hardtack and perhaps two or three could be imbedded in the—well, cracker. But after being on board for some time I could munch them equal to any vet, without examining the interior."[44] Another sailor described the weevils in his ship's biscuits as "having a proboscis or trunk like an elephant and were the size of a small ant that hopped about like a flea."[45]

Periodically the cooks made out of hardtack a dish called "dandyfunck." The cook soaked the hardtack in freshwater and then baked it with salt pork and molasses. As a substitute for hardtack, the ship's cook occasionally baked fresh bread or used the flour ration to make a unique dish called "duff"—a flour pudding boiled in a bag with raisins, when available.[46] Sailors slowly tired of the never-ending salted meat and hardtack. When opportunity availed itself ships sometimes turned to the land or sea to augment the ration and satisfy the men's palates.

Constitution, at anchor at Port Mahon, Minorca, in the late 1820s, purchased for the crew live geese, sixty chickens with their legs tied, pigs, sheep, and rabbits, all enclosed by a partition on the forward part of the gun deck. (The ship had other live animals on board as well, as pets—a donkey, dogs, pigeons and other birds, and a goat.)[47] *Columbus* fared just as well twenty years later at anchor in Yeddo (Tokyo) Bay. The ship received alongside two junks that sold it sweet potatoes, eggplants, carrots, pumpkins, and a large quantity of apples. Later in the cruise, in the Sandwich (Hawaiian) Islands, the sailors purchased bananas, coconuts, limes, and watermelons. Also, as Charles Nordhoff reported, "There is, however, another fruit, the taro, . . . which is one of the most delicious of vegetables. It grows to about the same size as a large coconut, and is round and hard, cutting precisely like a firm potato. They are boiled as potatoes, or with milk."[48]

If sailors enjoyed a wide variety of exotic foods deployed around the world, the men of the Union navy during the Civil War benefited from the local cuisine of the coastal islands of the South. Early in the war, when combined naval and army forces occupied coastal islands of the Carolinas and Georgia, freed slaves established small businesses that sold a variety of amenities. By the summer of 1862, the officers and enlisted men were paying five cents for a quart of milk or a dozen ears of corn. Eggs sold for twelve cents a dozen, and one chicken went for the same price. Shrimp sold for a steep ten cents apiece, but fish were only two cents a pound.[49] On shore, the men also enjoyed superb dinners prepared by local inhabitants trying to establish livelihoods. One "contraband" (former slave), named Harry, opened a small dining establishment on Saint Simons Island, off the coast of Georgia. Harry charged the sailors only fifty cents for a meal of fresh pork, chicken, rice, green vegetables, and potatoes. Another contraband family, in competition with Harry, charged the men only twenty-five cents for fresh beef, fried fish, oysters, apple pie, and sassafras beer.[50]

While sailors certainly enjoyed the bill of fare available ashore, one item that became a staple of their diet on board ship by the early 1840s was coffee. Fresh, piping-hot coffee was their favorite nonalcoholic beverage. The ship's cook received the coffee beans either fresh (green) or roasted and prepared the coffee in a large kettle, out of which the men ladled it into their cups. One advantage steam-powered vessels had over sailing ships was a constant source of heat to boil coffee. Standard shipboard procedure required the extinguishing of galley stoves during combat and in hours of darkness; on sailing ships, during these periods the men were without hot coffee, but not on steamships. Ingenious sailors heated their coffee over hot coals removed from the boilers or even drew scalding-hot water directly from the main condenser.[51] Unfortunately, not all coffee served on board ship met with the satisfaction of the crew. One tar wrote disgustedly about creatures that inhabited his coffee: "One thing that I never got used to, and that was finding cockroaches in my coffee, although after picking out a few from my cup, I could manage to worry the liquid down."[52]

Throughout the period of sail and the early days of steam, the Navy realized the integral part food played in the success of the fledgling American fleet. To that end, senior Navy officials, Congress, and most important, individual ship commanding officers made a concerted effort to ensure that sailors received a balanced and nutritious diet. The success of the Navy during this period, which included conflicts with France, Barbary pirates, Great Britain, Mexico, and the Confederacy, can in part be attributed to the sailor's daily ration, which in turn established a precedent that is enjoyed by the service today. In January 1991 the frigate USS *Cook* (FF 1083), after taking on fuel and provisions, departed Seattle, Washington, en route to its home port of San Diego, California. During its four-day transit the crew dined on fresh salmon, Alaskan king crab, lasagna, and "surf and turf."[53] The U.S. Navy, thanks to the efforts of the men serving during the age of sail and the introduction of steam, remains the best-fed and healthiest navy in the world.

NOTES   1 Hugh A. Mulligan, "Military Turkeys Do Tasty Duty Overseas," *Detroit Free Press,* 24 November 1996, sec. F, p. 7.

2 "Life on a Blockader," *Continental Monthly* 6 (August 1864), p. 50.

3 *Naval Documents Related to the Quasi-War between the United States and France* (Washington, D.C.:

U.S. Government Printing Office [hereafter GPO], 1935–38) [hereafter QW], I, pp. 7–8.

4 QW, II, p. 116.

5 Margaret S. Chaney and Margaret Ahlborn, *Nutrition,* 3rd ed. (Boston: Houghton Mifflin, 1943), pp. 168–73.

6 "Vitamin and Mineral Chart No. 5612-11," General Nutrition Corporation, Pittsburgh, Pa., 1985; Chaney and Ahlborn, *Nutrition,* pp. 232–44.

7 James Lind, MD, "A Treatise of the Scurvy," reprinted in *The Health of Seamen: Selections from the Works of Dr. James Lind, Sir Gilbert Blane, Dr. Thomas Trotter,* ed. Christopher Lloyd (London: Navy Records Society, 1965), pp. 7–62; Clayton L. Thomas, ed., *Taber's Cyclopedic Medical Dictionary,* 15th ed. (Philadelphia: F.A. Davis, 1985), p. 1536.

8 Harold D. Langley, *A History of Medicine in the Early U.S. Navy* (Baltimore: Johns Hopkins Univ. Press, 1995), pp. 60, 64.

9 Ibid., pp. 89, 327–29.

10 Samuel P. Boyer, *Naval Surgeon: Blockading the South, 1862–1866,* ed. Eleanor Barnes and James A. Barnes (Bloomington: Indiana Univ. Press, 1963), p. 196.

11 Langley, *History of Medicine in the Early U.S. Navy,* pp. 56–72, 89, 326–33.

12 Ibid., pp. 55–56.

13 Ibid., pp. 89–90.

14 QW, II, pp. 152–232.

15 "Frequently Asked Questions: Navy Regulations, 1814," *Naval History and Heritage Command,* www.history.navy.mil/.

16 Langley, *History of Medicine in the Early U.S. Navy,* p. 70.

17 Thomas, *Taber's Cyclopedic Medical Dictionary,* p. 1795.

18 Boyer, *Naval Surgeon,* p. 91; William J. Clark to his mother, 3 March 1863, Clark Papers, vol. 1, Historical Society of Pennsylvania, Philadelphia, Pa.

19 K. Jack Bauer, ed., *The New American State Papers,* vol. 1, *Naval Affairs* (Wilmington, Del.: Scholarly Resources), pp. 30–31; Stephen R. Brown, *Scurvy: How a Surgeon, a Mariner, and a Gentleman Solved the Greatest Medical Mystery of the Age of Sail* (New York: Thomas Dunne Books, 2003), p. 228.

20 Bauer, *Naval Affairs,* pp. 518, 528.

21 Langley, *History of Medicine in the Early U.S. Navy,* pp. 327–29.

22 *An Act to Establish and Regulate the Navy Ration,* chap. 267, *Statutes at Large* 5 (1856), pp. 546–47.

23 Rich Cohen, "Sugar: Why We Can't Resist It," *National Geographic,* August 2013, p. 84.

24 *An Act to Alter and Regulate the Navy Ration,* chap. 7, *Statutes at Large* 12 (1863), pp. 264–65.

25 QW, II, pp. 115–16.

26 QW, I, p. 166.

27 QW, IV, pp. 522–23.

28 Ibid., p. 534.

29 Ibid., pp. 590–91.

30 *Report of the Secretary of the Navy with an Appendix Containing Reports from Officers* (Washington, D.C.: GPO, December 1861), pp. 10–11.

31 U.S. War Dept., *Official Records of the Union and Confederate Navies in the War of the Rebellion* (Washington, D.C.: GPO, 1894–1927) [hereafter *ORN*], vol. 1, pp. 27, 357.

32 QW, II, p. 116.

33 "Frequently Asked Questions: A Short Account of the Several General Duties of Officers, of Ships of War . . . by Thomas Truxtun," *Naval History and Heritage Command,* www.history.navy.mil/.

34 "Frequently Asked Questions: Navy Regulations, 1814."

35 George Jones, *Sketches of Naval Life, with Notices of Men, Manners and Scenery, on the Shores of the Mediterranean, in a Series of Letters from the* Brandywine *and* Constitution *Frigates* (New Haven, Conn.: Hezekiah Howe, 1829), p. 238; F. A. Roe, *Naval Duties and Discipline, with the Policy and Principles of Naval Operations* (New York: D. Van Nostrand, 1865), p. 30; Alvah Folsum Hunter, *A Year on a Monitor and the Destruction of Fort Sumter,* ed. Craig Symonds (Columbia: Univ. of South Carolina Press, 1987), p. 43; W. M. C. Philbrick, Journal, vol. 3, 7 October 1862, record group 45, National Archives and Records Administration, College Park, Md.; James A. Chelsey to the People of Wakefield, 6 February 1862, Library of Congress, Manuscript Division, reprinted in David L. Valuska, "The Negro in the Union Navy" (PhD dissertation, Lehigh University, Bethlehem, Pa., 1971), p. 129; DeWitt Papers, in Reuben Elmore Stivers, *Privateers and Volunteers: The Men and Women of Our Naval Forces, 1776–1866* (Annapolis, Md.: Naval Institute Press, 1975), p. 371.

36 Charles Nordhoff, *Man-of-War Life,* series ed. Jack Sweetman (repr. Annapolis, Md.: Naval Institute Press, 1985), p. 119, available at www.navyandmarine.org/.

37 Charles Poole Papers, 31 October 1863, in Stivers, *Privateers and Volunteers,* p. 371.

38 Hunter, *Year on a Monitor,* pp. 42–43.

39 Stephen F. Blanding, *Recollections of a Sailor Boy; or, The Cruise of the Gunboat* Louisiana (Providence, R.I.: E. A. Johnson, 1886), p. 88.

40 Philbrick, Journal, vol. 3, 21 and 25 December 1862.

41 Nordhoff, *Man-of-War Life,* pp. 29–30.

42 Ibid., p. 74.

43 James M. Sanderson, *Camp Fires and Camp Cooking, or Culinary Hints for the Soldier* (Washington, D.C.: GPO, 1862), p. iv; Palmer H. Boeger, "Hardtack and Burnt Beans," *Civil War History* 4 (1958), pp. 73–92.

44 Blanding, *Recollections of a Sailor Boy,* p. 66.

45 Nordhoff, *Man-of-War Life,* p. 154.

46 U.S. Navy Dept., *Civil War Naval Chronology, 1861–1865* (Washington, D.C.: Naval History Division / GPO, 1971), vol. 6, pp. 53–64.

47 Jones, *Sketches of Naval Life,* vol. 1, p. 194.

48 Nordhoff, *Man-of-War Life,* pp. 187, 199–200.

49 *ORN,* vol. 1, pp. 13, 139.

50 Boyer, *Naval Surgeon,* p. 69.

51 Hunter, *Year on a Monitor,* pp. 36, 48.

52 Blanding, *Recollections of a Sailor Boy,* p. 66.

53 Author's personal experience as executive officer of the frigate USS *Cook* (FF 1083), as a lieutenant commander, U.S. Navy.

VI *Portable Soup to Peruvian Bark*
Medicinal Trials in the Royal Navy, 1750–1800

CORI CONVERTITO

For the eighteenth-century Royal Navy, disease was the ultimate adversary, because of the drain on manpower that it created. The Admiralty recognized the benefits of sustaining healthy crews, since they made for a fleet far more valuable than one replete with sick men operating at half strength. When it proved necessary to send men halfway around the world in defense of British colonial interests, it became essential to consider the methods and medicines needed to treat a variety of diseases. The Royal Navy became increasingly concerned with the preservation of seamen's health as the century drew to a close. It established the Sick and Hurt Board, under the direction of which the navy carried out a revolution that reduced the preference for remedial care and transferred attention to preventative medicine. In shifting its efforts the navy vaulted to the forefront of medical development in the late eighteenth century.

This paper will survey the Royal Navy's approach to treating sick seamen between 1750 and 1800. It will then briefly discuss the medical branch's break with Hippocratic teachings and its transition to preventative care. This will be followed by an in-depth investigation of a number of remedies tested and employed by the navy during this period. Surgeons relied on observation and experimentation to determine the best treatments for diseases. Naval life allowed these surgeons to carry out trials in a "controlled" environment and record the results. The most significant of these involved portable soup, Peruvian bark, and several remedies for scurvy. If it had not been for these trials and the subsequent distribution of Peruvian bark and the juice of lemons and limes, the devastating effects of both malaria and scurvy would have undoubtedly continued for a number of years.

The Sick and Hurt Board was established by the Admiralty to operate as the navy's medical branch and oversee a multitude of medical duties, including disease management. This was no easy task for the board, because before 1793 its commissioners had no formal medical training; by and large, they were bureaucrats with experience in other government departments and had been appointed solely to handle the finances of the office.[1] Nevertheless, the commissioners were accountable for the medical decisions of that office. External assistance was available from the Royal College of Physicians, the Company of Surgeons, the Society of Apothecaries, and the Royal Naval Hospital at Greenwich.

As part of its duties, the Sick and Hurt Board was expected to decide which medicines were suitable for use on board ships. It was also responsible for considering proposals for new medicines and remedies submitted by surgeons, physicians, and members of the general public. Given their lack of medical training, the commissioners principally relied on the Society of Apothecaries to guide them on what treatments seemed most trustworthy before expending funds on medicinal trials. When the society felt there was merit in a proposal, the board designed guidelines for a trial either at one of the naval hospitals or on board designated ships. Naval surgeons selected to undertake the trials were required to document the treatment's distribution to patients and report their findings to the board. When medicinal trials of a particular treatment were deemed successful, the board added it to the list of mandatory remedies carried in surgeons' chests.

Before delving into specific treatments, it is essential to highlight the changes in medicine and medical practice at the end of the eighteenth century. They ultimately influenced the Sick and Hurt Board's decision to trial new medications in the hope of preventing disease rather than treating it; this was a groundbreaking concept, as most physicians and surgeons thought only in remedial terms, not preventative.

At the beginning of the eighteenth century, medical practices were rudimentary; medicine had hardly advanced for centuries. Physicians were taught a number of beliefs and philosophies rooted in a traditional concept that the body was composed of four "humors" and that illnesses resulted from their imbalance, an idea that dated back to Hippocrates (c. 460–377 BC). These humors were blood, choler, phlegm, and black bile. It was believed that each of these humors was responsible for specific life functions. Blood was the source of vitality, choler was the gastric juice that aided in digestion, phlegm constituted all colorless excretions from the body (including sweat and tears), and black bile represented "melancholy," which tainted the other humors during times of illness. If a person was in good health, that meant, it was believed, that the four humors existed in a harmonious balance; ailments stemmed from the increase or diminishment of one of them. For example, if the body produced too much blood, sanguineous disorders and fevers resulted. A deficiency of blood, by contrast, meant reduced vitality, potentially giving rise to fainting, coma, or even death.

During the middle to late eighteenth century, however, occurred a clear divergence from Hippocratic teachings, in a period of medical revolution known (like the broad Western European intellectual movement of which it was a part) as the "Enlightenment." Preference grew among certain surgeons and physicians for scientific experimentation and observation. The "contagionist" theory gained momentum and offered a more accurate model of disease transmission than did the idea (which it replaced, to some degree) of miasmas, or "bad airs," that had coevolved with the humoral theory.[2] Variation in opinion on medical concepts and philosophies among these men, however, resulted in several conflicting diagnoses, treatments, and remedies for naval diseases in the eighteenth century.

The medical Enlightenment not only influenced the ways in which surgeons and physicians viewed the source of diseases but impacted recommended remedies and treatments. The navy contributed to the innovative approach to medicine by relying heavily on observation, experience, and experimentation in its hospitals. Ship's surgeons too recognized the potential for observation and experimentation in the controlled environment, or "closed populations," that existed on board. Discoveries and advancements in medicine largely stemmed from the work of naval surgeons, particularly those experimenting during long voyages in regions far from home waters.

The navy frequently looked to revise the contents of the standardized medicine chest for surgeons to provide the most appropriate relief for seamen's illnesses. Proposals for medicines employed outside the navy frequently arrived at the Sick and Hurt Board office, where, as previously mentioned, the commissioners decided whether to test them in hospitals or on ships. By such progressive methods, the navy launched itself to the forefront of medical development in the years leading up to the wars with revolutionary France. A number of treatments that the navy utilized or experimented with during that period will be investigated here in more detail.

Portable Soup

One of the most noteworthy treatments in the mid-eighteenth century was the "portable soup" tablet. Portable soup was, in the simplest terms, a gelatinous bouillon cube that was prepared by boiling bones and offal from oxen to create a beef broth. Vegetables were added, and the broth was then allowed to simmer for hours until it reduced to a syrupy consistency and the vegetables had virtually dissolved into the mixture. The soup was then poured out into shallow trays and allowed to dry and harden until it could be carved into small tablets designed for easy storage. On board naval ships, they were reconstituted by dissolving them in hot water and served to sick men as a type of instant soup.[3]

Portable soup was first proposed to the Admiralty by the Sick and Hurt Board in 1756 for use by convalescent seamen. The board supposed it would be particularly useful in scurvy cases, although it recognized potential for use with other illnesses as well.[4] The Admiralty requested that the board establish what quantity of soup should be allowed per man for a four-month period and that a trial be carried out. The board determined the amount to be a "pint and a half each to ten men in a hundred for every day of the said four months."[5] It would assess the feedback provided by surgeons and adjust the quantity as necessary.

By 1758 reactions from the trials reached the Sick and Hurt Board. Mr. Carruthers, surgeon of HMS *Burford,* asserted his overwhelming approval for the soup:

> Under God the portable broth preserved many of the weakly and scorbutic [scurvy-stricken] patients, until our sickness obliged the ship to make for Portsmouth, where they were sent to their respective hospitals. . . . Every British seafaring man in His Majesty's navy ought to be thankful for this great refreshing benefit, so wisely calculated for a palatable diluting nourishment as well as to have a tender regard for the inventor and proposer of a thing so likely to support and revive the feeble. . . . The intention is certainly noble, and I hope success will crown the design.[6]

Aside from the antiscorbutic effects the board hoped portable soup would have on sick seamen, its commissioners were also eager to determine whether it was efficacious against other ailments. In 1759, Mr. Poole, surgeon of HMS *Barfleur,* described a serious malignant fever that had taken hold of a large portion of the crew: "many of the men were reduced to the lowest ebb" and, had they not been given the soup, "must have perished through a marasmus [malnutrition]," since most refused to eat any other food offered to them. "There is nothing in the navy instituted for the use of the sick equal [in] utility with the portable broth."[7]

Perhaps one of the more significant voyages on which portable soup was trialed was that of Capt. James Cook in HMS *Discovery* and *Resolution.* It has been documented in various academic sources that the health of Cook's crews was quite remarkable given the medical knowledge of the time. His attention to cleanliness, hygiene, and proper diet contributed to their overall good condition.[8] Cook found the portable soup valuable when fresh foods were not available, and it was well liked by his crews. When *Resolution* returned to London after the five-year expedition, leftover portable soup tablets were forwarded to the Sick and Hurt Board so their serviceability following such a lengthy voyage could be tested. The commissioners were pleased to report that although the soup tablets had been stored in canisters that "appeared to have been opened and some remained loose in the box," those tested had been found to make good-quality soup that retained much of its original virtue.[9] Such resounding results emphasized the value of manufacturing the tablets to be stored until needed, which could be a number of years in the future.

Portable soup continued to be crucial to naval service well into the 1790s, even after the order to distribute lemon juice to treat scurvy was given. The soup remained exceedingly popular for the duration of the Napoleonic Wars and was administered to sick men well into the nineteenth century.

Elixir of Vitriol

One of the more favored and widely circulated naval medicines was elixir of vitriol, a combination of sulfuric acid and alcohol regularly administered to men suffering from scurvy.[10] Elixir of vitriol was first recommended for naval use in 1740 and was endorsed by the Royal College of Physicians in London. On that basis, the navy agreed to include the medicine in surgeons' chests. Once quantities of it reached naval ships, captains and surgeons conveyed satisfactory feedback, speaking of the elixir's great benefit to scorbutic seamen and those weakened by fevers and fluxes. J. Martin, surgeon of HMS *Shoreham,* believed that it was effective against additional diseases as well; he reported good results in treating ardent and intermittent fevers and fluxes and considered it to "greatly contribute towards preventing those diseases."[11]

In 1747, less than a decade following its inclusion in the surgeon's chest, Dr. James Lind, a highly regarded naval surgeon, used elixir of vitriol in experiments on board HMS *Salisbury.* Lind concluded that the elixir was in fact not effective against scurvy, although his findings were largely ignored because reports from various other medical men, including members of the Royal College of Physicians, continued to assert that it was beneficial. Aside from Lind, Adm. George Rodney disapproved of the elixir, writing the Sick and Hurt Board in 1781 that "every man has his favourite antiscorbutic, which he presses upon the public with great earnestness, and extols with exaggerated praise. In the beginning the cure of this disease was not sought for from food but from medicine and elixir of vitriol was to be the infallible cure; it was introduced into the navy and is now universally known to be of no manner of service in the cure of the scurvy."[12] Lind's and Rodney's negative verdicts were not incorrect. Testimonies from other surgeons and physicians of the elixir's ineffectiveness continued to come in until the Sick and Hurt Board was finally forced to reexamine its value to naval service. Elixir of vitriol, having spent over half a century in the naval surgeon's chest, was finally discontinued in the 1790s.

Dr. James's Fever Powder

Another widely popular medicine available to surgeons was Dr. James's Fever Powder. Its origins are somewhat disputed, but it is known to have been sold by John Newbery, the publisher of children's books after whom the Newbery Medal was named.[13] The antimony powder was believed to have the capacity to cure not only fevers but gout, rheumatism, and even scurvy.

Not long after its patenting in 1752, the navy evaluated the suitability of including Dr. James's Fever Powder in the surgeon's chest. The powder was trialed at naval hospitals to ascertain what benefit, if any, was to be had by using it to treat fevers.[14] It clearly proved largely effective, because the Sick and Hurt Board agreed to distribute it to the entire fleet at no cost to surgeons, with more on board ships bound for the coast of Africa and the West Indies, which suffered from fevers regularly.

Not all surgeons considered James's Fever Powder advantageous; some claimed that it was of little use in fever cases. The medicine quickly earned a number of adversaries, including James Lind. Despite such negative feedback, the navy continued to dispense the powder for over forty years. In early 1796 the Sick and Hurt Board was still recommending James's powder, although, according to their own correspondence, its members were unsure why they advocated its use when "more than three editions of the London Pharmacopoeia [had] been published during the present century and . . . no notice whatever [was] taken of James' powder in any of them."[15] It seems that the navy was one of a limited number of supporters of the medicine. The board discontinued the distribution of the antiquated remedy in mid-1796 in the hopes of discovering a treatment better suited for treating fevers.[16]

Peruvian Bark

What Dr. James's Fever Powder lacked, the Peruvian bark compensated for. This medicine, sometimes referred to as Jesuit's bark or cinchona, was first brought to Europe from South America in 1631.[17] Gathered from the cinchona trees native to Peru, the bark was shown to Jesuit missionaries as a cure for the "ague," or "intermittent fever" (malaria).[18] Unlike other treatments that were directly recommended to the Sick and Hurt Board, the Peruvian bark came to the navy's attention by way of one of its captains. Capt. Thomas Collingwood of HMS *Rainbow* had been ordered to the west coast of Africa in 1773. He was fortunate enough to have on board the surgeon Robert Robertson, who saw fit to carry out his own trial of the bark, a test that "was attended with great success."[19] Since it was his duty to "use every prudent method to obviate fevers amongst [men] who are employed on . . . shore duty," he distributed a dosage of bark to men heading ashore on wood-gathering and watering duties. Robertson believed the bark would eliminate, or at least alleviate, the threat of intermittent fever.

He successfully administered the treatment on Saint Thomas, an island off Sierra Leone, in West Africa. He later recounted what occurred: "When at St. Thomas's . . . our officers and men, about fifty in number on duty[,] were obliged to stay ashore all night from a great tornado, I sent a dose of tincture of bark for each of them in the morning after, to be taken in a glass of wine[;] . . . few of them were afterwards [taken] with fevers [compared] to what were expected, and in all probability would have been had they not got that medicine."[20]

Robertson continued to dispense bark to each crew member every morning before they went ashore. Seeing results atypical for ships stationed in that region, Collingwood strongly recommended that the Sick and Hurt Board order the bark be administered, diluted in a glass of wine, in all future operations on that coast.[21] Collingwood's and Robertson's correspondence on their experience with the medicine elicited the Admiralty's approval for the distribution of Peruvian bark to treat fever outbreaks to all ships bound for the coast of Africa.

Another advocate of administering bark to seamen serving in tropical climates was James Lind. He found that circulating the bark among those suffering from either intermittent or remittent fevers "proved the most certain means of cure" and felt that "the bark [was] . . . the best remedy."[22] Even more pioneering was his view that since bark appeared to curtail relapses, it could conceivably also be used to *prevent* fevers. His advice appears to have been overlooked for some time, however;

the bark was issued only sporadically to the African coast and was administered only once fevers set in.

It was up to admirals, captains, and surgeons to request the medicine if they required it in any other region of the world. In 1780 Sir Peter Parker wrote from Jamaica reporting several complaints by his captains about the lack of bark and alleging that "several men [had] died from the want of a proper quantity of [it]."[23] Echoing Parker's letter, Admiral Rodney insisted he be supplied with a quantity of bark before sailing for the Leeward Islands. His request denied, Rodney purchased five hundred pounds of Peruvian bark and divided it among the ships in his squadron. According to Rodney's letter to the Sick and Hurt Board justifying the expenditure, the hospital at Jamaica could not accommodate the number of sick men from his fleet who had fallen ill upon arrival in the West Indies; it appeared to him that the only way to combat the fever was to procure the bark himself. Once the medicine was in hand, he claimed, fever patients recovered more rapidly.

Eventually, with testimonies from a number of captains and surgeons attesting to the good effects of Peruvian bark, the Admiralty authorized its distribution to vessels bound for all tropical regions, to answer the devastating effects of fevers.[24]

Flux, Dysentery, and Diarrhea Cures

Nutritional deficiencies and foul drinking water in these years resulted in digestive and intestinal problems. The most common of these diseases were diarrhea, fluxes, and dysentery. There were few effective medicines to alleviate the symptoms, and even less could be done to prevent them. So long as seamen were given salted meat and not provided regular supplies of fresh provisions or clean water, the navy was in effect increasing the likelihood that seamen would experience difficulties with digestion.

Having no real combatants against diarrhea, dysentery, or fluxes, the navy continually sought them. It is not surprising that when Edward Hogben submitted a proposal for a cure for flux in 1758, the Sick and Hurt Board was pleased to allow a trial of it. Hogben was authorized to carry out his trial at two naval hospitals, where he was allocated a total of twelve patients. The board required him to record his progress and forward the results once the trial finished. According to Hogben's report, four of the men died, and one was removed from the ward when he became consumptive (tubercular). Of the remaining men, only two were cured, and one of those, it was suspected, would have been cured of the flux anyway by ordinary means. His results did not persuade the Sick and Hurt Board to perform further trials of his medicine.[25]

Additional remedies were offered to the board, but none seemed to be of any value. Richard Dunn claimed that his powder, a family secret, was infallible, although he was unable to produce any evidence attesting to cures. M. Pinto, who had at one time served in the navy, argued that his external medicine could "expel the venom, comfort the bowels and restore the patient his health."[26] Another method purported to cure the disorders by bleeding the patient, relieving him of some six to eight ounces of blood, followed by an induced vomiting.[27] While the navy searched for a definitive cure-all for digestive disorders, naval surgeons carried, at their own discretion, an assortment of remedies to treat bowel complaints. This meant that success was typically disparate from ship to ship; no surgeon could pinpoint an exact cure.

Fever Cures

The complex nature of fevers and lack of understanding of their causes made diagnosing them incredibly difficult. Although as the Sick and Hurt Board recognized, Peruvian bark was effective against ague (malaria), that was not the only type of fever to which seamen were exposed; for instance, there was no remedy for yellow fever or jail fever. Fevers were widely believed to be caused by "bad airs," and therefore most cures were based on purifying air. A favored method was to "sweeten" the air in spaces on overcrowded vessels. Once diseases such as jail fever appeared among ships' companies, cleaning and purifying both the air and the ship were valuable in dampening outbreaks. One of the earliest recommendations for fumigation came from Dr. Maxwell, a naval surgeon. To eradicate fevers Maxwell proposed that all ships periodically smoke their hammocks and bedding using charcoal and brimstone for periods of ten or twelve hours. After smoking, he suggested, all bedding and clothing should be washed to ensure any illness had been eliminated.[28]

Ventilation seemed of the utmost importance, as any fresh-flowing air had the potential to dispel bad vapors. The most notable name associated with shipboard ventilators was Stephen Hales. He had originally designed an air-circulation device installed on the roof of London's Newgate Prison. Hales improved on this idea and produced "Ship's Lungs," essentially bellows in huge boxes with hinged sides that could be opened and shut by means of rods and the bellows worked by hand. The results from Hales's ventilators were so promising that the Admiralty immediately organized their distribution to all naval hospitals and ships of the fleet.[29]

Despite such advancements in ventilation, fevers continued to ravage the fleet for the remainder of the eighteenth century. Jail fevers appeared to lessen a bit, but mainly because of tests by captains, physicians, and surgeons of various methods to achieve cleanliness. As for yellow fever, no cure was forthcoming. Naval personnel had neither any expectation of escaping the disease in the tropics nor any real hope of treating it on a considerable scale.

Scurvy Cures

Depicted as one of the most serious threats to seamen's health during the age of sail, scurvy has been studied and written about more than any other maritime disease. Scurvy was by no means the principal killer of seamen; it did, however, routinely debilitate them. Also, once scurvy had weakened their immune systems, men became susceptible to other illnesses, such as fevers, ulcers, fluxes, and dysentery. Present-day narratives on the causes of and cures for scurvy have essentially a single theme—that James Lind discovered a cure but the Admiralty refused to heed him. The result, some claim, was that seamen suffered unnecessarily from scurvy for an additional forty years until the navy recognized that lemon juice warded off the disease.[30] Although this is an oversimplification of published material, it is fairly representative of the overall current perception of Lind's attempt to cure scurvy. The true situation was much more complex. The Sick and Hurt Board was introduced to the curative properties of citrus juice during Lind's time, but the same was claimed for a number of other cures. Presented with so many supposed remedies, it was difficult for the board commissioners to establish which were helpful and which were ineffective.

Brian Vale quite rightly challenges the view, held by many historians, that Lind should be credited with the cure.[31] When Lind carried out his well-documented trials on board HMS *Salisbury,* not even he was convinced of the lemon's effectiveness. If the Sick and Hurt Board commissioners had heeded his advice to use a "rob" of lemons and oranges, they would have found it inadequate. To make the rob one boiled the fruit, reducing the juice to a syrup—and in the process destroying its vitamin C, making the rob ineffective against scurvy.

It is worth briefly summarizing some of the proposed cures to comprehend fully the challenging decisions the Sick and Hurt Board had to make. Elixir of vitriol was, as noted above, recommended for curing scurvy and was perceived to be successful, although in reality it provided no relief. Next to come to the attention of the Sick and Hurt Board was the proposal from James Lind. By that time, he had already carried out his systematic experiment on board *Salisbury,* in which men suffering from scurvy were issued various distinct cures to determine which worked best.[32] According to Lind, the men who were administered citrus fruits recovered from scurvy the quickest and were able to return to service first.

When Captain Cook's first voyage to the Pacific was in the planning stage, the Sick and Hurt Board saw a chance to put this issue to rest. If provided with a variety of treatments for scurvy, Cook could carry out a trial on each of them, keep meticulous records of outcomes, and eventually report back to the board. Cook's ship, HMS *Endeavour,* carried sauerkraut, malt of wort, and rob of oranges and lemons, among other purported remedies.[33] During his voyage, as noted, Cook's crews remained relatively healthy, largely because of the level of cleanliness he demanded. Scurvy rarely made an appearance; such of his men as became ill generally suffered from fever or dysentery. Upon his return he erroneously attributed the absence of scurvy to the malt of wort, a finding that further complicated the scurvy issue for the Sick and Hurt Board.

Thoroughly unsatisfied with medicines trialed by the navy, surgeons and captains took it upon themselves to purchase their own fresh provisions, which they believed promoted health better than recommended treatments. Captain Caldwell of HMS *Hannibal* demonstrated this proactiveness. Caldwell, arriving off the coast of Ireland with 120 men suffering from scurvy, was induced by his surgeon to purchase ashore seventeen boxes of lemons and sweet oranges. Once these had been distributed, the sick men recovered so fast "that many returned to their duty, and only two died."[34] Captain Curtis of HMS *Brilliant* transmitted a similar account, on behalf of his ship's surgeon and that of HMS *Porcupine*.[35] According to those men, lemon juice was the most effective antiscorbutic they tried, and on both ships virtually no one was now suffering from scurvy.

It took the Sick and Hurt Board until the mid-1790s to accept genuinely the effectiveness of lemon juice (not the "rob" of lemons as proposed by Lind). The board then ordered it administered daily on board ships as a preventative. Finally, the dreaded scurvy could be managed effectively. Although it had taken the Sick and Hurt Board some time to agree on the cure, the delay would not necessarily have been avoidable even if it had heeded the advice of James Lind half a century earlier.

Conclusion

One of the major duties of the Sick and Hurt Board was to facilitate the selection and distribution of medicines throughout the fleet. Unfortunately, for a long period of the board's history, its commissioners were not medically trained and so lacked sufficient knowledge to make decisions about treatments. During the middle to late eighteenth century, medicine underwent a period of significant reform that occasioned several surgeons and physicians to question Hippocratic teachings. These men relied on observation and experimentation to determine the best treatment for disease. For naval surgeons, conditions on board ship allowed them to experiment with treatments in a "controlled" environment. Further, and befitting this atmosphere of reform, the Sick and Hurt Board as a matter of policy held trials to test remedies that appeared to have merit. Sometimes these trials proved useful, although on a number of occasions the board was left more perplexed than before by the results. The best it could do was assess the individual qualities of each proposal, as well as the credentials of the submitters.

By taking this vigorous approach, the Royal Navy launched itself to the forefront of medicine. If not for naval surgeons and their captains taking proactive stances on the issuance of Peruvian bark or the juice of lemons and limes, the devastating effects of both malaria and scurvy would have undoubtedly been felt for years longer. The Sick and Hurt Board deserves recognition for promoting shipboard trials, advancing cleanliness, conquering scurvy, and subduing other diseases. It was not able to suppress all naval diseases; however, it was during this period, the latter half of the eighteenth century, that the groundwork was laid for the near-total suppression of virtually all naval diseases in the ensuing century.

NOTES   1 See Stephen F. Gradish, *The Manning of the British Navy during the Seven Years' War* (London: Royal Historical Society, 1980), p. 21. During the Seven Years' War, there had been medical men employed as commissioners on the Sick and Hurt Board, although they had little influence in the Admiralty and struggled to make sweeping changes to medical practices. As Gradish points out, "from 1756 onwards . . . the Admiralty thought that some medical men should be appointed to the Sick and Wounded Board. Their [the Admiralty's] choice of Dr. James Maxwell in February 1756 illustrated this. The Admiralty told the Sick and Hurt Board that they had appointed Maxwell precisely because he was a person qualified in medicine and 'well acquainted with the nature of hospitals' and this was the type of person needed at this time to inspect the naval hospitals." An additional medical man joined the board later that year who had previously served as chief surgeon of Plymouth Hospital. At the conclusion of the war, it appears, medical men were notably absent from the board until 1793.

2 Several surgeons and physicians believed that air could become charged with an epidemic influence from the presence of emissions from organic decomposition of the earth. The resulting gases, or miasmas, produced diseases. See Roy Porter, *Blood and Guts: A Short History of Medicine* (London: Penguin Books, 2002), p. 86.

3 Charlotte Mason, *The Ladies' Assistant for Regulating and Supplying the Table; being a Complete System of Cookery, &c.* 6th ed. (London: n.p., 1787), p. 199; Janet MacDonald, *Feeding Nelson's Navy: The True Story of Food at Sea in the Georgian Era* (London: Chatham, 2006).

4 Sick and Hurt Board to Admiralty, 14 September 1756, ADM/F/13, Board of Admiralty In-Letters, Caird Library, National Maritime Museum, London [hereafter NMM].

5 Sick and Hurt Board to Admiralty, 28 March 1757, ADM/F/15, Board of Admiralty In-Letters, Caird Library, NMM.

6 Sick and Hurt Board to Admiralty, 4 January 1758, ADM/F/17, Board of Admiralty In-Letters, Caird Library, NMM.

7 Sick and Hurt Board to Admiralty, 24 January 1759, ADM/F/19, Board of Admiralty In-Letters, Caird Library, NMM.

8 For examples see K. J. Carpenter, *A History of Scurvy and Vitamin C* (Cambridge, U.K.: Cambridge Univ. Press, 1986); Glyn Williams, *Death of Captain Cook: A Hero Made and Unmade* (London: Profile, 2008);

Vanessa Collingridge, *Captain Cook: The Life, Death and Legacy of History's Greatest Explorer* (London: Ebury, 2003).

9 Sick and Hurt Board to Admiralty, 12 January 1781, ADM/FP/24, Board of Admiralty In-Letters, Caird Library, NMM.

10 "Mynficht's Elixir of Vitriol," in *London Pharmacopoeia* (1770).

11 J. Martin to Sick and Hurt Board, 7 March 1746, ADM 97/114/4, Sick and Hurt Board In-Letters, The National Archives, Kew, U.K. [hereafter TNA].

12 Sick and Hurt Board to Admiralty, 18 December 1781, ADM 98/14, Sick and Hurt Board Out-Letters, TNA.

13 It is traditionally accepted that the powder was created by Dr. Robert James and patented at Chancery, although there is some dispute that he may have thieved the recipe from William Schwanberg. The latter invented both a liquid shell (used to cure stones and gravel) and a fever powder. Following Schwanberg's death in 1744, his friend Dr. James applied for a patent on his own fever powder, which proved to be a very well-liked medicine. Walter Baker, an administrator for Schwanberg, accused James of stealing the recipe, even going so far as petitioning the king to revoke the patent, but his petition was denied. See Sidney Lee, ed., *Dictionary of National Biography 1885–1900* (London: Elder Smith, 1892), vol. 29, pp. 220–21.

14 Admiralty to Sick and Hurt Board, 27 September 1752, ADM/E/13, Sick and Hurt Board In-Letters, Caird Library, NMM; Admiralty to Sick and Hurt Board, 20 December 1752, ADM/E/13, Sick and Hurt Board In-Letters, Caird Library, NMM.

15 Sick and Hurt Board to Admiralty, 2 February 1796, ADM/F/26, Board of Admiralty In-Letters, Caird Library, NMM.

16 Admiralty to Sick and Hurt Board, 6 February 1796, ADM/E/45, Sick and Hurt Board In-Letters, Caird Library, NMM.

17 Fiammetta Rocco, *The Miraculous Fever-Tree: The Cure That Changed the World* (London: HarperCollins, 2003), p. xviii.

18 Ibid., pp. 55–57. There is some speculation that the cinchona tree was named in honor of the Countess of Chinchón. According to various sources, the wife of the viceroy had fallen ill with a tertian fever while in Peru and word had spread into rural areas as far as present-day Ecuador. The prefect of Loja was said to have written to the viceroy that he had a cure for the countess composed of bark from a local tree. When the prefect arrived with the remedy, it is said, the countess made a full recovery. Upon her return to Europe, she is said to have carried the bark with her, causing Carolus Linnaeus, a Swedish botanist, to name the genus of the Peruvian bark after her, in 1742. Sadly, this story is simply not true. The viceroy's private diary, which resurfaced in the 1930s, does not mention any illness endured by the countess, at least not malaria. The diary also records that the countess died suddenly in Cartagena before ever returning to Europe.

19 Admiralty to Navy Board, 21 November 1774, ADM/A/2685, Navy Board In-Letters, Caird Library, NMM. See also Robert Robertson, *A Physical Journal Kept on Board His Majesty's Ship* Rainbow, *during Three Voyages to the Coast of Africa, and West Indies, in the years 1772, 1773, and 1774. To Which is Prefixed, a particular Account of the Remitting Fever, which happened on board of His Majesty's Sloop* Weasel, *on that Coast, in 1769* (London: n.p., 1777).

20 Admiralty to Sick and Hurt Board, 17 September 1773, ADM/E/41, Sick and Hurt Board In-Letters, Caird Library, NMM.

21 Ibid.

22 James Lind, *A Treatise of the Scurvy* (Edinburgh: 1753), unpaginated.

23 Sir Peter Parker to Admiralty, 15 December 1780, ADM/E/42, Sick and Hurt Board In-Letters, Caird Library, NMM.

24 Captain Countess to Sick and Hurt Board, 14 October 1796, ADM/F/27, Board of Admiralty In-Letters, Caird Library, NMM.

25 Sick and Hurt Board to Admiralty, 14 April 1758, ADM/F/17, Board of Admiralty In-Letters, Caird Library, NMM.

26 Admiralty to Sick and Hurt Board, 27 September 1752; Gulielmi Pinto to Admiralty, 26 March 1762, ADM/E/35, Sick and Hurt Board In-Letters, Caird Library, NMM.

27 *The Ship-Master's Medical Assistant; or Physical Advice to all masters of ships who carry no surgeons; particularly useful to those who trade abroad in hot or cold climates. Containing a brief description of diseases, especially those peculiar to seamen in long voyages. With a concise method of cure, the result of many years practice and experience in all climates* (London: 1777), unpaginated.

28 Dr. Maxwell to Sick and Hurt Board, 16 May 1757, ADM/F/15, Board of Admiralty In-Letters, Caird Library, NMM.

29 Christopher Lloyd and Jack L. S. Coulter, *Medicine and the Navy 1200–1900* (Edinburgh: E&S Livingstone, 1961), vol. 3, pp. 72–73.

30 See Christopher Lloyd, ed., *The Health of Seamen: Selections from the Works of Dr. James Lind, Sir Gilbert Blane and Dr. Thomas Trotter* (London: Navy Records Society, 1965), vol. 107; Lloyd and Coulter, *Medicine and the Navy.*

31 Brian Vale, "The Conquest of Scurvy in the Royal Navy 1793–1800: A Challenge to Current Orthodoxy," *Mariner's Mirror* 94 (May 2008), pp. 160–75.

32 Joan Druett, *Rough Medicine: Surgeons at Sea in the Age of Sail* (New York: Routledge, 2001), p. 145.

33 Cdr. S. H. S. Moxly, "Scurvy" answer, *Mariner's Mirror* 39, no. 1 (1953), pp. 69–70.

34 Admiralty to Sick and Hurt Board, 12 February 1781, ADM/E/43, Sick and Hurt Board In-Letters, Caird Library, NMM.

35 Dr. Coleman to Captain Curtis, 30 March 1782, ADM/E/43, Sick and Hurt Board In-Letters, Caird Library, NMM.

VII *The First Gunboat Diplomacy*
The U.S. Navy, Haiti, and the Birth of American Interventionism, 1798–1800

ANDREW J. FORNEY

D uring the summer of 1798, President John Adams received his mail at his personal residence in Quincy, Massachusetts. Summering at Quincy both allowed him and his family the opportunity to escape the miasmal season in Philadelphia and provided a restful retreat for his sick wife, Abigail. A vast amount of his correspondence dealt with the undeclared naval war, known as the Quasi-War, that the Adams administration had inaugurated the preceding May. Accounts of "depredations" had filled the air since before Adams's presidency. The administration, feeling political pressure from its own Federalist party, had authorized a response to the seizure of American merchantmen by French privateers at the end of May; the president had forwarded instructions to his new Department of the Navy to "seize take and bring into any port of the United States . . . any armed vessel sailing under the Authority or Pretence of Authority from the Republic of France, which shall have committed, or which shall be found hovering on the Coasts of the United States, for the purpose of committing Depredations on the Vessels belonging to the citizens thereof."[1] In response, Congress passed several acts that focused on defending American merchant vessels and expanding the Navy to take the offensive against piracy and privateering, a task to be overseen by the new Secretary of the Navy, Benjamin Stoddert.[2]

Writing to Adams directly during late July, Secretary Stoddert now pled for a strategic shift in the ongoing hostilities; as the heat of deep summer enveloped Philadelphia, he had become restive. After assuming the role of secretary, Stoddert had fully backed the administration's policies and had mobilized the still-small Navy to protect the coastline of the republic. Now, in July, he theorized that the impending hurricane season would drive French privateers back into the protection of West Indian harbors. This reprieve from attacks on the nation's coast would allow the Navy the opportunity to reshape the course of the conflict. Stoddert preferred fighting French privateers in French colonial waters, not within range of American cities. "By keeping up incessant attacks upon the French Cruisers on their own ground," Stoddert believed, "they will in a degree be prevented from coming on ours."[3]

This idea not only served a strategic end but also spoke to another facet of the conflict, one that had been slowly emerging among men with prominent ties to the administration. Henry Knox, Revolutionary War hero and Secretary of War under Washington, had a month before Stoddert's request penned a notable letter to Adams, obviously agitated about the situation with France. Knox opined that "posterity will be astonished, at the constant perseverance of the different succession of French Rulers rising upon the ruins of each other, and yet holding steadily the same unjust conduct towards us." The citizenry of the United States would follow the president's lead, rallying around him during this time of potential strife and providing the virtuous fortitude to end the depredations of the anarchic French Directory.[4]

For all of his bombast, however, Knox voiced caution. Rather than solely advocating naval expansion to protect American merchantmen and attack rapacious French privateers, he also outlined the steps necessary to protect the nation from invasion. Knox concerned himself most with the southern states, which he believed were "vulnerable . . . to an alarming degree." He acknowledged that currently only the wooden walls of the British navy kept the wily Jacobins from launching a force of "blacks and people of color" onto the shores of the slave South. "Under such circumstances," Knox warned, "the slaves would instantly join them, and greatly encrease their force." Fearing that he would sound alarmist, Knox reminded the president that "the event [black/mulatto invasion of the South] is possible, and whatever is possible the enemy will have the enterprise to attempt."[5]

These two disparate ideas—a desire to shift the area of battle to the West Indies and a fear of Jacobin invasion—animated Stoddert's recommendation to President Adams, as well as the plans he enacted in the next month to execute his strategy. In the process of this transition, the Adams administration completely reconfigured the Quasi-War with France and recast the foreign policy of the United States. The Navy became the primary tool to execute this policy, and it acted far beyond the stated goals of stopping French depredations. By 1799 all but one ship in the Navy had orders to sail south and assume station somewhere in the Caribbean. After the spring of 1798, the American coastline never again faced the scourge of privateering and depredations it had before, and commerce rebounded handily in the year leading to the end of the century.

This paper will argue that the Navy became an extension of a national policy that sought to eradicate instability in the West Indies during the Quasi-War, dallying in imperial politics along the way. American actions toward Saint-Domingue and Toussaint L'Ouverture's government during the conflict provide the prime example of this new interventionist predilection. As opposed to simply executing an antiprivateering campaign in the Caribbean, the Adams administration quickly moved to support L'Ouverture in his bid to consolidate power in the French colony, providing both diplomatic and military support to him and his forces. Secretary of State Timothy Pickering led the move to unite Atlantic diplomacy with naval might; his primacy in the cabinet not only animated the legislative actions taken to support L'Ouverture but helped shape naval operations. Harking back to earlier fears of popular unrest and slave revolts, the Federalists quickly transitioned the Quasi-War with France to a West Indian war for antirevolutionary stability.

The French Caribbean appeared to be the nexus of revolutionary fervor during the 1790s. The Washington administration handled the Haitian Revolution unevenly, and understandably so. It grew increasingly difficult to determine which side represented the light of liberty on the island.[6] During 1793, free blacks and mulattoes, swept up by the Jacobin fury of the revolution in the home country, unseated the white, planter aristocracy that had governed the colony. As the fighting between the two factions slowly moved toward a stalemate, the revolt created a schism in the social hierarchy that helped to inaugurate a slave rebellion that in turn quickly spread throughout the colony. Outsiders perceived the formation of a race war in the now-floundering colony, but a war that still maintained vestiges of revolutionary idealism and unity with the wider cause of liberty. A British invasion and the subsequent arming and support of General in Chief Toussaint L'Ouverture, the leader of the ascendant slave faction on the island, further muddied the water.[7]

During early November 1798, L'Ouverture petitioned Adams directly for the resumption of American trade. Pickering immediately divined the import of this outreach. The British still maintained a series of forts on the island's western shore, but little else, and L'Ouverture's resistance to declaring independence from France had slowly soured their relationship with him.[8] All Saint-Dominguan ports had been blockaded from French vessels by the British navy, and the United States joined in an active antiprivateering campaign with its British pseudo-allies in the waters around the colony.

L'Ouverture's letter to President Adams evinced a policy *shift* for the ex-slave general. The "War of the Knives" against André Rigaud, the mulatto general opposed to L'Ouverture, continued to grind on in the southern portions of the colony. The French agents sent to represent imperial control contributed nothing to the war effort; in conjunction with his request to the American president, L'Ouverture expelled the remaining ones from the island, hoping that this exhibition of renunciation of France would have the necessary effect on the Adams administration. Secretary Pickering took notice; in a letter to the consul at Cap François dated 30 November 1798 he drew the distinction that the last Congress had passed legislation prohibiting trade "with places *under the acknowledged power of France*." Logically, "if the inhabitants of St. Domingo have ceased to acknowledge this power, there will not, as I conceive, be any bar to the prompt and extensive renewal of trade between the United States and the ports of that Island." This is the first recorded outline of a new policy to Jacob Mayer, the consul in Cap François, but Pickering had obviously brought this idea up with others, most likely fellow merchants from New England (Pickering was from Massachusetts and had briefly been a merchant). He noted later on in his dispatch, "our merchants . . . are already preparing to renew that commerce."[9]

Mayer must have forwarded this information to L'Ouverture quickly, for the general dispatched Joseph Brunel, a close comrade and personal representative, before the end of 1798 to present his views in person to President Adams. While Pickering fought to secure the votes to amend the prohibitive legislation then in effect, Adams intended to display his regard for L'Ouverture and his cause. Secretary Stoddert, in letters to Capts. John Barry and Thomas Truxtun, requested that they modify their ships' routes to include time on station off Cap François, for "General L'Ouverture has a great desire to see some of our Ships of War" off his coast—and, the secretary added for emphasis, "the President has a desire that he [L'Ouverture] should be satisfied." Stoddert recommended to the two captains that they ingratiate themselves with the general, telling Truxtun, "Should you see the General, it would be well to cultivate a good understanding with him."[10] Stoddert, either wooed by Pickering's ideas or feeling the weight of Adams's intentions, believed it important that his captains begin building working relationships with General L'Ouverture.

President Adams signed an act that legislated this policy transition on 9 February 1799. The act was aptly titled "Toussaint's Clause," and its genesis had been a few months before its signing. Secretary Pickering had led the international and national negotiations that brought the act to fruition, and he cherished the idea of a more expansive role for U.S. power in the Caribbean. As the vessels of the U.S. Navy prepared to determine the function of the new "Santo Domingo Station," Congress designed a series of benchmarks that offered French colonies a way to reintroduce American merchantmen into their ports, a process emphasizing the necessity of suppressing the privateering enterprises in the respective islands' waters. Pickering nominated Dr. Edward Stevens, a close friend of Alexander Hamilton and an avowed Federalist, to the new position of "consul general" to Saint-Domingue upon the passage of the act. Stevens's primary task upon arriving on the island involved communicating the provisions of the act to L'Ouverture. They obliged the Saint-Dominguan leader to allow all U.S. vessels, including ships of war, to enter Saint-Dominguan ports for "victuals, water, and refit"—common practice for merchantmen, but Pickering was changing the game by including military vessels.[11] By making the resumption of commerce contingent on allowing the Navy to refit in L'Ouverture's ports, Pickering had turned a French possession into a supply depot for the U.S. Navy, allowing Stoddert to increase the range and time at sea of his fleet.

Pickering did not believe that such a stricture was too much to request, particularly given his recent battle in the cabinet to wed more closely the policies of the United States with L'Ouverture's designs in Saint-Domingue. Brunel, at his meeting with Adams, forwarded an appeal from L'Ouverture for supplies and provisions. The British blockade and the inability of the French to break it had left L'Ouverture's army lacking common goods, particularly uniforms, food, and parts needed to mend weapons. Agreeing to this request would pull the United States directly into the conflict in Saint-Domingue, and not as an impartial observer. Forwarding supplies to L'Ouverture would provide him the means necessary to end the vicious stalemate in the French colony. In the complicated context of the Quasi-War Caribbean, the United States would actually be arming an ex-slave general who still proclaimed ties (albeit loose ones) to the French Republic, in return for a promise to halt future depredations of privateers ostensibly under his control.

Adams considered the question before forwarding it to his cabinet for review. Attorney General Charles Lee, from Virginia, dissented from the remainder of the cabinet. He believed that for the United States to send provisions to L'Ouverture was "neither lawful or expedient," although he conceded that a private merchant might forward the articles to L'Ouverture for a price. Such a maneuver also opened the executive department to criticism from the public over perceptions of "interests in adventures." Lee closed by roundly declaring, "I have no more confidence in the black Frenchmen than the white, and am willing they should suffer in St. Domingo till they actually refrain from depredations on our commerce."[12]

Pickering wrote the majority decision for Adams, as well as a gruff reply to Lee. "Having been more than any other gentlemen in the way of receiving information of the real situation of Toussaint," Pickering wrote Lee, he was convinced that not to supply L'Ouverture's army "endangers [L'Ouverture's] authority and the peace of the island of St. Domingo." As he stated in this letter, the secretary equated supporting L'Ouverture with the eventual stabilization of the internal affairs of the island. More than that, however, Pickering believed that such an immediate measure would soothe the aggressive nature of the "blacks." Harking back to the fears of Jacobin or ex-slave invasion of the South that Knox had described to Adams less than a year before, Pickering declared that "to delay relief . . . might render the blacks *impatient and unbelieving,* especially as L'Ouverture himself for some time past have [*sic*] been feeding them with *promises.*"[13] An expansion of privateering seemed a more likely response to delaying the shipping of supplies, Pickering admitted, but his description of the restive nature of L'Ouverture's undersupplied "black" army left unsaid an undercurrent of concern for the spread of Jacobin, and emancipatory, revolutionary fervor. President Adams approved the supplies.[14]

In early 1800, in execution of Adams's request to provide naval assistance to L'Ouverture, Commodore Silas Talbot, captain of *Constellation* and commander of the naval forces around Saint-Domingue, ordered Capt. Christopher Raymond Perry to sail his vessel *General Greene* around the island of Hispaniola, "paying more particular attention to the South side of the island." Hispaniola, particularly the hotly contested southern portion of Saint-Domingue, continued to roil with pirates and privateers. Some of their vessels belonged to L'Ouverture; the general in chief had scrounged together some barges to break Rigaud's grip on the southern portion of the island. Rigaud depended on privateering for supplies, which were much needed, particularly since L'Ouverture could soon expect to receive a trickle of goods from the United States. Rigaud had retreated to the port of Jacmel in an effort to keep his supply lines open and maintain access to his privateering fleet as it continued to prey on American and English merchants in the Caribbean. Under no circumstances, Talbot ordered, should Perry "capture any Vessels (except those from Rigaud[']s Ports) within one league of any part of the Island under General Tou[s]sa[i]nt[']s Command, or do any one thing, that may Justly give cause to disturb the Harmony between him, and the People of the United States."[15] *General Greene* arrived in the waters off Jacmel during the last week of February and quickly began to interdict Rigaud's privateers, capturing a "French armed schooner" with a crew of fifty, "mostly white," on 11 March.[16]

L'Ouverture repeatedly singled out Captain Perry in his correspondence. "Nothing could equal his kindness, his activity, his watchfulness and his zeal in protecting me, in unhappy circumstances," he avowed, adding, "he has contributed not a little to the success by his cruise, every effort being made by him to aid me in the taking of Jacmel, also in seeing order restored in this colony."[17] Such words betray an active partnership between L'Ouverture and Perry, more than the simple antiprivateering duty that Perry's orders to the Santo Domingo Station stipulated. In fact, Perry's ship's log indicates that L'Ouverture's aides arrived early after the frigate's arrival, after which they made several trips to confer with Captain Perry. Accounts of these discussions either never existed or have been lost, but future actions taken by Captain Perry and *General Greene* hint at what might have been agreed on. A letter from an officer on board *General Greene,* later reprinted in a stateside newspaper, acknowledged the standing order from Talbot to sail around the entirety of Hispaniola but admitted that the cruise took longer than planned, delayed "for the purpose of aiding Gen. Toussaint in the capture of Jacmel." As the officer recounted, "we engaged three of Rigaud's forts warmly for 30 or 40 minutes; in which time we obliged the enemy to evacuate the town and two of the forts." Perry even prepared a boarding party of Marines and sailors to "take possession of the place," stopping only when a potentially enemy ship came into view and he decided to forgo the ground assault in the hope of capturing a French prize. Rigaud suffered "several men killed and wounded" and, shortly after the bombardment, fled his fortifications.[18]

Far from simply attempting to capture or destroy privateers in accordance with a collection of legal sanctions passed by Congress in an attempt to regulate the ongoing Quasi-War with France, Captain Perry had attacked militants engaged in a civil war alongside forces loosely affiliated with republican France and had been prepared to seize terrain and place it under the flag of the United States. Such actions barely resembled the context in which the Adams administration inaugurated the Quasi-War in 1798, let alone Perry's own orders published in January 1800. While one could claim that Captain Perry carried out his Jacmel assault of his own volition, being more a loose cannon than a by-the-book Navy man, a court of inquiry was to tell a different story.

After returning from Hispaniola Perry faced an official inquiry into his actions, the court formally convening in the beginning of October 1800. In the listing of official charges brought against him, however, no mention was made of the bombarding of Jacmel or the transgression of orders that such cannonading involved. Rather, Perry faced censure for conduct in connection with the Danish merchant schooner *William and Mary*, which, its captain stated, during early March 1800 Perry had detained off Jacmel until L'Ouverture's own privateers could seize it. From the hold of *William and Mary* L'Ouverture had transferred a sizeable amount of coffee (rumored to be ten thousand pounds) into the hold of *General Greene*. Such a give-and-take must have developed quickly between Perry and L'Ouverture, for the fourth bullet in the charge list described the loading of a "large number of swine [along with the coffee] for the use of his [Perry's] Father's farm."[19] Finding Perry guilty of all the charges brought against him, the court of inquiry recommended his removal as captain of *General Greene* and a three-month suspension without pay. President Adams approved the recommendation.[20] If this case served as a barometer of appropriate conduct for captains in the Navy during the Quasi-War, it seems clear that pushing the intent of orders to include active kingmaking in foreign civil wars could be overlooked but that interrupting regular commerce or besmirching one's honor through graft could not.

Reverberations from Perry's actions rippled throughout Saint-Domingue, as well as the Navy. L'Ouverture appeared ascendant following the capture of Rigaud's bastion at Jacmel. By May, his army of former slaves had marched overland and seized Petit and Grand Goâve, immediately after which he announced the blockading of all ports in the southern portion of Saint-Domingue. His drive to consolidate control over the French colony now approached its final stages.[21] Stoddert mobilized the rest of the Navy, hoping that its guns might provide the necessary leverage for L'Ouverture's final victory. During mid-July 1800, Commodore Talbot ordered *Augusta, Trumbull,* and *Herald* to Jacmel to resupply L'Ouverture's forces and then to Aux Cayes, where Rigaud's remaining large ships were anchored. Talbot went so far as to instruct the commander of *Trumbull* to utilize his bread room for extra gunpowder earmarked for L'Ouverture's forces, as the supply the ship was to carry to the general in chief's army most likely would overflow the magazine.[22]

Talbot further instructed all U.S. ships of war operating off Saint-Domingue to blockade Rigaud's remaining portion of the island. He intimated that their focus should be determining the location of Rigaud's larger ships and either hemming them into their anchorages or capturing them if they attempted to break for open water. In the meantime, the American vessels would take all necessary measures to support L'Ouverture and his campaigns. Talbot's instructions to Archibald MacElroy of *Augusta* best outline the new phase of operations for the Navy in relation to L'Ouverture: MacElroy was to "favor General Toussaint[']s operations against Rigaud, and to protect his small armed vessels, which are cruising before said ports, in order to stop the supplies going to Rigaud." By preventing supplies from reaching Rigaud the Navy would render L'Ouverture's foe "more distressed, and the sooner reduced to submission." The most striking element in Talbot's correspondence, however, regards his perception that Rigaud's downfall "*is of great consequence. . . .* [Rigaud] has hitherto kept up a constant and cruel warfare on the lives, and property of the citizens of the United States." In a later dispatch sending *Trumbull* to assist L'Ouverture, Talbot labeled Rigaud "one of our most cruel and barbarous enemy's [*sic*]."[23]

The work of L'Ouverture and Pickering and their adherents in the U.S. government to refashion the narrative of depredations is remarkable. In little less than eighteen months (using the debate over arming L'Ouverture as a start point), the ex-slave general had completely shifted the onus of privateering and chaotic, murderous warfare onto Rigaud. By appealing to the United States to open commerce and painting himself as the force of moderation in the internecine civil war that raged in the French colony, L'Ouverture reversed the roles that had prevailed in the preceding years of the revolution. The general in chief had determined that the United States craved stability in the West Indies and that if he could allay the fear of emancipatory Jacobin revolution or shift the embodiment of this ideal from the ex-slave to the mulatto, the economic, diplomatic, and military power of the American nation would gravitate toward his faction. He expertly commandeered the issue of privateering, not only agreeing to halt depredations stemming from his supporters but inaugurating a campaign of antiprivateering himself, receiving supplies and armament from the United States to effect this goal. Never mind that L'Ouverture's own former privateers constituted his antiprivateering naval force nor that they used their newfound legitimacy to interdict supplies to Rigaud more than to halt privateering.

Most important for L'Ouverture, he capitalized on the physical proximity of the U.S. Navy, engendering a warmness that, as Perry's actions and Talbot's orders both show, paid large dividends during the course of the campaign. A letter from Capt. Alexander Murray to L'Ouverture, dated 25 July 1800 (sent upon Murray's ascension to command of the Santo Domingo Station), best epitomizes this transition: "I deem it a Duty incumbent on me to offer you my most zealous services in cooperation with you & the meritorious cause in which you are now engaged to bring about order, Peace & Harmony in the island of Hispaniola." The commander went on that "time and experience hath evinced to us the importance, & necessity of a close and firm Friendship between our respective countries, so proximate with each other, for the purpose of mutual exchange." As long as L'Ouverture's requests did not infringe on the standing orders of the Navy, Murray assured him, "you may freely command me."[24] In the eyes of Murray and many of his countrymen, L'Ouverture's deliberate refashioning as a father of independence, protector of liberty, and possible descendant of America's own revolution appeared to be complete.

French and American ministers signed the Convention of 1800 in Paris toward the end of September 1800, effectively ending a war that had never been declared. The two nations agreed to practice free and open trade and would immediately halt depredations and attacks on each other's vessels, armed or otherwise. The final draft of the convention makes no direct mention of the situation in the West Indies, but several subtle inclusions appear relevant. If American or French officials determined that a merchant ship possessed war material from a clearly defined list of goods agreed on by the two countries, that vessel could be seized. The civilians on board, however, were to be treated humanely and fairly. To guarantee this, the convention ordered that would-be privateers possess between seven and fourteen thousand dollars, depending on size of crew, toward compensation to dispossessed captains and sailors before home governments could issue letters of marque. Such a stricture would force France to regulate its privateering activities in the Caribbean and end the haphazard issuance of letters of marque that had typified its policy during the 1790s.

At the same time, foreign privateers could not provision in French or American ports, and their captures would be reclaimed by their owners in the ports of the two nations. At first glance, such an article appears superfluous. The United States did not enlist privateers during the Quasi-War, so such a policy would refer to it only if it allowed the enemies of France to arm and refit in its ports. The British had no need for privateers; their navy owned the seas by 1800. France had no declared allies, so no privateers arrived at its ports for sustenance. This new Franco-U.S. policy makes sense only if one realizes that France had decided, in the wake of its reverses at the hands of the U.S. Navy during the Quasi-War, to strengthen imperial control in the West Indies. No longer allowing such chaotic situations as existed in Saint-Domingue or ignoring actions by ambitious colonial officials contrary to governmental policy, France sought to realign and demarcate factions in the West Indies. No longer abiding middle ground, France forced participants of the emancipatory Jacobin movement to declare firmly for the home country or find themselves outside the pale.[25]

The U.S. Navy played one more role in the Quasi-War West Indies, one much more personal and more indicative of the conflict's nature than was the convention that ended it. The U.S. naval schooner *Experiment* fought and silenced the privateer *Diane* on 1 October 1800, ironically the day after the signing of the convention. The vessel's captain informed *Experiment*'s boarding party that General Rigaud was aboard, having fled his losing cause in Saint-Domingue. The boarding officer, Lt. Charles Stewart, exhibiting the changing perception of Rigaud, fairly crowed at the general's apprehension, stating that he had "wrested millions from my countrymen; the depredations, the piracies, plunder, and murders he has committed on my fellow-citizens are but two [sic] well known in the United States; and now the supreme ruler of all things has placed him in the hands of that country he has most injured."[26] Stewart transferred Rigaud to the supervision of his commanding officer, Captain Truxtun, who in turn deposited him on Saint Kitts until he had arranged a proper parole. The truculence of the Saint Kitts population forced Truxtun to send a Marine escort to guarantee Rigaud's safety; he was certain that they "would have murdered him when passing through the streets."[27] Conferring with the colonial officials in Guadeloupe, Truxtun agreed to parole Rigaud there, trusting him on his honor to remove himself from further affairs in the West Indies. But the French citizens on Guadeloupe "were so uneasy at his being at large," Truxtun later recounted, "that they made application to the Governor for his close confinement, and he was committed to jail."[28] A former Jacobin revolutionary, Rigaud now languished in a French colonial prison, a victim of the American search for West Indian stability.

NOTES 1 "Instructions to Commanders of Armed Vessels, 28 May 1798," in *Naval Documents Related to the Quasi-War between the United States and France,* ed. Dudley W. Knox (Washington, D.C.: U.S. Government Printing Office, 1935–38) [hereafter *NDQ*], vol. 1, p. 88.

2 Timothy Pickering, Report to Congress, 27 December 1797, *NDQ,* vol. 1, pp. 20–36.

3 "To President John Adams from Secretary of Navy," 30 July 1798, *NDQ,* vol. 1, pp. 255–56.

4 Henry Knox to the President of the United States [John Adams], 26 June 1798, *NDQ,* vol. 1, p. 139.

5 Ibid., p. 140.

6 Alexander DeConde, *Entangling Alliance: Politics and Diplomacy under George Washington* (Westport, Conn.: Greenwood, 1958), pp. 270–74; Forrest McDonald, *The Presidency of George Washington* (Lawrence: Univ. of Kansas Press, 1974), pp. 134–35.

7 Arthur Scherr, *Thomas Jefferson's Haitian Policy: Myths and Realities* (Lanham, Md.: Lexington Books, 2011), pp. 60–69; Thomas O. Ott, *The Haitian Revolution, 1789–1804* (Knoxville: Univ. of Tennessee Press, 1973), pp. 76–99.

8 For a dynamic contemporary view of Toussaint L'Ouverture, see Philippe R. Girard, "Black Talleyrand: Toussaint Louverture's Diplomacy, 1798–1802," *William and Mary Quarterly,* 3rd ser., 66, no. 1 (January 2009), pp. 87–124.

9 Timothy Pickering to Jacob Mayer, 30 November 1798, Consular Dispatches: Cap Hatien, reel 1, record group [hereafter RG] M0009, National Archives and Records Administration, College Park, Md. [hereafter NARA].

10 Benjamin Stoddert to John Barry, Benjamin Stoddert to Thomas Truxtun, 16 January 1799, *NDQ,* vol. 2, pp. 242–43.

11 Timothy Pickering to Edward Stevens, 7 March 1799, Consular Dispatches: Cap Hatien, reel 1, RG M0009, NARA.

12 Charles Lee to John Adams, 20 February 1799, Consular Dispatches: Cap Hatien, reel 1, RG M0009, NARA.

13 Timothy Pickering to Charles Lee, 20 February 1799, Consular Dispatches: Cap Hatien, reel 1, RG M0009, NARA.

14 Provisions list, 28 August 1799, Consular Dispatches: Cap Hatien, reel 1, RG M0009, NARA.

15 Commodore Silas Talbot to Christopher Perry, 18 January 1800, *NDQ,* vol. 5.

16 Christopher Perry to Edward Stevens, 17 March 1800, *NDQ,* vol. 5.

17 Toussaint L'Ouverture to Edward Stevens, 16 March 1800, *NDQ,* vol. 5.

18 Perry to Stevens, 17 March 1800.

19 "Concerning Capture of the Danish Schooner *William & Mary* by the U.S. Ship *General Greene,* Captain Christopher R. Perry, U.S. Navy, Commanding," 23 June 1800, *NDQ,* vol. 5, pp. 266–67; "Court of Enquiry Convened to Investigate Conduct of Captain Christopher Raymond Perry, U.S. Navy," 13 October 1800, *NDQ,* vol. 6, pp. 472–73.

20 Benjamin Stoddert to Christopher Perry, 28 November 1800, *NDQ,* vol. 6, p. 559.

21 Robert Richie to Timothy Pickering, 3 May 1800, *NDQ,* vol. 5; "News Item Concerning Proclamation of Toussaint L'Ouverture Blocking All the Southern Departments of St. Domingo," 8 May 1800, *NDQ,* vol. 5.

22 Silas Talbot to Commander of *Trumbull,* 22 July 1800, *NDQ,* vol. 6, pp. 165–66.

23 See orders dispatching *Augusta, Herald,* and *Trumbull* to the Saint-Domingue station, *NDQ,* vol. 6, pp. 139–40, 153–54, 165–66 [emphasis supplied].

24 Alexander Murray to Toussaint L'Ouverture, 25 July 1800, *NDQ,* vol. 6, pp. 178–79.

25 "Convention of Amity and Commerce between the United States and France," 30 September 1800, *NDQ,* vol. 6, pp. 393–409.

26 "Extract from Letter from Lieutenant Charles Stewart, U.S. Navy," 3 October 1800, *NDQ,* vol. 6, pp. 422–23.

27 "Extract from Log Book of U.S.S. *President,* Captain Thomas Truxtun, U.S. Navy, Commanding, Friday, 3 October 1800," *NDQ,* vol. 6, pp. 430–31.

28 Thomas Truxtun to Mr. Myers, 27 October 1800, *NDQ,* vol. 6, p. 506.

VIII   *Overcoming "Hydrophobia"*
John Adams and the War of 1812

R. M. BARLOW

When the United States declared war on Great Britain in 1812, John Adams, former president and diplomat, was enduring his retirement from public life. As one of America's senior statesmen, whose son John Quincy would eventually negotiate the peace treaty in 1814, Adams did not hesitate to voice his opinion. Although he questioned the wisdom of invading Canada, he insisted the war was "necessary." Adams accused the Republicans of "hydrophobia" and presented an alternative strategy that depended on naval power and drew from his success fighting the Quasi-War with France from 1798 to 1800. Although Adams does not normally spring to mind as a strategic thinker, his understanding of the effectiveness of asymmetric warfare on the Atlantic and of the need for command of the Great Lakes before attempting an invasion of Canada invites comparison with the principles of Alfred Mahan, Julian Corbett, and the Jeune École. Attention to Adams's counterfactual explains why, when so many other New Englanders opposed the war, John Adams could see it as "necessary"—but disagree with how the Republicans had chosen to fight it.

Adams had been in the forefront of American independence in 1776, and it could be argued that his Anglophobia was reason enough to advocate a second round with Great Britain. But Adams saw both France and Britain as powers from which the United States needed to be independent, and he worried about both pro-British and pro-French factions in American politics. He explained to Dr. Benjamin Rush, "This our beloved country, my dear friend, is indeed in a very dangerous situation. It is between two great fires in Europe, and between two ignited parties at home, smoking, sparkling, and flaming ready to burst into a conflagration."[1] Key to Adams's independent American foreign policy was rejection of the temptation to depend on European military or naval power for American defense. Adams argued that, ideally, the United States should form no military alliances with European powers. If necessary, an alliance was permissible, like the Franco-American alliance that had brought French support against Great Britain during the War of Independence. Since Adams considered Britain to be America's "natural enemy," he considered its enemy France to be America's "natural ally," but one that was looking out for its own interests. Adams looked instead to the American union as a source of security. If the states did not remain united, they would become pawns of the European powers and fight each other. If they did remain united, they could resist entanglement in European quarrels and possess strategic depth if attacked by European armies. Adams opposed the creation of a large standing army. His aim was to provide a cost-effective defense for the United States, one that would permit it to have an independent foreign policy based on naval strength and on careful maneuvering in the European balance of power.[2]

Adams was annoyed at both the High Federalists and the Republicans for their failure to grasp the potential of American naval power. He complained that High Federalists like Timothy Pickering wanted to cower behind the shield of the Royal Navy.[3] Adams argued that Americans did not need to depend on Great Britain for their defense. The Republicans—rightly, in his opinion—rejected closer ties with Britain but feared British naval power. Their resort to the embargo had crippled revenue and threatened to split the country. Adams scoffed at Republican timidity, telling Dr. Rush, "I wish you would cure our Rulers of the Hydrophobia!"[4]

In 1796 Adams had become the second president of the United States. The Directory in France brought a new challenge to Adams, with France, the natural ally, attacking American merchant ships and Britain, the natural enemy, restrained by the Jay Treaty. As president, Adams dealt with France through a combination of diplomacy and asymmetrical naval power. First, he permitted merchantmen to arm themselves. Second, he issued letters of marque to privateers. Third, he continued the building of "superfrigates"—ships not only effective against pirates and privateers but formidable enough to take on any foreign frigates in single combat and fast enough to sail away to safety if they met ships of the line. Fourth, he avoided an actual declaration of war against France. Fifth, he accepted unofficial cooperation with the Royal Navy in preference to a binding alliance with Britain. Adams saw no benefit to the United States in declaring war on France, and the possibility of much harm because of sectional tensions. He feared that a declaration of war would justify and institutionalize Hamilton's army, an expensive enterprise that many Americans would refuse to support. The result would be rebellions against the required taxes.[5] He likewise saw no value in an official military alliance with Great Britain against France. Years later he insisted, "My invariable principle for five-and-thirty years has been, to promote, preserve, and secure the integrity of the Union, and the independence of the nation, against the policy of England as well as France."[6]

Adams understood that an effective naval strategist considered not only the number and class of warships the enemy possessed but also whether that enemy had merchantmen vulnerable to attack. The strategist also needed to consider the vulnerability of his own shoreline, the challenge of keeping open his own ports, and the protection of his own merchantmen. Adams adjusted his views on naval policy for the United States as the challenges altered. During the War of Independence, Adams emphasized breaking the British blockade of American ports and encouraged attacks on British transports and whalers.[7] When dealing with the Barbary pirates, Adams advised paying them rather than fighting them, for the pirates had no ships worth seizing as prizes and could not be defeated so long as powers such as Great Britain continued to pay them.[8] In the wake of the Jay Treaty, when the American share of the carrying trade increased dramatically, Adams shifted his attention to protecting that trade.

Adams, of course, never read the works of naval strategists such as Alfred Mahan or Julian Corbett or of the Jeune École. Mahan was, however, to write a two-volume study of the War of 1812. His sources included *The Works of John Adams,* which unfortunately does not collect all of Adams's criticism of Republican naval policy. But Mahan, like Adams, recognized that although the early American republic could not match British naval strength, the United States was capable of a much more effective naval establishment than the Republicans supported. Like Adams, he argued that a small frigate navy was preferable to dependence on foreign naval power, which might be withdrawn when interests altered. Like Adams, he saw commerce as the foundation of naval power. But Mahan praised Gouverneur Morris for his support for building American ships of the line and faulted Adams as too defensive.[9] Adams's naval policy was therefore not "Mahanian" either in the modern simplification of Mahan's ideas or in terms of what Mahan himself thought appropriate for the early American republic.

Adams's focus on the protection of commerce and on limiting warfare suggests the viewpoint of Mahan's alternative, Julian Corbett. Like Corbett, Adams did not favor seeking out an enemy squadron in the hopes of obtaining a decisive result through a climactic sea fight. Adams's reasoning, however, was different from Corbett's. Adams opposed building ships of the line because he feared that a great naval establishment would, like Hamilton's army, result in tax revolts. His focus with respect to commerce was not on securing sea-lanes but rather on reducing insurance rates. He was determined to fight only a limited war with France to avoid civil war between the factions at home. Adams understood that although America possessed the people and the resources to become the greatest naval power on earth, the competing interest in westward expansion would prevent such a development.[10] He would not have been surprised to see a great American navy arise in the wake of the closing of the frontier.

Adams's asymmetric attempt to counter the superiority of British naval power invites comparison with the ideas of the Jeune École. Its theoreticians' emphasis on indirect attacks, torpedo boats and destroyers, and a more sophisticated application of the *guerre de course,* however, was to rest on important distinctions between France in the late nineteenth century and the early American republic.[11] As the

U.S. share of the carrying trade exploded, Adams focused on protecting American merchantmen rather than attacking British commerce. Second, Adams consistently looked to the security of the Atlantic fisheries. He insisted that Americans had a right to those fisheries "from God and our own swords," because New Englanders had forced concessions from the French through the conquest of Louisbourg in 1745. This fishery was also secured, twice, by treaty.[12] Third, his view that the fishery and carrying trades were the nurseries of the navy numbers him with the eighteenth-century British defenders of imperialism.[13] Adams's views on seapower are complex—divided between the ideal and the affordable but more like those of his contemporaries from the days of fighting sail than those of Mahan, Corbett, or the Jeune École.

Although Adams complained that his concern for his country did not win him a second term as president, he was proud that he left it prosperous and at peace.[14] Whatever the political ramifications for himself, Adams's policy in the Quasi-War was a significant military success. Although American merchantmen remained vulnerable to attack, the figures are impressive: for a cost of six million dollars to build his frigates and operate his navy, Adams protected two hundred million dollars' worth of commerce, and the government collected over twenty-three million from duties on imports. His naval strategy brought down the cost of insurance and enabled the operation of a profitable merchant marine.[15] This success would be a sharp contrast to the financial hardships and sectional animosity that were to be the results of the Republican embargo.

Adams placed the blame for the War of 1812 squarely on Thomas Jefferson and his "neglect of the navy."[16] In Adams's judgment, Jefferson had squandered resources on useless gunboats and, without an effective navy, tried to force Britain's hand with the equally useless embargo.[17] Adams was not entirely against the embargo but thought it should be a temporary measure, used only to recall merchantmen for the purpose of allowing them to arm themselves. Arming merchantmen, Adams observed, took away the reason for merchants to complain: if they were permitted to defend themselves, they could take care of their own defense. The Atlantic trade was a danger zone; those who chose to take the risk should be permitted to defend themselves and their property. This self-reliance would insulate the government from complaint.[18]

As justification for this self-defense, Adams cited his 1769 court case where he had successfully defended Michael Corbet and three other sailors who had killed a British lieutenant trying to press them into the Royal Navy. Adams had been prepared to argue that a sailor had the right to resist impressment, even to the point of killing the officials who were trying to impress him. The British court did not comment on his argument but simply found Corbet and the three others to have committed justifiable homicide. Adams conceded that the British king had the right to summon his subjects to fight for him but not the right to force them to answer the summons. Adams ridiculed the British action, asking why officers in Canada and Nova Scotia did not come into New England itself and try to take men: "The right would stand upon the same principles; but there is this difference, it would not be executed with so little danger."[19]

He was confident that his legal argument for resisting impressment was sound according to the law of nations, and he was convinced that it was unlikely that either England or France would declare war on account of a merchantman's victory for fear that the United States would abandon neutrality.[20] Adams even insisted that if the United States had to fight both France and England, its situation would not differ significantly from fighting England alone. A glance at the map shows his reasoning: England had colonies in North America, and France did not; England had command of the Atlantic, and France did not; therefore England was the real threat, since France was unable to project power.

In Adams's view, James Madison had merely continued Jefferson's hydrophobic policies of commercial coercion. There was, however, an important distinction between France in 1798 and Britain in 1812. Adams was well aware of the overwhelming preponderance of British naval power that had resulted from the victories on the Nile, at Copenhagen, and at Trafalgar and that the same lack of French naval power that had meant a French army would indeed land in heaven before it landed on the American mainland also meant that the French would not be able to cooperate with the Americans as the Royal Navy had during the Quasi-War.[21] In the Quasi-War Adams had confronted a great land power at sea and accepted a quasi-alliance with a great sea power. In 1812, he would have confronted a great sea power at sea and accepted a quasi-alliance with a great land power.[22] How much Adams would have had to expand his frigate navy to offer the same degree of protection to American commerce is uncertain, but clearly the effort would have been much greater.

The idea of Adams fighting the great naval power at sea is not as hubristic as it first appears. As in the Quasi-War, he would not have considered the guaranteed safety of each and every American merchant ship necessary for victory. Part of Adams's strategy would have been avoidance of an actual declaration of war, giving Britain no excuse to blockade American ports or seize American merchantmen. Adams would have permitted American seamen to arm themselves and resist impressment. Adams also pointed to the example of Commodore John Rodgers, who had famously taken a squadron to sea at the outbreak of war: "Rodgers has shown the universe that an American squadron can traverse the ocean in spite of the omnipotence, omniscience, and omnipresence of the British navy."[23] Adams therefore could have continued to build his superfrigates and sought a diplomatic solution at the same time.[24]

Most historians think that had the United States received the news that the new British foreign secretary had recommended repeal of the Orders in Council on 16 June 1812, the Senate would not have voted for war.[25] Adams's strategy, which did not require a declaration of war, would have been much more flexible than Madison's in accommodating this sudden shift in British policy. But as with all counterfactuals, one cannot know for certain whether Adams's alternative strategy would have worked. What is clear is that Adams thought it would have and that it would have been a wiser strategy than that chosen by Madison.

Adams did not limit himself to a counterfactual based on Republican maintenance of his naval strategy. He also dealt with the realities that the navy had been neglected and that Madison had nevertheless declared war and intended to invade Canada. Adams expressed sympathy for Madison and the partisan attacks that were crippling him:

> When I was exerting every nerve to vindicate the honor, and demand a redress of the wrongs of the nation against the tyranny of France, the arm of the nation was palsied by one party. Now Mr. Madison is acting the same part, for the same ends, against Great Britain, the arm of the nation is palsied by the opposite party. And so it will always be while we feel like colonists, dependent for protection on France or England; while we have so little national public opinion, so little national principle, national feeling, national patriotism; while we have no sentiment of our own strength, power, and resources.[26]

In the Senate debates, some Federalists were advocating a naval strategy but apparently were more interested in either opposing Madison or delaying any armed conflict with Great Britain.[27] Madison seemed to favor seizing Canada, because those "few acres of snow" were rapidly becoming important suppliers of food for the West Indies and seriously undermining the Republican strategy of forcing Britain to terms because of a need for American produce. Worse yet, his government was powerless to prevent smugglers from defying his trade restrictions and taking advantage of the Saint Lawrence.[28] Also, Upper Canada had replaced the Baltic as the Royal Navy's source for timber.[29] Other Republicans, such as Peter B. Porter and Henry Clay, also supported a land war.[30] Paul Hamilton, Madison's Secretary of the Navy, relying on the reports from naval officers, argued that the Navy required a substantial investment if a naval option were to be pursued.[31]

Once war was declared in 1812, Adams wrote that "the present war with Great Britain [is] just and necessary."[32] Less than two months later he wrote, "The war I justify, but the conduct of it I abhor."[33] Adams faulted the proposed invasion of Canada and thought an attempt to conquer Canada without first securing naval superiority on the Great Lakes had been a serious failure to understand the reality of warfare.[34] William Hull, in command at Detroit, had recommended building up naval forces on the Great Lakes before an attempt to invade Upper Canada yet had also suggested that an army at Detroit might convince the British to abandon both their ships and the province.[35] The Americans proceeded with an invasion without command of the Lakes. After the surrender of Detroit, Henry Clay admitted that British naval superiority on the Lakes had been key to American defeat. Hull was court-martialed and given a death sentence, but even before the trial began Adams growled, "If any Body is Shot, they ought to be those who have neglected the command of the Lakes and Rivers."[36] Madison overruled Hull's death penalty; Hull was dishonorably discharged.

The depressing defeats of the army highlighted the encouraging success of the frigates in single encounters. Federalists and Republicans alike took pride in the victories of the navy they considered Adams's.[37] Adams was pleased but understood these exciting sea fights could not win the war. The British were effectively shutting down American efforts on the Atlantic, and Adams lapsed into apocalyptic visions of Britain commanding the Atlantic, the Great Lakes, and the Mississippi and landing armies that would drive from those points into the interior. However, he did not think the British armies would conquer the United States, since its vast territory would prove too challenging for their logistics. The real horror would be the man of iron who would rise to save the nation and make himself dictator, thus destroying the republic.[38]

Fortunately for the United States, the Duke of Wellington realized that Britain could not get command of the Great Lakes and counseled against a prolonged war in North America.[39] President Madison summoned John Quincy Adams from his place as minister to Saint Petersburg to help negotiate a peace with Britain. With the conflict over and the union intact, Adams took a surprisingly optimistic and conciliatory view of Mr. Madison's war, considering that his navy had been neutralized and American commerce severely damaged. Adams pointed out that the government of the republic had survived, Great Britain had won some battles but had been unable to take any territory permanently, the Army and Navy had performed adequately, and the new western states had shown themselves worthy of the original thirteen. Madison had not tried to make an alliance with France, and the war in North America had been fought by Americans for Americans.[40] Although the strategy had been wrong—owing to neglect of his navy—Adams could take satisfaction in the efforts of Americans on their own behalf.

The War of 1812 justified Adams's criticism of Republican foreign policy. In his annual message in 1823, Republican James Monroe announced that the Atlantic trade was beneficial to all Americans and that therefore all had an interest in naval power to protect American shipping. His emphasis on adequate coastal defense and his vision of the acquisition of the Great Lakes, the Mississippi, and Florida as the collective foundation of national defense could have come straight out of Adams's writings.[41] The partnership of Monroe and John Quincy Adams and their successful diplomacy with both Spain and Great Britain would secure American interests in the Gulf of Mexico and in the Northwest. For old John Adams, war with

Great Britain had been "necessary," though of course it should not have been waged as the Republicans had—but the outcome, so compatible with his own vision of American security, was vindication.

NOTES   1 John Adams to Benjamin Rush, 25 July 1808, micro-film edition of the Adams Family Papers, reel 118, Massachusetts Historical Society, Boston [hereafter Adams Family Papers, reel number].

2 John Adams to James Lloyd, 29 March 1815, in *The Works of John Adams, Second President of the United States,* ed. Charles Francis Adams (Boston: Little, Brown, 1856) [hereafter *Works*], vol. 10, p. 147.

3 Timothy Pickering, *A letter from the Hon. Timothy Pickering, a Senator of the United States from the State of Massachusetts and Secretary of State under Gen. Washington, Exhibiting to his Constituents a view of the Imminent Danger of an Unnecessary and Ruinous War with Great Britain. Addressed to His Excellency James Sullivan, Governor of the said State* (Boston: 1808), p. 15.

4 John Adams to Benjamin Rush, 28 December 1807, Adams Family Papers, reel 118.

5 John Adams to James Lloyd, 21 February 1815, in *Works,* vol. 10, pp. 126–31.

6 John Adams to Joseph Lyman, 20 April 1809, in *Works,* vol. 9, pp. 619–20.

7 Commissioners to the Comte de Vergennes, 9 January 1779, in *Papers of John Adams,* ed. Gregg L. Lint et al. (Cambridge, Mass.: Harvard Univ. Press, 1989), vol. 7, pp. 305–11; John Adams to the Massachusetts Council, 13 September 1779, in ibid., vol. 8, pp. 145–47.

8 John Adams to Thomas Jefferson, 31 July 1786, in *The Papers of Thomas Jefferson,* ed. Julian P. Boyd (Princeton, N.J.: Princeton Univ. Press, 1954), vol. 10, pp. 176–78.

9 Alfred Thayer Mahan, *Sea Power and Its Relations to the War of 1812* (Boston: Little, Brown, 1919), vol. 1, pp. 71–74; vol. 2, p. 213.

10 Entry by John Adams, 13 December 1779, in *Diary and Autobiography of John Adams,* ed. L. H. Butterfield (Cambridge, Mass.: Harvard Univ. Press, 1961), vol. 2, pp. 196–99.

11 Theodore Ropp, "Continental Doctrines of Sea Power," in *Makers of Modern Strategy: Military Thought from Machiavelli to Hitler,* ed. Edward Mead Earle (Princeton, N.J.: Princeton Univ. Press, 1952), pp. 446–56.

12 John Adams to William Cranch, 3 March 1815, in *Works,* vol. 10, pp. 131–33.

13 N. A. M. Rodger, *The Command of the Ocean: A Naval History of Britain, 1649–1815* (London: Allen Lane, 2004), p. 327.

14 John Adams to F. A. Vanderkemp, 28 December 1800, in *Works,* vol. 9, pp. 576–77.

15 *Naval Documents Related to the Quasi-War between the United States and France* (Washington, D.C.: U.S. Government Printing Office, 1935–38), vol. 7, pp. 313–14. See Stanley M. Elkins and Eric L. McKitrick, *The Age of Federalism* (New York: Oxford Univ. Press, 1993), p. 653: "Insurance savings alone, according to the House Naval Affairs Committee report of January 17, 1799, already amounted to more than three times the total cost of the navy since the appropriations of 1794." See also pp. 890–91 note 24.

16 John Adams to Thomas Jefferson, 28 June 1812, Adams Family Papers, reel 118.

17 John Adams to Benjamin Rush, 25 December 1811, in *Works,* vol. 10, p. 10.

18 John Adams to J. B. Varnum, 26 December 1808, in *Works,* vol. 9, pp. 604–608.

19 John Adams, "The Inadmissible Principles of the King of England's Proclamation of October 16, 1807, Considered," in *Works,* vol. 9, pp. 312–30.

20 Madison apparently did consider arming merchantmen. See J. C. A. Stagg, *Mr. Madison's War: Politics, Diplomacy and Warfare in the Early American Republic, 1783–1830* (Princeton, N.J.: Princeton Univ. Press, 1983), p. 80 note 120.

21 John Adams to James Lloyd, 27 March 1815, in *Works,* vol. 10, p. 145.

22 Michael A. Palmer, *Stoddert's War: Naval Operations during the Quasi-War with France, 1798–1801* (Columbia: Univ. of South Carolina Press, 1987), p. 233.

23 John Adams to Benjamin Rush, 4 September 1812, Adams Family Papers, reel 118.

24 For a study of asymmetric warfare see Ivan Arreguin-Toft, *How the Weak Win Wars: A Theory of Asymmetric Conflict* (Cambridge, U.K.: Cambridge Univ. Press, 2005).

25 Leland R. Johnson, "The Suspense Was Hell," *Indiana Magazine of History* 65, no. 4 (1969), p. 264.

26 John Adams to William Keteltas, 25 November 1812, in *Works,* vol. 10, pp. 23–24.

27 Johnson, "Suspense Was Hell," p. 250.

28 J. C. A. Stagg, "James Madison and the Coercion of Great Britain: Canada, the West Indies and the War of 1812," *William and Mary Quarterly* 38, no. 1 (1981), pp. 25, 33.

29 Stagg, *Mr. Madison's War,* p. 40.

30 J. C. A. Stagg, "Between Black Rock and a Hard Place: Peter B. Porter's Plan for an American Invasion of Canada in 1812," *Journal of the Early Republic* 19, no. 3 (1999), pp. 385–422.

31 Stagg, *Mr. Madison's War,* p. 146.

32 John Adams to Benjamin Rush, 18 July 1812, Adams Family Papers, reel 118.

33 Adams to Rush, 4 September 1812.

34 John Adams to Richard Rush, 13 June 1813, in "Some Unpublished Correspondence of John Adams and Richard Rush, 1811–1816," ed. J. H. Powell, *Pennsylvania Magazine of History and Biography* [hereafter *PMHB*] 60, no. 4 (1936), pp. 438–39. For a series of essays focused on the significance of the Great Lakes in this period see David Curtis Skaggs, ed., *The Sixty Years War for the Great Lakes* (East Lansing: Michigan Univ. State Press, 2001).

35 Stagg, *Mr. Madison's War,* pp. 191–92.

36 John Adams to Richard Rush, 12 December 1813, in "Some Unpublished Correspondence of John Adams and Richard Rush, 1811–1816, II," ed. J. H. Powell, *PMHB* 61, no. 1 (1937), p. 31.

37 Richard Rush to John Adams, 29 June 1813, in Powell, "Some Unpublished Correspondence," *PMHB* 60, no. 4 (1936), p. 440.

38 John Adams to Richard Rush, 12 December 1813 and 14 September 1814, in Powell, "Some Unpublished Correspondence, II," *PMHB* 61, no. 1 (1937), pp. 29–32, 52–53.

39 Samuel Flagg Bemis, *John Quincy Adams and the Foundations of American Foreign Policy* (Westport, Conn.: Greenwood, 1949), p. 216.

40 John Adams to Thomas McKean, 6 July 1815, in *Works,* vol. 10, pp. 167–68.

41 James Monroe, *Annual Message,* 2 December 1823, in *The Writings of James Monroe,* ed. Stanislaus Murray Hamilton (New York: G. P. Putnam's Sons, 1898–1903), vol. 6, p. 333.

IX Brown Water, Blue Water
The Naval Battle for New Orleans

GENE ALLEN SMITH

On 8 January 1815, Andrew Jackson's multiracial, heterogeneous, rag-tag assemblage of troops confronted British Peninsular War veterans—soldiers who had forced Napoleon into exile on the island of Elba only a few months earlier—some nine miles south of New Orleans on the Plains of Chalmette. Within two hours British killed and wounded numbered more than two thousand, American casualties less than thirty. The battle represented a turning point for American democracy and for the development of the United States, and it finally ended British aspirations for renewed American colonization. Andrew Jackson became a national hero and the battle of New Orleans the crowning moment for a young country. No role for the U.S. Navy appears in the commonly accepted narrative. Yet Jackson could not have won the laurels he did without the Navy. He himself understood the importance of the Navy's role, but subsequent generations have minimized, overlooked, or even forgotten that the Navy contributed to this victory.

One of the main reasons the Navy has been omitted from the narrative of the battle of New Orleans is that the mere mention of the "Golden Age of Sail" conjures up images of majestic, seventy-four-gun ships of the line and swift, powerful frigates roaming under full sail across the open seas. This romantic vision, enhanced by the late-nineteenth-century writings of Alfred Thayer Mahan, does not fit the U.S. Navy during the early republic. In fact, any investigation of the Navy during the early nineteenth century reveals not a fleet dominated by seagoing vessels but rather a national flotilla of gunboats whose duties included defending the nation's ports and harbors and upholding domestic political policy.

The gunboats of the Jeffersonian era were not large, heavily armed vessels or designed for blue-water operations. They had several common characteristics, despite wide variations in their design. Generally forty to eighty feet long, fifteen to twenty feet in beam, and four to seven feet deep in the hold, they usually carried one or two long twenty-four- or thirty-two-pound cannon, plus assorted smaller guns. They were one- or two-masted, shallow-draft vessels designed to maneuver and fight in coastal waters as defensive rather than offensive craft.[1]

Upon assuming the presidency in March 1801, Thomas Jefferson faced the desire for maintaining national security. He also felt an overwhelming need for further reductions in governmental spending. These were conflicting goals, especially since the Republicans had inherited an $82,000,000 debt, or "moral canker," from the outgoing Federalist administration. So as president, Jefferson wanted a naval program that satisfied Republican fiscal concerns and prejudices concerning a permanent military establishment but more importantly one he believed assured national security without provoking war. In his mind a naval militia supplementing a gunboat program offered a partial solution to his naval and economic problems. Yet as all presidents have learned, Jefferson found it impossible to satisfy all concerns, because congressional ideology concerning defense needs constantly changed as domestic and international events warranted, and because economic concerns sometimes become secondary to national security in times of trouble.[2]

Jefferson's attitude toward the Navy has certainly been misinterpreted when compared with the pro-navy ideas of John Adams's administration. The marked contrast in naval ideology has led many to believe that because of Jefferson's affinity for gunboats manned by a naval militia, the Navy "had always been . . . his abhorrence." That was not the case; he did not oppose a navy in principle or intend to eliminate the fleet or replace it with gunboats, especially since a naval force served as such an important aspect of national defense. Had Jefferson opposed the Navy and been obstinate about its elimination he would not have sent naval squadrons to the Mediterranean to face the Barbary pirates and restore American honor. In fact, Thomas Jefferson was neither anti-navy nor a pacifist.[3]

Yet the navy Jefferson wanted was not the same one his predecessor had created. In the attempt to secure command of the sea and a balance of sea power, Adams and the Federalists had created the Navy Department and a fleet much larger than Republicans expected or wanted. Yet on 3 March 1801, the day before Jefferson's inauguration as president, the lame-duck Federalist Congress passed an Act Providing for the Naval Peace Establishment. Fearing the even more stringent measures the new Republican administration might propose, the Federalist majority preserved the fleet on the statute books while discharging all but forty-five officers and selling more than twenty vessels. In reality the Federalists actually began what anti-Jeffersonians and naval supporters blame on Republicans. It is true that the rationale given by Federalists for the passage of the naval-reduction bill was the fear that Republicans would totally disband the Navy. Yet that fear was unfounded; Jefferson had no intention of eliminating the fleet or of converting it, as many have maintained, to a "white water," "brown water," or "gunboat navy."[4]

The composition of the Navy during the Jeffersonian period reflected Republican theories of defense. Ships of the line and frigates were necessary only if a country was protecting trade and projecting offensive power. During Thomas Jefferson's years as president, 1801–1809, the United States was predominantly an agricultural nation, focused on internal concerns. The country seemed preoccupied with protecting its own territorial integrity from the uncertainties of a world at war, and its gunboats embodied a natural political-defensive response aimed at preserving the American identity. Defense was Jefferson's major concern, and gunboats represented but a means to that end. Also, while it is true that the gunboats were designed for defensive service, they also had usefulness in nontraditional roles, such as revenue enforcement, the suppression of piracy along the coastal frontier, and the fight against the international slave trade.[5]

Jefferson's small naval force stressed passive coastal defense rather than control of the seas to protect trade. He wanted a modest blue-water force to complement coastal fortifications, gunboats, and other defensive works, because he understood that war, as the "greatest scourge of mankind," could never be eliminated and that a nation's leaders must bolster its defense to preserve the freedom and the security of its citizens.[6]

Even though Jefferson knew the nation needed to stress defense, the rabidly anti-navy Republican Congresses of the first decade of the nineteenth century did not support the construction of seagoing vessels for that purpose. They embraced gunboats as an alternative for defending the country. Since Jefferson was the leader of the Republican Party, he has been accused of making the Navy dependent on gunboats. Historians have noted, however, that despite Jefferson's leadership of his party, he could not overcome congressional opposition to a seagoing navy. Thus the president had to reconcile the defense problem in the only way Congress would approve—the gunboat program. What becomes apparent is that Jefferson's attitude toward the Navy has been stereotyped, just as his gunboat program has been oversimplified.[7]

Jefferson believed that as long as gunboats protected the coast in the defensive manner he prescribed, the vessels minimized the possibility of provoking potential conflicts.[8] He explained in his "Special Message on Gun-Boats," presented to the Senate and House on 10 February 1807, that the craft were not to be the nation's only defense, nor would they replace a navy. They were instead "proposed merely for defensive operations." More importantly, he declared, the nation's defenses should be based on a combination of land batteries, movable artillery, floating batteries, and gunboats.[9] Yet this message, coming near the end of his second term, did not do justice to his defense doctrine. All instruments called for in this report were solely defensive, and he offered no reference to a seagoing navy.[10]

The Jeffersonian system, formulated piecemeal over many years, attempted to create a balanced defense for security. It included not only a navy of seagoing ships and gunboats but also a system of coastal and harbor fortifications stretching from Maine to Louisiana. Jefferson was not the only one to recognize the need for defending the nation's seaports. Congress had first authorized a system of simple and inexpensive earthwork forts in March 1794. Yet by contemporary European standards these works were too simple and thus weak, and they quickly fell into disrepair after 1800. There were other attempts to complete works at locations of primary importance, but the building appropriations were always negligible. It was not until November 1807 that the country embarked on another major program of fortress construction. These works, consisting of open batteries, masonry-faced earth forts, and all-masonry forts, helped to prepare the country for the War of 1812.[11]

To supplement the system of fortifications, Jefferson wanted "land batteries, furnished with heavy cannon and mortars." Although these would not foil enemy vessels entering a harbor, he believed they would do much to prevent a port town from being damaged. Stationary land batteries sited opposite a fort prevented a vessel from passing without coming into range of at least some guns, be they the fort's or the battery's.[12] Capt. John Shaw, naval commander of the New Orleans flotilla, 1806–1808 and 1810–13, recognized the importance of a fixed land battery for the protection of Mobile Harbor on the Gulf of Mexico. He argued that fifteen cannon on Mobile Point working in cooperation with gunboats offered "the best mode of defense that can be devised, against maritime invasion."[13] As a part of the overall system, stationary land batteries limited an enemy's approach and made positions more defensible.

For locations that did not warrant a fixed battery or a fort, Jefferson advocated the use of "moveable artillery," consisting of "heavy cannon on traveling carriages." He argued that cannon and mortars could quickly be moved to the bank of a river or beach to frustrate a landing or drive a vessel back to sea. In addition, these weapons could be lent to seaport towns and militia could be trained in their use, thus perpetuating the militia tradition while lessening defense costs for the federal government.[14] Moreover, they could serve in conjunction with harbor forts and stationary batteries.

"Floating batteries" would represent another integral part of Jefferson's maritime defense. Cannon on floating batteries, he argued, stationed to prevent enemy vessels from penetrating a harbor or to drive them out once they had entered, could create difficulties for an attacker. Jefferson believed that cannon, mortars, rockets, or "whatever else could . . . destroy a ship" could block the approach to a harbor and force the enemy to sacrifice valuable resources to remove the obstacles before assaulting the target.[15] In turn, this necessity limited the resources the enemy could bring to bear on the port itself.

Other statements illustrate that Jefferson's theory of defense did not necessarily exclude a seagoing navy. He believed the country needed seagoing vessels to harass and demoralize enemy ships before they assaulted American defenses. Commenting before the October 1805 British victory at Trafalgar, Jefferson charged that "brigs and schooners" should "be free to cruise," especially "in time of war," because they could serve as a disruptive factor. Frigates too represented an important feature of the nation's sailing force. Jefferson insisted that the country needed "the wooden walls of Themistocles" and that seagoing ships would complement defensive coastal vessels. In 1806 Jefferson even halfheartedly remarked that "building some ships of the line" was "not to be lost sight of." For as he understood, "a [seagoing] squadron properly composed" was necessary "to prevent the blockading [of] our ports" and permit American commerce to sail the seas. Yet he also acknowledged that construction of larger vessels depended on congressional approval rather than any action he alone could take, and this problem became apparent early in 1806 when Congress overwhelmingly defeated legislation for building capital ships. An anti-navy Congress, rather than Jefferson, sealed the seagoing navy's defeat.[16]

Jefferson's naval policy cannot be reduced to a black-and-white dichotomy between seagoing vessels and gunboats; it is far more accurate to depict it as a dichotomy between defensive and offensive power and vessels to be used for those respective purposes. Assertions that Jefferson's naval program represented choices between seagoing vessels and gunboats are groundless, as evidenced by Secretary of the Treasury Albert Gallatin's statement that "federal papers" had tried to spread the idea that Jefferson "intended [gunboats] as a substitute to the navy." Some charged that Jefferson was "prepared to let the nation's magnificent Humphreys frigates [i.e., six ships designed in the 1790s by Joshua Humphreys] rot at the wharves and . . . build a 'mosquito fleet' of gunboats in their place." But these assertions were far from the truth, as even John Adams recognized that, although not ardently pro-navy, Jefferson did believe in a navy. As president, however, Jefferson focused on maintaining national security, and a navy oriented to littoral defense rather than blue-water offense represented his response to that need. Had Jefferson wanted to eliminate the Navy altogether, there would have been no reason for him to advocate a fleet at all, whether of gunboats or any other vessel, and he certainly would not have sent four fleets to the Mediterranean in quick succession from 1801 to 1805. As components in a sophisticated overall defensive system, gunboats and seagoing ships served as means to the same end—national security, or national defense.[17]

The Jeffersonian gunboat program represented a classic example of the functioning of early American democracy. In a narrow sense the gunboats represented a naval policy, but in a more comprehensive way they embodied a political-military program upholding broader governmental decisions. The program initially enjoyed nearly overwhelming popular and congressional support. Nevertheless, many still opposed the craft. Federalists and navalists alike ridiculed the "whirligigs of the sage of Monticello," "Jefferson boats," or "Jeffs," as the visionary ideas of an idealistic anti-naval president. Many quickly pointed out the debacle of gunboat *No. 1,* blown ashore into a southern Georgia cornfield during a September 1804 storm, quipping, "If our gunboats are no use on the water, may they at least be the best on earth!" Others emphasized the "wasteful imbecility" of "money thrown away." Despite the opposition, Congress still implemented the program. It did so because, embroiled in the much larger naval/anti-naval debate of the period and convinced of the economic and political considerations of gunboats, it concluded that if the craft were unquestionably naval vessels, they at least placated the fears of some about a large, permanent flotilla.[18]

For Jefferson's administration the "great desideratum in building gunboats [was] to prepare them well for fighting." Gunboats provided "for home defense," whereas "ships [were] for distant expeditions." Jefferson acknowledged that gunboats were "proposed merely for defensive operations" and that it was for that reason that those "who wished for engines of offense" ridiculed them. A gunboat had indeed limited offensive potential. Many maintained that the most gunboats could do, whether working alone or in groups, was be an "annoyance." They could not scour the open seas waiting for their prey, for on the open seas they themselves became prey. As long as they protected the coast, Jefferson maintained, gunboats escaped the possibilities of unintended conflicts, thereby saving the country money as well as human lives. If the gunboats worked within the confines of Jefferson's coastal defensive system, they were, he insisted, "the humble, the ridiculed, but the formidable gunboats" that ultimately made American harbors *hors d' insulte*."[19] In fact, in his study *Navalists and Antinavalists* historian Craig Symonds has posited that "coastal defense was always the complete *raison d'etre* for the gunboats."

Military operations at New Orleans in December 1814 and January 1815 constitute one of the best examples during the War of 1812 of Jefferson's ideas concerning a multifaceted defense. The Crescent City, commanding the great Mississippi watershed, sat about 150 miles north from the mouth of the river. It was and still is today surrounded by swamps, marshes, shallow lakes, and bayous. Access to New Orleans was impractical except by water. Master Commandant Daniel Patterson, commanding the New Orleans flotilla immediately prior to the battle, found his defensive position exposed to several possible routes of attack by water, including Bayou Lafourche, Barataria Bay, River aux Chenes and Bayou Terre aux Boeufs, the Mississippi River itself, and three routes via Lake Borgne.

Bayou Lafourche, a deep, narrow stream running from the Mississippi River north of New Orleans to the Gulf, would not serve the British as a route of attack, because of its length, narrowness, and ease of obstruction. Barataria Bay, seventy miles west of the mouth of the Mississippi, with numerous channels running north to the river across from New Orleans, also appeared unfeasible, unless the British procured experienced pilots familiar with the narrow, shallow, treacherous passages. In fact, during September 1814 the British approached privateer/pirate Jean Laffite and his Baratarian associates to secure their help; the plan failed when

Laffite and the Baratarians reported the British offer to Andrew Jackson and joined him. River aux Chenes and Bayou Terre aux Boeufs, small streams running almost from English Turn and emptying into the Gulf of Mexico just east of the river's mouth, were also winding, narrow, and easily defended.[20]

The main channel of the Mississippi River provided a possible alternative and in hindsight was probably the best route the British could have taken. The river was the only option for deep-draft vessels, but even so its shallow mouth denied access to ships of the line. A strong current forced vessels to make a long beat upstream, during which they would be exposed to fire from the river's banks. Fort Saint Philip had been constructed about thirty miles from the river's mouth and Fort Saint Leon some seventy miles upstream. Moreover, Fort Saint Leon commanded English Turn, an S-shaped passage where sailing vessels had to wait for a change in wind before proceeding upstream. While it was possible to sail upriver, the time spent tacking and waiting for favorable winds would leave an enemy flotilla exposed to a constant barrage.[21]

Patterson, like the flotilla commanders before him, understood the importance of the river and had made plans for such an attack. When David Porter had commanded the station (1808–10), he designed gun rafts with both oars and sails. Each was to be armed with one heavy gun, and the rafts would supplement gunboats on the river in much the same manner as Thomas Jefferson had intended for his floating batteries. These vessels, acting in conjunction with gunboats, shore batteries, and permanent fortifications, would discomfit an enemy and make the Mississippi River virtually impassable. Yet those craft were never constructed.[22]

A more ambitious project had started during John Shaw's second tenure as commander (1810–13). Shaw began construction of a blockship, or barge, 148 feet in length and forty-two feet in beam, that would draw only six and a half feet of water. This vessel's size and draft would have permitted it to navigate the river as well as the shallow waterways. Designed to carry twenty-six thirty-two-pound cannon—as many guns as a small frigate—it would have been the most heavily armed craft in the Gulf region. Shaw argued that it was "better calculated to defend our waters than all the forts and batterys [sic] erected for the defense of the country."[23] Governor William C. C. Claiborne agreed, declaring that not only would the blockship and a few gunboats be a "formidable defense" for the area lakes, but "two large Block Ships . . . on the Mississippi . . . would *give greater security*" than any other defense that could be erected.[24] The blockship would have served in the same manner as Jefferson's floating batteries, but Secretary of the Navy William Jones believed the project a waste of money and decided in early 1814 to discontinue construction.[25]

When Daniel Patterson replaced Shaw as commander at New Orleans in October 1813 he found the station virtually undefended. "The approaches to this city . . . by water are so numerous," he claimed, "that they require many vessels and vigilant officers to guard them effectively." Yet he had neither; the station was always short of both vessels and personnel. This lack of resources forced Patterson to use all the means at his disposal to frustrate the invasion that he believed to be inevitable. Patterson intended to use the converted merchant sloop *Louisiana* and schooner *Carolina* in the Mississippi River, in cooperation with the two forts and the shore batteries, to confront an enemy approaching via the river and to cover land attacks along the river. Some of the gunboats would support Fort St. Philip, and fireships would be used to disperse an enemy assault via the river. Patterson would station most of the flotilla's gunboats, however, on the bays and estuaries east of New Orleans to prevent an attack along those water avenues.[26]

In light of the routes available and the defensive measures taken by Patterson, Lake Borgne became the most feasible option for a British attack. Besides, the saltwater estuary provided three possible approaches. The first was through Lake Borgne's Rigolet's Pass into Lake Pontchartrain. This avenue, combined with Bayou Saint John, would have permitted the English to move by water within two miles of New Orleans. But this route necessitated many light, shallow-draft vessels that the British had problems securing, and Fort Petites Coquilles, which the British believed to have over five hundred men and forty guns, guarded the approach. The second alternative was through Lake Borgne to the Plain of Gentilly. From there British troops could march on the Chef Menteur Road to the city. Because of its ease of accessibility, Andrew Jackson had it defended with both men and artillery; a pitched battle there would have allowed the Americans to fall back and construct other lines of defense well away from the city.[27]

The last route, and the one the British ultimately chose, called for using Bayou Bienvenue, which drained the area east of New Orleans and stretched from Lake Borgne to within a mile of the Mississippi River. From there the British could proceed north nine miles along the river levee, a narrow strip of land through sugar plantations, toward New Orleans. While this approach appeared to be the path of least resistance, it too had obstacles. The route was shallower than expected, thus prohibiting British ships from entering the estuary or providing gunfire support to cover the barges' advance. Furthermore, the distance from Cat Island, at the mouth of Lake Borgne, to Bayou Bienvenue was sixty-two miles, thirty-six hours of hard rowing. Yet perhaps the most serious obstacles, according to British midshipman Robert Aitchison, who was present at Lake Borgne, were the "five American gunboats, of great strength" that commanded the shoal waters.[28]

Patterson had sent Thomas ap Catesby Jones to Lake Borgne in early December with gunboats *Nos. 5, 23, 156, 162, 163,* schooner *Sea Horse,* and tender *Alligator.* Jones's seven-vessel flotilla numbered in all just twenty-six guns and 204 men. Patterson had also provided Jones with simple instructions: wait for the enemy outside the Rigolet islets, between Ship and Cat Islands; confront British barges and small boats unless assaulted by a superior force; if attacked, withdraw to the Rigolets and the protection of land batteries at Fort Petites Coquilles. The Rigolets were to be Jones's last line of defense, where he should "sink the enemy, or be sunk." In accordance with his orders, Jones sent gunboats *Nos. 23* and *163* to Dauphin Island, while the others remained off Saint Mary's Island anticipating the arrival of the British fleet. After three days of watching the British forces grow, Jones decided it was "no longer safe or prudent" to remain in his position. He planned his retreat westward to safety.[29]

British vice admiral Alexander F. I. Cochrane ordered his barges to advance against the American gunboats on the morning of 13 December 1814; Jones responded by sending *Sea Horse* to destroy channel markers and supplies at Bay Saint Louis. By 2:00 PM the British barges had secured the Pass Christian as they slowly continued westward toward Jones's becalmed gunboats. A strong westerly wind that had blown for several days before the assault had reduced the lake's depth, leaving Jones's *No. 156* and the other gunboats grounded. Jones ordered his men to throw overboard "all articles of weight that could be dispensed with," and by 3:30 that afternoon the tide "commenced," permitting the gunboats to withdraw toward the Rigolets. Otherwise, all Jones could do was watch as the British inched closer.[30]

As Jones retreated westward, he saw that the British had sent three barges against *Sea Horse* as it destroyed the supplies at Bay Saint Louis. The American schooner, armed with its one six-pounder and supported by two six-pounders on shore, fought off the initial British assault. Four other British barges soon joined the attack, and the Americans held off the seven barges for more than thirty minutes before realizing their situation was hopeless. With no other options, the American commander burned the storehouse and supplies ashore, ignited *Sea Horse* to prevent its capture, and retreated overland toward New Orleans.[31]

Jones continued his retreat westward until about 1 AM on the morning of 14 December, when the winds finally died, the tide changed, and the gunboats ran aground near the Malheureux Island passage. At dawn Jones saw that the British had steadily advanced. He estimated that they were now nine miles away, rowing hard and closing fast. A lack of wind combined with a strong eastward ebb tide forced Jones to anchor his craft. He placed them in a line-abreast defensive position to "give the enemy as warm a reception as possible." Jones wanted to concentrate his craft, but a strong current drove his flagship, *No. 156,* and also *No. 163* about a hundred yards east of the other three gunboats, leaving the two exposed in the center of the American line.[32]

At 9:30 AM British barges overwhelmed *Alligator,* which had been forced to anchor some distance southeast of Jones's squadron. Thirty minutes later British captain Nicholas Lockyer, who commanded the assault, anchored his flotilla just beyond the range of Jones's guns and gave his men a much-needed rest and the opportunity for breakfast. After a half-hour, Lockyer resumed his advance toward Jones, who could not restore his defensive line, because of the tide. Jones's *No. 156* became the first gunboat to face the British attack.

As the enemy approached, Jones counted, aside from three light gigs, forty-two barges armed with light carronades. He estimated that the craft had upward of a thousand men and officers. In reality the British force numbered more than 1,200 men, whereas Jones had but 183 men; in his gunboat he had only thirty-six. At 10:39 AM the British barges came within cannon range of the gunboats, and Jones ordered his vessels to fire. For more than ten minutes Jones's flotilla discharged its long guns with little effect on the approaching enemy. By 10:50 the smaller British guns came within range of the Americans' shorter-range weapons and began firing and, as Jones noted, the "action became general and destructive on both sides."[33]

Jones had instructed his sailors to rig boarding nets, and when shortly before noon three British barges tried to board they were unsuccessful. Jones's sailors fired their cannon and small arms, killing or wounding nearly every enemy officer and sinking two barges. As Jones recalled, the "unfortunate enemy" barely escaped drowning by clinging to the capsized barges until other vessels came to their aid. Soon four more British barges came forward, and after a spirited fight they too were driven back. During this second assault Jones shot with his pistol a soldier trying to board his gunboat and then mortally wounded Lt. George Pratt, the officer who reportedly had defaced the naval monument at the Capitol during the British occupation of Washington, D.C., in August 1814. But as Pratt fell back into his barge, a soldier behind him fired a musket. The ball penetrated Jones's left shoulder, and as he fell to the deck several others passed through his clothes and cap. Jones continued screaming orders as he lay on the deck of his gunboat, covered with blood. A few minutes later he fainted, and Master's Mate George Parker assumed command. Parker soon suffered a wound too. Once the smoke of the battle cleared some minutes later, the British counted eighteen killed or wounded Americans aboard gunboat *No. 156*, including both Jones and Parker.[34]

After capturing Jones's vessel, the British turned its cannon on the others, which one by one succumbed to the numerically superior force. The British victory over *No. 156* had been the turning point of the battle of Lake Borgne. Yet the victory had not come without great loss. When Jones wrote his report some months later, he asserted that British losses had been staggering, though the British reported only seventeen killed and seventy-seven wounded. Meanwhile, American casualties for the entire squadron amounted to only six killed, thirty-five wounded, and remainder captured. The battle of Lake Borgne had been a costly tactical defeat for the United States, because it allowed the British to choose their point of attack against Jackson at New Orleans.[35]

Jones had followed Patterson's orders explicitly. He had harassed the British, then withdrawn against a superior force, and when his vessels had become becalmed he had tried to give the British a "warm reception." Jones's sacrifice provided much-needed time for Jackson and demonstrated his unquestioned bravery; the engagement also proved the gunboats' true value in waters that larger ships could not navigate. Thereafter Jones always believed that the battle was the crowning point in his long career; even Patterson later boasted that Jones's "action will be classed among the most brilliant of our Navy."[36]

After defeating the American naval vessels on Lake Borgne, British forces traversed the almost seventy miles to the Mississippi River levee south of New Orleans. Sailors laboriously rowed the sixty-two miles to land soldiers at the Bienvenue Canal. Then engineers and sappers hacked their way through the cane fields, cleared paths and canals for the army, and then dragged barges and launches through to the shore of the Mississippi River. When the British army finally arrived on the river, the two-week land campaign for New Orleans began, culminating with the 8 January 1815 engagement on the Plains of Chalmette.[37]

During the campaign at Chalmette, Daniel Patterson's sloop *Louisiana* and schooner *Carolina* contributed greatly to Andrew Jackson's land defenses. During the important night fighting of 23 December 1814, both vessels sailed downriver to fire on the British left flank while Jackson's army attacked the British center and right. The presence of these vessels distressed British commanders, who tried thereafter to destroy them. Four days later British heated shot struck the becalmed *Carolina* anchored on the west side of the river; the fire quickly engulfed the schooner, and the American captain and crew evacuated shortly before it blew up. On 28 December British forces tested Jackson's defensive line at Chalmette for seven hours, during which *Louisiana* maintained "a tremendous and well-directed fire" that broke the attacking columns and then silenced the British artillery. Three days later the British began a concentrated artillery barrage (from 31 December 1814 to 1 January 1815) hoping to damage Jackson's line and destroy *Louisiana* as they had *Carolina*; yet they accomplished neither. During the fateful and climactic attack of 8 January 1815 *Louisiana* remained anchored in the Mississippi River to the right of the American position, its guns enfilading British lines as they advanced against Jackson's entrenched army. It contributed greatly to the devastating British defeat.[38]

The Navy's role during the battle of New Orleans is generally obscured or overlooked because Jackson's land forces inflicted such staggering casualties on the British. Yet the Navy is central to this narrative. The role the gunboats played in defending New Orleans was characteristic of their intended purpose within Jefferson's multifaceted defense. Gunboats represented one part of the overall system, and in this instance they were well suited for their intended task. Because of the river defenses and the risk the British would have had to endure attacking through the numerous bayous surrounding New Orleans, Lake Borgne became the most viable route for the invasion. Daniel Patterson had positioned on Lake Borgne five shallow-draft gunboats with armament that made them "dangerous to anything under a fifty-gun ship." Therefore, the British believed, this "formidable flotilla" had to be considered as a serious threat and either captured or destroyed.[39]

The capture of the American gunboats on Lake Borgne has been proclaimed by some as "an American disaster," one that could have brought defeat to a commander with less fortitude than Andrew Jackson, or at least one that, by enabling the British "to chuse [*sic*] his point of attack," at the strategic level "rendered a very dear advantage to the foe."[40] Others have charged that Thomas ap Catesby "Jones sacrificed his small flotilla to gain [albeit much-needed] time for [General] Jackson." While it is true that, as noted, the capture of the gunboats represented an American tactical setback, it did contribute to a strategic victory. Lieutenant Jones and his fellow American prisoners fed British intelligence faulty information about the locations and strength of Jackson's troops, forcing British commanders to proceed with caution and thereby providing the general an unexpected advantage of time.[41]

It is true that the gunboats did not win the engagement on Lake Borgne or prevent the battle of New Orleans from being fought. Had twenty operable craft been stationed at New Orleans as called for by the Navy Department, the British might have never been able to cross Lake Borgne. But because of hurricanes, tornadoes, decay, and the Navy Department's unwillingness to dispatch more craft, the American flotilla on the lake had only five gunboats in service when the British began their assault. Furthermore, had the flotilla been equipped with oars, as had been ordered by the Secretary of the Navy, the British barges most likely would not have caught the gunboats. Some have argued "that if the Block ship . . . had been finished, and in the Lakes, we should not have lost our flotilla—and had our flotilla been preserved the Enemy would not have dared to land where he did." Such was not the case and the capture of the American vessels unfortunately provided fodder for those who despised the gunboat program.[42]

There are valid reasons to condemn Jefferson's gunboat program as it developed, and the program can be viewed as a failure in light of the president's original conception of how the vessels were to be integrated into the nation's defense. Also, on another level, the craft did not inspire confidence, among either their commanders and crews or the people.[43] Nonetheless, the battle of New Orleans provides the most succinct example of Jefferson's concepts of defense. Forts, small seagoing vessels, and artillery—stationary, movable, and floating—were all positioned along the river to guard the most obvious route of attack. Patterson stationed gunboats in the shoals to the east of the city, where they could be most useful. The hardened and determined Andrew Jackson cobbled together a cosmopolitan assemblage of militiamen, Native Americans, and lawless privateers/pirates, with a handful of regular soldiers. This ragtag defense used the advantages offered by Louisiana's terrain to provide a defense for New Orleans that was effective in that it forced the British to sacrifice valuable resources and precious time as well as the element of surprise before they could launch an assault against the city. Had Jefferson's defensive system been fully implemented and the whole complement of gunboats present on the lake and outfitted, perhaps the battle of Lake Borgne would not have taken place at all.

Naval historians and American politicians have not heeded the lessons that they should have learned from Jefferson's gunboat navy. History instead declared the gunboats to have represented an aberration that provided no benefits, and the country thereafter moved toward larger and more-advanced technological machines, in the belief that bigger is better. Yet throughout the nineteenth, twentieth, and twenty-first centuries, Jefferson's vision reemerged in new forms adapted to then-current technology. During the nineteenth-century Seminole War the importance of small shallow-draft vessels became obvious, as they were the only craft that could infiltrate the shallow swamps of southern Florida. At the same time, a "mosquito fleet" plied the Caribbean waging war on piratical activity. During the early 1840s Secretary of the Navy Abel P. Upshur even proposed using smaller steam gunboats to defend American harbors, especially those along the shallow Gulf of Mexico. Even the Civil War saw shallow-draft riverine vessels help shape the outcome of that conflict. During the twentieth century small shallow-draft vessels played useful contributive roles in World War II and the Vietnam conflict. The twenty-first century has witnessed new lessons about the vulnerability of large seagoing vessels, whether at sea or in restrictive waters, as well as about the attributes of littoral and amphibious vessels, further illustrating the merits of small, inexpensive craft. A U.S. Chief of Naval Operations, Adm. Vern Clark, acknowledged in early January 2005 that the era of climactic major naval engagements is long past and that building a floating force to deal only with major combat operations represents faulty logic. The Mahanian age of "blue water" ships and control of the seas appears to be giving way to an age of littoral warfare.[44]

So, there are valid reasons to condemn Jefferson's gunboat and naval program as it developed. It was generally ridiculed; few acknowledged that the small craft had any capabilities then or later. Thomas Jefferson's comment to ideologue Thomas Paine proclaiming that "gun-boats are the only *water* defence which can be useful to us and protect us from the ruinous folly of a navy" did not truly describe the dichotomy between blue-water and brown-water vessels or between defending the nation's shores or controlling sea-lanes. Coming from a pragmatic politician, Jefferson's note more accurately represented the one end rather than the two possible choices—that one end being the freedom and security of his United States. The battle of New Orleans truly describes, for the age of Jefferson as well as for ours, the value of brown-water and blue-water vessels working in conjunction with other defense forces, and this is a lesson relevant in any age.

NOTES   1 Howard I. Chapelle, *History of the American Sailing Navy* (New York: Bonanza Books, 1949), pp. 179–241; Craig Symonds, *Navalists and Antinavalists: The Naval Policy Debate in the United States, 1785–1827* (Newark: Univ. of Delaware Press, 1980), pp. 105–30; Gene A. Smith, "The Ruinous Folly of a Navy: A History of the Jeffersonian Gunboat Program" (PhD dissertation, Auburn Univ., 1991), pp. 154–96.

2 Alexander Balinky, "Albert Gallatin, Naval Foe," *Pennsylvania Magazine of History and Biography* 82 (1958), p. 293; "A Statistical Table for the United States of America, for a Succession of Years," October 1803, Jefferson Manuscripts, Library of Congress, Washington, D.C. [hereafter Jefferson MSS, LC]. This table indicates that the country's expenditures rose from $8,740,329 in 1796 to $12,945,455 in 1801.

3 John T. Morse, *Thomas Jefferson* (Boston: Houghton, Mifflin, 1898), p. 259; Chapelle, *History of the American Sailing Navy,* p. 181; Harold Sprout and Margaret Sprout, *The Rise of American Naval Power* (Princeton, N.J.: Princeton Univ. Press, 1946), pp. 58–61; Forrest McDonald, *The Presidency of Thomas Jefferson* (Lawrence: Univ. of Kansas Press, 1976), p. 44; William M. Fowler, Jr., *Jack Tars and Commodores* (Boston: Houghton Mifflin, 1984), p. 145; Jefferson to John Adams, 27 May 1813, in *The Writings of Thomas Jefferson,* ed. Andrew A. Lipscomb and Albert Ellery Bergh (Washington, D.C.: Thomas Jefferson Memorial Association, 1904), vol. 13, p. 249; J. G. de Roulhac Hamilton, "The Pacifism of Thomas Jefferson," *Virginia Quarterly Review* 31 (1955), p. 616; Julia H. Macleod, "Jefferson and the Navy: A Defense," *Huntington Library Quarterly* 8 (1944–45), pp. 169–70; Smith, "Ruinous Folly of a Navy," pp. 14–50.

4 Frederic H. Hayes, "John Adams and American Sea Power," *American Neptune* 25 (January 1965), p. 42; Robert F. Jones, "The Naval Thought and Policy of Benjamin Stoddert, First Secretary of the Navy, 1798–1801," *American Neptune* 24 (January 1964), pp. 61–62; Macleod, "Jefferson and the Navy," pp. 159–60; Walter Millis, *Arms and Men* (New York: G. P. Putnam, 1956), p. 56; Russell F. Weigley, *The American Way of War* (Bloomington: Indiana Univ. Press, 1973), pp. 43–44; David M. Cooney, *A Chronology of the U.S. Navy: 1775–1965* (New York: Franklin Watts, 1965), p. 24; Christopher McKee, *A Gentlemanly and Honorable Profession: The Creation of the U.S. Naval Officer Corps, 1794–1815* (Annapolis, Md.: Naval Institute Press, 1991), pp. 36–37. The act provided for nine captains and thirty-six lieutenants, but it did not set any limit on master commandants; Charles Oscar Paullin, *Paullin's History of Naval Administration, 1775–1911* (Annapolis, Md.: Naval Institute Press,

1968), p. 128; *Public Statutes at Large of the United States* (Boston: Charles C. Little and James Brown, 1845), vol. 2, pp. 110–11.

5 Sprout and Sprout, *Rise of American Naval Power,* p. 60; Alfred Thayer Mahan, *Sea Power and Its Relations to the War of 1812* (1905; repr. New York: Haskell House, 1969), vol. 1, pp. 187–88, 296; Jefferson, "Special Message on Gun-Boats" to the Senate and House of Representatives, 10 February 1807, in *A Compilation of the Messages and Papers of the Presidents,* ed. James D. Richardson (New York: Bureau of National Literature, 1897), vol. 1, pp. 407–409; Mary P. Adams, "Jefferson's Military Policy with Special Reference to the Frontier, 1805–1809" (PhD dissertation, Univ. of Virginia, 1958), pp. v–vi; Macleod, "Jefferson and the Navy," p. 176.

6 Adams, "Jefferson's Military Policy with Special Reference to the Frontier," p. iii; Jefferson to Mr. [James] Bowdoin, 10 August 1806, Jefferson MSS, LC.

7 Jefferson, "Special Message on Gun-Boats." Jefferson reveals in this message that his strategy for defense was a multifarious plan, consisting of more than just gunboats; Dumas Malone, *Jefferson the President: Second Term* (Boston: Little, Brown, 1974), p. 496; Macleod, "Jefferson and the Navy," p. 153.

8 Jefferson to James Madison, 21 May 1813, in Lipscomb and Bergh, *Writings of Thomas Jefferson,* vol. 13, p. 234; Jefferson to Bowdoin, 10 July 1806, Jefferson MSS, LC.

9 Jefferson, "Special Message on Gun-Boats."

10 Dumas Malone claims that "Jefferson's opinion, especially after Trafalgar, that a strong seagoing navy would have been an utter waste was not as silly as certain later enthusiasts for seapower were to claim"; Malone, *Jefferson the President,* pp. xx, 496. Marshall Smelser exclaims, "After Trafalgar, a lonely, micro-scopic American fleet would have been gold cast into the sea"; Marshall Smelser, *The Democratic Republic, 1801–1815* (New York: Harper and Row, 1968), p. 229. Jefferson realized that anti-navalist Republicans would not approve the construction of a seagoing navy, despite his pleas.

11 Emanuel Raymond Lewis, *Seacoast Fortifications of the United States,* 2nd ed. (Annapolis, Md.: Leeward, 1979), pp. 21–25. Lewis provides (pp. 25–31) a basic description of the three types of fortifications, their differences and similarities. Open batteries were small works in positions of secondary importance or located near forts as supporting adjuncts. Masonry-faced forts utilized a combination of earth and an exterior scarp reinforced with masonry. All-masonry forts were granite-constructed, high-walled harbor defenses with casemated gun emplacements.

12 Jefferson to DeWitt Clinton, 29 January 1805; Jefferson to Nicholson, 29 January 1805; Jefferson to Governor Lewis, 2 May 1806; all Jefferson MSS, LC. Jefferson, "Special Message on Gun-Boats."

13 John Shaw to Gen. James Wilkinson, 9 May 1813, 4 June 1813, John Shaw Papers, Naval Historical Foundation Collection, Library of Congress, Washington, D.C. [hereafter NHF, LC].

14 Jefferson to Nicholson, 29 January 1805; Jefferson to Henry Dearborn, 27 January 1806; both Jefferson MSS, LC. Jefferson, "Special Message on Gun-Boats."

15 Jefferson to Nicholson, 29 January 1805; Jefferson, "Special Message on Gun-Boats"; Jefferson to Governor Wilson C. Nicholas, 2 April 1816, in Lipscomb and Bergh, *Writings of Thomas Jefferson,* vol. 14, pp. 446–47.

16 Jefferson to Secretary of the Navy, 19 June 1805, Jefferson MSS, LC; Jefferson to Robert Smith, 19 May 1806, Jefferson MSS, LC, quoted in Joseph G. Henrich, "The Triumph of Ideology: The Jeffersonians and the Navy, 1779–1807" (PhD dissertation, Duke Univ., 1971), p. 360; B. L. Rayner, *Sketches of the Life, Writings, and Opinions of Thomas Jefferson* (New York: A. Francis and W. Boardman, 1832) [hereafter *Sketches*], p. 442 (Themistocles is credited with rebuilding the Athenian fleet and the land walls that protected the city and its port, both of which played important roles in the Athenian victory over Sparta at Salamis); Jefferson to Jacob Crowninshield, 13 May 1806, Jefferson MSS, LC. Julia Macleod has argued ("Jefferson and the Navy," p. 176) that Jefferson wanted ships of the line, yet Frederick Leiner concludes that if Jefferson wanted capital ships, he certainly sent mixed and confusing signals; Frederick Leiner, "The 'Whimsical Philosophic President,' and His Gunboats," *American Neptune* 43 (Fall 1983), pp. 250–51, 253. See also *Annals of the Congress of the United States,* 9th Cong., 1st sess., 23 December 1805 (Washington, D.C.: Gales and Seaton, 1834), p. 302, and 25 March 1806, pp. 842–47.

17 Albert Gallatin to Jefferson, "Remarks on Jefferson's Fourth Annual Message," 29 October 1804, in *The Writings of Thomas Jefferson,* ed. Paul Leicester Ford (New York: G. P. Putnam, 1892–99), vol. 4, p. 327; McDonald, *Presidency of Thomas Jefferson,* p. 44; Fowler, *Jack Tars and Commodores,* p. 145; Sprout and Sprout, *Rise of American Naval Power,* p. 58; John Adams to Jefferson, 15 October 1822, cited in Rayner, *Sketches,* pp. 442–43; Jefferson to Samuel Harrison Smith, 2 March 1808, Samuel Harrison Smith Manuscript Collection, Library of Congress, Washington, D.C.

18 *Baltimore Federal Gazette,* 22 January 1806; Jefferson to Wilson Cary Nicholas, 6 December 1804, in Ford, *Writings of Thomas Jefferson,* vol. 10, p. 124; William Plumer, 8 November 1804, in William Plumer, *Memorandum of the Proceedings in the United States Senate, 1803–1807,* ed. Everett Somerville Brown (New York: Macmillan, 1923), p. 188; George F. Emmons, *The Navy of the United States: From the Commencement 1753 to 1853, with a Brief History of Each Vessel's Service and Fate as Appears upon Record* (Washington, D.C.: Gideon, 1853), p.

23; Samuel Eliot Morison, *The Oxford History of the American People* (New York: Oxford Univ. Press, 1965), p. 371; editorial, *Washington Federalist,* 11 March 1807; Thomas Truxtun to Timothy Pickering, 8 December 1807, Timothy Pickering Papers, Massachusetts Historical Society, Boston; William Augustus Fales, *An Oration Pronounced at Lenox, July 4, 1807* (Pittsfield, Mass.: Phinehas Allen, 1807), p. 16; *Early American Imprints,* series II, no. 12535; Spencer C. Tucker, *The Jeffersonian Gunboat Navy* (Columbia: Univ. of South Carolina Press, 1993), p. 181.

19 Secretary of the Navy to Alexander Murray, 29 January 1808, p. 173, "Gunboat Letters," record group [hereafter RG] 45, National Archives, Washington, D.C. [hereafter NA]; Thomas Paine, "Of the Comparative Powers and Expense of Ships of War, Gun-Boats, and Fortifications," in *The Complete Writings of Thomas Paine,* ed. Philip S. Foner (Minneapolis, Minn.: Book Sales, 1984), p. 1075; Jefferson, "Special Message on Gun-Boats"; Jefferson to Madison, 21 May 1813, p. 233; Samuel Barron to Jefferson, 8 February 1807, in *The American State Papers: Naval Affairs, 3 March 1789–5 March 1825,* ed. Walter Lowrie and Walter S. Franklin (Washington, D.C.: Gales and Seaton, 1834), p. 164; Jefferson to Bowdoin, 10 July 1806; Symonds, *Navalists and Antinavalists,* p. 109.

20 John Shaw to Daniel Patterson, 21 December 1813, Captains' Letters, RG 45, M125, NA; Frank Lawrence Owsley, Jr., *Struggle for the Gulf Borderlands: The Creek War and the Battle of New Orleans, 1812–1815* (Gainesville: Univ. Press of Florida, 1981), pp. 126–27; Tucker, *Jeffersonian Gunboat Navy,* p. 164.

21 Shaw to Patterson, 21 December 1813; Owsley, *Struggle for the Gulf Borderlands,* pp. 126–27; Tucker, *Jeffersonian Gunboat Navy,* p. 164.

22 David Porter to the Secretary of the Navy, 28 November 1808, Letters Received by the Secretary of the Navy from Commanders, 1804–1886, microfilm, RG 45, M147, NA [hereafter Commanders' Letters].

23 John Shaw to Secretary of the Navy, 11 September 1813, Letters Received by the Secretary of the Navy: Miscellaneous Letters, 1801–1884, microfilm, RG 45, M124, NA.

24 William C. C. Claiborne to James Madison, 9 July 1813, in *Official Letter Books of W. C. C. Claiborne, 1801–1816,* ed. Dunbar Rowland (Jackson, Miss.: State Department of Archives and History, 1917), vol. 6, p. 238.

25 Secretary of the Navy to Daniel Patterson, 25 January 1814, Miscellaneous Letters Sent by the Secretary of the Navy, 1798–1886, microfilm, RG 45, M209, NA.

26 Daniel Patterson to Secretary of the Navy, 27 December 1814, Commanders' Letters; E. M. Eller, W. J. Morgan, and R. M. Basoco, *Sea Power and the Battle of New Orleans* (New Orleans, La.: Battle of New Orleans, 150th Anniversary Committee of Louisiana, 1965), pp. 17–19; Edwin N. McClellan, "The Navy at the Battle of New Orleans," U.S. Naval Institute *Proceedings* 50 (December 1924), p. 2045; Daniel Patterson to the Secretary of the Navy, 20 January 1815, in *Niles' Weekly Register* 7, 18 February 1815,

p. 389; James D. Little, Jr., "The Navy at the Battle of New Orleans," *Louisiana Historical Quarterly* 54 (Spring 1971), p. 23.

27 Shaw to Patterson, 21 December 1813; Owsley, *Struggle for the Gulf Borderlands,* pp. 126–27; Wilbur S. Brown, *The Amphibious Campaign for West Florida and Louisiana* (Tuscaloosa: Univ. of Alabama Press, 1969), p. 83.

28 Brown, *Amphibious Campaign for West Florida and Louisiana,* p. 48; Eller, Morgan, and Basoco, *Sea Power and the Battle of New Orleans,* pp. 17–19; McClellan, "Navy at the Battle of New Orleans," p. 2045; Little, "Navy at the Battle of New Orleans," p. 25; Alexander Cochrane to John Wilson Coker, 9 March 1815, in *Naval Chronicle* 23 (1815), p. 337; "Autobiography of Admiral R. Aitchison" (original manuscript in Historic New Orleans Collection [hereafter HNOC], New Orleans, Louisiana), p. 64.

29 Jones to Patterson, 9 December 1814, Letters Received by the Secretary of the Navy from Officers below the Rank of Commander, 1802–1884, RG 45, M148, NA; "Statement of Lt. Thomas ap C. Jones Concerning the Engagement on Lake Borgne on 14 December 1814 to Daniel T. Patterson, 12 March 1815" [hereafter Jones Statement], HJ box 181, 1814–15, RG 45, NA, and reproduced in A. Lacarriere Latour, introduction to *Historical Memoir of the War in West Florida and Louisiana in 1814–15* (Philadelphia: John Conrad, 1816), p. xxxiii.

30 Jones Statement.

31 Memorial of Thomas Shield, Congressional Report No. 66, 4 January 1819, copy in the Andrew Hynes Papers, HNOC, New Orleans, Louisiana; Jones Statement; Lieutenant Moore to John, 13 December 1814, Kean-Prescott Papers, Southern Historical Collection–University of North Carolina, Chapel Hill.

32 Jones Statement.

33 Ibid.

34 Ibid.; Clericus, "Biographical Sketch of Thomas ap Catesby Jones," *Military and Naval Magazine* (1834), pp. 130–31.

35 Capt. Sir John Henry Cooke, *Narrative of Events in the South of France and of the Attack on New Orleans in 1814 and 1815* (London: T&W Boone, 1835), pp. 162–63; Nathaniel Herbert Claiborne, *Notes on the War in the South; with Biographical Sketches of the Lives of Montgomery, Jackson, Sevier, the Late Gov. Claiborne, and Others* (Richmond, Va.: William Ramsay, 1819), pp. 56–57; Andrew Jackson to James Monroe, 27 December 1814, in *Niles' Weekly Register* 7, 4 February 1815, p. 357.

36 Patterson to Secretary of the Navy, 16 December 1814, Commanders' Letters; Jones Statement; John Shaw to James Wilkinson, 12 September 1812, Captains' Letters, RG 45, M125, NA; "British Troops Landed in New Orleans in 1815," John Shaw Papers, NHF, LC; Robert J. Hanks, "'. . . The Ruinous Folly of a Navy,'" in *America Spreads Her Sails,* ed. Clayton R. Barrow, Jr. (Annapolis, Md.: Naval Institute Press, 1973), pp. 3–6; Brown, *Amphibious Campaign for West Florida and Louisiana,* pp. 78–81; Dean R. Mayhew, "Jeffersonian Gunboats in the War of 1812," *American Neptune* 42 (Spring 1982), pp. 116–17; Spencer Tucker, "Mr. Jefferson's

Gunboat Navy," *American Neptune* 43 (Spring 1983), pp. 140–41.

37 George Laval Chesterton, *Peace, War, and Adventure: An Autobiographical Memoir of George Laval Chesterton* (London: Longman, Brown, Green, and Longmans, 1853), p. 205; Robert Aitchison, *A British Eyewitness at the Battle of New Orleans: The Memoir of Royal Navy Admiral Robert Aitchison,* ed. Gene A. Smith (New Orleans, La.: HNOC, 2004), pp. 61, 64; Journal of A. Emment, Royal Engineers (p. 50, 4601-57/1), and Journal of John Fox Burgoyne, Royal Engineers M68, Entry 8 January 1815, both in Royal Engineers Museum, Chatham, U.K.; Alexander Dickson, "Artillery Services in North America in 1814 and 1815," *Journal of the Society for Army Historical Research* 8 (April 1929), pp. 97, 152–54.

38 Patterson to the Secretary of War, 28 December 1814, pp. 227–28; John Henley to Daniel Todd Patterson, 28 December 1814, p. 233; and Patterson to the Secretary of the Navy, 13 January 1815, pp. 243–46; all in Latour, *Historical Memoir.*

39 Mayhew, "Jeffersonian Gunboats in the War of 1812," p. 117; Cochrane to Coker, 9 March 1815.

40 *Niles' Weekly Register* 7, 4 February 1815, pp. 357–58; Brown, *Amphibious Campaign for West Florida and Louisiana,* p. 81.

41 Battle of New Orleans Sesquicentennial Commission, *Battle of New Orleans Sesquicentennial Celebration, 1815–1965* (Washington, D.C.: U.S. Government Printing Office, 1965), pp. 46–47; Brown, *Amphibious Campaign for West Florida and Louisiana,* p. 81; Owsley, *Struggle for the Gulf Borderlands,* p. 141.

42 C. S. Forester, *The Age of Fighting Sail* (Garden City, N.Y.: Doubleday, 1956), pp. 267–69; Owsley, *Struggle for the Gulf Borderlands,* pp. 139–40; Daniel Patterson to William Jones, 22 November 1813, 7 December 1813, 21 January 1814, 31 January 1814, Commanders' Letters; Paul Hamilton to John Shaw, 25 September 1812, and William Jones to Daniel Patterson, 18 October 1813, Letters Sent by the Secretary of the Navy to Officers, 1798–1868, microfilm, RG 45, M149, NA; Bartholomew S[c]haumburg to James Wilkinson, 25 January 1815, S[c]haumburg Letter, HNOC, New Orleans, Louisiana; Tucker, *Jeffersonian Gunboat Navy,* p. 163.

43 McKee, *Gentlemanly and Honorable Profession,* pp. 156–57; Henry Adams, *History of the United States of America* (New York: Scribner's, 1891; repr. New York: Literary Classics of the United States, 1986), p. 1036; William S. Dudley and Michael J. Crawford, *The Naval War of 1812* (Washington, D.C.: Naval Historical Center, 1985), vol. 1, p. 12 note.

44 Robert W. Tucker and David C. Hendrickson, *The Empire of Liberty: The Statecraft of Thomas Jefferson* (New York: Oxford Univ. Press, 1990), pp. 224–25; George E. Buker, *Swamp Sailors: Riverine Warfare in the Everglades, 1835–1842* (Gainesville: Univ. of Florida Press, 1975), passim; E. B. Potter and Chester W. Nimitz, *Sea Power* (New York: Prentice Hall, 1960), pp. 231–32, 275–311; Weigley, *American Way of War,* pp. 170–78; Michael Bruno, "Navy Not 'Correctly Balanced' for Future, Clark Says," *Aerospace Daily & Defense Report,* 12 January 2005.

X "Unquestionably There Is an Organized Band of Incendiaries"

Confederate Boat Burners on the Lower Mississippi River

LAURA JUNE DAVIS

The fifteenth of July, 1864—the city of St. Louis lulled in the predawn stillness of another day. At nearly four o'clock in the morning, startled citizens awoke to the sound of clanging bells. Watchmen had discovered a fire "issuing from the aft part of the new steamer *Edward F. Dix*." Local firemen rushed to the scene, but despite "herculean efforts," the conflagration advanced at unimaginable speeds. Between the delay in sounding the alarm, the crowding of the docks, and "the intense heat of the sun of the previous day [the vessels were left as] dry and inflammable as timber." Five boats met fiery ends—*Northerner, Sunshine, Glasgow, Cherokee,* and *Edward F. Dix*—while *Welcome* escaped with minimal damage. *Cherokee*'s porter was not so fortunate; his charred remains were found amid the glowing embers. The fire also incinerated eighty tons of government provisions, twenty tons of Indian annuities, three hundred bales of hemp, several hundred sacks of corn, over 250 tons of private freight, and assorted cargo. The economic loss was substantial; reports claimed that the "total loss cannot fall short of a half million dollars." The largest steamboat fire in almost fifteen years, this conflagration was the presumed exploit of Rebel boat burners. In the days just prior to the inferno, Federal officials had received several dispatches about boat burners operating out of St. Louis. Within a few days, the Union military had arrested two men on suspicion of starting the fire.[1]

Often overlooked by scholars, this incendiary method of Confederate warfare does not fit into the conventional modes of regular, or even irregular, combat. Not mainstream sailors, boat burners did in fact take their cause to the water, making steamboats and river ports their battlefields of choice. Referred to as "incendiaries" or "naval guerrillas" by contemporaries, boat burners differed from "bushwhackers." While irregular fighters such as William Quantrill and "Bloody Bill" Anderson flaunted their exploits, bushwhackers wore flamboyant shirts, and partisan rangers operated under the authority of the Confederate government, naval guerrillas intentionally operated in the shadows; they skulked along the docks, secreted themselves on board vessels, or insinuated themselves as steamboat crew members. Preferring secrecy and anonymity, naval guerrillas engaged in a stealthy game of subterfuge, targeting Union steamboats and setting them ablaze via fire or "torpedo" (what would now be called mines or limpets). They usually besieged merchant and civilian vessels rather than Federal gunboats, exemplifying nineteenth-century irregular *guerre de course* and terrorism. In a February 1865 letter to President Jefferson Davis, W. S. Oldham advised that the Rebels should "burn every transport and gunboat on the Mississippi river, as well as devastate the country of the enemy, and fill his people with terror and consternation."[2] Notably, all of this was done under the veil of maximum secrecy; the boat burners never sought publicity or fame for their exploits.

While their methods varied, boat burners had the same aim as their landlocked counterparts; they too "distracted the Federals from their primary objectives, caused them to alter strategies, injured the morale of Union troops, and forced the reassignment of men and resources to counter threats" along the lower Mississippi River. Furthermore, they caused hundreds of thousands of dollars' worth of damage—destroying the livelihoods of civilian steamboat owners as well as vital war materiel destined for Union troops. The victimization of innocent women and children only worsened the incendiaries' crimes. Naval guerrillas challenged the Union's control of the waterways, regularly denying "Northerners complete freedom to use the river by mounting many small-scale attacks on steamers for the remainder of the war."[3]

While many naval guerrillas may have acted alone, evidence suggests that an organized gang of boat burners operated out of St. Louis during the latter half of the war. Federal officials received reports that Rebel authorities were paying incendiaries; Union officials even found a list of all the boats traveling the Mississippi, as well as their estimated worth, among the belongings of captured boat burners. The Confederate government incentivized the burnings by offering to pay naval guerrillas up to 60 percent of the damaged boats' estimated value.[4]

William Murphy, a member of the organized incendiaries, later gave a full confession to Provost Marshal J. H. Baker. According to Murphy, Edward Frazor led a band of nineteen secret agents whose mission was to destroy Federal property and steamboats. Murphy further "confessed that they were employed by the rebel authorities" and that the Confederate president and secretary of state sanctioned their actions. Murphy told Union officials that in exchange for destroying steamboats, the St. Louis boat burners "were paid at Richmond by the Rebel Secretary of State." He also claimed to have enjoyed a private audience with Jefferson Davis.[5]

Evidence of intentional boat burning along the lower Mississippi came to light during the summer of 1863. With the fall of Vicksburg in July, the Union had seemingly gained unfettered control of the Mississippi; President Abraham Lincoln even proclaimed that "the Father of Waters again goes unvexed to the sea." But while conventional naval battles were ending, brown-water irregular warfare was just beginning. The Southerners realized that while they had failed to maintain control of the Mississippi River, they might be able to employ irregular warfare to thwart Federal jurisdiction over this essential waterway. The Confederate naval war, consequently, took on a more aggressive posture.[6]

For example, on 4 August 1863 an extensive conflagration arose when the Federal steamer *Ruth* caught fire while traveling between Cairo and Vicksburg. Carrying more than standard cargo, *Ruth* was also transporting much-needed funds to Maj. Gen. Ulysses S. Grant in Vicksburg. Seven paymasters, eight clerks, and thirty-one soldiers accompanied Union paymaster Nathan S. Brinton and his well-guarded coffer of $2,600,000. Unfortunately, *Ruth*'s incineration resulted in the complete loss of the greenbacks as well as thousands of dollars in damage. More gruesome were the resulting deaths of twenty-six people—including one Union paymaster, three Yankee clerks, one woman, and three African Americans. Most of the casualties were drowning victims who fell into the water when the fire caused the ship's planking to collapse. Only *Ruth*'s crew managed to survive the inferno. While early reports claimed that "there is no satisfactory theory as to how the fire originated," locals believed it to be the work of a Rebel saboteur working on behalf of the Confederate government.[7]

For the next several weeks, details of *Ruth*'s conflagration trickled in, raising ire and constantly reminding citizens of the mounting dangers of river travel. None of the newspaper accounts named specific suspects, leaving boat burning a constant, albeit shadowy, threat. An October 1863 court of inquiry determined that an incendiary had set the fire in the carpenter's shop. Assistant Adjutant General E. D. Townsend ruled that the intentional burning of *Ruth* was "not for the particular purpose—although that may have been an additional object—of destroying the public funds on board, but in conformity with what appears to be a plan of the rebels for the destruction of the water transportation in the valley of the Mississippi, and thus crippling the movements of our armies." At one time or another, provost marshals attributed *Ruth*'s burning to William Murphy, John McKennon, Robert Louden (or Lowden), and Isaac Aleshire (or Elshire)—all members of the St. Louis boat burners—though none claimed responsibility for the act.[8]

On 13 September another massive steamboat fire broke out in St. Louis. Around six o'clock in the evening, a dense cloud of smoke descended on the port. Alarm bells clamored. Dozens flocked to the riverbank. Within minutes the steamboat *Imperial* disintegrated into "a mass of flame and burning coal from stem to stern." The fire soon spread across the docks, making "such headway that it was impossible to stop" it. Confusion abounded. The combustible nature of the steamboats only exacerbated matters. The expanding inferno resulted in the demise of *Hiawatha, Post Boy,* and *Jesse K. Bell.* One newspaper claimed that "the sluggish river seemed a party in the plot to engender misfortune to the doomed" craft, moving so slowly that the endangered vessels could not escape their fiery fate. For hours, locals could see "cinders and smoke . . . dancing and whirling fantastically in the air." The real culprits, however, were naval guerrillas—or as the *Daily Missouri Republican* declared, a "devilish spirit which actuated some scoundrel to set fire" to the boats. While no lives were lost, damage totaled two hundred thousand dollars.[9]

Despite two years of warfare and professed Union control of the Mississippi River, Federal officials realized that river towns such as St. Louis were hotbeds of Confederate sympathizers. While Missouri never officially left the Union, many from St. Louis favored secession, and several thousand locals joined the Confederate military. Boat burners were just a small subset of Missourians who remained steadfast to the Rebel cause. For those who remained loyal to the Union, it was becoming evident that a great conspiracy to destroy all steamers along the lower Mississippi River was wreaking havoc on their own lives, livelihoods, shipping, and commerce.

It is not surprising that Confederate boat burners focused their efforts on the Mississippi River. Spanning 2,350 miles from Lake Itasca, Minnesota, to the Gulf of Mexico, the river bisects the United States into east and west, flowing into the very heart of America. By the dawn of the Civil War, the Mississippi was the nation's premier economic, transportation, and communications highway. Cotton, grain, hogs, chickens, sugar, and people traveled from St. Louis to New Orleans (and vice versa) in as little as four days. With the advent of steamboats, 160,000 tons of shipping carried $200 million worth of goods on board seven hundred vessels. St. Louis alone saw a million pounds of fodder pass through its ports each month. Secessionists familiar with the waterway employed a network of spies, saboteurs, and mail runners. Confederate guerrillas traveled up- and downstream to harass Yankee occupiers, while Rebel incendiaries took to the water to destroy commercial vessels carrying supplies, civilians, and correspondence.[10]

Provost Marshal Baker noted that "it would be impossible to obtain a correct account of the property destroyed by these parties." Yet he believed them to be responsible for the burning of at least ten vessels, including the previously mentioned *Imperial, Hiawatha, Post Boy,* and *Jesse K. Bell.* Hearing of these and similar incidents, Robert Allen, the chief quartermaster of the Union army, reported that "there is evidently a band of incendiaries organized for the destruction of our own transports." In October 1863, Allen elaborated, "The continued destruction of steamboats, by fire, on these waters is assuming a very alarming feature. Unquestionably, there is an organized band of incendiaries, members of which are stationed at every landing." Unfortunately, the mayhem only continued. As Allen noted, the "increase of watchmen and extra vigilance do not seem to arrest this insidious enemy." In the end, naval guerrillas destroyed forty steamers between the fall of 1863 and the winter of 1864. These conflagrations resulted in dozens of civilian casualties and ultimately led to the arrest of six incendiaries, including William Murphy and Robert Louden.[11]

Adding fuel to the fire—so to speak—reports emerged that the boat burners were employing "infernal machines." Union officers learned that "amongst other devilish inventions [of the Confederacy] is a torpedo resembling a lump of coal, to be placed in coal piles and amongst the coal put on board vessels." Such innovations may have aided the naval guerrillas in their cause, allowing them to sneak on board ships, hide their explosive devices, and escape long before the steamers exploded. In December 1863, Union authorities actually captured two presumed boat burners carrying a homemade incendiary device. One of the Rebels carried "a thing in the similitude of a tobacco pouch, filled up with a combustible fluid capable of burning under water, lighted with fuses calculated to burn one, two, three, or four hours." Such a destructive device could be lit and thrown into a ship's hold, providing the naval guerrilla with a delay and a distraction to escape the scene prior to the fire's eruption. Such intelligence underscored Robert Allen's belief that "the incendiary, when it serves his purpose, becomes one of the crew, and thus secures himself from detection. I apprehend that there are disloyal men in disguise in the employ of every steamer, and it will be difficult to eliminate them." While such universal deception was unlikely, the terror created by even a handful of confirmed boat burnings was immeasurable—an outcome desired by the incendiaries. W. S. Oldham claimed, "I believe we have the means at our command, if promptly appropriated and energetically applied, to demoralize the Northern people in a very short time." Fear—it would seem—was the naval guerrillas' greatest achievement.[12]

The psychological effects of boat burnings on the citizens of St. Louis and other river towns were overwhelming. Frightened by the repeated conflagrations and frustrated by the Federal government's seeming ineptitude at protecting its citizens, the writers of the *Daily Missouri Republican* implored Union military officials "to use special means and vigilance to detect the perpetrators of these hellish wholesale murders and burnings, and to consign them to speedy and exemplary punishment." The paper cast the boat burners as "monstrous and murderous," especially in the case of *Ruth,* which had involved the deaths of innocent civilians. William Tecumseh Sherman shared the populace's frustration over irregular naval warfare. He bluntly "exclaimed, 'It is not war.' Any boat captain who caught incendiaries should 'drop them overboard and let them find the bottom in their own way.'"[13]

By the fall of 1863, the Union military had finally taken concerted action to stop the plague of boat burning. The Union pursued a two-pronged defense of the river: Federal gunboats from the Mississippi River Squadron patrolled the river, while local police on land extended protection for commercial steamboats. In October 1863, Federal authorities began placing undercover agents in port towns and on steamers. Rear Adm. David Dixon Porter also ordered several precautions "to prevent fire to public vessels by incendiaries." These included the stationing of sentries at major ports, refusal to allow anyone nighttime access to public property, and stopping of all small boats seen traversing the river after dark. Porter reiterated that "it behooves every officer and man to be watchful at this time and see that no attempt to burn the property under their charge shall succeed." Lastly, the Federals restricted river trade to confirmed Unionists.[14]

The local populace, however, was not happy with such measures. Many citizens of river towns did not trust the Union government to ensure their safety. They often criticized Federal troops for their inability to protect steamboats, safeguard civilian passengers, or hold the saboteurs accountable for their nefarious actions. In September 1863, the *Daily Missouri Republican* focused its ire on the Union defenders, commenting, "We never hear of [the guerrillas] being attacked by any vessels belonging to the Brigade." Despite the enormous expense of such a river defense fleet, it seemed to fail in its duties. The *Republican* attributed such shortcomings to the squadron "lying all together at some port doing nothing" rather than conducting regular patrols of the river.[15]

Feeling unprotected, the local populace took matters into its own hands. Steamboat owners living in St. Louis gathered on 10 October 1863 to discuss "the danger which now surrounds steamboat property from fire, and to endeavor by concerted action to remove [said] evil." Desperate to make the river waterways and steamboats safer for commercial and leisure travel, they too increased the number of watchmen on the docks. Unfortunately, neither the Federal government nor the steamboat captains succeeded. Charles F. Vogel, a member of the 29th Missouri Infantry Regiment stationed in St. Louis, confessed that "the steam boat incendiaries since I have been here burnt [eleven] steamers, all at the time in Gov't service"; there was little he or his fellow soldiers could do to stop them. For the duration of the war, the naval guerrillas evaded authorities, targeting steamers traveling the lower Mississippi River.[16]

Unfortunately for historians, there is no formal list of naval guerrillas. Instead, we must paint a collective portrait from old newspaper reports, provost marshal investigations, and official records—sources that so vilified the incendiaries as to make it difficult to take their human measure. For example, newspapers described the culprit behind the 15 July inferno as "some Devil, in the shape o' a human Being." Robert Louden was between five feet eight inches and five feet ten, with dark hair, large blue eyes, and a build of 160 to 170 pounds; but on that slight basis, the historical record vilifies him. One newspaper cast him as "surly," while the provost marshal caricaturized him as a villain with "square shoulders, [fair complexion, and] large blue eyes constantly rolling [who displayed] a great deal of white, fair hair and whiskers." If the rolling eyes were not dubious enough, reports claimed that Louden frequently wore a false mustache and backward hat—marked signs of wickedness. Such a demonic description was a far cry from the faithful friend whom the infamous Confederate spy Absalom Grimes characterized as one who "had unlimited courage and judgement [sic] for any dangerous work." Meanwhile, the provost marshal described Isaac Aleshire as five feet six with a slim build, wicked-looking eyes, dark brown hair, a small nose, and, worst of all, a "slouchy and care-less" appearance. But even such vivid and exaggerated descriptions of incendi-aries were rare. Most remained undetected—or worse yet, misidentified, as one William Murphy found out when he was mistaken for the boat burner of the same name.[17]

In reality, as we have noted, most naval guerrillas operated in the shadows. While the majority pursued anti-Union agendas, some may have burned North-ern steamers for their own amusement—if mail runner Absalom Grimes is to be believed. Many of the St. Louis boat burners were from river towns and therefore familiar with the local geography, people, and vessels. For example, William Mur-phy was from New Orleans. John G. Parks was from Memphis, Tennessee. Isaac Aleshire, originally from Indiana, worked as a mate of a steamboat out of St. Louis. John R. Barrett, Harrison Fox, Peter Mitchell, and Robert Louden were also from St. Louis. However, as Grimes revealed, getting on board ship was relatively sim-ple. In his memoirs, Grimes recounted how he had been able to board a Memphis steamboat simply because he knew the crew. Grimes also "managed to get half of [his] command on board as deck hands and deck passengers," stating that it "was easy to get the others aboard on various pretexts." Boat burners like Aleshire with previous experience on board steamboats could have easily insinuated themselves as members of a crew. The rest likely followed Grimes's method and utilized their personal relationships to gain unquestioned access on board a commercial vessel. Whether their friends knew of their incendiary intent is unknown.[18]

Furthermore, knowing who was responsible and bringing them to justice were two entirely different matters. Despite public outcries to punish the incendiaries for their treasonous actions, most eluded authorities. The provost marshal cap-tured and imprisoned four at Gratiot State Penitentiary in St. Louis, but most of these broke out before the war ended. General Orders 41 of 1864 sentenced Rob-ert Louden to hang for steamboat burning. However, Louden managed to escape prison—and his death sentence—heading south to Mobile, Alabama. No subse-quent action was taken to recapture him, and according to Absalom Grimes, Lou-den became a painter before dying several years later of yellow fever.[19]

By war's end, newspapers were reporting that "the evidence on file [at] the Bu-reau of Military Justice against the gang of Rebel incendiaries . . . implicates about thirty-five persons," including President Davis. Newspapers also elevated the dam-age caused by naval guerrillas, claiming that "during the war over two hundred steamers of all kinds valued at from $15,060 to $150,000 each, were destroyed by this chivalrous band, involving not only an immense pecuniary loss to the Govern-ment but the sacrifice of hundreds of valuable lives." While the true cost of irregular naval warfare may never be determined, Confederate boat burners certainly in-flicted substantial economic, psychological, and material damage.[20]

Ultimately, William Murphy became the scapegoat for all naval guerrillas. Between January 1863 and February 1864, Murphy had admittedly conspired with nineteen others to perpetrate at least three distinct acts of arson along the lower Mississippi River. Perhaps motivated by greed—or at the very least, the promise of riches—Murphy now became a turncoat. He informed Col. J. H. Baker, provost marshal general of the Department of the Missouri, that he had vital information on the boat burners operating out of St. Louis. In exchange for intelligence, Murphy received one hundred dollars and a promise of protection. Instead, in March 1864 Murphy absconded from St. Louis and headed to New Orleans, in hopes of leaving the country by boat. His duplicity resulted in a September 1865 appearance before the Missouri Military Commission, which tried him for intentional boat burning. Despite claims that "the burning and destruction [of steamboats] was a military measure of the rebel Government," Murphy was eventually convicted. General Court Martial Order 107 of 1866 declared Murphy guilty on two charges: first, "conspiracy to burn and destroy steamboats and other property belonging to or in the service of the United States of America"; and second, "violation of the laws and customs of war." E. D. Townsend, assistant adjutant general, sentenced Murphy to ten years' imprisonment at hard labor. President Andrew Johnson himself approved the conviction, in an executive order dated 30 March 1866. In the end Murphy was, the historical record indicates, the only boat burner held accountable for his crimes. Fortunately, Murphy did not serve the whole ten years. During his 1867 circuit ride, Supreme Court justice Samuel Freeman Miller heard William Murphy's habeas corpus case and overturned his conviction, thereby freeing him.[21]

Ultimately, the St. Louis boat burners left a fiery mark on the lower Mississippi River. While one historian comments that "despite their spectacular mode of operation, the boat burners accounted for only 8.8% of the total number of boats lost during the war," this statistic is misleading. It does not take into consideration the vital role that shipping played in nineteenth-century America, the millions of dollars in materiel consumed by the conflagrations, the dozens of innocent lives lost, or the criticality of the Mississippi to the war's outcome. The integral relationship between man and the Mississippi remained a constant in the Rebels' minds— explaining why they altered their tactics from conventional, defensive action to aggressive, irregular warfare. Furthermore, the boat burners represented a distinct group of actors; they were not afraid to challenge conventions and codes of combat, harass Federal authorities, disrupt the Union economy, psychologically terrorize Northern populations, or perform in the shadow of secrecy. They remind us that the fall of Vicksburg was not the end of fighting along the Mississippi; rather, it was the start of a new chapter in naval warfare. The Confederates never accepted the fall of the river, nor did they go quietly into the night; instead, they pursued a violent and fiery defense of the waterway until the war's end.

NOTES   An extended version of this paper was published as "Irregular Naval Warfare along the Lower Mississippi" in *The Guerrilla Hunters: Irregular Conflicts during the Civil War*, edited by Barton A. Myers and Brian McKnight (LSU Press, 2017). The author would like to thank Stephen Berry, Joseph M. Beilein, and Nicholas Benson for their feedback and David J. Gerleman for his invaluable assistance. Generous grants from the Willson Center for Humanities and Arts, the University of Georgia Graduate School and History Department, the Greg and Amanda Gregory Graduate Studies Enhancement Fund, and the Vincent J. Dooley Graduate Research Award supported this project.

1 "River News," *Daily Missouri Republican,* 16 July 1864, p. 4; "Destructive Fire at the Wharf," *Daily Missouri Republican,* 16 July 1864, p. 3; "Steamboat Fire in St. Louis," *Daily Intelligencer,* 16 July 1864, p. 3.

2 Daniel E. Sutherland, *A Savage Conflict: The Decisive Role of Guerrillas in the American Civil War* (Chapel Hill: Univ. of North Carolina Press, 2009), p. 70. While historians such as Richard Brownlee, Michael Fellman, Mark Grimsley, Robert Mackey, and Daniel Sutherland have demonstrated the pivotal role of guerrillas in the Civil War, none have considered naval guerrillas or boat burners. Fellman, Grimsley, and Mackey fail even to mention this type of irregular fighter, while Sutherland classifies them as either privateers or sailors on board torpedo gunboats. Sutherland dismisses the import of infernal machines and commerce raiders when he asserts that neither "constituted a guerrilla war at sea." Ibid., p. 165; W. S. Oldham to Jefferson Davis, 11 February 1865, Record Group 94, entry 12, General Records of the Adjutant General's Office, Correspondence, 1800–1947, Letters Received by the Office of the Adjutant General (Main Series), 1861–1870, National Archives Building, Washington, D.C.

3 Earl J. Hess, *The Civil War in the West: Victory and Defeat from the Appalachians to the Mississippi* (Chapel Hill: Univ. of North Carolina Press, 2012), p. 199; Sutherland, *Savage Conflict,* p. ix.

4 "Every Steamboat Navigating the Lower Mississippi and Ohio Rivers to Be Destroyed by Rebel Emissaries," *Daily Missouri Republican,* 8 October 1864, p. 3. In this case, the boat burners were former Memphis policemen operating apart from the organized band.

5 "By Telegraph," *Nashville Daily Union,* 18 October 1863, p. 3; "The Latest News," *Nashville Daily Union,* 24 December 1863, p. 2; U.S. War Dept., *The War of the Rebellion: A Compilation of the Official Records of the Union and Confederate Armies* (Washington, D.C.: U.S. Government Printing Office [hereafter GPO], 1880–1901), series 1, vol. 48 [hereafter OR, citing series and volume], p. 196. Other documents within the OR indicate that the Confederate government did sponsor and pay boat burners for their service. See OR, II:8, p. 516; U.S. Navy Dept., *Official Records of the Union and Confederate Navies in the War of the Rebellion* (Washington, D.C.: GPO, 1894), series 1, vol. 26 [hereafter ORN, citing series and volume], p. 186; and "Every Steamboat Navigating the Lower Mississippi and Ohio Rivers," p. 3. Also "More Steamboat Incendiarism: Attempt to Burn Boats at Carondelet," *Daily Missouri Republican,* 4 October 1863, p. 2; and Hess, *Civil War in the West,* p. 238.

6 Abraham Lincoln, *Collected Works of Abraham Lincoln,* ed. Roy P. Basler (New Brunswick, N.J.: Rutgers Univ. Press, 1953), vol. 6, p. 409.

7 "Terrible Calamity," *Daily Missouri Republican,* 6 August 1863, p. 3; "Burning of the Ruth: Additional Particulars," *Daily Missouri Republican,* 7 August 1863, p. 2; "Affairs Down River," *Daily Missouri Republican,* 11 August 1863, p. 3.

8 *Reports of Committees of the House of Representatives Made during the First Session Thirty-Eighth Congress, 1863–64* (Washington, D.C.: GPO, 1864), p. 91; U.S. War Dept., "United States, Union Provost Marshal Files of Individual Civilians, 1861–1866," entries for John McKennon on roll 1200, William Murphy on roll 1249, Isaac Elshire on roll 1311, and Robert Lowden on roll 1363.

9 "Extensive Conflagration," *Daily Missouri Republican,* 14 September 1863, p. 3; "River News," *Daily Missouri Republican,* 14 September 1863, p. 3. Surprisingly, some of the owners of the burned steamers bought replacement boats a day after the conflagration.

10 For the economic importance of the Mississippi River, see Walter Johnson, introduction to *River of Dark Dreams: Slavery and Empire in the Cotton Kingdom* (Cambridge, Mass.: Harvard Univ. Press, 2013); Louis C. Hunter, *Steamboats on the Western Rivers: An Economic and Technological History* (New York: Dover, 1993); and "The Commercial Growth and Greatness of the West," *Hunt's Merchants' Magazine* 17 (1847), pp. 495–503. For Civil War–era New Orleans, see Chester G. Hearn, *When the Devil Came Down to Dixie: Ben Butler in New Orleans* (Baton Rouge: Louisiana State Univ. Press, 2000), and Catherine Clinton, "'Public Women' and Sexual Politics during the American Civil War," in *Battle Scars: Gender and Sexuality in the American Civil War,* ed. Catherine Clinton and Nina Silber (New York: Oxford Univ. Press, 2006), pp. 61–77. For Civil War–era St. Louis, consult Louis G. Gerteis, *Civil War St. Louis* (Lawrence: Univ. Press of Kansas, 2004), and Michael Joseph Whaley, "'It Was a Hostile City': Disloyalty in Civil War St. Louis" (PhD dissertation, Southern Illinois Univ. at Carbondale, 2008).

11 OR, I:48, pp. 195–96; OR, I:30, part 3, p. 664; OR, I:22, p. 607; "Destructive Fire at the Wharf," p. 3.

12 ORN, I:26, p. 186; OR, I:22, p. 607; "Latest News," p. 2; Oldham to Davis, 11 February 1865. The December 1863 arrest occurred twenty-five miles above the mouth of the White River. Secret service agent S. B. Morehouse arrested Mr. Brown and Mr. Tinley, two notorious secessionists, carrying Confederate letters of marque, matches, and a torpedo-like device.

13 "More Steamboat Incendiarism," p. 2; Hess, *Civil War in the West,* p. 238; "Every Steamboat Navigating the Lower Mississippi and Ohio Rivers," p. 3.

14 "Letters from Canton, Miss.," *Memphis Daily Appeal,* 29 September 1863, p. 2; Hess, *Civil War in the West,* p. 238; ORN, I:25, pp. 463–64.

15 "River News," *Daily Missouri Republican,* 16 September 1863, p. 3.

16 "Meeting of Steamboat Owners," *Daily Missouri Republican,* 6 October 1863, p. 4; Charles F. Vogel, diary, 4 October 1863, Z/0656.000: Vogel (Charles F.) Diary, Mississippi State Archives, Jackson, Miss.

17 "River News," 16 July 1864, p. 3; "From Missouri," *Daily Ohio Statesman,* 7 October 1864, p. 3; U.S. War Dept., "United States, Union Provost Marshal Files of Individual Civilians, 1861–1866," entries for Robert Lowden on roll 1363, Isaac Elshire on roll 1311, and William Murphy on roll 1249; Absalom Grimes, *Confederate Mail Runner* (New Haven, Conn.: Yale Univ. Press, 1926), p. 63.

18 OR, I:48, pp. 194–95; Grimes, *Confederate Mail Runner,* p. 63. For Confederate mail running see LeeAnn Whites, "'Corresponding with the Enemy': Mobilizing the Relational Field of Battle in St. Louis," in *Occupied Women: Gender, Military Occupation, and the American Civil War,* ed. LeeAnn Whites and Alecia P. Long (Baton Rouge: Louisiana State Univ. Press, 2009); and Grimes, *Confederate Mail Runner,* p. 134.

19 OR, I:48, pp. 195, 197; Grimes, *Confederate Mail Runner,* p. 190. Upon his deathbed, Robert Louden purportedly admitted to having been the saboteur behind the infamous *Sultana* explosion. The veracity of the claim seems doubtful. However, the lingering correlation between the St. Louis boat burners and intentional steamboat fires highlights the enduring legacy of their fear campaign. For more on the Louden-*Sultana* connection, see Deb H. Rule, "*Sultana*: A Case for Sabotage," *North and South* 5, no. 1 (December 2001), pp. 76–87.

20 "The Rebel Boat-Burners," *American Citizen,* 27 September 1865, p. 2.

21 "Extensive Conflagration," p. 3. See also OR, I:30, pp. 3, 641; OR, I:22, p. 607; "Local News: The Arraignment of William Murphy," *Daily Missouri Republican,* 20 September 1865, p. 3; "Local News," *Daily Missouri Republican,* 22 September 1865, p. 3; and *In re Murphy,* 17 F.Cas. 1030 (C.C.D. Mo. 1867).

XI *Building a Sugar Empire*
Slave Trafficking on the Rivers of Antebellum America

DEBRA JACKSON

The cultivation of sugarcane in the colonies of the New World created great wealth for white settlers and for the mother countries from which they came. Indeed, "the centrality of sugar to the development of the early Atlantic world is . . . well known. Sugar was the 'green gold' [on which planters staked their fortunes] and it was the commodity that became linked . . . to the rise of the Atlantic slave trade." Threats to the viability and security of the sugar islands of the Caribbean came from attacks by pirates and privateers prowling the waters of the Spanish Main, and the maritime power exerted to ensure the continued prosperity of these islands was considerable. British planters in particular relied on the Royal Navy to keep the islands safe from invasion—especially from the French—and gratefully paid tribute, in the forms of gifts, to naval commanders.[1]

Sugar plantations were a relatively late development in the United States after the Revolution, but settlers cultivating sugar and other crops in the southern interior relied just as heavily on the vessels that plied the rivers of that region as the British sugar planters relied on the Royal Navy and British merchant marine. And although the U.S. dependence on such crops was not jeopardized by threats of foreign invasion, the viability and economic success of the plantations of the southern interior were nonetheless at stake.

To what geographic area do we refer in using the phrase "southern interior"? In the postrevolution years this would have been the land area west of the Allegheny Mountains, east of the Mississippi River, and south of the Ohio River. This region provided fertile ground on which countless fortunes were built. One such fortune was built by entrepreneur Andrew Hynes (1785–1849). His life and career illustrate, on the micro level, how economic growth in the young republic began and how it evolved. Hynes was a soldier, land speculator, merchant, and slave trader. He understood, as did others of his time, that men of energy and vision might prosper. Indeed, the creation of Hynes's personal empire paralleled that of the burgeoning nation: just as the new United States exploited vast areas to the south and west for their potential in producing such slave-grown staples as hemp, cotton, and sugar, so the activities of Hynes took him south to Iberville, Louisiana, as he exploited slave labor in the cultivation of sugarcane and its by-products.

One benefit of the shift of focus from the general to the particular—from the growth of the young republic to the spotlight on one man's business activities—is the opportunity it offers to uncover some of the effects of the forced resettlement of slaves into the southern interior. As a viable source of cheap labor, slavery ensured the profitability of the frontier lands being developed. As more land became available throughout the antebellum period for white settlement and the demand for slaves increased, the domestic slave trade to the regions of the southern interior grew exponentially.

In the United States no area has been shaped more decisively by rivers than the South. The river system in the interior centered on the Mississippi, and the key streams of the region—the Ohio, Missouri, Cumberland, Tennessee, and Red Rivers—constituted a freshwater empire of agricultural production and commerce, a riverine network that moved raw materials, furniture, foodstuffs, and slaves throughout the area. Tobacco and rice were the staple products for early settlers in the area of the Chesapeake Bay and in the Carolinas. But the invention of the cotton gin at the end of the eighteenth century led to expansion into lands previously unknown to white settlement—areas that became the states of Kentucky, Tennessee, Mississippi, and Alabama, as well as inland Georgia. When in 1803 the Louisiana Purchase suddenly made available an immense swath of territory that seemed promising for sugarcane cultivation, enterprising businessmen and speculators began to explore their options for acquiring land in the region.

With the availability of vast areas of cheap land came the problem of how to cultivate it at a profit, a problem that was solved by the domestic slave trade. It is difficult to overestimate the importance of the trade in fostering growth and prosperity during the antebellum period. The demands for labor required a massive transfer of enslaved people from the Upper South to the frontier regions of the Southeast and West. Slaves were tasked with the backbreaking work of clearing the land, constructing living quarters for themselves and their masters, and, finally, with cultivating staple crops for market. This forced migration highlighted one of the domestic trade's ugliest features: the slave coffle. Slaves chained together moving overland presented a spectacle that disgusted even the staunchest defenders of slaveholding property rights.

The movement of slaves along the nation's waterways, initially less visible than overland coffles, increased as the domestic trade grew, uprooting hundreds of thousands of black people while enriching planters and speculators. The riverine network that existed in the southern interior certainly facilitated the movement of slaves, but at the beginning of the nineteenth century these rivers were traveled only by a variety of such slow-moving vessels as rafts, keelboats, and flatboats. With the advent of steam power the movement of waterborne slave coffles became more efficient for the slave trader. In the estimation of one scholar, "steamers . . . were a quick and efficient way to coordinate the commerce in human beings."[2]

In summary, then, the situation that developed during the postrevolutionary period was a confluence of circumstances that created the climate for phenomenal growth and prosperity in the country. The first circumstance was technological innovation; the invention of the cotton gin facilitated the separation of the cotton, and the introduction of Robert Fulton's steam-powered boats allowed the easy transference of ginned cotton and other commodities to and from the interior through the country's major ports. The second was the physical expansion of the country, represented by the Louisiana Purchase in 1803 and also the newly vacated lands of the Southeast as the result of President Andrew Jackson's policy of forced Indian removal. The final circumstance was the massive displacement of enslaved blacks, the largest forced migration of people in the nation's history. These conditions form the backdrop to the story of Andrew Hynes; they are some of the factors that occasioned his economic prosperity and subsequent rise to prominence.

Andrew Hynes was a veteran of the War of 1812 and a public official in his adopted state of Tennessee. He was also a land speculator and slave trader, and he engaged in economic ventures that took him far beyond his Nashville base, as he and his associates sought lucrative opportunities in the newly opened lands of the Deep South. Hynes became one of the largest sugar planters in Louisiana; the maritime shipment of slaves, food stores, building materials, and manufactured goods was critical to the creation and maintenance of his substantial personal empire.

His story began like those of so many young white men "on the make" at the beginning of the nineteenth century. He was the younger son of a moderately prosperous family, born in 1785 in Bardstown, Kentucky, where his parents had settled after migrating west from Maryland. By 1808, at the age of twenty-three, Andrew Hynes was already a small-scale slave trader; in that year he purchased a boy named Louis for $425. The bill of sale was witnessed by Andrew's father, Thomas, and the seller, one Armstead Hubbard, receipted for money "in hand paid."[3] This phrase might indicate that the transaction was settled with cash, which would suggest that Hynes, perhaps with some financial aid from his father, was already a man of some means. But despite his apparently comfortable circumstances and a job as postal clerk at Bardstown, Hynes decided to emigrate from Kentucky and make his home in Nashville.

Hynes's slave-trading activities increased as he became more invested in the business affairs of Joseph Erwin, a Nashville merchant. When Hynes married Erwin's daughter Nancy in 1817 he became an even closer associate of the merchant, now his father-in-law, and assumed greater responsibility for land sales and other transactions. In addition, Hynes became more directly involved with the operations at "Home," the sugar plantation owned by Erwin at Plaquemine (in Iberville Parish), Louisiana. The U.S. census of 1820 records that the Hynes's Tennessee household included seven enslaved young people: two boys and four girls under the age of fourteen and a female between the ages of fourteen and twenty-five. As these young slaves are unnamed in the census, only enumerated by gender and age group, it is difficult to trace their movements. Hynes may have intended them to labor in Nashville temporarily while awaiting transport south to Plaquemine and the Erwin plantation. A document from the following year, 1821, confirms that Hynes had by this time been granted the authority to make slave purchases on Erwin's behalf for eventual shipment to Home.[4] Slaves shipped from Nashville, on the Cumberland River, would have had a direct trip west to the Mississippi River town of Cairo, Illinois, and from Cairo south to Plaquemine. Cairo was indeed well situated, at the point of convergence of two of the West's greatest rivers, the Mississippi and the Ohio.

Upon the death of Joseph Erwin in 1829, Andrew Hynes inherited an interest in Home plantation, and it was this circumstance that transformed him into a large-scale planter. He began to divide his time between Nashville and Plaquemine, Louisiana, the better to regulate his business affairs and settle the estate of his late father-in-law. Home plantation was located on the west bank of the Mississippi—just south of Baton Rouge—and some miles upriver from the port of New Orleans. The sugar production operations at Home were dependent on the commodities supplied by riverboats—and not just those traveling along the Mississippi. The riverine system allowed the efficient movement of goods up the Mississippi, then east up the Ohio River to Cincinnati and even as far as Wheeling and Pittsburgh, then back again downriver to the port of New Orleans.

It is difficult to imagine the Home plantation as a successful enterprise without steamers, for goods and people moved at a regular, steady pace, as the records kept by Lavinia Erwin—Hynes's mother-in-law and the widow of Joseph Erwin—demonstrate. During the early months of 1831 the accounting records of Lavinia Erwin include several trips by Hynes on the steamboat *Pacific* between Nashville, the Home estate, and New Orleans. These records also include freight transport of a headstone for the grave of Joseph Erwin, deck passage for the stonemason brought in to set the headstone in place, and also deck passage for three slaves whom Hynes purchased for $750 from his mother-in-law: a twenty-year-old man named John, a woman of thirty-five named Sucky Todd, and her child Lethe.[5]

Service by a particular riverboat might be disrupted for a variety of reasons, including delays due to inclement weather and low water. But other problems came up as well, as happened when in May 1833 Hynes wrote from Clarksville (near Nashville) to a business associate to explain why three wagons and a cotton-spinning machine Hynes had shipped from Nashville on the steamboat *Cotton Plant* had not arrived at Plaquemine. Acknowledging that a full month had passed, Hynes reported that the steamer had "lost nine persons with the cholera, all the hands abandoned her, and it has been impossible to get hands ever since, and I hardly know now if we can get her off." Disease that traveled via steamers was a major cause of concern. Hynes ended his letter with the news that "some scattering cases of cholera continues [sic] at Nashville."[6]

There were other problems that caused delays as well, and an intriguing example occurred in August 1838, when the brokers Yeatman & Company informed Hynes that the "steamboat *Servant* positively refused to take or land freight at your plantation." The firm offered no explanation, but if the dispute could not be amicably resolved, Hynes and his business associates would have had plenty of alternative transport options. There were literally scores of steamers plying the southern interior during this period. Steamboat construction and operation grew at a tremendous rate, reaching a high point of activity during the 1850s, after which it began to decline.[7]

Some of the details of the personal and business interests of Andrew Hynes offer glimpses into the world of the transplanted slaves, who, having endured the pain of forced separation from loved ones, were compelled to rebuild broken relationships and forge new extended family connections under radically different circumstances. One such view is provided by the story of ten-year-old Edmund, for whom Sally Hamilton (of Logan County, Kentucky) sought a buyer because she was strapped for cash. Through an agent Hamilton stipulated in a letter that she desired to sell Edmund locally, as his parents lived in Nashville and she had no wish to separate him from them. Left unsaid but nevertheless understood was that Hamilton would proceed with the sale whether or not a local buyer could be found for Edmund. Hynes purchased the child for $250 in July 1829. In the census of 1830 his household included seven male slaves between the ages of ten and twenty-three;[8] it is unclear whether young Edmund was among them or whether he had been sent away from his parents after all and loaded onto a southbound steamer to Home at Plaquemine.

Close inquiry into the slave-trading activities of Hynes also reveals the experiences of Maria, whom as a thirteen-year-old Hynes had purchased (with two other children) and presented as a gift to his eldest daughter, Lavinia.[9] Upon her marriage to Edward Gay of St. Louis in 1840, Lavinia prepared to move to St. Louis and made arrangements to take Maria with her. As Lavinia dealt with her own emotions at her imminent departure, she wrote her father that Maria was "at first a good deal distressed" at the prospect of leaving Nashville. Lavinia considered the matter closed as she further observed to her father that "she will I expect get over it."[10] The historian may yearn for direct evidence from Maria herself about what she felt at a moment such as this. But certainly one can surmise how profound her sense of loss must have been, for Maria had already experienced at least one separation, having as a young teenager (very likely) been sold away from her parents when Hynes purchased her in 1829. It is interesting to observe that Lavinia, while exploring her own feelings as she prepared to depart Nashville and begin life as a married woman, was incapable of conceiving that Maria might be experiencing similar emotions when faced with the move away from friends and loved ones. One might be tempted to speculate that Maria was consoled by the thought that the river that carried her north to St. Louis and away from home might just as easily convey her back again, if the woman who controlled her life and prospects could be persuaded to allow her the privilege. Or perhaps Maria might have considered a more desperate option, in flight, a try for the freedom that the river had offered to others before her. But the Hynes records provide no hint of her fate.

When Andrew Hynes died in 1849 he owned 223 slaves and one of the largest sugar plantations in Iberville Parish. The business continued to prosper under the management of Hynes's son-in-law Edward Gay. With the coming of the Civil War, Gay moved his family from St. Louis to Home, which became the permanent residence. Gay continued to direct his business affairs as best he could during the war years. When Union threats to seize his property or naval activity on the Mississippi became too intense, Gay negotiated a "safeguard" for himself and his family with the authority of the Union army's Department of the Gulf.

One might note the irony in the observation that the very waters that fostered economic success in the Mississippi River valley during peacetime became with the coming of war a liability. The mighty river bore the gunboats of the Union navy and thereby delivered the means of destruction of the South's slaveholding empire.

NOTES 1 Quotation from conference description, "Beyond Sweetness: New Histories of Sugar in the Early Atlantic World," 24–27 October 2013, available at blogs.brown.edu/sugarandbeyond/. The sugar merchants at Kingston, Jamaica, for example, presented a gift of silver to Vice Adm. Sir John Thomas Duckworth, commander in chief at Jamaica, the principal British West Indian naval station.

2 Aaron Fogelman, "Women on the Trail in Colonial America: A Travel Journal of German Moravians Migrating from Pennsylvania to North Carolina in 1766," *Pennsylvania History* 61 (1994), pp. 206–234; quote in Robert Gudmestad, *Steamboats and the Rise of the Cotton Kingdom* (Baton Rouge: Louisiana State Univ. Press, 2011), p. 56. See also Walter Johnson, *River of Dark Dreams: Slavery and Empire in the Cotton Kingdom* (Cambridge, Mass.: Belknap of Harvard Univ. Press, 2013).

3 Bill of sale dated 26 February 1808 for Louis, F. C. Brown Slavery Collection [hereafter Brown Collection], box 1, folder 1, Princeton University Archives, Princeton, N.J. [hereafter PUA].

4 1820 U.S. Federal Census, Nashville, Davidson County, Tennessee; bill of sale dated 10 February 1821 for Edmund, Brown Collection, box 1, folder 2, PUA.

5 Business accounts, 1828–1831, box 3, series I, Edward Gay and Family Papers, Mss. 1295, Louisiana and Lower Mississippi Valley Collections, Louisiana State University Libraries, Baton Rouge, La. [hereafter Gay Family Papers]; bill of sale dated 7 May 1831 for Sucky Todd and her child, Brown Collection, box 1, folder 4, PUA.

6 Andrew Hynes to John B. Craighead, 2 May 1833, Gay Family Papers.

7 Gudmestad, *Steamboats and the Rise of the Cotton Kingdom,* p. 24, table 1; accounting note from Yeatman & Company, 22 August 1838, Gay Family Papers.

8 Sally Hamilton to Loflin & Wilson, 20 July 1829, and bill of sale dated 30 July 1829 for Edmund, Brown Collection, box 1, folder 4, PUA; 1830 U.S. Federal Census, Nashville, Davidson County, Tennessee.

9 Bill of sale dated 6 August 1829, Brown Collection, box 1, folder 4, PUA. A notation on the document reads, "Maria given to Lavinia and the others sold."

10 Lavinia Hynes Gay to Andrew Hynes, 19 July 1841, Hynes Family Papers, 1804–1870, Tennessee State Library and Archives, Nashville, Tenn.

XII Tinclads, Torpedoes, and Levees
Using Environmental History to Understand the Civil War's Western Theater

ROBERT GUDMESTAD

There has been a recent spurt of books concerning the Civil War's naval conflict; Craig Symonds and James McPherson have recently published monographs that cover the war on the waters, while Myron Smith, Jr., has examined the Yazoo River campaign. These studies, along with earlier examinations of the navy's role in the Civil War, have done much to advance our understanding of the importance of Civil War gunboats for the fighting in the western theater and, by extension, the war itself. Symonds's work, for instance, situates Union and Confederate navies within the context of nineteenth-century technological developments and draws on a historiographical tradition that examines Civil War technology.[1]

Simultaneously, a number of Civil War scholars have used environmental history as an organizing principle. Lisa Brady's book on Union war strategy and its consequences for the landscape is an excellent example of how environmental history can bring a fresh perspective to a well-worn subject. But Brady's book concentrates on Union armies and has relatively little to say about Civil War navies. This paper hopes to sketch out what a combination of the more traditional technological history and the environmental upstart would look like in the context of the struggle to control the western waters. Because of space constraints, I will focus on Union activities and strategy and only obliquely mention the Confederacy. Moreover, I will use the terms *nature* and *environment* interchangeably and follow Brady's definition of the former: "the physical environment and the nonhuman elements—animate and inanimate—that it comprises."[2]

The origins of the Union's strategy in the West are murky, but one starting point is James B. Eads's 22 April 1861 letter to Secretary of the Navy Gideon Welles. Eads, who had made his fortune salvaging steamboats, recommended that the Union regulate access to the Mississippi, Ohio, Tennessee, and Cumberland Rivers. He argued that this strategy would cut off food to the South and bring the Confederacy to its knees in six months. A few weeks later, Winfield Scott gave specific recommendations on how to implement Eads's idea when he ordered George B. McClellan to prepare for "a powerful movement down the Mississippi to the ocean" in conjunction with a coastal blockade. Scott estimated that the army would need anywhere from twelve to twenty "steam gun-boats" and sixty thousand troops to do the job. As the Union force proceeded downriver, it would establish forts that would guard its supply line and keep the river open. The ideas of Eads and Scott would eventually constitute one of the guiding principles for the war in the West: deny the Confederacy the bounty of nature. To do so, the Union army needed a sudden infusion of technology.[3]

Naval Constructor John Lenthall, the man initially responsible for figuring out how to build those "steam gun-boats," was skeptical that recent advances in naval technology could be adapted to the western waters' environmental constraints. Steam propulsion, rifled ordnance, shell guns, metal armor, and the screw propeller had become cutting-edge advances for the world's navies in the mid-nineteenth century but were better suited for blue-water navies than freshwater forces. Lenthall gloomily concluded that "it does not seem very practicable to make an armed steam vessel for the Mississippi that will be very efficient." He predicted that thick armor plating would make a gunboat too heavy to operate in shallow water. Instead, Lenthall proposed a fleet of small, unarmored gunboats—what he called "batteau" (i.e., bateaux)—that would carry four eight-inch guns. While such craft would certainly float, they would not float for very long; shell guns fired projectiles that would have shredded Lenthall's batteau.[4]

But if Lenthall's plans seemed stillborn, the Union was desperate to get boats—any boats—in the water. The army, acting more from motives of urgency than careful planning, bought three commercial steamboats, slathered them with oaken planks, and turned them into floating stockades. These "timberclads," as they became known, were vulnerable and of limited value. The army bought five other steamboats and bolted iron plates onto jury-rigged casemates. Three of the latter boats incorporated a curious feature, a backing of gutta-percha behind their casemate armor. Presumably the inch-thick "India rubber" was meant to give the armor a bit of spring, the more easily to deflect cannon balls, but the innovation rotted in the South's humid environment. In other respects, the converted ironclads performed reasonably well, but they were huge targets and could barely steam upstream.[5]

It was at this point that institutional confusion and interservice infighting achieved tangible benefits for the Union war effort. The Mississippi Squadron was the bastard child of a contentious relationship between the army and navy: while the navy constructed and commanded the vessels, the army outfitted and paid for them. This arrangement caused vexatious problems but did have the serendipitous result of involving the army's quartermaster general, Montgomery Meigs. When Meigs saw Lenthall's batteau recommendation—he had to pay for it, after all—he insisted that at least one or two of the vessels be plated with armor. Meigs also took

Lenthall's suggestion to bring Samuel Pook, a naval constructor, into the process. Pook drafted plans for the ironclads that eventually became the City-class vessels.[6]

Designed to pound Confederate forts into oblivion, the City-class boats became the backbone of the Mississippi Squadron. Each of the seven ironclads had 122 tons of armor plating, which protected the casemate, pilothouse, and wheelhouse. One boat was equivalent to a land-based artillery battery, and the combined fire of five or six of them could be massive. For all their power, though, the City-class ironclads had difficulty with important features of the western environment. Among the tremendous advantages enjoyed by Confederate emplacements on high ground, such as Fort Donelson and Vicksburg, was that the tops of the ironclads were not armored, making them vulnerable to plunging fire.[7] More troubling, the fluctuating water levels of the western waters were a challenge. One Union sailor later remembered that water levels on the Mississippi River could drop as much as fifteen feet from their highest stage. The City-class boats' draft was about five feet, even after the builder lightened them by reducing the cannon from twenty to sixteen. A five-foot draft was acceptable when water levels were high, but the dry season in late summer—a crucial time for military action—severely limited the gunboats' range.[8]

The peculiar geography of the lower Mississippi River also affected other Union activities. Rear Adm. David Farragut is well known for capturing New Orleans, an accomplishment that owes as much to the Confederacy's poor preparedness as it does to Farragut's audacity. The inadequacy of New Orleans's defenses more than offset the inappropriateness of Farragut's ships, which were oceangoing vessels with deep keels. Farragut complied with orders to send some of his fleet upriver past Baton Rouge. But privately, Farragut was keenly aware that his vessels were not ideally suited to operations on the inland rivers, that he had the wrong technology to cope with the unfamiliar conditions of the lower Mississippi. In an 1862 letter to a fellow officer he complained that "I am now up the Mississippi again, and when I will go down God only knows. It appears that the Department is under the impression that it is easier for me, with my dilapidated vessels, to encounter the difficulties of the Mississippi and ascend a thousand miles against a strong current than it is for [Andrew Hull] Foote or [Charles H.] Davis, with vessels peculiarly constructed for the river, to come down the stream, and therefore I am compelled to do it, at what sacrifice time will show."[9]

Farragut's essential premise—that shallow-draft ironclads were uniquely suited to carry the war to the Confederacy on the inland rivers—was absolutely correct. Union military planners pushed the City class into situations that seemed to defy the laws of physics. During the expedition into Steele's Bayou in March 1863 (an effort to outflank Vicksburg), Acting Rear Adm. David D. Porter took five ironclads into Black Bayou. The crews had to pull up trees, knock down others, and cut away branches. "It was terrible work," Porter explained, but he gloated that the boats' presence shocked Southerners who thought the environment protected them from military incursions. "Never did those people expect to see ironclads floating where the keel of a flat boat never passed," he chuckled.[10]

Even while the ironclads were pushing the frontier of war, the navy improvised a new class of gunboats that could take the place of the blue-water vessels on the lower river and also make more Southern civilians experience Northern military power. The swarm of new boats—the Union eventually converted seventy-four commercial riverboats—were lightly armored, with boiler plates an inch thick riveted to the fronts of their casemates and around the engines. These "tinclads" drew about thirty inches of water and carried six to eight light cannon; they were the Union high command's response to low water levels and the necessity to exert military power all across the western river system. As one historian has noted, light-draft Union gunboats were like Viking ships—they could appear anywhere, anytime, causing panic among civilians.[11]

The tinclads were necessary to "suppress the active guerrilla movements on the Ohio and Tennessee Rivers," as Rear Adm. Charles H. Davis put it. The tinclads' construction coincided with the turn from a Union strategy that shielded civilians from military depredations to a "hard war" against Southerners, whether or not in uniform. As Porter explained to Maj. Gen. William T. Sherman, the man most closely associated with the hard-war doctrine, the tinclads would "carry the war into the heart of the country." Tinclads were part of a nasty little conflict where Southern partisans sniped at Union boats and captured sailors who ventured out on foraging expeditions. Southern attacks became so brazen that Porter authorized each tinclad commander to "fire back with spirit, and to destroy everything in that neighborhood within reach of his guns." And fire back they did. Sailors in the Mississippi Squadron became notorious for not only shooting at Southern civilians with particular zeal but also plundering "wealthy plantation[s] and carry[ing] off everything of value, from the piano to the tea urn."[12]

The Mississippi Squadron complemented the activities of the Union land forces. Lisa Brady has argued that Ulysses S. Grant's Army of the Tennessee tried to exert control over the environment during its campaign to take Vicksburg. Grant used a number of strategies, including a failed plan to reroute the Mississippi River and a successful series of raids against the region's agricultural productivity. She is correct, but Union naval strategy was more than just controlling the land or turning it back into a wilderness. With the fall of Vicksburg and Port Hudson, the Union navy in particular tried to detach the Confederate war effort from the fruits of the land. The constant patrolling of tinclads along the western waters limited the Confederacy's ability to use produce from Arkansas, Louisiana, and Texas to feed its armies in the eastern and western theaters. Once the Union ran its gunboats past

Vicksburg—and before the city's surrender—Confederate general John C. Pemberton concluded that "I regard the navigation of the Mississippi River as shut out from us now. No more supplies can be gotten from the trans-Mississippi department."[13]

Even before Pemberton wrote his glum words, the Union navy was tightening the noose around the Confederacy. Porter's General Order No. 21 explicitly outlined the Union strategy to deny the Confederacy the fruits of the land. It directed commanders of all Porter's vessels to prevent any unauthorized commerce and "break up the carrying of anything into rebel ports." Suddenly cotton, clothing, food, shoes, salt, saddles, medicines, and munitions were contraband. Union boats were, in the words of one Union commander, "constantly scouring the river," looking for scofflaws. The Mississippi Squadron seized wheat, lard, whiskey, and meat, captured herds of cattle, encouraged slaves to run away, and generally delighted in tormenting Southern civilians. The crew of USS *Benton* reveled in "throw[ing] some shells" above a herd of cattle and frightening the poor beasts, which, presumably, were intended to be converted into Confederate calories. Union gunboats contributed to the shortage of supplies and low morale in Southern armies in the last two years of the war.[14]

The Union effort to control access to the western rivers provoked a strong response from Southern guerrillas, who used the levees as cover. This pursuit of asymmetrical warfare was appropriate for an undermanned and underequipped belligerent against a better-armed and more numerous foe. Particularly along the lower Mississippi River, partisans built gun platforms for artillery, slicing embrasures in the levees and covering the openings with boards. Sharpshooters nearby either stood on the levee or perched in trees. When Union vessels or merchant ships steamed by, hidden gunners dropped the boards and started shooting. It seemed as if the very landscape, man-made in this case, came alive. The commander of USS *Sciota* described levees as "strong, safe, and ready-made breastwork[s] for sharpshooters." The commander of another noted, "We are constantly now under fire of the covert kind as we pass up and down the river." When USS *Kineo* came under fire near Donaldsonville, Louisiana, its commander swung the boat around and ordered "shrapnel and grape" against the ambushers. The cannonade succeeded only in driving off the attackers, who hauled away their four artillery pieces in a mad dash that exposed above the top of the levee "nothing except the tips of horses' ears running away." The Union navy was engaged in a deadly game of Whack-A-Mole: Confederate guerrillas would pop up from behind the levee, and the sailors would try, usually in vain, to smite them. When water levels were particularly low, the Union boats were at an even greater disadvantage: twenty feet below the levee's crest, they could not angle their guns upward to meet the threat.[15]

But if the levees could be effective shelters for the Confederates, they were imperfect ones. Union commanders turned the levees—or more precisely, the waters the levees held back—into a weapon against guerrillas and troublesome civilians. For instance, guerrillas congregated near Greenville, Mississippi, because steamboats were easy targets when they slowed down while navigating the Mississippi River's four S-turns just above the town. Their attacks became such a nuisance that Porter ordered USS *Tyler* to go to the town and "cut the levee, so that the whole country may be overflowed." In March 1862, Capt. Thomas Selfridge of USS *Conestoga* steamed to Bolivar, Mississippi, and cut fifty feet of the levee. His purpose: "drown out Mrs. Monley and Old Topp." While the identities of Monley and Topp are unclear, it is obvious that Selfridge was delighted to hear that the water was "pouring through [the opening] very rapidly." The purpose in these and other cases was to restore the landscape to its condition prior to the levee system. The rushing waters would wash away any fields, farms, or produce that stood behind the levees in comparative safety. By altering the landscape, Union sailors were turning nature against the Confederacy and converting the region into a swampy wilderness. Northern gunboats struck a powerful blow against the Southern agro-ecosystem— the new ecological system that humans create when they "draw sustenance or profit from nature through agriculture and animal husbandry." Southern planters had worked for years—or at least forced their slaves to work for years—to create a system that drew sustenance and wealth from the land. Union gunboats interrupted or destroyed this complex system and thereby sapped the Confederate ability to sustain war.[16]

The environmental aspects of the Civil War in the West can be discerned as well by looking below the surface of the water. Just as levees seemed to come alive and attack Union vessels, so did the water. Torpedoes, or what we call mines, were one of the Confederacy's more potent weapons. Southerners deployed the underwater weapon—or as Union sailors called it, the "infernal machine"—on an ad hoc basis. The torpedo used most often in the western waters was typically made from five-gallon glass demijohn bottles. Bomb makers filled the bottle with black powder, inserted a primer into the neck, attached waterproof copper wires to the primer, and then ran the wires to a pit on shore. Intrepid swimmers then anchored torpedoes below the opaque surface of the water. A volunteer would detonate the torpedo, usually as the prelude to an ambush.[17]

Torpedoes blended into the environment so well that Union commanders had to temper their aggressive strategy. Porter expressed their frustration when he wrote that the "torpedo lifting [removal, i.e., "minesweeping"] has been carried on under extreme difficulty and firing from the rebels." Torpedo hunting was particularly nerve-racking; Union sailors dragged the water and "scrape[d] the banks" with boat hooks and spars.[18] But the environment that hid torpedoes also threatened them. Fast-moving western rivers carried logs, debris, and other flotsam that could detonate the torpedoes or cut their wires or bring them to the surface. In any case, the Confederacy could not build enough torpedoes and deployed them too late in the war to impair the Northern war effort.[19]

The environment, then, was not simply a backdrop against which the war played out; it influenced the development and application of technology. Both sides recognized the importance of controlling the western rivers. Confederate leaders adopted the relatively passive strategy of building forts, placing obstacles in the rivers, and building large ironclads that proved virtually immobile. Union leaders employed technology in a more aggressive way that tilted the war in their favor. They built ironclads and tinclads that were suited to specific environmental conditions and then used them to neutralize the Confederacy's technology. Once the Union had fastened a fairly strong grip on the western waters, it made a concerted effort to separate Southern society from nature's bounty. Despite the efforts of guerrillas and torpedo makers, Union dominion over the environment eventually helped wear down the Confederate war effort.

NOTES 1 Craig L. Symonds, *The Civil War at Sea* (Santa Barbara, Calif.: Praeger, 2009); James M. McPherson, *War on the Waters: The Union and Confederate Navies, 1861–1865* (Chapel Hill: Univ. of North Carolina Press, 2012). Surprisingly, there is no single scholarly volume that examines Civil War technology. Most scholarly studies look at discrete technologies, particularly rifled muskets, railroads, and USS *Monitor* and CSS *Virginia*. The traditional sources on the Civil War's naval conflict waters are too numerous to mention here but will appear in subsequent notes.

2 See Lisa M. Brady, "The Future of Civil War Studies: Environmental Histories," *Journal of the Civil War Era* 2, no. 1 (March 2012), p. 8; idem, *War upon the Land: Military Strategy and the Transformation of Southern Landscapes during the American Civil War* (Athens: Univ. of Georgia Press, 2012), p. 12; Jack Temple Kirby, "The American Civil War: An Environmental View," in *Nature Transformed: The Environment in American History* (Research Triangle Park, N.C.: National Humanities Center, rev. 2001), nationalhumanitiescenter.org/; Theodore Steinberg, *Down to Earth: Nature's Role in American History* (New York: Oxford Univ. Press, 2002), pp. 89–98; Mark Fiege, "The Nature of Gettysburg: Environmental History and the Civil War," in *The Republic of Nature: An Environmental History of the United States*, ed. Brian Allen Drake (Seattle: Univ.

of Washington Press, 2012), pp. 199–227; Andrew McIlwaine Bell, *Mosquito Soldiers: Yellow Fever, Malaria, and the Course of the American Civil War* (Baton Rouge: Louisiana State Univ. Press, 2010); and Kathryn S. Meier, "'No Place for the Sick': Nature's War on Civil War Soldier Health in 1862 Virginia," *Journal of the Civil War Era* 1, no. 2 (June 2011), pp. 176–206.

3 James B. Eads to Gideon Welles, 22 April 1861, in *Official Records of the Union and Confederate Navies in the War of the Rebellion* (Washington, D.C.: 1894–1917) [hereafter ORN], ser. 1, vol. 22, pp. 278–79; Winfield Scott to George B. McClellan, 3 May 1861, in *The War of the Rebellion: A Compilation of the Official Records of the Union and Confederate Armies* (Washington, D.C.: 1880–1914), ser. 1, vol. 51, pp. 369–70 (quotation); Earl J. Hess, *The Civil War in the West: Victory and Defeat from the Appalachians to the Mississippi* (Chapel Hill: Univ. of North Carolina Press, 2012), pp. 1–11; Symonds, *Civil War at Sea*, pp. 89–91.

4 "Memorandum for General Totten by Mr. Lenthall, June 1, 1861," in *The War of the Rebellion*, ser. 3, vol. 2, pp. 814–15; Symonds, *Civil War at Sea*, pp. 6–10; James Phinney Baxter, *The Introduction of the Ironclad Warship* (Hamden, Conn.: Archon Books, 1968), p. 3; John D. Milligan, "From Theory to Application: The Emergence of the American Ironclad War Vessel," *Military Affairs* 48 (July 1984), p. 126.

The name "Mississippi Squadron" did not become official until 1 October 1862; see Gary D. Joiner, *Mr. Lincoln's Brown Water Navy: The Mississippi Squadron* (Lanham, Md.: Rowman & Littlefield, 2007), p. 90.

5 John D. Milligan, *Gunboats down the Mississippi* (Annapolis, Md.: Naval Institute Press, 1965), pp. 5–7, 31; Joiner, *Mr. Lincoln's Brown Water Navy*, pp. 21–23; McPherson, *War on the Waters*, pp. 70–71; Report of David D. Porter, 16 February 1864, in *ORN*, ser. 1, vol. 25, p. 760; Donald L. Canney, *The Old Steam Navy*, vol. 2, *The Ironclads, 1842–1885* (Annapolis, Md.: Naval Institute Press, 1993), pp. 38–45. For a more charitable interpretation of the timberclads' role in the war, see Myron J. Smith, Jr., *The Timberclads in the Civil War: The* Lexington, Conestoga, *and* Tyler *on the Western Waters* (Jefferson, N.C.: McFarland, 2008). The converted ironclads were *Essex, Benton, Eastport, Choctaw,* and *Lafayette.*

6 Canney, *Ironclads*, pp. 47–48. For a good introduction to Meigs's life, see David W. Miller, *Second Only to Grant: Quartermaster Montgomery C. Meigs* (Shippensburg, Pa.: White Mane, 2000).

7 Milligan, *Gunboats down the Mississippi*, pp. 24, 29–30; Milligan, "From Theory to Application," pp. 126–27; Joiner, *Mr. Lincoln's Brown Water Navy*, pp. 25–29; Edwin C. Bearss, *Hardluck Ironclad: The Sinking and Salvage of the* Cairo (Baton Rouge: Louisiana State Univ. Press), pp. 13–15; Earl J. Hess, "Northern Response to the Ironclad: A Prospect for the Study of Military Technology," *Civil War History* 31, no. 2 (June 1985), p. 135. The City-class vessels were *Cairo, Carondelet, Cincinnati, Louisville, Mound City, Pittsburgh,* and *St. Louis* (renamed *Baron de Kalb*).

8 E. J. Huling, *Reminiscences of Gunboat Life in the Mississippi Squadron* (Saratoga Springs, N.Y.: printed for private circulation, 1881), pp. 10–11; Bearss, *Hardluck Ironclad*, pp. 29–31.

9 "Letter from Flag-Officer Farragut, U.S. Navy, to Captain Bailey, U.S. Navy, regarding Affairs in the Mississippi River," 11 June 1862, in *ORN*, ser. 1, vol. 18, p. 551; McPherson, *War on the Waters*, pp. 50–69. For more on Farragut, see Chester C. Hearns, *Admiral David Glasgow Farragut: The Civil War Years* (Annapolis, Md.: Naval Institute Press, 1998).

10 "Joint Expedition to Steele's Bayou, Miss.: Detailed Report of Acting Rear-Admiral [David D.] Porter," 26 March 1863, in *ORN*, ser. 1, vol. 24, pp. 474, 477.

11 Michael J. Bennett, *Union Jacks: Yankee Sailors in the Civil War* (Chapel Hill: Univ. of North Carolina Press, 2004), pp. 87–90. For an overview of the tinclads, see Myron J. Smith, Jr., *Tinclads in the Civil War: Union Light-Draught Gunboat Operations on Western Waters, 1862–1865* (Jefferson, N.C.: McFarland, 2010).

12 Charles H. Davis to Gideon Welles, 19 August 1862, in *ORN*, ser. 1, vol. 23, p. 305 (first quotation); David D. Porter to Andrew H. Foote, 6 November 1862, in *ORN*, ser. 1, vol. 23, p. 466; David D. Porter to William T. Sherman, 24 November 1861, in *ORN*, ser. 1, vol. 23, p. 500 (second quotation); "General Order of Acting Rear-Admiral Porter, U.S. Navy," 18 October 1862, in *ORN*, ser. 1, vol. 23, p. 421 (third quotation);

Gideon Welles to David D. Porter, 11 January 1864, in *ORN*, ser. 1, vol. 25, p. 682 (final quotation). For more on guerrilla warfare, see Daniel E. Sutherland, *A Savage Conflict: The Decisive Role of Guerrillas in the American Civil War* (Chapel Hill: Univ. of North Carolina Press, 2009), esp. pp. 147–51; Mark Grimsley, *The Hard Hand of War: Union Military Policy toward Southern Civilians, 1861–1865* (New York: Cambridge Univ. Press, 1995); and Hess, *Civil War in the West*, pp. 199–202.

13 Brady, *War upon the Land*, pp. 24–71; John C. Pemberton to Brig. Gen. James Chalmers, 18 April 1863, in *ORN*, ser. 1, vol. 24, p. 717.

14 "General Order of Acting Rear-Admiral Porter, U.S. Navy," 2 December 1862, in *ORN*, ser. 1, vol. 23, p. 528 (first quotation); "Extract from Diary of Lieutenant Roe, U.S. Navy," 24 October 1862, in *ORN*, ser. 1, vol. 19, p. 775 (second quotation); "Order of Acting Rear-Admiral Porter," 3 June 1863, in *ORN*, ser. 1, vol. 25, pp. 58–59 (final quotation); "Report of Lieutenant-Commander Fitch, U.S. Navy," 4 December 1862, in *ORN*, ser. 1, vol. 23, pp. 530–31; "Joint Expedition to Steele's Bayou, Miss.," pp. 474–78; John D. Milligan, ed., *From the Fresh-Water Navy: 1861–64; The Letters of Acting Master's Mate Henry R. Browne and Acting Ensign Symmes E. Brown* (Annapolis, Md.: Naval Institute Press, 1970), pp. 145, 235, 245; Stephen E. Woodworth, *Decision in the Heartland: The Civil War in the West* (Westport, Conn.: Praeger, 2008), pp. 66–67. Tinclads became very closely associated with "confiscating" cotton and plundering Southern civilians; the captain of USS *Rattler* even tried to sell his boat, for $250,000 and a hundred bales of cotton; Bennett, *Union Jacks*, p. 97; Smith, *Tinclads*, pp. 263–65.

15 R. B. Lowry to D. G. Farragut, 4 October 1862, in *ORN*, ser. 1, vol. 19, pp. 250–51 (first quotation); "Extract from Diary of Lieutenant Roe, U.S. Navy," p. 776 (second quotation); Lt. Cdr. George M. Ransom to David G. Farragut, 23 October 1862, in *ORN*, ser. 1, vol. 19, p. 314 (remaining quotations); F. A. Roe to D. G. Farragut, 29 September 1892, in *ORN*, ser. 1, vol. 19, p. 215.

16 Rear Adm. D. D. Porter to Lieutenant Prichett, 26 January 1863, in *ORN*, ser. 1, vol. 24, p. 198 (first quotation); Capt. Thomas Selfridge to Lieutenant Bishop, 12 March 1862, in *ORN*, ser. 1, vol. 24, p. 468 (second quotation); report of Lieutenant Commander Selfridge, 14 March 1863, in *ORN*, ser. 1, vol. 24, p. 472 (third quotation); report of Lieutenant Commander Selfridge, 4 April 1863, in *ORN*, ser. 1, vol. 24, pp. 527–28; Brady, *War upon the Land*, pp. 10 (final quotation), 97–98.

17 Timothy S. Wolters, "Electric Torpedoes in the Confederacy: Reconciling Conflicting Histories," *Journal of Military History* 72, no. 3 (July 2008), p. 775; Bearss, *Hardluck Ironclad*, p. 97; Raimondo Luraghi, *A History of the Confederate Navy* (Annapolis, Md.: Naval Institute Press, 1996), pp. 234–49.

18 Report of Charles Rivers Ellet, 3 January 1863, in *ORN*, ser. 1, vol. 23, pp. 593–94.

19 Milton F. Perry, *Infernal Machines: The Story of Confederate Submarine* (Baton Rouge: Louisiana State Univ. Press, 1965), pp. 4, 45–46.

XIII Technical Human Capital and Retention in the U.S. Navy during the Second Industrial Revolution

DARRELL J. GLASER and AHMED S. RAHMAN

A cross nearly all industries, firms worry about retaining their most skilled workers. As technological progress becomes increasingly more skill intensive, retention grows ever more critical. To keep pace, companies provide their labor forces with requisite training and experience or else potentially suffer the exodus of their quality workers. While "skill biased" technological change, skill upgrading, and retention are often associated with twentieth- and twenty-first-century labor markets, their origins are to be found in the nineteenth century.[1] This paper adds to the body of empirical research by economists on job skills and turnover by focusing on the job retention of a particular group of skilled workers—U.S. naval officers during the Second Industrial Revolution. This group is an apt one to explore, for the concerns over human-capital retention of the U.S. Navy of the late nineteenth century were quite similar to those of private firms today.

Using data on naval officers' careers, we study the accumulation of technical human capital and its impact on worker separations from the Navy. All U.S. naval officers during this era graduated from the Naval Academy in Annapolis, Maryland. Using archival material housed at the Naval Academy we track entire careers in order to construct measures both of initial levels of human capital and of human capital accumulated over time. Our principal results indicate that officers with more technical job experience separated from the Navy at rates that are economically and statistically significant. Officers with more Navy-specific human capital, however, were less likely to separate.

Background

David M. Blank and George J. Stigler, along with Michael Edelstein, analyze how formal technical training arose in response to the need for a labor force that could master complex technologies and manage production during the Second Industrial Revolution.[2] Like many private manufacturers, the Navy needed technologically advanced workers and managers who understood metallurgy, chemistry, and the applied sciences. In spite of the growing need from industry for and commitment by institutions of higher learning to technical education, Blank and Stigler estimate, of the approximately 4 percent of the population that by 1900 was enrolled in college a mere 3.3 percent earned engineering degrees.[3] This demand from private industry and the lack of suitable output from colleges gave graduates of the Naval Academy excellent potential for manufacturing and managerial jobs in the private sector.

Advances in naval technology coincided with economy-wide advances in manufacturing, chemicals, and electricity.[4] This confluence enabled officers to understand the processes behind nationwide industrial growth. Beyond the rudimentary understanding of new technologies, naval officers also developed skills useful as liaisons to manufacturing. This included work in iron and steel foundries, the building of ships, management of supply chains, lighthouse inspection, and general bureaucracy. Their skills in diplomacy and negotiation, mathematics, chemistry, electricity, telecommunications, and numerous other fundamentals would be useful to firms in the private sector. Much of this capability is what economists refer to as "general human capital," by implication skills that were transferable to jobs outside the Navy. Officers could take their human capital elsewhere at any time, and conceivably they would be motivated to do so if their naval pay did not keep pace with external wage growth. Of course, many officers may have viewed patriotism as a strong payoff for military service. But for the right price, outside options would have existed, especially if the Navy would not compensate individuals appropriately with respect to their skill levels.

Prior to the turn of the century, line officers (that is, "seaman officers" eligible for command at sea) and engineers often spent years without promotions. Although the very best officers could find themselves on career fast tracks, the bulk of them remained stuck in an ill-conceived system in which promotion partly depended on class rank at graduation from Annapolis and was heavily weighted by seniority.[5] With no system to clear out personnel periodically, morale sank. Not until President William H. Taft's administration did the Navy begin to alleviate the problem and improve processes for promotion and the separation of "deadwood." At the same time, an excess supply of officers competed for a limited number of positions at sea. This imbalance also affected pay, since serving at sea was the only means by which officers might receive a (modest) bump in wages. Indeed, the best way for a young officer or engineer to increase earnings was often not through a promotion-based pay bump but to exit the Navy and enter the private labor market.

Data

To conduct our statistical analysis of officer job retention, we compiled data on naval officer careers from records stored in the historical archives of the Naval Academy library. Among those archival materials is the *Navy Register,* which, published annually, contains data on job assignments, ranks, and stations of officers. We used this information to construct measures of human capital. We also had information about each officer's time at the Naval Academy, information that provides us a standardized measure of academic ability.

Summary statistics of accumulated human capital appear in table 1 below. Each column reports means and standard deviations of each statistic, conditional on the number of years that an officer served. For example, officers with ten years of experience had an average of 0.63 years of technical experience. Add another five years in the fleet, and the average officer would have served 1.32 years in a "technical" position. The standard deviations are also relatively large, which indicates how wide a variation in technical experience is exhibited in the sample of officers.

Also of note, the distribution of Academy "order of merit" (the relative ranking of academic ability) among remaining officers does not change as each cohort ages. The distribution of raw academic ability does not change over the length of careers. In other words, the best students at Annapolis are no more or less likely than their classmates to stay in the Navy at any given point in time.

These simple statistics show several interesting and contrasting trends on the accumulation of human capital for naval personnel. First—all such observations hereafter refer to this historical sampling—the average officer serves one out of every five years on vessels in domestic waters, regardless of total time served. But other kinds of experiences vary dramatically with job tenure. These include time served on vessels in international waters, service in command, or service in technical jobs. Specifically, as officers progress in their careers they tend to serve less in international waters and more in positions of command. The proportion of engineers and constructors (both categories that are separate from line officers) tends to be constant across tenure.[6]

Technical jobs include assignments to a technically oriented bureau (e.g., the Bureau of Construction and Repair, Bureau of Ordnance, or Bureau of Steam), in shipyards (for the construction and maintenance of ships), in privately operated iron or steel foundries (to oversee steel production), as lighthouse inspectors, in jobs at the Naval Observatory, or to additional schooling at one of a handful of top universities in Europe or the United States. For the average officer, technical

Table 1
Sample Statistics (conditional on years served)

Variable	10 Years	15 Years	20 Years	25 Years
Experience in "technical jobs" average years (std. dev.)	0.63 (1.32)	1.32 (1.90)	2.22 (2.54)	2.93 (2.88)
Engineer or constructor % of total personnel (std. dev.)	0.16 (0.37)	0.13 (0.34)	0.14 (0.35)	0.13 (0.34)
Ship experience (domestic) average years (std. dev.)	1.85 (1.50)	2.82 (2.06)	3.81 (2.56)	4.70 (2.83)
Ship experience (international) average years (std. dev.)	4.29 (1.70)	5.78 (2.13)	7.14 (2.39)	8.91 (2.66)
Command experience average years (std. dev.)	0.06 (0.32)	0.13 (0.52)	0.24 (0.72)	0.43 (1.03)
Academy order of merit average (std. dev.)	0.52 (0.28)	0.53 (0.28)	0.54 (0.28)	0.53 (0.29)
# of observations	1,104	829	606	455

experience as a percentage of service time nearly doubles between the tenth and twentieth years of careers. At the same time, officers who choose to leave the Navy have half a year more of technical experience than the officers who stay. Over the years from 1891 until 1905, this result becomes even stronger. During this period, officers who leave the Navy average one more year of technical experience than those who stay.

We define the relative earnings for each officer, *i*, during year τ as the percentage difference

$$e_{i\tau} = \left[\frac{w_{i\tau} - w_\tau}{w_\tau}\right] \times 100.$$

Each individual *i*'s year-specific pay, $w_{i\tau}$, is constructed by combining information on his rank, years in rank, and type of job (sea, international shore, domestic shore, or awaiting orders) with annual pay tables published in the *Navy Register*. We use two alternative measures for w_τ, the first being average skilled wage from external labor markets during the year τ, drawing on historical wage statistics published by Clarence Long and by Albert Rees.[7] Rees draws from information originally published in Paul H. Douglas.[8] We use Douglas's estimates for the specific labor market of skilled unionized workers, foundry workers, and machinists. This covers the years from 1890 to 1905. The growth rates of wages in the Douglas data appear generally consistent with engineer wages in the late 1890s and early 1900s imputed by Blank and Stigler.[9]

For an earlier set of estimates, we turn to an earlier stretch of skilled-labor earnings data that spans the years from 1866 to 1890. These wage data originally appeared in an 1893 document known as the Aldrich report, compiled by the Labor Department for Senator Nelson W. Aldrich.[10] In particular, the Aldrich report summarized actual payroll data on over five thousand employees in thirteen manufacturing industries from 1860 to 1890. We focus on Long's summary of annual weighted averages from five skilled occupations (blacksmiths, carpenters, engineers, machinists, and painters);[11] these were compiled for firms located in the northeastern and mid-Atlantic states.[12] The time span covered by the Douglas data includes the early and middle careers of the most technologically educated graduates of the Naval Academy. The Aldrich data cover the early and middle careers of the less technologically educated officers who graduated prior to 1886.

Several historical factors affect measures of relative wages (earnings). First, the U.S. economy underwent a severe depression from 1873 to 1879, and wages in the external labor market generally declined. Since naval officer wages did not change during this time, the relative wages of officers rose. Less severe recessions hit in 1893 and 1896 as well, spiking the relative wage of officers again as the nineteenth century drew to a close. Figure 1 supplements this story with year-over-year earnings growth rates for each subset of data and displays the volatility

Annual Manufacturing Earnings Growth
1866–1905

Fig. 1
Changes in w_τ across time

of earnings in careers outside of the Navy.

Statistical Estimation and Results

To estimate the impacts of officer attributes on retention in the late-nineteenth-century Navy, we specify a statistical duration model. This type of statistical specification generates an estimate of the conditional probability of separation at any given point in a career. For example, we can ask about the conditional probability of an officer exiting the Navy in his tenth year of service, given that he has already served nine years and that five of those years were in technically intense positions. After controlling for a wide set of factors, including the wage earned by the officer, his time of service in the Navy, and his general ability, we can estimate which officer attributes impact the likelihood to exit. This method of estimation follows from work outlined extensively in J. D. Kalbfleisch and R. L. Prentice and further developed by James Heckman and B. Singer.[13]

The retention decision is defined by the conditional probability that an officer separates for a private-sector job during year $t + 1$ of his career, given that his career has lasted t years. During the postbellum period the Navy system did not systematically force officers from service (e.g., after nonselection for promotion) unless they were sixty-two years old or physically unable to perform. Most decisions about whether an officer stayed or left were thus one-sided ones—that is, made by officers themselves. The statistical specification estimates the log-likelihood function for N officers as follows:

$$\log L(\gamma, \beta) = \sum_{i=1}^{N} \left[\delta_i \log[1 - \exp\{-\exp[x_i(T_i)'\beta_x + \gamma(T_i)]\}] - \sum_{t=1}^{T_i - \delta_i} \exp[x_i(t)'\beta_x + \gamma(t)] \right].$$

The estimates discussed below follow from careers lasting at least six years.[14] Some careers in this data last as long as thirty-six years.[15] A step function controls for blocks of overall naval experience. The steps of this function follow five-year intervals [(6, 10), (11, 15), . . . (31, 35)]. In the log-likelihood function specified above, these "job tenure" steps follow from estimates for the Greek letter γ (gamma).

Other control variables include the percentage difference in wages between officers and aggregated measures of wages from the overall economy, cumulative experience at sea or in command, an indicator variable to designate stagnation within rank, an indicator variable capturing status as an engineer, cumulative experience in various types of technical jobs, and variables that control for an officer's physical constitution.

Table 2 includes estimates from the likelihood function on a subset of officers who had careers between 1871 and 1905. Earnings gaps for the years from 1871 to 1890 are based on the average wages of workers in skilled occupations, and results for this time frame appear in column 1.[16] For the years from 1890 to 1905, earning gaps are estimated from the average wage of skilled and unionized workers employed in foundries and machine shops.[17] Estimates of the likelihood function for this second time frame appear in column 2.

The odds ratios reported in table 2 reveal how the probability of job separation changes when the variable of interest changes by one unit. If the odds ratio exceeds 1, the variable has a positive impact on officer exits from the Navy. For example, over the period from 1890 to 1905, the odds ratio for technical job experience is 1.045. This implies that each additional year of job experience in a technical position increases the probability that an officer exits the Navy by 4.5 percent.[18] If the odds ratio is less than 1, then the variable has a negative impact on officer exits from the Navy. From 1871 to 1890, the odds ratio for technical experience is 0.997. This conversely indicates that each year of technical job experience decreases the probability that an officer exits the Navy by 0.3 percent.[19] Each reported p value indicates the probability of rejecting the null hypothesis when it is true. For table 2, the null hypothesis states that the regression coefficients equal zero. A small p value indicates strong evidence that the variable is statistically important. A large p value, by contrast, indicates that the control variable does not likely affect retention.[20] Given this, the only frame of time where technical job experience impacted job separations appears to have been from 1890 to 1905.

Exploring the results further, we can see that engineer training for both stretches of time increase the probability of separation (the hazard) by about 33 percent. Regardless of other training or experience, at any given point during their careers engineers were about 33 percent more likely to leave the Navy than other officers.

Results on overall job experience (tenure) support suggestions on a concave hazard elaborated by Henry S. Farber.[21] That is, the probability of job switching (the hazard) gradually increases over the early part of a career, but it also ultimately decreases from a peak. The conditional probability of leaving the Navy, based on the amount of time served, follows a concave (hill-shaped) form. This is most dramatic for the years from 1890 to 1905. Rather than appearing in the early part of a career, however, this concave hazard function underlines how late the search for a better job occurs for these officers (after at least twenty years in the Navy). One possible

Table 2
Separation Odds Ratios, 1871–1905

Variable	1871–1890	1890–1905
Technical job experience	0.997 (0.470)	1.045 (0.020)
Engineer or constructor	1.346 (0.068)	1.331 (0.048)
% difference in earnings	0.993 (<0.001)	0.991 (<0.001)
11–15 years in fleet	1.666 (0.014)	1.056 (0.425)
16–20 years in fleet	2.589 (0.001)	1.269 (0.238)
21–25 years in fleet	2.598 (0.021)	2.882 (0.001)
26–30 years in fleet	—	4.264 (0.002)
31–35 years in fleet	—	3.780 (0.021)
5 years stuck in rank	0.779 (0.114)	0.573 (0.006)
Overall USNA class percentile	0.684 (0.076)	1.159 (0.263)
Ship experience (domestic)	0.943 (0.114)	1.049 (0.025)
Ship experience (international)	0.986 (0.348)	0.980 (0.267)
Command experience	0.733 (0.011)	1.087 (0.026)
Cumulative years sick leave	1.384 (<0.001)	1.437 (<0.001)
Sick in year t	9.476 (<0.001)	8.667 (<0.001)
Log-likelihood	−358	−340
Observations : officers : separations	7,362 : 766 : 209	10,002 : 1,013 : 313

• Odds ratios reported with *p* values shown in parentheses.
• Standard errors used to construct *p* values estimated on clusters by USNA graduating class.

explanation for this could be that job-search costs for grizzled veteran officers decrease over time. Officers with longer careers have more time to develop job contacts in private industry. Another reason follows from the time demands of daily job responsibilities. As officers move higher up the chain of command, they might move into jobs with fewer time-intensive duties. While serving as younger officers and doing more time-intensive work, perhaps they simply had less time to search for outside jobs. Without more-refined time-use data, however, we cannot measure exactly whether or to what extent either of these conjectures rings true.

Another possible reason for delayed concavity in the hazard relates to pensions, although this is unlikely. For the time frame researched here, Navy pension eligibility (typically 75 percent of base pay) envisioned two scenarios: an officer could apply for retirement and an associated pension after forty years of service, or a retirement board could find an officer incapable of service due to disability or infirmity.[22] Since data limitations restrict career lengths in the sample to less than forty years, only instances of the latter case are applicable for this study. Our estimated hazard rates remain essentially the same when we exclude this group from the analysis.

As one might expect, when officers earned higher wages the likelihood of leaving the Navy decreased. This result exists in both time periods. Every 1 percent increase in wages relative to the external labor market decreases the probability of exiting by between 0.7 and 0.9 percent. Even though this wage effect is relatively small, it appears that the Navy could have easily used the right mix of incentives to retain the most highly trained officers. A 5 percent raise in relative pay for each year in a high-tech job might have mitigated the loss of workers who best understood the new technology. Unfortunately, Congress did not adjust pecuniary incentives to the market realities of the demand for high-tech workers.

Permanent pay could increase as a result of either of two events, promotion or prolonged rank stagnation. With respect to the latter, a 10 percent pay increase occurred every five years that officers did not receive promotions. Given this, we expect that these five-year bumps in earnings influence decisions as would promotion-based increases in wages. At the approach of every fifth year, the incentive to stay in the fleet would grow stronger. This within-rank-stagnation effect is accounted for in the model with a dummy variable for every fifth year an officer is stuck in the same rank. Our results indicate that this effect changed the conditional probability of exits by 22 percent prior to 1890 and by 43 percent afterward. The result over later years is particularly strong and statistically significant. An impending pay increase most certainly decreased separations.

Other measures of nontechnical human capital also appear to have impacted separation decisions, but these differ substantially for each measure. Overall academic ability, indicated by an officer's class ranking upon graduation from the Naval Academy, drops the conditional probability of an officer's exiting prior to 1890. After 1890, the result is not statistically significant. Also after 1890, a year of service on a domestically stationed ship increases the separation probability by about 5 percent. This result reverses for years prior to 1890, during which service on domestic-water ships decreases the hazard by approximately 6 percent per year of experience. From 1866 until 1890, the Navy confined most of its operations to domestic waters, so it should not surprise us that the only means of enhancing job-specific human capital during this era also decreased job mobility. International experience had no statistically significant effect in either time period.

Conclusion

In this work we explore the historical dynamics of job turnover among naval officers with heterogeneous forms of human capital. We demonstrate that the accumulation of very specific types of technical human capital alter job-separation probabilities by substantial margins. When we consider the effects from more-detailed forms of experience, we see that officers after 1890 with accumulated skills particular to steel, metallurgy, and electricity had strong incentives to leave for nonmilitary jobs. Those with technical-bureaucratic experience separated less rapidly. We also find that relative wage decreases boosted the likelihood of separation.

This study demonstrates that factors affecting worker-mobility decisions over a century ago remain very relevant today. Skilled workers trained to work with newer and more-transferable technologies are more likely to take their human capital elsewhere. This is true for workers in both private and military-sector industries, and it is true historically as well as now.[23]

NOTES 1 Claudia Goldin and Lawrence Katz, "The Origins of Technology-Skill Complementarity," *Quarterly Journal of Economics* 113, no. 3 (1998), pp. 693–732.

2 David M. Blank and George J. Stigler, *The Demand and Supply of Scientific Personnel,* General Series, no. 62 (Cambridge, Mass.: National Bureau of Economic Research, 1957); Michael Edelstein, "The Production of Engineers in New York Colleges and Universities: Some New Data," in *Human Capital and Institutions: A Long-Run View,* ed. David Eltis, Frank D. Lewis, and Kenneth L. Sokoloff (New York: Cambridge Univ. Press, 2009), pp. 179–219.

3 Blank and Stigler, *Demand and Supply of Scientific Personnel.*

4 Joel Mokyr, *The Lever of Riches: Technological Creativity and Economic Progress* (New York: Oxford Univ. Press, 1990).

5 For career fast tracks, see Darrell J. Glaser and Ahmed S. Rahman, "Human Capital and Technological Transition: Insights from the U.S. Navy," *Journal of Economic History* 71, no. 3 (2011), pp. 704–29.

6 In empirical specifications we also control for physical constitution, with measures of sickness and cumulative sickness. For the sake of brevity, we do not include these illness statistics in our summary of these data.

7 Clarence Long, *Wages and Earnings in the United States: 1860–1890* (Princeton, N.J.: Princeton Univ. Press, 1960); Albert Rees, *Real Wages in Manufacturing: 1890–1914* (Princeton, N.J.: Princeton Univ. Press, 1961).

8 Paul H. Douglas, *Real Wages in the United States, 1890–1926* (Boston: Houghton Mifflin, 1930).

9 Blank and Stigler, *Demand and Supply of Scientific Personnel.*

10 Subsequently summarized in Long, *Wages and Earnings in the United States.*

11 Ibid.

12 Most naval bases existed in these regions, and we suggest that localized relative earnings are what would matter most to workers considering job switches.

13 J. D. Kalbfleisch and R. L. Prentice, *The Statistical Analysis of Failure Time Data* (New York: Wiley, 1980); James Heckman and B. Singer, "A Method for Minimizing the Impact of Distribution Assumptions in Econometric Models for Duration Data," *Econometrica* 52, no. 2 (1984), pp. 271–320.

14 For the method of estimating duration models, see Heckman and Singer, "Method for Minimizing the Impact of Distribution Assumptions." For the methods and theoretical considerations underlying this economic model and U.S. naval economic history, see Darrell J. Glaser and Ahmed S. Rahman, "Benchmarking Job Mobility and Returns to Technical Skill for an Era with Rapid Innovation" (working paper, U.S. Naval Academy, Annapolis, Md., 2014).

15 Congress dictated that officers could not work beyond sixty-two years of age or serve more than forty years.

16 These data follow from the Aldrich report, discussed and outlined in Long, *Wages and Earnings in the United States.*

17 Wage data used from Rees, *Real Wages in Manufacturing.*

18 When the odds ratio, *or,* exceeds 1, the change in the probability of separation, Δ, is calculated as $\Delta = (or-1) \times 100\%$.

19 When the odds ratio, *or,* is less than 1, the change in the probability of separation, Δ, is calculated as $\Delta = (1-or) \times 100\%$.

20 A "small" p value will typically be less than 0.1.

21 Henry S. Farber, "Mobility and Stability: The Dynamics of Job Change in Labor Markets," in *Handbook of Labor Economics,* vol. 3B, ed. Orley Ashenfelter and David Card (Amsterdam: Elsevier, 1999), pp. 2439–83.

22 Robert L. Clark, Lee A. Craig, and Jack W. Wilson, *A History of Public Sector Pensions in the United States* (Philadelphia: Univ. of Pennsylvania Press, 2003).

23 Empirical evidence of job mobility among military personnel remains scant. Only a few dynamic models analyze job-mobility decisions of officers. See Darrell J. Glaser, "Time-Varying Effects of Human Capital on Military Retention," *Contemporary Economic Policy* 29, no. 2 (2011), pp. 231–49; Glenn A. Gotz and John J. McCall, *A Dynamic Retention Model for Air Force Officers: Theory and Estimates,* R-3028-AF (Santa Monica, Calif.: RAND, 1984); and Michael Mattock and Jeremy Arkes, *The Dynamic Retention Model for Air Force Officers: New Estimates and Policy Simulations of the Aviator Continuation Pay Program* (Santa Monica, Calif.: RAND, 2007).

XIV Great-Power Apprenticeships
Naval and Maritime Operations of the United States and Japan, 1898–1905

CARL CAVANAGH HODGE

P ower, like nature, abhors a vacuum. Between 1898 and 1905 the United States and Japan filled vacuums of power, the first occasioned by a revolt against the colonial regime of Spain in the Caribbean, the second by the failing hold of China's Qing dynasty on Korea and Manchuria. The resulting Spanish-American and Russo-Japanese Wars represent pivotal conflicts between declining and emerging powers at the dawn of the twentieth century. Because in each case naval capacity was fundamental to victory, these conflicts accelerated the global naval arms race and intensified great-power competition in the decade leading to World War I. Additionally, both wars involved the application of maritime strategy, defined loosely in a classic of the time as "the principles which govern a war in which the sea is a substantial factor."[1]

A Mania Born in America

Navalism, the idea that possession of an oceanic navy constitutes an essential attribute of great-power status, was a strategic vogue of the late nineteenth century.[2] It was legitimated intellectually by, above all, the writings of Alfred Thayer Mahan, who argued that the sea power of Great Britain had provided it with both security and a command of ocean lanes sufficient to make it the preeminent global power.[3] American navalists ultimately succeeded in launching the United States on a century of expanding sea power owing to the catalyst of the Spanish-American War and the political consensus that Theodore Roosevelt crafted as president in the years directly following.[4] Victory in that war projected the United States into the western Pacific and changed its relationship with another emerging naval power, Japan, fundamentally. Mahan's philosophy of sea power may in fact have exerted its most profound influence on the oligarchs of Japan's Meiji regime. Ever since Commodore Matthew C. Perry's ships had sailed into Edo Bay in 1853, Japan had been painfully aware of its vulnerability to seaborne aggression. Naval weakness was prominent among the factors favoring the toppling of the shōgunate by means of the restoration of the Meiji emperor, a state-sponsored drive toward industrialization and administrative rationalization. After 1898 the appearance of the U.S. Navy in the Philippines lent intellectual coherence to the arguments of Japanese navalists in pressing the case for a modern navy.[5]

Characteristic of American strategic ambition in the nineteenth century, by contrast, was a precocity outrunning capacity. Before and after the Civil War the United States articulated sphere-of-interest doctrines it could redeem only with the convergence of luck and circumstance.[6] With the crisis of Spanish colonialism in Cuba, the Monroe Doctrine of 1823 required an American response; the news of the repression of rebellion in Cuba stirred public opinion in the United States to such a froth of indignation that Progressive sentiment demanded an application of righteous might for which the United States of 1898 was ill prepared.[7] When President William McKinley asked Congress to authorize the use of force to protect American interests, the legislature exceeded him with a joint resolution declaring Cuba sovereign and demanding the withdrawal of Spanish troops.[8] The opportunism in evidence here was present also in Japan's much larger war with Russia, 1904–1905, if not in the invocation of a humanitarian cause then certainly in the choice of an adversary against whom national capabilities could be tested. Although a comparison of the apprenticeship of American and Japanese naval power in these conflicts recommends itself for this reason alone, lessons learned and not learned in the prosecution of the wars tell us a good deal about the nature of emerging Pacific rivalry between the United States and imperial Japan over the following decades.

States of Readiness

By the 1890s both Spain and tsarist Russia were ripe for humiliation at the hands of more-vigorous states. The Spanish fleet had never recovered from its joint defeat (with that of Napoleonic France) under the cannon of the Royal Navy off Cape Trafalgar in October 1805. That the Spanish navy of 1898 was no longer capable of battle with a first-rank power was revealed in the opening gambit of the war with the United States, not in the Caribbean, but in the western Pacific, where a second-rate power defeated it with aplomb.[9] Japan's foe of 1904, Russia, was a vastly more capable state than Spain yet only circumstantially able to prevail in a war with Japan in Korea and Manchuria. Prominent among Russia's liabilities was the nature of the tsarist regime, which made Russian Far Eastern policy ambiguous, its attitude to the prospect of war with Japan casual, and the prosecution of the war uncertain.

By the 1870s Meiji Japan had by contrast developed a variant of parliamentary government, a professional bureaucracy, independent courts, armed forces with universal conscription, and an education system dedicated to literacy and numeracy.[10] Japan's immediate foreign-policy concern was the waning of the Qing dynasty in China and its implications for Korea and Manchuria, especially the prospect of European predations on the Asian mainland following the defeat of the Boxer Rebellion—a concern heightened by subsequent Russian behavior in signing a convention with China over Manchuria yet failing to abide by its commitment to withdraw some two hundred thousand troops from the region. On the eve of the war with Russia the Imperial Navy had six battleships less than ten years old, seven armored cruisers, and seven protected cruisers of the same age.[11] Japan offered to declare Manchuria beyond its sphere of interest if Russia would do the same for Korea, yet it was primed for war before and during the dance of diplomacy. And note: Japan made a formal declaration of war on 10 February 1904, after the navy had sailed on 6 February. During the night of 8–9 February Japanese destroyers launched a torpedo attack on Russian ships anchored at Port Arthur. Troops meanwhile occupied Fusan, Masan, and Chinhae Bay, on the south coast of Korea, while the navy supported the landing of troops at the port of Chemulpo, on the west coast. The Combined Fleet's commander, Vice Adm. Heihachirō Tōgō, had sent the destroyers against the Russian fleet at Port Arthur, while the Second Fleet, under Vice Adm. Sotokichi Uryū, took four cruisers to escort merchant vessels carrying three thousand troops to the Chemulpo landing.[12]

At the time of the Cuban crisis the American republic had only recently begun to strengthen the capacity of government to cope with the economic and social rigors of industrial maturity. One of the ways in which government was to become more purposeful was symbolized in the power of the New Navy. When the popular indignation over Spain's abuse of its colonial subjects turned openly bellicose following the destruction of the battleship *Maine* in Havana Harbor on 15 February 1898, the U.S. Navy facilitated the coming-out of the United States as a great power.[13] However, the McKinley administration was not as unified as the Meiji oligarchy of 1904 on the need for war; nor was Congress united on the means to wage it. The condition of the U.S. Army, after all, gave grounds for pause. At the time of the war declaration its strength stood at 28,747 officers and enlisted men, a pale expression of the martial potential of an industrial nation of seventy-three million people. A bill to authorize a force of a hundred thousand men immediately ran into headwinds from congressmen voicing the traditional distrust of a large standing army and from state governors who feared that the constitutional right of states to maintain their own militias might be impaired.[14] A compromise permitted the federal army to recruit up to sixty-five thousand men for a period of two years, and an additional bill authorized the president to call for volunteers above that ceiling. McKinley issued a call for 125,000 and was rewarded with mass enthusiasm, but the expeditionary force thereby raised created a decentralized system of recruiting, uneven standards for training, and "too many men chasing too little equipment, weapons and accommodation."[15] Logistical ligatures were not up to the sudden demand placed on them.[16] Operational planning was haphazard. The force was assembled to depart from Tampa, Florida, land in the vicinity of Santiago de Cuba, and then assist the Navy in the destruction of the Spanish fleet in the harbor. Tampa had the advantage of proximity to Cuba, but it was a comparatively small port and was more modestly endowed with railway connections than Charleston, South Carolina, or the Gulf cities of Mobile, Alabama, and New Orleans, Louisiana. The invasion force languished in Tampa Bay for five days, leaving at last on 14 June because of a report that Spanish warships were prowling off the northern coast of Cuba.[17]

The Beachheads of Expansion

The war's first engagement was nonetheless joined in its secondary theater, the Philippines, and that engagement was decisive in the very sense intended by Mahan's theory of sea power—aided at every step by the incompetence of the Spanish command at Manila Bay, where Adm. George Dewey sank three Spanish warships and set six ablaze at a cost of negligible damage to his own squadron.[18] In the Caribbean, American naval power was equally central to the war's outcome, yet not by virtue of its maritime operations.[19]

The invasion convoy sent against Cuba, consisting of twenty-six transport vessels and six supply ships carrying 16,058 men, 819 officers, 959 horses, and 1,336 mules, arrived unmolested off Santiago de Cuba on 20 June. Maj. Gen. William Shafter, at the head of the Fifth Army Corps and in command of land operations, thereupon surprised Rear Adm. William Sampson with the news that he intended not to assault the heights at the harbor entrance but rather to land his force at Daiquirí and strike an inland route toward Santiago de Cuba to capture the city from the rear. The calculation that a landing at Daiquirí would meet with only modest resistance was well founded.[20] Yet the lack of good docking facilities forced the transports to land the force over the beach, whereas a heavy surf made it impossible for them to navigate close to shore, so that supplies were loaded onto boats and ferried to the beach. Heavy artillery intended for attacking the fortifications of Santiago de Cuba was abandoned; the challenge of getting hundreds of horses and mules ashore was answered by pushing them overboard in the hope they would swim there.[21] Then, in its advance toward Santiago de Cuba the army labored in winter-weight wool against tropical heat, insects, disease, and roads turned to mud by afternoon rains.[22]

The critical engagements came at El Caney and San Juan Hill on 1 July. A Spanish force of 520 under Gen. Joaquín Vara del Rey y Rubio defended the fortified village of El Caney against some 6,600 Americans commanded by Gen. Henry Ware Lawton. At San Juan Hill the numerical odds were more balanced: 10,400 Spaniards and 8,400 Americans. In both instances the Americans carried the day, but these successes had little to do with a unity of conception or execution. Envisioning the capture of El Caney in no more than two hours, Shafter expected that American force then to march westward and join the right flank of the main attack on the San Juan Heights. The plan unraveled when the Spanish garrison at El Caney offered spirited resistance, so that an action peripheral to the main objective imperiled the operation.[23] An attack on San Juan Hill originally scheduled for 10:00 AM did not move off until long after noon, delayed waiting for the El Caney force (which would not arrive until the next day); in the meantime the Spanish on the heights poured fire on the Americans below, crouching behind what cover they could find, ridges and small rises. At 1:00 PM Lt. John D. Miley, General Shafter's aide, seized the initiative. With no order from his superior on when his men should move, he instructed the anxious generals around him to take the heights "at all hazards."[24] They did, but although Shafter had planned then to move on directly against Santiago de Cuba, his troops were now in no condition to advance farther. Only three thousand of the fifteen thousand men of the American force occupied the position immediately following the assault; they were delirious with exhaustion, had no artillery support, and were thinly strung out along the crest of the San Juan Heights.[25] The plan had been too clever. Not that the war's outcome was in doubt—in 1898, American forces in and around Cuba were going to prevail one way or another. But a national embarrassment due to the comic-opera incompetence of the U.S. Army was eminently possible.

The San Juan engagement so rocked Shafter's confidence that on 2 July he asked Admiral Sampson, whom only two weeks earlier he had treated as his junior, to launch a naval attack on Morro Castle on the eastern side of the entrance to Santiago's harbor and on the Socapa batteries on the opposing side. At this point the Spanish general Ramón Blanco y Erenas informed Adm. Pascual Cervera y Topete that his fleet should sortie from the harbor and run the blockade, as the Americans, having captured the San Juan Heights, were in a position to attack the entrance to the harbor. Happily, this meant that responsibility for the American cause now swung back to the U.S. Navy.[26] Of Cervera's six warships none were battleships and only four were armored cruisers. The heaviest of these, *Almirante Oquendo* and *Vizcaya,* displaced only 6,890 tons and would face in the worst scenario Sampson's armored cruisers *Brooklyn* and *New York,* both of which displaced more than eight thousand tons, and his battleships, *Indiana, Iowa,* and *Oregon,* all of which exceeded ten thousand tons. By the time Cervera was ordered to run the blockade, on 3 July, the U.S. North Atlantic Fleet had arrived to reinforce it. Sampson's advantage in firepower alone might have been decisive—18,847 to 6,014 pounds of broadside—but tactical circumstance compounded his advantage. After a quixotic attempt by the armored cruiser *Infanta Maria Teresa* to ram *Brooklyn,* Cervera's squadron ran westward along the coast and was completely destroyed, at the cost of minor damage to *Brooklyn, Texas,* and *Iowa* and one death, against 323 Spanish killed and 151 wounded.[27] Following two weeks of siege by Shafter's army the Spanish garrison at Santiago de Cuba surrendered, and on 12 August Spain's representation in Washington agreed to preliminary terms.

As hostilities wound down in Cuba, they graduated to a new stage in the Philippines. In January 1899 a constituent assembly declared the Philippine Republic under President Emilio Aguinaldo; because the United States had sought and re-ceived help from Filipino insurgents in the effort against Spain, Aguinaldo rea-soned that Filipinos were owed an assurance against American rule. This assur-ance Maj. Gen. Elwell S. Otis, the U.S. Army's man on the spot, lacked the political authority to offer. His position was not helped by the McKinley administration's insistence that the insurgents must submit to the authority of the United States or by instructions that the Army protect people and property only in and around Ma-nila. The first American troops—115 officers and 2,386 enlisted men of what was later designated the Eighth Corps—had arrived in the Philippines in June 1898 and were thereafter reinforced only in trickles, because of a scarcity of transport; when a third contingent arrived on 25 July the force totaled 10,946 officers and men, mostly state militia.

In the meantime, fighting broke out between Aguinaldo's men and the Ameri-cans in a nighttime skirmish around Manila, during which Dewey's warships pro-vided artillery support.[28] In November Otis was able to hazard an offensive with thirty-five thousand men intended to defeat the Filipino army and occupy the main island of Luzon. The war then entered a difficult guerrilla phase. In early 1900 Gen. Arthur MacArthur, father of Douglas MacArthur, took over Otis's command with a determination to coerce respect from the population wherever affection was ab-sent.[29] By the end of 1900 MacArthur's army had reached a total strength of seventy thousand, and the U.S. Navy blockaded foreign arms shipments to the guerrillas. Isolating rebel units geographically from each other, the Navy facilitated American mobility with an amphibious capacity to land troops anywhere the coast permitted.[30]

As a result of this apprenticeship in counterinsurgency, the Philippines were destined to assume a central role in American strategic thinking. The U.S. Navy had taken Midway Atoll in 1867; the annexation of Hawaii followed the war with Spain, in 1898. By the outbreak of World War I, Hawaii had been transformed into a major Army and Navy base for the protection of America's colonial Pacific empire. Still, the Philippines were a possession in the *western* Pacific, some 6,454 nautical miles from California and 4,612 from Hawaii. Although there were voices raised in Washington that Japan represented a threat to the Philippines, as long as the Meiji regime remained preoccupied with Russian encroachment in Manchuria the regional balance of power was acceptable. The astonishing performance of the Japanese fleet in 1904–1905 overthrew this assumption.[31]

The Japanese attack on Port Arthur in 1904 sought to prevent the main Russian squadron—six battleships and six cruisers—from leaving the harbor to challenge the Japanese seizure of the Yellow Sea and Korea Bay. The Japanese operation has been criticized because its failure to destroy the Port Arthur squadron forced the Combined Fleet to impose a protracted blockade;[32] nonetheless, the Imperial Japa-nese Navy had control of the sea around Korea and the Liaodong Peninsula while the invading army was put ashore. The shock effect of the preemptive move against Port Arthur became a cornerstone of Japanese strategic culture, an underappreciated one until its reappearance in the skies over Pearl Harbor in 1941.[33] With the Russian navy temporarily neutralized, Japan was with ease and speed able to transport troops over water to the theater of war and supply them. Additionally, Japan had advantages of seaborne access to Korea similar to those enjoyed by the United States in transporting troops to Cuba, with the difference that its coastline directly across from Korea was studded with fine harbors connected directly by rail with garrisons in the interior.[34]

By the time the First Army, under the command of Gen. Tamemoto Kuroki, met the tsar's forces for the first major land engagement of the war, at the Yalu River in late April, it could bring to bear three divisions. This force, composed of two thousand cavalrymen, twenty-eight thousand infantry, and 128 field guns, including some brand-new Krupp 4.7-inch howitzers, faced the Russian Eastern Detachment of five thousand cavalry, fifteen thousand infantry, and only sixty guns.

This balance of forces did not reflect the strategic depth of the adversaries. In 1904 the manpower of the Japanese army stood at 850,000, but the standing army had only 380,000 troops at its immediate disposal; active Russian strength, meanwhile, totaled over a million men, backed by reserve of over two million. The initial disparity of strength tilted in Japan's direction in the place and at the time where numbers truly mattered—at the Yalu in the spring of 1904—because Japan was able to seize and maintain the offensive initiative with efficient naval and maritime operations.[35]

As the two armies converged on the Yalu River, the tsar's government continued to believe that Japanese intentions were confined to Korea and gave explicit directions to Adm. Eugene Alexeiev, in overall command of Russian forces in Manchuria, to undertake no action against the Japanese as long as they remained on Korean soil south of the Yalu.[36] Alexeiev had little appreciation for the tactical sophistication of the Japanese navy, a sophistication based in part on an Anglo-American tutelage of early generations of its officers and in part on the influence at the Naval Staff College of Akiyama Saneyuki, a naval intellectual in the mold of Mahan who had spent two years in the United States.[37] In 1904, however, naval support of army operations was more important than battle-fleet tactics. Russia could benefit from the superior size of its army only if it could mobilize quickly enough to offset the speed of the Japanese advance, but in 1904 the Trans-Siberian Railway buoyed imperial spirits much more effectively than it transported troops. A typical Russian army corps required 267 trains to reach the front.[38] As a consequence, Japan's opening naval and maritime operations paid an enormous strategic dividend; they had in effect turned the war into a local conflict, while Russia had only two of its twenty-nine army corps east of the Urals.

As Japan's First Army crossed into Manchuria, the Second managed its land-ing only sixty miles east of Port Arthur on 5 May. By the night of 13 May all three divisions of the Second Army were safely ashore.[39] Japanese forces now threatened to cut off Port Arthur's garrison from any relief by Russian forces in Manchuria. Its capture, left to the Third Army under Gen. Nogi Maresuke, was not urgent. More importantly, Gen. Nozu Michitsura's Fourth Army, landed at Takushan, was to proceed north with the Second to join Kuroki's First Army for the main land en-gagements of the war, at Liaoyang and Mukden. As the three Japanese armies in the Manchurian interior converged south of Liaoyang in July 1904, Field Marshal Iwao Oyama arrived to assume overall command. This change reflected the size of the combined armies and the scale of their operations over broad territory, but it also testified to an urgent awareness that the passage of time favored the enemy. Where-as Spain in 1898 had been helpless to reinforce its Cuban garrison once Ameri-can naval power had the sea approaches, Russia was able to buttress its position in Manchuria by railway as long as its army was able to avoid a debilitating defeat.[40]

The battle of Liaoyang postponed that day. The Russian army suffered 3,611 killed and 14,301 wounded yet inflicted 5,537 killed and 18,063 wounded on Oya-ma.[41] It is true that Russia's railway lifeline was extremely vulnerable, owing to its ex-tension deep into the zone of conflict.[42] Still, without a convincing Japanese victory continued hostilities advantaged Russia. The tsar's government now took measures to reverse the tide of military fortune, in the short term with a counteroffensive at Sha-ho, between Liaoyang and Mukden, and in the long term by dispatching the Russian navy's Baltic Fleet to relieve Port Arthur. From preliminary skirmishes on 19 February and the Russian evacuation of the town itself three weeks later, Muk-den evolved into the largest land battle to date, involving nearly a half-million men along some hundred miles of contested front. Japanese forces entering Mukden on 10 March were able to take some twenty thousand Russian prisoners yet failed in the effort to encircle and annihilate the remaining force. Mukden cost the tsar ninety thousand men to death, wounding, or capture, but Japanese casualties ran to seventy-five thousand, a quarter of the total force.[43] The Baltic Fleet meanwhile was completing its long voyage to the theater of war.

Only superficially were the Japanese and Russian battle fleets equal in capability. Although each had four modern battleships and Rear Adm. Zinovy Rozhestvenski had older capital ships in addition, Vice Admiral Tōgō had eight modern armored cruisers against Rozhestvenski's one. The Russian squadron had an advantage in ten- and twelve-inch guns, but the Combined Fleet's secondary armament more than compensated for this by contributing to an overall greater firepower. Addi-tionally, Rozhestvenski's older ships, slower by virtue of design and propulsion, were encumbered by tons of coal, while Tōgō's faster ships were made faster still when he ordered any coal superfluous to the coming battle thrown overboard.

Superior speed, aided by the coordination of the ships made possible by better use of wireless communications, turned the great naval battle in the Strait of Tsushima on 27 May 1905 into a series of Japanese maneuvers around the Russian squadron's plodding progress to the northeast and then northwest. Most critical to the outcome was Tōgō's risky turn of his entire line into the fire of the Russian fleet to prevent the latter's escape and to engage it at close range while running a parallel course.[44] When Rozhestvenski attempted to turn his ships away to the starboard, Tōgō used his speed to pull ahead on the outside of the turn, maintain his range, and continue to pour shells into the Russian line.[45] As Tōgō's fleet closed to within three thousand meters and changed to armor-piercing rounds, the Russian formation quickly lost all coherence. As night came, Japanese destroyers and torpedo boats attacked under cover of darkness the remaining Russian ships limping for Vladivostok. By noon of the following day, thirty-four of the thirty-eight ships Rozhestvenski commanded had been sunk, scuttled, captured, or interned. Tōgō had chalked up the greatest naval triumph since Trafalgar.[46]

The oligarchy therefore wasted no time in seeking mediation from Theodore Roosevelt, now president of the United States. Roosevelt was a superb mediator—informed, patient, understanding, and objective. But he could not be entirely disinterested. The felicity with which the little island empire had humiliated Russia, notes his biographer, "made him wonder what future expansion Japan was capable of."[47]

The Large Lesson of a Little War

The reader will be struck by the difference in the scale of land engagements of the Spanish-American and Russo-Japanese Wars, the latter anticipating World War I in the numbers of troops involved and the level of carnage entailed. As far as the strategic consequences of the two conflicts are concerned, the difference is irrelevant. Internationally, Japan's victory enhanced the vogue of naval power, and governments felt compelled to grapple with technological, economic, and political challenges inherent in preparing battle fleets for future Tsushimas. Few felt more vindicated in their ambitions for national naval power than Roosevelt, who saw the lessons of Manila and Santiago Bay confirmed in spectacular fashion at Tsushima and seized the political moment by pressing on Congress the case for battleship construction. In the following years, furthermore, the United States learned more from its battle-fleet operations and its awkward apprenticeship in maritime operations in 1898 than did Japan from the extraordinary feats of 1904–1905.

By most measures the Japan faced by Russia in 1904 was a remarkable success in state-driven modernization. The Meiji state's success in making the war into a collective patriotic endeavor appears in fact to have been constitutive for Japan's approach to war later in the twentieth century, possibly to a greater extent than the oligarchs would have wished. At Liaoyang, Mukden, and Port Arthur the Imperial

Japanese Army had demonstrated a willingness to accept appalling casualties in its attempt to secure a clear decision over the Russian army.[48] Meanwhile, the Imperial Navy's comparative standing was hugely improved by the war, but naval planners such as Akiyama drew lessons from Tsushima concerning fleet concentration and decisive engagement that later influenced—with baleful consequences—designs for war in the Central Pacific. In short, the Japanese army and navy cultivated myths about the Russo-Japanese War that subsequently degenerated into strategic pathologies.[49] In 1904–1905, moreover, Japan was punching above its weight. Russia's decision to agree to peace terms came just as the Meiji state was reaching its fiscal limits, and the blood sacrifice of its troops in Manchuria had exceeded a scale that could ever be compensated by a diplomatic dividend. Japan did not possess the industrial depth to match the strategic ambition that Mukden and Tsushima inspired. It was not until 1909 that the Kure Navy Yard laid down Japan's first dreadnought, *Settsu;* Japan's greatest warship of the pre–World War I era, the twenty-seven-thousand-ton *Kongo,* was built by the British firm Vickers.[50]

By contrast, the United States had all the resources it needed to build a first-class battle fleet and had only just begun to bend them to the effort. Steel came from the Bethlehem and Carnegie works in Pennsylvania; ordnance from Pennsylvania but also from the Gatling Gun Company and the Colt factory in Hartford, Connecticut; projectiles from Crucible Steel in Newark, New Jersey, and Miami Cycle and Manufacturing in Ohio. Warships took shape at Cramp and Sons in Philadelphia, and at Newport News, Virginia, but also at Moran Brothers in Seattle, the Union Iron Works of San Francisco, and the Columbia Iron Works of Baltimore. Bethlehem Steel Corporation, established in 1904, quickly became a major supplier of the national arsenal. During Roosevelt's presidency the United States launched fourteen battleships; in the thirty-seven months between 2 April 1902 and 1 May 1905, American shipyards laid down no fewer than twelve and achieved an acceleration of the average building time of one year per ship.[51]

When the Japanese immigration issue turned into a diplomatic crisis in the summer of 1907, the president's discussions concerning the disposition of American warships with Secretary of the Navy Victor Metcalf, Capt. Richard Wainwright of the General Board, and Col. W. W. Wotherspoon, acting president of the Army War College, were leaked to the *New York Herald.* So began the public debate about possibly radical changes to naval policy, changes that culminated in the world cruise of the sixteen battleships later referred to as the "Great White Fleet."[52] That fleet's fourteen-month and forty-five-thousand-mile world tour became a political and diplomatic triumph. Naval planners reduced their estimates of the time required to mount operations against Japan from 120 to ninety days and decided that the main American naval base in the Pacific should be located at Pearl Harbor.[53]

Although in the Root-Takahira Agreement of 1908 the United States acknowledged Japan's vital interest in Korea in exchange for an affirmation that Japan had no design on the Philippines, the initial discussions that produced War Plan ORANGE, a draft blueprint for Japan's defeat in a future Pacific war, date to 1906. Before 1906 the prospect of a Japanese threat to American interests in the Pacific was given little attention, but the ravaging of the Russian Baltic Fleet at Tsushima demonstrated the vulnerability of a fleet operating at great distance from its home base.[54] Plan ORANGE accepted that the Philippines were indefensible against a determined Japanese attack and would be lost in the opening phase of a Pacific war yet asserted that they could be retaken by naval power operating from a secure base such as Pearl Harbor. This would necessarily involve naval support for a succession of amphibious operations across the Pacific requiring transport ships superior to the ragtag formation sent against Cuba and an approach to amphibious landings infinitely more sophisticated than had been on display at Daiquirí.

In other words, ORANGE featured the conceptual rudiments of the American conquest of the western Pacific after 1941. Its reasoned realism transcended Mahan's stress on decisive battle in its acceptance of the inherent vulnerability of western Pacific bases and the advocacy of a long conflict of attrition. World War I technology then rendered the battle fleet itself obsolete and furnished the United States with carrier-borne airpower as the workhorse of a Pacific offensive.[55] Thanks partly to the naval preferences of another Roosevelt in the 1930s, the U.S. Army remained a junior party to the U.S. Navy in the Pacific. Although the two services maintained a split command until the end of World War II, the operation of the Army in the Southwest Pacific and the Navy in the Central Pacific ran in parallel and conformed to the logic of ORANGE.[56]

The paradox is that the United States, fresh from its splendid little triumph over Spain, should in the ensuing months and years have taken such sober stock of the perils inhering in its new role in the world while Japan failed to do so after a conflict of immensely greater cost and carnage. After 1905 the Japanese government never developed a coherent strategic vision of the country's future, in large part because the Imperial Army, having sacrificed so much for the nation's foothold on the Asian continent, insisted that Japan aspire to a dominant role on the mainland, a role in which the army's claim on national resources was justified by its garrison duties in Korea and Manchuria. Its leadership developed a corporate obsession with Manchuria as amounting to its own, rather than Japan's, sphere of interest. No alliance among competing interests of the Japanese state was strong enough to offset the army's influence, so that by the 1930s both Manchuria and the army exerted a perversely expansionist influence on Japanese foreign policy.[57]

The navy did nothing to amend the army's strategic vision. It merely developed its own. After all, if the navy leadership was to be mindful of its duty to national policy after the triumphs of 1904–1905 had bestowed on it new prestige and influence, it could hardly overlook the fact of growing American naval power in Japan's backyard. The alternative to the army's northward/over-land perspective was the navy's southward/over-sea strategic vision, the one service having little to say to the other while the two competed over budget share and "the strategic axis of advance."[58] Although the Imperial Navy was in most respects a more progressive institution than the Imperial Army, the intellectual legacy of Tsushima corrupted Japan's future in the Pacific to the same degree as the army's on the mainland. Akiyama continued to influence thinking on naval strategy. To his eminently practical ideas on organization he added the conviction, based on Tsushima, that Mahan's notion of decisive battle represented the essence of naval war, as well as a stress on moral intangibles in war that borrowed heavily from the mysticism of classical texts.[59] Without going so far as to assert that "the war plan with which Japan went to war in 1941 was a case of Akiyama re-incarnated," it is important to note that after Tsushima Japanese naval thought tended to confuse tactical doctrine with strategic planning to an extent that severely hampered its understanding of the likely realities of war with an adversary of greater strategic depth.[60]

Fundamental to the national disaster of the twentieth century was that no compromise over the strategic axis of advance was ever reached between the two Japanese services. Instead, Japan fought two wars. World War II began for Japan in 1931, with the misadventure of the Kwantung Army in the "Manchurian Incident," after which a succession of other "incidents" led to a mounting commitment of men and materiel to operations in Manchuria and China. By 7 December 1941 Japan had already lost 185,000 fighting men on the Asian mainland, whereupon the navy struck against the U.S. Pacific Fleet at Pearl Harbor—a strike executed with preemptive shock that had been on display at Port Arthur in 1904—to expel the United States from the western Pacific long enough to permit amphibious operations against the Netherlands East Indies and the Philippines in pursuit of resources needed for a protracted conflict.[61] There are few instances of a nation so clearly distilling exactly the wrong lessons from one war for application to another.

NOTES 1 Julian S. Corbett, *Principles of Maritime Strategy* (London: Longmans, Green, 1911), p. 13.

2 The definition comes from the glossary of John Keegan, *The Price of Admiralty* (London: Hutchinson, 1988).

3 Philip A. Crowl, "Alfred Thayer Mahan: The Naval Historian," in *Makers of Modern Strategy from Machiavelli to the Nuclear Age,* ed. Peter Paret (Princeton, N.J.: Princeton Univ. Press, 1986), pp. 444–77.

4 George Baer, *One Hundred Years of Sea Power: The U.S. Navy, 1890–1990* (Stanford, Calif.: Stanford Univ. Press, 1993), pp. 9–48.

5 David C. Evans and Mark Peattie, *Kaigun: Strategy, Tactics, and Technology in the Imperial Japanese Navy, 1887–1941* (Annapolis, Md.: Naval Institute Press, 1997), pp. 4–24, 134–35; Edward J. Drea, *Japan's Imperial Army: Its Rise and Fall, 1853–1945* (Lawrence: Univ. of Kansas Press, 2009), pp. 1–7.

6 See Carl Cavanagh Hodge, "A Whiff of Cordite: Theodore Roosevelt and the Transoceanic Naval Arms Race, 1897–1909," *Diplomacy & Statecraft* 19, no. 2 (2008), pp. 712–31, and James R. Reckner, *Teddy Roosevelt's Great White Fleet* (Annapolis, Md.: Naval Institute Press, 1988).

7 Walter A. McDougall, *Promised Land, Crusader State: The American Encounter with the World since 1776* (Boston: Houghton Mifflin, 1997), pp. 110–11; Frank Freidel, *The Splendid Little War* (New York: Dell, 1958), pp. 10–11; Sean Dennis Cashman, *America in the Age of the Titans: The Progressive Era and World War I* (New York: New York Univ. Press, 1988), p. 7; Walter Mills, *The Martial Spirit: A Study of Our War with Spain* (Boston: Houghton Mifflin, 1931), pp. 42–43.

8 McDougall, *Promised Land, Crusader State,* pp. 110–11; H. W. Brands, *TR: The Last Romantic* (New York: Basic Books, 1997), pp. 321–29.

9 G. J. A. O'Toole, *The Spanish War: An American Epic, 1898* (New York: W. W. Norton, 1984), p. 177.

10 W. G. Beasley, *The Meiji Restoration* (Stanford, Calif.: Stanford Univ. Press, 1972); Martin van Creveld, *Rise and Decline of the State* (New York: Cambridge Univ. Press, 1999), p. 323; Shumpei

Okamoto, *The Japanese Oligarchy and the Russo-Japanese War* (New York: Columbia Univ. Press, 1970).

11 Lisle Rose, *Power at Sea: The Age of Navalism, 1890–1918* (Columbia: Univ. of Missouri Press, 2007), pp. 97–98.

12 The Combined Fleet (the Japanese First and Second Fleets) consisted of six battleships, ten cruisers, forty destroyers, and forty smaller vessels.

13 Lewis L. Gould, *The Presidency of William McKinley* (Lawrence: Regents Press of Kansas, 1980), pp. 59–80; Brands, *TR,* pp. 323–26.

14 Joseph Smith, *The Spanish-American War: Conflict in the Caribbean and the Pacific* (New York: Longman, 1994), pp. 98–99; Russell F. Weigley, *History of the United States Army* (Bloomington: Indiana Univ. Press, 1984), pp. 290–92.

15 Smith, *Spanish-American War,* pp. 99–100.

16 Ibid., p. 105.

17 Ibid., pp. 106–17; Weigley, *History of the United States Army,* pp. 300–304; Dean Chapman, "Army Life at Camp Thomas, Georgia, during the Spanish-American War," *Georgia Historical Quarterly* 70, no. 4 (1986), pp. 633–56; Gary R. Mormino, "Tampa's Splendid Little War: Local History and the Cuban War of Independence," *OAH Magazine of History* 12, no. 3 (1998), pp. 37–42.

18 Ivan Musicant, *Empire by Default: The Spanish-American War and the Dawn of the American Century* (New York: Henry Holt, 1998); James M. McCaffrey, *Inside the Spanish-American War: A History Based on First-Person Accounts* (Jefferson, N.C.: McFarland, 2009), pp. 8–9.

19 H. P. Willmott, *The Last Century of Sea Power* (Bloomington: Indiana Univ. Press, 2009), vol. 1, p. 38; Brian M. Linn, "The US Military and Expeditionary Warfare," in *Battles Near and Far: A Century of Overseas Deployment,* ed. Peter Dennis and Jeffrey Grey (Canberra, ACT: Army History Unit, 2005), pp. 80–81.

20 David F. Trask, *The War with Spain in 1898* (New York: Macmillan, 1981), pp. 203–208; Smith, *Spanish-American War,* pp. 130–31.

21 Trask, *The War with Spain in 1898,* p. 214.

22 Gerald F. Linderman, *The Mirror of War: American Society and the Spanish-American War* (Ann Arbor: Univ. of Michigan Press, 1974), p. 104.

23 McCaffrey, *Inside the Spanish-American War*, pp. 94–95; Trask, *The War with Spain in 1898*, pp. 236–37.

24 McCaffrey, *Inside the Spanish-American War*, pp. 103–105. Miley's own account, remarkably self-effacing, was published in 1899. See John D. Miley, *In Cuba with Shafter* (New York: Scribner's, 1899), pp. 101–28.

25 Trask, *The War with Spain in 1898*, p. 244; O'Toole, *Spanish War*, p. 319.

26 Trask, *The War with Spain in 1898*, p. 259; Smith, *Spanish-American War*, pp. 145–47.

27 David F. Trask, "The Battle of Santiago," in *Great American Naval Battles*, ed. Jack Sweetman (Annapolis, Md.: Naval Institute Press, 1998), pp. 202–203, 209–14.

28 Brian McCallister Linn, *The Philippine War, 1899–1902* (Lawrence: Univ. of Kansas Press, 2000), pp. 3–29.

29 Ibid., p. 213.

30 Ibid., p. 325; Glenn Anthony May, *Battle for Batangas: A Philippine Province at War* (New Haven, Conn.: Yale Univ. Press, 1991).

31 Baer, *One Hundred Years of Sea Power*, p. 44; William Braisted, "The Philippine Naval Base Problem," *Mississippi Valley Historical Review* 41, no. 1 (1954), pp. 21–40.

32 Willmott, *Last Century of Sea Power*, vol. 1, p. 81.

33 Ibid., pp. 79–81.

34 *Official History (Naval and Military) of the Russo-Japanese War* (London: Historical Section of the Committee of Imperial Defence, 1910), vol. 1, p. 45.

35 Bruce W. Menning, "Miscalculating One's Enemies: Russian Military Intelligence before the Russo-Japanese War," *War in History* 13, no. 2 (2006), pp. 141–70.

36 Ibid., pp. 163–64; Denis Warner and Peggy Warner, *The Tide at Sunrise: A History of the Russo-Japanese War, 1904–1905* (New York: Charterhouse, 1974), p. 256; Richard Connaughton, *Rising Sun and Tumbling Bear: Russia's War with Japan* (London: Cassell, 2003), p. 67.

37 Evans and Peattie, *Kaigun*, pp. 11–13, 67–74; Willmott, *Last Century of Sea Power*, vol. 1, p. 125.

38 J. N. Westwood, *Russia against Japan: A New Look at the Russo-Japanese War* (Albany: State Univ. of New York Press, 1986), pp. 122–23; Connaughton, *Rising Sun and Tumbling Bear*, pp. 29–30; Dietrich Beyrau, *Militär und Gesellschaft im vorrevolutionären Russland* (Cologne: Böhlau Verlag, 1984), p. 442.

39 *Official History*, vol. 1, pp. 137–38; Evans and Peattie, *Kaigun*, p. 101.

40 Okamoto, *Japanese Oligarchy and the Russo-Japanese War*, pp. 101–102.

41 Warner and Warner, *Tide at Sunrise*, pp. 378–99; David T. Zabecki, "Liao-Yang: Dawn of Modern

Warfare," *Military History* 16, no. 5 (December 1999), pp. 54–61.

42 Evans and Peattie, *Kaigun*, pp. 102–107; Connaughton, *Rising Sun and Tumbling Bear*, p. 115; *Official History*, vol. 3, p. 814.

43 Warner and Warner, *Tide at Sunrise*, pp. 498–513.

44 Evans and Peattie, *Kaigun*, pp. 126–27.

45 Julian S. Corbett, *Maritime Operations in the Russo-Japanese War, 1904–1905* (Annapolis, Md.: Naval Institute Press, 1994), vol. 2, p. 249; Evans and Peattie, *Kaigun*, p. 63.

46 Willmott, *Last Century of Sea Power*, vol. 1, pp. 115–19; Evans and Peattie, *Kaigun*, pp. 116–24. See also H. W. Wilson, *Battleships in Action* (Toronto: Ryerson, 1926), vol. 1, pp. 240–65.

47 Edmund Morris, *Theodore Rex* (New York: Random House, 2001), p. 397.

48 Yoshihisa Tak Matsusaka, *The Making of Japanese Manchuria, 1904–1932* (Cambridge, Mass.: Harvard Univ. Press, 2001), pp. 17–59, 180–82.

49 Willmott, *Last Century of Sea Power*, vol. 1, pp. 124–25.

50 J. Charles Schenking, *Making Waves: Politics, Propaganda, and the Emergence of the Imperial Japanese Navy, 1868–1922* (Stanford, Calif.: Stanford Univ. Press, 2005), pp. 110–12, 223–28; Evans and Peattie, *Kaigun*, pp. 159–61.

51 Willmott, *Last Century of Sea Power*, vol. 1, p. 56.

52 Reckner, *Teddy Roosevelt's Great White Fleet*, pp. 10–11.

53 Ibid., p. 161.

54 Edward S. Miller, *War Plan Orange: The U.S. Strategy to Defeat Japan in the Pacific, 1897–1945* (Annapolis, Md.: Naval Institute Press, 1991), pp. 21–32.

55 Craig C. Felker, *Testing American Seapower: U.S. Navy Strategy Exercises, 1923–1940* (College Station: Texas A&M Univ. Press, 2007), pp. 134–43. See also Thomas C. Hone and Trent Hone, *Battle Line: The United States Navy, 1919–1939* (Annapolis, Md.: Naval Institute Press, 2006), and John T. Kuehn, *Agents of Innovation: The General Board and the Design of the Fleet That Defeated the Japanese Navy* (Annapolis, Md.: Naval Institute Press, 2008).

56 Felker, *Testing American Seapower*, pp. 327–28; Weigley, *History of the United States Army*, pp. 417, 490.

57 Matsusaka, *Making of Japanese Manchuria*, pp. 405–408.

58 Drea, *Japan's Imperial Army*, pp. 254–55; Evans and Peattie, *Kaigun*, pp. 185–91; David Gordon, "Historiographical Essay: The Japan-China War, 1931–1945," *Journal of Military History* 70, no. 1 (2006), pp. 137–82.

59 Evans and Peattie, *Kaigun*, pp. 73–74, 129–32.

60 Willmott, *Last Century of Sea Power*, vol. 1, p. 125; Evans and Peattie, *Kaigun*, pp. 129–32.

61 Meirion Harries and Susie Harries, *Soldiers of the Sun: The Rise and Fall of the Imperial Japanese Army* (New York: Random House, 1991), pp. 288–99; Drea, *Japan's Imperial Army*, pp. 207–21.

XV Two Ships Passing in the Night
The United States, Great Britain, and the Immunity of Private Property at Sea in Time of War, 1904–1907

ALAN M. ANDERSON

The principle of the immunity of private property at sea in time of war provides that all privately owned ships and cargoes not contraband of war, regardless of the citizenship of the owner, belligerent or neutral, are immune from capture unless attempting to violate a blockade.[1] This principle implicates the associated issues of effective blockade, the definition of contraband, and the doctrine of continuous voyage. Historically, nations promoting or accepting the principle have had small or no naval forces, especially in comparison with their seaborne commerce or potential adversaries. For the United States, the immunity of private property at sea during war was a fundamental maritime and naval policy from virtually the founding of the Republic. In contrast, Great Britain, with the Royal Navy as the undisputed master of the seas, especially during the nineteenth century, strongly opposed the immunity of private property at sea during war. The principle was a contentious issue between the United States and Great Britain throughout the 1800s.[2]

This paper reviews and analyzes the positions of the United States and Great Britain on the principle of the immunity of private property at sea during the 1904–1907 period. It addresses the efforts in both countries to change their traditional positions prior to the 1907 Hague Conference and the reasoning behind those efforts. The consequences that flowed from their decisions to maintain their customary policies and the conflicts that developed at the 1907 conference are reviewed. This analysis sheds new light on a previously understudied period of the development of the U.S. Navy and American/British naval relations, as well as the civilian/military conflicts that existed in each nation over this important naval issue.

On 21 October 1904, Secretary of State John Hay sent a circular to representatives of the various countries that had attended the 1899 Hague Conference. On behalf of President Theodore Roosevelt, Hay called on the nations to hold a second conference. He specifically raised the issue of the immunity of private property at sea, pointing out that on 28 April 1904 the U.S. Congress had adopted a resolution calling on the president to "bring about an understanding . . . incorporating into the permanent law of civilized nations the principle of the exemption of all private property at sea, not contraband of war, from capture or destruction by belligerents."[3] Ultimately, the conference was postponed in light of the Russo-Japanese War, but the issue was now on the table for discussion in both the United States and Great Britain.

Although long retired from the navy, Alfred Thayer Mahan began efforts to get the United States to reconsider and change its traditional position. In a letter to President Roosevelt dated 27 December 1904, Mahan stated he had "seen with concern" that the country had placed the issue of immunity of private property "in the foreground of subjects for consideration." He urged the president to reconsider the nation's traditional position, recognizing that the issue was inextricably tied to the size of the navy.[4] Roosevelt equivocated but indicated he would discuss the matter with the Secretary of State.[5] Hay did not equivocate. He told the president that Mahan's arguments were "the professional sailor's view of the question. I do not think the considerations he brings to bear are weighty enough to cause us to reverse our traditional policy for the last century."[6] With that, Mahan's initial effort to change America's position failed.

Great Britain too began a review, in late 1904, of its traditional policy opposing the immunity of private property at sea. Because Britain had recognized in the 1856 Paris Declaration that a neutral flag covers an enemy's goods and that an enemy's flag covers neutral goods, except in both cases for contraband of war, the scope of its right to search and capture neutral ships was limited to those containing contraband or attempting to violate an effective blockade. But no recognized definition of "contraband of war" existed. Indeed, both as a belligerent and as a neutral, Britain had felt the impact of, and conflicts arising from, a broad application of the right of search and seizure.[7]

Prime Minister Arthur Balfour, who in late 1898 and again in 1899 had questioned Britain's traditional opposition to the immunity of private property at sea, requested a study of the issue in late 1904.[8] Sir George Clarke, the secretary to the Committee of Imperial Defence (CID) authored the response. Clarke's memorandum considered the value to Britain of the right to search and capture *neutral* ships. Despite tilting his methodology in favor of Britain's traditional position, Clarke determined that "not only would no real advantage accrue to Great Britain from the exercise of the right of search and seizure of neutral shipping carrying contraband as defined in the extreme form, but grave danger of incurring the active hostility of" neutrals, such as the United States, would occur.[9] But the Royal Navy disagreed. The Admiralty told the Foreign Office, in response to Hay's circular, that while "the inviolability of private property at sea would confer great benefits upon our mercantile marine, . . . so long as the fleet has command of the sea the danger to our commerce will be small." Any position "which tends to reduce the influence exerted by [the Royal Navy's command of the sea] is detrimental to the interests of the country."[10] However, the Admiralty's position against reconsideration was not universally held. On

9 June 1905, Capt. Edmond Slade, then serving as commander of the Royal Naval College in Greenwich, told the assistant naval secretary to the CID that "having signed the Treaty of Paris, and agreed to the proposition that the Flag covers the cargoes, we ought to go the whole hog and allow it in the case of all cargoes, except of course in the case of blockade."[11] Politicians also disagreed with Britain's traditional position. In a letter to the *Times,* Sir Robert Reid argued Britain should exempt private property at sea from capture unless it was contraband of war or intended to violate a blockade.[12]

Balfour's government left office in early December 1905 and was replaced by Henry Campbell-Bannerman's Liberal Party. Foreign Secretary Sir Edward Grey soon decided an expert committee should be appointed to reconsider Britain's traditional opposition to the immunity of private property at sea. Known as the Walton Committee for the last name of its chair, it began its work in May 1906.[13]

Russia reinvigorated the call for a second peace conference on 3 April 1906.[14] Mahan showed he did not lack persistence as a virtue, interrupting a holiday in Germany to write Hay's successor, Elihu Root. In a lengthy letter, Mahan argued that adherence to the immunity of private property at sea, "derived from the expediencies of our early weakness, has been too easily continued by successive Administrations to the present day, and to very different conditions." He asked for a reexamination of the subject and suggested that the issue be submitted to a panel of experts, such as the General Board of the Navy.[15]

This time Mahan's plea found somewhat more fertile ground. Root told Mahan that while he personally had "serious doubts" about the policy, "the United States has advocated the immunity of private property at sea so long and so positively that I cannot see how it is possible to make a *volte face* at the Hague."[16] Nevertheless, Root forwarded Mahan's letter to the Secretary of the Navy, raising the point that "the liability of private property to seizure in time of war insures a strong and powerful class in every commercial country deeply interested in the preservation of peace." However, Root also noted that "the necessity for protecting a merchant marine is undoubtedly an important consideration, leading to the enormous increase of naval armament now in progress." He asked for the views of the General Board of the Navy on the subject.[17]

Less than a month later, the General Board responded. The board recognized that American support for the policy had stemmed from the historical weakness of the navy, especially vis-à-vis the size of the country's maritime commerce. It stated the policy should be viewed from both the moral and military standpoints, that continuation of America's traditional policy had recently been advocated "from moral considerations," and "that the military or practical considerations have not received the attention in framing the United States policy which they deserve." The board then reviewed the military aspects of the immunity principle, analyzing the impact on war with various powers, including Great Britain. On the basis of its analysis, the board concluded that because a relatively small amount of American commerce was carried in domestic ships in contrast to that of potential enemies, by virtue of which greater injury might be done to enemy commerce during war, the United States should not give up the military advantage it possessed by continuing to argue for the immunity of private property at sea. Oddly, however, the board did not recommend complete renunciation of the principle but instead urged the adoption of regulations almost identical to the provisions in the 1856 Paris Declaration.[18] The board had rushed its response and was not of one mind regarding its recommendations.[19] Three months later, in a supplemental memorandum, the General Board argued that the United States should tie itself to England and work to persuade it not to change its traditional opposition to the principle, which gave it advantages over Germany.[20]

Perhaps not satisfied with the General Board's failure to recommend wholesale rejection of the immunity policy, Mahan again directly raised the issue during a meeting with President Roosevelt in late July 1906 in connection with Mahan's preparation of a history of the General Board. Roosevelt still was not impressed with Mahan's arguments.[21] Afterward, Mahan wrote Roosevelt, again laying out his arguments but this time asking permission to take his case to the court of public opinion.[22] Roosevelt consented.[23] Mahan then embarked on a concerted writing campaign, authoring articles and eventually combining some of them into a book.[24] He clearly hoped that his efforts would result in the United States dropping its traditional position.[25]

Meanwhile, the Royal Navy had been fighting any change in Britain's traditional policy. Indeed, the Admiralty did not want the matter discussed *at all*.[26] The First Sea Lord, Adm. Sir John Fisher, opposed any change in Britain's policy. He described Britain's policy as "our great special anti-German weapon of smashing an enemy's commerce."[27] The Admiralty's view was that "the right of capture of private property at sea is of great value to [Great Britain], and ought to be firmly maintained."[28] On 14 May 1906, Clarke, the author of the earlier CID study, submitted a new analysis focused on the "immunity of the private property of a belligerent under his flag." Thus, the subject of his new study, while linked to his earlier memorandum on the immunity of *neutral* ships in time of war, was different. Clarke concluded that Britain had "nothing to gain and much to lose by abandoning" the right to capture a belligerent's private property at sea. However, "if there were any reason to suppose that by abandoning an immemorial right [Britain] could secure a general reduction of naval armaments and check the naval competition which is heavily pressing upon the nations, a valid argument for change of British policy might be established."[29] Britain's traditional policy, it seemed, was now a potential bargaining chip to be used at The Hague.

In July, Clarke approached the American military attaché in London and the army's judge advocate general, who was visiting, and asked what the U.S. view was on the immunity principle. He offered to share the extensive data he had collected on the issue. Informed of the approach, Secretary of State Root responded through the American ambassador, saying he would be glad to review the data on a confidential basis. But nothing further was heard at the time.[30] Root remained anxious to learn what Britain's position would be at the conference. In October, he wrote Whitelaw Reid, the ambassador in Britain, to ask Foreign Secretary Grey what his views were on the immunity of private property. Root stated that he now harbored "grave doubts" about the traditional American policy.[31]

The views of the United States and Great Britain on the issue of the immunity of private property at sea appeared to be converging, but on which side of the issue was not clear. In early December 1906, the United States learned that the British government was divided, with some members favoring immunity and others opposing it. Clarke informally proposed a compromise to the United States, that an enemy's property in an enemy ship would continue to be subject to capture but that the concept of "contraband" would be abolished, thereby leaving a belligerent the right to conduct a blockade and to capture ships and their cargoes, regardless of whether they were neutral or belligerent, that tried to violate the blockade.[32] Learning of the British government's divided views and compromise proposal, Adm. Charles S. Sperry, who had already been designated the U.S. naval representative for the conference, wrote to the American Assistant Secretary of State to make clear that he agreed entirely with Mahan's views and those of the General Board.[33]

At nearly the same time, Prime Minister Campbell-Bannerman received a petition, signed by 168 members of the House of Commons, urging the government to adopt the exemption of private property at sea in time of war.[34] Clarke responded with a note to the prime minister, providing ammunition to use against the petitioners. He noted that "the view of the United States is changing on this point, and this was certain as soon as their Navy became more formidable."[35] Mahan would have entirely agreed with Clarke's position.

In February 1907, the Admiralty made a further submission to the Walton Committee, reiterating its unyielding opposition to any change in British policy.[36] The Board of Trade previously had agreed with Clarke's December 1904 view that opposition to the immunity of private property at sea regarding neutral vessels provided few benefits and many disadvantages to Britain.[37] A year later, it conceded that the Admiralty's views should prevail.[38] As a result, the Walton Committee's final report of 21 March 1907 appeared to decide the issue for Great Britain, concluding that the country should not abandon its traditional opposition to the immunity of private property at sea in time of war, even if other nations adopted the principle.[39] Great Britain seemed to have come full circle, back to its starting point—or had it?

Commercial interests again petitioned the government to adopt the immunity principle.[40] The Lord Chancellor, Lord Loreburn, as Sir Robert Reid became in late 1905, wrote a well-argued memorandum to the cabinet urging that the country drop its opposition to the immunity of private property at sea.[41] The result was indecision. On 26 April, the cabinet met and was unable to reach any decision.[42] On 2 May, the American ambassador learned from Foreign Secretary Grey that the cabinet had decided on the instructions for the British delegation to The Hague on every issue *except* the question of immunity of private property at sea.[43] Three days later, a decision still had not been reached. The prime minister told one of the British delegates that "he had read both sides of the controversy, and at the end of each paper perused he found himself agreeing with the writer."[44] On 16 May Mahan reentered the debate, asking if the British government would bring to the attention of its delegates his recent article against the immunity of private property at sea.[45] On 3 June Grey circulated draft instructions on the issue that after summarizing the arguments on both sides concluded, "His Majesty's Government cannot authorize . . . any Resolution which would diminish the effective means which the navy has of bringing pressure to bear upon an enemy."[46] However, if some agreement on the diminution of military and naval armaments became dependent on adoption of the principle of immunity, the government might change its position.[47] The final instructions to the British delegation were the same.[48]

At the same time, the United States was struggling to reach a final decision on its position. At a daylong meeting held at the State Department on 20 April 1907, Root initially stated that he "was not wholly clear as to the position the Government should take on this important question" but that taking a new position on immunity now was precluded by the position taken by the United States at the 1899 conference. Admiral Sperry and Gen. Horace Porter, the navy and army delegates, spoke extensively, arguing that rejection of the principle would be a significant restraint on war. Joseph Choate, the designated head of the delegation, spoke in favor of immunity, arguing that the government "should examine the question from the humanitarian and international standpoint rather than weigh the doctrine solely in the scale of self-interest." The discussion ended when Root concluded, "although he had great doubt on the question, he felt it his duty to instruct the delegation in favor of the immunity."[49] The final instructions of 31 May unequivocally told the American delegation to "maintain the traditional policy of the United States regarding the immunity of private property of belligerents at sea."[50] The United States too had come full circle.

Prior to the 1907 conference, Great Britain hoped it would be able to coordinate its positions with the United States.[51] Not unlike Mahan and his efforts to influence the views of the British delegation, First Sea Lord Fisher sent Choate a copy of an article by naval strategist Julian S. Corbett arguing against the principle. Fisher later thought the article had "done splendid service with Choate."[52] But he was wrong.

At a meeting at the Foreign Office in London with the primary American and British delegates to the conference, Grey tried to gain unanimity on a number of subjects, including the issue of the immunity of private property at sea.[53] Choate, however, "rather startled the Minister for Foreign Affairs by holding before him the prospect of all nations against the British position—inquiring whether under these circumstances Great Britain would still feel disposed to maintain its ground."[54] President Roosevelt, while confirming that he held "to our traditional American view, but in rather tepid fashion," was "astounded" by Choate's words and asked his ambassador in Britain whether he should say something to Secretary Root or Choate.[55] Unfortunately, by the time he learned of Choate's action and views, significant damage had been done to the relations between the two countries at the 1907 conference.

Once at the conference, Choate aggressively asserted America's position. Choate tried to get Great Britain to change its position, arguing that adoption of the immunity principle was inevitable. He told one of Britain's delegates he would make a significant speech in support of immunity.[56] In his speech, Choate indeed spoke at length in support of America's traditional position, but in doing so he directed his arguments primarily against Great Britain and was highly critical of any nation that opposed the immunity of private property at sea in time of war.[57] Great Britain recognized the speech was aimed largely against it.[58] Choate received praise for his speech from a variety of sources.[59] Britain spoke against America's proposal and tried to delay consideration of the U.S. proposal until the issue of contraband was considered. Choate opposed any such delay, doggedly insisting on a vote on the proposal. When the vote was taken on 17 July, twenty-one nations, including Germany, voted with the United States, while eleven countries voted with Great Britain against the immunity of private property at sea.[60]

Although Britain had not been isolated on the immunity issue, it quickly became viewed as the obstacle to progress at the conference.[61] The United States and Germany were firmly seen as "pulling together" against Great Britain.[62] The United States and Germany joined in opposing Britain's proposal to abolish contraband, resulting in a sharp exchange between British and American delegates.[63] Foreign Secretary Grey offered to speak to the American ambassador if the British delegation found "that you are having difficulties with the United States Delegates which you think are unreasonable."[64] Moreover, the United States became viewed as a potential opponent of Great Britain in war. Fisher advised King Edward VII, "The only *one* thing in the world that England has to fear is Germany and the United States *combining* against England, and the Hague Conference and the Algeciras Conference over Morocco brought them nearer than ever before."[65]

Fisher acted on his concerns about the United States combining with Germany against Great Britain. He told the Director of Naval Intelligence to prepare war plans assuming that the U.S. Navy would voyage across the Atlantic to join the Imperial

High Seas Fleet.[66] Multiple plans were prepared in 1908. War Plans 4 and 5 posited the United States and Germany fighting Britain. War Plan 6 included an alternative scenario involving the United States and Germany against Britain.[67] All were fully developed war plans for possible execution in 1908, with detailed directions to the various fleets and units of the Royal Navy. Each plan envisioned that the Royal Navy would await the arrival of the American fleet and intercept and defeat it before it could rendezvous with the German navy.[68] Even the War Office studied the possibility of war with the United States;[69] it concluded, "The growth of the United States and of the German empire and the development of their fleets constitute the most serious problem which confronts the people of the United Kingdom."[70] The 1909 war plans also presented a scenario of war with the United States allied with Germany.[71] Fortunately for both the United States and Great Britain, this "serious problem" never materialized.

Thus, in anticipation of the 1907 Hague Conference, the United States and Great Britain undertook extensive reconsideration of their respective positions vis-à-vis the immunity of private property at sea in time of war. The United States started from its traditional support of this principle. The navy, led by Alfred Thayer Mahan and the General Board, nearly brought about a reversal of the country's long-standing adherence to the inviolability of private property. In the end, an inability to change from the status quo caused the United States to enter the 1907 conference with its position unchanged. In contrast, Britain's civilian leadership led the arguments that the country should drop its opposition to the immunity principle. The Royal Navy led the defense of the country's traditional policy. In late 1906 and early 1907, the two nations came tantalizingly close to realizing how near their positions were. Instead, as a result of the aggressive support by the United States for immunity at the 1907 conference, Britain became concerned that it might face war with Germany allied with America. The United States and Great Britain had gone from two ships passing in the night to nearly a collision course. Fortunately, the two nations avoided a crash.

NOTES   1 Bryan Ranft, "Restraints on War at Sea before 1945," in *Restraints on War: Studies in the Limitation of Armed Conflict,* ed. Michael Howard (Oxford, U.K.: Oxford Univ. Press, 1979), p. 44.

2 John W. Coogan, *The End of Neutrality: The United States, Britain, and Maritime Rights, 1899–1915* (Ithaca, N.Y.: Cornell Univ. Press, 1981), pp. 18–25.

3 Hay to foreign ambassadors, 21 October 1904, John Hay Papers, no. 15,213-23P, reel 23, vol. 36, Library of Congress, Washington, D.C. [hereafter Hay/LC Papers].

4 Mahan to Roosevelt, 27 December 1904, in *Letters and Papers of Alfred Thayer Mahan,* ed. Robert Seager II and Doris D. Maguire (Annapolis, Md.: Naval Institute Press), vol. 3, pp. 112–14.

5 Roosevelt to Mahan, 29 December 1904, A. T. Mahan Papers, no. 19,175-12P, container 4, reel 3, Library of Congress, Washington, D.C. [hereafter ATM/LC].

6 Hay to Roosevelt, 31 December 1904, reel 2, vol. 2, Hay/LC Papers.

7 Coogan, *End of Neutrality,* pp. 30–54.

8 The earlier paper is Balfour, note, 24 December 1898, p. 82, CAB 17/85, f. 224, The National Archives, Kew, U.K. [hereafter TNA].

9 Sir George Clarke, "The Value to Great Britain of the Right of Search and Capture of Neutral Vessels," 12 December 1904, pp. 2–6, CAB 4/1/41B, TNA.

10 Admiralty to Foreign Office, 31 December 1904, p. 225, CAB 17/85, TNA.

11 Slade to Nicholson, 9 June 1905, p. 307, CAB 17/85, TNA.

12 R. T. Reid, "Capture of Private Property at Sea," *Times* (London), 14 October 1905, p. 4.

13 Foreign Office to Colonial Office, Admiralty, and Board of Trade, 19 April 1906, p. 15, FO 412/86, TNA.

14 Benckendorff to Grey, 3 April 1906, in *Correspondence Respecting the Second Peace Conference Held at The Hague in 1907* (London: His Majesty's Stationery Office, 1908), pp. 1–4.

15 Mahan to Root, 20 April 1906, in *Letters and Papers,* ed. Seager and Maguire, vol. 3, pp. 157–59.

16 Root to Mahan, 21 May 1906, quoted in Richard W. Turk, *The Ambiguous Relationship: Theodore Roosevelt and Alfred Thayer Mahan* (New York: Greenwood, 1987), p. 73.

17 Root to Secretary of the Navy, 21 May 1906, Charles S. Sperry Papers, MSS 40923, box 9, folder 1, Library of Congress, Washington, D.C. [hereafter Sperry/LC].

18 General Board to Secretary of the Navy, 20 June 1906, pp. 1, 14–17, 25–26, box 9, folder 1, Sperry/LC.

19 Barnette to Mahan, 27 July 1906, reel 2, box 2, ATM/LC.

20 General Board to Secretary of the Navy, 26 September 1906, box 1, vol. 4, Record Group 80, National Archives and Records Administration (I), Washington, D.C.

21 Robert Seager II, *Alfred Thayer Mahan: The Man and His Letters* (Annapolis, Md.: Naval Institute Press, 1977), p. 509; Turk, *Ambiguous Relationship,* p. 73.

22 Mahan to Roosevelt, 14 August 1906, in *Letters and Papers,* ed. Seager and Maguire, vol. 3, p. 164.

23 Roosevelt to Mahan, 16 August 1906, container 4, reel 3, folder "Theodore Roosevelt," ATM/LC.

24 See, generally, A. T. Mahan, *Some Neglected Aspects of War* (Boston: Little, Brown, 1907).

25 See Mahan to Maxse, 5 March, 15 April, and 30 April 1907, in *Letters and Papers,* ed. Seager and Maguire, vol. 3, pp. 207, 209–10.

26 F.A.C., Foreign Office Minute, 15 January 1906; W.E.D., Foreign Office Minute, 19 January 1906; both CAB 17/85, ff. 232–33, TNA.

27 Fisher to Fortesque, 14 April 1906, in *Fear God and Dread Nought: The Correspondence of Admiral of the Fleet Lord Fisher of Kilverstone,* vol. 2, *Years of Power, 1904–1914,* ed. Arthur J. Marder (London: Jonathan Cape, 1956) [hereafter *FGDN,* vol. 2], p. 72.

28 Remarks by Admiralty to The Hague Conference, 12 May 1906, p. 17, CAB 4/2/75B, TNA.

29 Sir George Clarke, "The Capture of the Private Property of Belligerents at Sea," 14 May 1906, pp. 10–11, CAB 4/2/73B, TNA.

30 See Davis to Sperry, 12 December 1906, box 9, folder 2, Sperry/LC.

31 Root to W. Reid, 24 October 1906, Reid Family Papers, MSS 65491, Part I: series A, reel 176, Library of Congress, Washington, D.C. [hereafter Reid/LC].

32 Davis to Sperry, 12 December 1906.

33 Sperry to Bacon, 15 December 1906, box 9, folder 2, Sperry/LC.

34 Petition to Sir Henry Campbell-Bannerman, December 1906, pp. 271–72, CAB 17/85, TNA.

35 Ibid., pp. 273–74.

36 Admiralty memorandum to Walton Committee, 4 February 1907, p. 11, CAB 37/86/14, TNA.

37 Board of Trade, remarks to The Hague Conference, 22 January 1906, p. 13, CAB 4/2/75B, TNA.

38 Board of Trade to Foreign Office, 12 March 1907, p. 123, FO 372/38, TNA.

39 Report of the Inter-Departmental Committee Appointed to Consider the Subjects Which May Arise for Discussion at the Second Peace Conference, 21 March 1907, CAB 37/87/42, TNA.

40 For example, Manchester Chamber of Commerce to Grey, 22 March 1907, p. 128, FO 412/86, TNA.

41 Lord Loreburn, "Immunity of Private Property at Sea in Time of War," n.d. (printed April 1907), CAB 37/88/58, TNA.

42 Campbell-Bannerman to Edward VII, 26 April 1907, CAB 41/31/16, f. 41, TNA.

43 W. Reid to Root, 4 May 1907, Part I: series A, reel 176, Reid/LC.

44 Ernest Satow Journal, 7 May 1907, PRO 30/33/16/10, ff. 17, TNA.

45 Crowe to Satow, 16 May 1907, PRO 30/33/10/13, TNA.

46 Grey, memorandum, 3 June 1907, CAB 37/89/65, TNA.

47 Ibid.

48 Grey to Fry, 12 June 1907, pp. 235–42, FO 412/86, TNA.

49 Minutes, 20 April 1907, pp. 10–14, Joseph Hodges Choate Papers, MSS 15768, box 21, folder "Hague Conference 1907," Library of Congress, Washington, D.C. [hereafter Choate/LC].

50 James Brown Scott, ed., *Instructions to the American Delegates to the Hague Peace Conferences and Their Official Reports* (New York: Oxford Univ. Press, 1916), p. 81.

51 See, for example, Grey to Durand, 17 October 1906, p. 462, FO 372/23, TNA.

52 Fisher to Corbett, 8 June 1907, Papers of 1st Lord Fisher of Kilverstone, GBR/0014/FISR, FISR 1/5, Churchill Archives, Cambridge, U.K.

53 See Satow Journal, 12 June 1907, p. 25, PRO 30/33/16/10, TNA.

54 W. Reid to Roosevelt, 19 July 1907, Part I: series A, reel 176, Reid/LC.

55 Roosevelt to W. Reid, 29 July 1907, Part I: series A, reel 176, Reid/LC.

56 Satow Journal, 26 June 1907, p. 31, PRO 30/33/16/10, TNA.

57 James Brown Scott, ed., *The Proceedings of the Hague Peace Conferences,* vol. 3, *The Conference of 1907* (New York: Oxford Univ. Press, 1921), pp. 748–67.

58 Satow Journal, 28 June 1907, p. 33, PRO 30/33/16/10, TNA.

59 See, for example, Carnegie to Choate, 1 July 1907; White to Choate, 12 August 1907; both box 21, folder "Hague Conference 1907," Choate/LC.

60 Scott, *Conference of 1907,* pp. 790, 801, 821–25.

61 Reay to Campbell-Bannerman, 21 July 1907, Add MSS 52514, ff. 89–92, Henry Campbell-Bannerman Papers, British Library, London, U.K.

62 Carnegie to Morley, 30 July 1907, Andrew Carnegie Papers, MSS 15107, box 143, Library of Congress, Washington, D.C.

63 Scott, *Conference of 1907,* pp. 865–66. See also Coogan, *End of Neutrality,* pp. 94–95.

64 Grey to Fry, 30 July 1907, FO 800/69, ff. 171, TNA.

65 Fisher to Edward VII, 7 October 1907, in *FGDN,* vol. 2, pp. 142–43 [emphasis in original].

66 Edmond Slade Diary, 22 July 1908, Edmond Slade Papers, MRF 39/2, Caird Library, National Maritime Museum, Greenwich, U.K.

67 War Plan W. 4, part 1, pp. 596–625, ADM 116/1043B, TNA; War Plan W. 5, part 2, pp. 482–576, ADM 116/1043B, TNA; War Plan W. 6, part 2, pp. 714–18, ADM 116/1043B, TNA.

68 See, for example, War Plan W. 4, part 2, pp. 865–77, ADM 116/1043B, TNA.

69 Maj. Grant Duff, "The Conditions of a War between the British Empire and the United States," 1907–1908, WO 106/40, TNA.

70 Duff, "Military Policy in a War with Germany," 1908, p. 27, WO 106/46, TNA.

71 "War Plan G.U.," 1909, MSS 253/84/3, Papers of Thomas Crease, National Museum of the Royal Navy, Portsmouth, U.K.

XVI *Strategy and Sustainment*
A Century of Australian Amphibious Operations in the Asia-Pacific

RHYS CRAWLEY and PETER J. DEAN

At dawn on 25 April 1915, soldiers of the Australian and New Zealand Army Corps (the ANZAC), along with their British, French, and Indian allies, landed on the Gallipoli Peninsula in what would become one of the most infamous amphibious assaults in military history. For some in Australia this action served as the origins of a national warrior ethos—what has become known as the "Anzac legend"—while for others, it symbolized the "birthplace" of the Australian nation.[1]

Rather than being indicative of a focus on joint amphibious expeditionary operations, the landing at Gallipoli was part of an expeditionary strategy, an example of the Australian tradition of committing its forces to the defense of its interests alongside its major alliance partner. As the Australian military historian Professor Jeffrey Grey has pointed out, Australia's approach to war has always been distinguished by the "quality of its expeditionary infantry, who are usually sent overseas as part of a wider coalition and depend on a larger ally for logistical and other support."[2] Such deployments have a long heritage in Australian military history, from the early colonial commitment to support Britain in the Sudan in 1885 to the Boer War, through the First and Second World Wars, to Korea, Vietnam, and more recently, Iraq and Afghanistan.

Australia's ability to commit its military forces to major operations in distant places has largely resulted from the relatively benign security environment of its immediate neighborhood. Specifically, it has required a stable Asia-Pacific region that is largely devoid of tension or major strategic competition. This has been an essential prerequisite to Australia's capacity to forward-deploy its forces alongside those of its "great and powerful friends," who in turn have guaranteed Australia's maritime security in Asia. Thus, for the bulk of its history Australia has used its military to support its interests and values—as operations in Europe and the Middle East highlight—as opposed to defending its sovereign territory.[3]

The strategic tension between an expeditionary strategy and regional operations has meant that when Australia has undertaken the latter, it has traditionally struggled with equipment, doctrine, and most significantly, the "lifeblood of war"—logistics. With the current rise of strategic competition and uncertainty in Asia, the drawdown of Australian forces from Afghanistan, and the U.S. "pivot," or "rebalance," to the Asia-Pacific region, these joint regional operations represent a major focus of Australia's future security threats. Hence, in addition to being able to continue to provide the niche, single-service deployments alongside its allies that Australia has traditionally undertaken, Australia must also possess capabilities to undertake self-sustaining maritime expeditionary operations in its immediate region.

This paper charts the vexed history of Australian amphibious operations in the Asia-Pacific region over the last century. Using examples from the First and Second World Wars and the Australian-led international deployment to East Timor in 1999, it argues that despite not being a central component of strategic policy for most of this period, amphibious warfare has been a constant and recurring theme in the history of Australia's defense needs. These case studies reveal how and why Australia used its amphibious capabilities in the past and why it needs to enhance its range of strategic and operational capabilities to deal with future threats and opportunities.

German New Guinea: 1914

Australia is the sixth-largest country in the world and the only one of the top six to be completely surrounded by water. Covering 7,618,493 square kilometers, with 59,736 kilometers of coastline, it is an island, a country, and a continent.[4] Moreover, it is a classic trade-dependent maritime state, with a strong Western cultural identity in international affairs. The clash between its Western cultural heritage and its location in Asia, in combination with the realities of its small population (less than 23.5 million at the beginning of 2014), its large landmass, and its rich natural resources, has meant that successive Australian governments have always felt an acute sense of distance from Western allies. Ever since British settlement in 1788, Australia has relied for its protection and security on a major Anglo-Saxon maritime power exerting dominance over the Asia-Pacific. The nation having outsourced its defense requirements to the British Empire in the period after Federation in 1901, Australia's rudimentary military forces were little interested in amphibious warfare. However, at the outbreak of the First World War Australia's regional interests and its support for the empire led to a strategic alignment that depended on the new nation's ability to project force in its immediate neighborhood.

On 6 August 1914, just days after declaring war on Germany, Britain requested that Australia "as a great and urgent imperial service" seize and destroy the German wireless stations in the southwest Pacific that were supporting Vice Adm. Graf von Spee's East Asiatic Squadron.[5] The Australian government agreed and in less than two weeks raised, equipped, and dispatched an expeditionary force of 1,500 men for overseas service.[6] Designated the Australian Naval and Military Expeditionary

Force (AN&MEF), Australia's first joint amphibious force landed near Rabaul, the capital of German New Guinea, on 11 September 1914. Facing only limited resistance, it located and captured the wireless station; surrender terms were signed within the week.[7] It was an impressive start to a lasting tradition of Australian amphibious warfare in the Asia-Pacific.

As well as being Australia's first amphibious operation, the destruction of the wireless station and the capture of Rabaul marked the first time an Australian military force had been responsible for its own logistics. One of the reasons that the force could be raised so rapidly was that its rifles and uniforms came from existing stocks. In spite of this logistic success, the initial departure of the AN&MEF from Sydney was delayed owing to problems loading supplies. When the force did sail, it did so without such basic equipment as mess tins or signaling devices. Nevertheless, as the commander of the force, Col. William Holmes, knew, until the islands were captured and normal commercial trade with New Guinea recommenced, supplies for his troops and the local population would have to be provided by the initial expeditionary task force.[8]

The AN&MEF had undertaken a remarkable display of force development, coupled with a high degree of strategic mobility provided by the ships of the Royal Australian Navy (RAN). For a force entirely dependent on seaborne resupply, it was fortunate to enjoy command of the sea, which ensured the safety of lines of communication and meant that sustainment was a comparatively easy task once the force was safely ashore and in command of Papua's major infrastructure facilities. Supplying the force was, however, one of the critical factors in shaping the size of the force and its conduct of operations. The saving grace for Colonel Holmes was the quick victory he was able to achieve over the German-led native troops, which in turn allowed his supplies to be brought ashore using existing piers and jetties. Because stores could be landed with ease, work soon began on a water-condensing plant near the wharf at Rabaul—a critical necessity, given the prevalence of mosquito-carried diseases, such as malaria, for which reason troops were forbidden from obtaining their water from existing tanks. Everything else had to be acquired and delivered from Australia, a distance of nearly two thousand sea miles.[9]

As the historian Ross Mallett writes, "That a force could be enlisted, equipped and shipped in little over a week must be considered extraordinary."[10] Indeed, it was a remarkable logistic achievement for a joint force comprising a fledgling navy and army that had no prior experience of working together. It is even more impressive given the 1911 estimation that it would take "at least 6 weeks" to enlist, organize, and train an expeditionary force for service outside Australia.[11] Militarily, the expedition to Rabaul "demonstrated the usefulness of joint forces in the defence of Australian interests."[12] However, this small and brief action was soon forgotten among the media coverage of the Gallipoli landings in 1915 and the maelstrom of the western front between 1916 and 1918. The lessons of amphibious warfare, including the experience of being responsible for its own logistics, would soon slip from memory. In most future wars Australia would be dependent on its allies for logistic support.

Southwest Pacific: 1942–1945

In the interwar period Australia continued to place its faith in the power of the Royal Navy to protect its interests in the Asia-Pacific. This meant that once again amphibious operations were almost entirely absent from Australian defense planning. There was in fact only one exercise in amphibious operations in this period —in 1935—and this was remarkable only "for [its] air of unreality."[13] The fall of Singapore, the Dutch East Indies, and Australian New Guinea in early 1942 radically changed Australia's strategic circumstances. During the course of 1943–45 the Australian military, in concert with its U.S. coalition partner, would conduct four division-sized amphibious assaults, one brigade-sized assault, dozens of battalion- or company-sized assaults, and hundreds of amphibious transportation operations in the Southwest Pacific Area of operations.[14]

Australia's first amphibious assault of the war—and its first since Gallipoli in 1915—was against the Japanese base at Lae in September 1943. Although it was a stunning strategic and operational success, Lae highlighted a number of tactical deficiencies, particularly in Australian training and logistics. Getting ashore was not a problem, especially given the limited Japanese resistance on land. However, soon after the landing got under way it became apparent that the limited American amphibious assets allocated for the maintenance of the beachhead were not sufficient for an operation of this size. In preparing for the landing the Australians had concentrated on the tactical assault phase as opposed to maintenance, supply, and logistics. So entrenched was the mistaken mind-set that the Australian commander actually rejected beforehand an offer of a beach ordnance detachment, believing that arrangements were already adequate.[15] To overcome the effects of this deficiency, he was forced to reduce his frontline combat power and reallocate troops from a pioneer battalion and two infantry battalions to the task of unloading resupply ships. This was a poor solution, and instead of fixing the situation it merely produced bottlenecks and blockages on the beaches. Supplies were placed alongside fuel and ammunition dumps—a major hazard, given the ongoing, if sporadic, Japanese air raids on the beachhead.[16] Poor logistic planning could have been disastrous had it not been for luck.

The operation at Lae revealed that while the Australian units and formations were adept in amphibious assault, logistics were their Achilles' heel. Lae highlighted the need for more specialized logistic units, the requirement for a beach master with overall authority in the landing zone, the desperate need for amphibious training for noncombat units, and the necessity to alter current operating procedures and doctrine to improve both logistics and the command-and-control arrangements between the three services. All of these needs could be met through structural changes and increased training in amphibious warfare. In late 1943 the Australian army established joint beach groups, each totaling 1,800 men and consisting of troops, engineers, pioneers, signalers, medical staff, and naval beach commandos. The role of these units was to clear the beach, liaise with the forces offshore, and unload the landing craft.[17] To improve training, an Australian/U.S. amphibious training school, the Joint Overseas Operational Training School, was established, with specialist training in logistics forming part of the program. Many of those in the beach groups attended the school, thus improving interservice logistics cooperation.[18] By the time Australia's military forces were tasked with the liberation of Borneo in July 1945—in what would include the final amphibious assault of the Pacific War—the lessons from Lae had been learned.

Balikpapan, the third and final of the Borneo landings, was Australia's largest and last amphibious assault of the war. The task was allotted to the 1st Australian Corps, ably supported by U.S. air, naval, and logistics forces. The operation was preceded by a preliminary bombardment lasting twenty days and involving three thousand tons of bombs and nearly forty thousand shells—the largest volume of ordnance ever in support of an Australian operation.[19] It destroyed the shore defenses and knocked out most of the enemy's field guns.[20] The way was set for the force of 33,500 men, in over a hundred ships, to begin its approach.

The importance and difficulty of resupply had not been lost on those planning the Balikpapan assault. The Australian divisional commander commanding the operations recognized that the problem was not in landing the troops "but in landing heavy equipment and stores since beaches may be vulnerable to shelling."[21] Such logistic considerations were at the forefront of his mind when he selected the landing site. The beach chosen had firmer sand than elsewhere along the coast and, more importantly, was closer to Balikpapan Bay, the use of which, he noted, "would ease the problem of supply over the beach and would be a safeguard against unfavorable weather."[22]

The voyage to the beaches on 1 July 1945 was quick, and the armored assault craft carried troops, stores, and weapons ashore. The beach group, which had received Gen. Douglas MacArthur's praise for its work during earlier assaults on Borneo, landed at Balikpapan with the second wave of troops and got to work marking out the beaches and directing the subsequent waves of troops. It was soon found that only one beach, code-named GREEN, was suitable for handling the tank landing craft (LCTs) and even there the LCTs could not get close enough to the beach to use their ramps. The beach groups therefore turned to the 2.5-ton amphibious

DUKW trucks to unload stores.[23] By the morning of 3 July the Americans had delivered and the Australian beach groups had unloaded nearly a thousand vehicles,
more than 16,500 men, and nearly two thousand tons of equipment and stores.[24]

With the beaches secure, work turned to creating docks for unloading stores.
The Australians constructed a pontoon dock, but by far the standout was the U-
shaped dock built at GREEN Beach by the U.S. Navy's 111th Naval Construction
Battalion. The dock's design gave it greater capacity and improved the speed at
which supplies could be brought ashore and stockpiled. On 10 July a new beach,
BROWN, was opened on the south side of Balikpapan Bay. This became the major logistic center for the rest of the campaign.[25] By 21 July the beach groups had
landed 5,562 vehicles, 36,291 personnel, and 32,127 tons of stores.[26] It was an effort that would not have been possible in 1943; training, experience, and doctrinal
development meant that by 1945 the Australians were flexible enough to adapt to
meet circumstances. This effort was also the result of plugging into and relying on
American resources. Despite Australian improvements on the beaches, Balikpapan
—and the other Borneo landings—would not have been possible without U.S. logistic assets, most importantly ships to transport men, munitions, and equipment
from Australia to the theater of operations. Australia's military was too small and its
industrial capacity too limited to sustain major operations in its own region. This
limitation would continue for another half-century.

INTERFET: 1999

The Australian Chiefs of Staff Committee in 1946 proposed that amphibious
capabilities become a major part of the force structure of the postwar Australian
military, but the government was not willing to fund this or other major projects.[27]
In time, the threat presented by the Cold War, the relative security of the South Pacific, and the fact that in 1950 Australia again found itself providing niche, single-
service contributions to an overseas coalition, this time in Korea, meant that amphibious operations drifted from priority. Australia moved into a period marked by
what was known as the strategy of "Forward Defence" (1955–72), one that would
once again see Australia concentrate on securing its interests and supporting Western values with its major alliance partners far from Australia's shores—in Malaya,
Malaysia, and Vietnam.

At the conclusion of the Vietnam War and with the establishment of the Nixon
Doctrine, Australian strategic policy shifted toward a focus on a strategy of "Defence
of Australia" (1973–97). This continental defense posture focused on the supposed
"air-sea gap" to Australia's north. The strategic focus on sea denial in the defense
of continental Australia meant that Australian strategic policy again showed little
interest in amphibious warfare. However, this strategic focus was soon revealed as
having major repercussions when it came to securing Australia's regional interest,

especially in the South Pacific. The first major deployment of Australian troops in this era, Operation MORRIS DANCE, was an amphibious demonstration conducted off Fiji in 1987. This deployment revealed the poor capacity of the Australian Defence Force (ADF) to conduct joint amphibious operations. Shortfalls included inadequate doctrine, poor interservice communications, and the lack of amphibious ships and craft and operating concepts needed to undertake such missions.

MORRIS DANCE highlighted the need to improve the ADF's ambitious warfare capabilities. The driving force behind these innovations accelerated in the post–Cold War era as regional insecurity in the South Pacific became a major area of concern for Australia. This period also saw a concurrent focus on deployments as part of Australia's traditional distant expeditionary strategy, through its participation in the first Gulf War. In spite of this important commitment, regional instability came to dominate the period of the middle-to-late 1990s. This insecurity heralded a new era in Australian strategic policy, that of "Regional Defence" (1997–2001). During this time Australia undertook its most significant military operation since Vietnam—the International Force East Timor (INTERFET) stabilization mission to East Timor in 1999.[28]

East Timor was the first time that Australia had been the lead nation in a large-scale operation, and as such the ADF had greater responsibility than ever before. Indeed, the chief of the ADF described the deployment to East Timor as "the most significant undertaking we have had since World War II."[29] Looking farther back, it was the first joint operation under Australian command since Rabaul in 1914.[30]

In the early hours of 20 September 1999, five C-130 Hercules aircraft, full of Australian and New Zealand Special Air Service troops, landed at Dili, the capital of East Timor. After securing the airport, the soldiers moved into the smoldering ruins of the town, and then, along with infantry from the 2nd Battalion of the Royal Australian Regiment, established contact with the Indonesian military and got to work clearing the port. Some 1,500 INTERFET troops, the bulk of whom were Australian, landed that day. The situation was tense, and there had been no telling how the militia or Indonesian military would react. Nonetheless, within days the situation had settled. Force numbers swelled to 11,500 by mid-November; the mission was accomplished by mid-December, and responsibility was handed to a UN peacekeeping force on 23 February 2000.[31] The five-month operation was a success, but logistically it had been "a close run thing."[32]

There had been some preliminary logistic planning prior to the final decision to form INTERFET, but this planning had been minimal and reflected the notion that it would be a short-term deployment. In reality, the ADF had two weeks' warning that it would be responsible for sustaining INTERFET, Australia's largest logistics commitment since Balikpapan.[33] In that time it had to get its own logistics in order

—no small feat, considering that Australian logistic units and systems had been cut back over the previous decade—and prepare to handle the logistics for an entire multinational force.[34]

Notionally, national contingents were meant to provide their own logistic support; but not all had the capacity to support operations away from their own countries, and some arrived without any supplies at all. In these cases, Australia as lead nation was forced to carry the logistic burden. This was not something for which the ADF was prepared—the ADF's processes and information technology systems were designed to support Australian forces operating in Australia, not national or other forces outside Australia—and it placed considerable strain on the ADF's logistics capabilities.[35] Maj. Gen. Peter Cosgrove, the INTERFET commander, later stated that "our logistic engine was under extreme pressure most of the time."[36] The political scientist Professor James Cotton goes farther: "Assuming the lead nation role stretched Australia's logistics capability to breaking point."[37]

The first hurdle in the logistic process was Darwin, in northern Australia. All INTERFET supplies went through Darwin before being sent to East Timor. The port and airport struggled to cope with the increased traffic that the deployment required.[38] Nonetheless, through constant hard work, supplies were dispatched. Some supplies were sent by air, but the overwhelming majority went by sea.[39] This burden was carried by civilian ships, without which, Cosgrove noted, logistics "would have been severely hampered."[40]

A lack of port facilities for transshipping and off-loading stores, however, meant that helicopters played an important role in getting material ashore.[41] The Australian CH-47 Chinook heavy-lift helicopters were inoperative at the commencement of operations, and Australia therefore relied on U.S. assets.[42] Initial American logistic support was provided by four CH-53 Sea Stallion helicopters from the 31st Marine Expeditionary Unit, based on the amphibious assault ship USS *Peleliu* (LHA 5) in Dili Harbor.[43] These helicopters enabled the rapid distribution of troops and supplies around East Timor and were particularly useful once patrols began pushing out from Dili.[44] To reduce its footprint in East Timor, the United States eventually decided to contract this work out.[45]

The complexity of logistic distribution increased as the force moved away from Dili. In the absence of suitable roads, most of the supplies for units spread throughout East Timor were delivered by amphibious craft over the shore and then, where possible, moved forward by vehicles.[46] INTERFET enjoyed control of the sea, and the sea lines of communication were secure. In spite of the tension and the need to tread carefully, there was no opposition to the landing, equipment was sufficient, and supplies could be off-loaded and distributed without the need for fire support. Yet the system still struggled. INTERFET was lucky that the situation did not escalate.

The deployment to East Timor provided some poignant lessons for Australian strategic policy about the capabilities required to operate in the region. Academic and East Timor veteran Bob Breen neatly summarizes the issues in his work on regional force projection:

> So, despite ending the twentieth century with one of Australia's most strategically important and risky military force projections, the lessons were not applied again. Intuitively, one might have expected that a force-projecting island nation like Australia would have become increasingly proficient, having had opportunities for both rehearsal and practice for more than a century. The reverse was true—especially when allies were not in a position to help.
>
> During the decade leading up to Operation Stabilise [the original East Timor mission], the ADF was neither as proficient as it believed it was, nor as competent as it should have been. Operation Stabilise once again exposed historically persistent weaknesses in the enabling functions of force projection. Australia had depended on good luck and the resilience of junior leaders and small teams at tactical tipping points in 1942, on the Kokoda Track, and in 1966, at Long Tan in Vietnam, and had to do so again in the streets of Dili in 1999.[47]

The East Timor experience was instructive, especially in 2006 when Australia once again found itself undertaking regional force projection operations concurrently with deployments as part of an expeditionary strategy, this time in Afghanistan. However, while Australia's commitment to Afghanistan was both important and the major focus of the ADF's operations for much of the last decade it did not stop the lessons from East Timor and other regional operations from being absorbed.

Conclusion: East Timor and Beyond

The post–East Timor period has witnessed a new era for amphibious warfare in Australian strategic policy. By 2000, two refurbished U.S. Navy LPAs (amphibious landing platforms), HMAS *Manoora* and HMAS *Kanimbla,* were available to the RAN, which with them and the heavy landing ship HMAS *Tobruk* was able to form its first amphibious ready group (ARG) since the end of the Second World War. The first operational deployment of the ARG was in 2006, when the ADF was again required to intervene in East Timor as the security situation in the country deteriorated. Unlike 1999, when the Dili Harbor facilities were secured, in 2006 the ADF operated entirely over the beach. HMAS *Tobruk* had previously played a critical role in the support for Australian operations in Somalia (1993) and Bougainville (1994), and the RAN's amphibious assets had made a central contribution to Australia's disaster-relief response to the 2004 tsunami in Aceh.

In light of lessons from Somalia, Bougainville, and East Timor the 2000 Defence White Paper committed the nation to purchasing two new amphibious vessels as replacements for *Tobruk, Manoora,* and *Kanimbla.*[48] By the time of the release of the 2004 Defence Capability Plan this commitment had evolved to the purchase of two 27,500-ton, Spanish-designed multipurpose amphibious assault ships (or Landing Helicopter Docks, LHDs), the largest vessels that the RAN has ever operated.[49] Each of these ships, when they become operational in 2015 and 2016, will be able to deliver ashore in three hours what the RAN's ARG needed three days to complete in East Timor in 2006.[50] This represents the most significant change to Australian amphibious capability since the reconfiguration of Australia's military forces following the strategic shock of the rapid Japanese advance through the Pacific in 1942.

The irony of the ADF's operational experience since 1914 is that while an "expeditionary strategy" has seen Australia consistently deploy its forces overseas to distant theaters, they generally have not undertaken self-sustaining joint amphibious expeditionary operations in the process; rather, such operations have occurred only in Australia's immediate vicinity. The historical distinction in Australian strategic policy between that of an "expeditionary strategy" and the "Defence of Australia" has only resulted in the neglect of the region around Australia—notably the South Pacific and Southeast Asia—when determining the ADF's force structure. More recently, however, Australia has moved toward ending this binary distinction. This move is a recognition and reflection of the reality that the vast maritime, littoral, and archipelagic region in which Australia sits presents the ADF with a land-sea-air operating environment, as opposed to an "air-sea gap." This reality requires an ADF capable of undertaking self-sustaining joint expeditionary operations in the region, as well as one that can deploy as part of a broader coalition.

The 2009 Defence White Paper recognized this need, noting that Australia required "an expeditionary orientation on the part of the ADF at the operational level, underpinned by requisite force projection capabilities."[51] The 2013 Defence White Paper that followed again emphasized this point, noting that the ADF needed to develop and maintain a robust amphibious capability as part of its overall maritime strategy focused on the "Indo-Pacific" region.[52] This is even more critical as the focus on global strategic competition and economic power moves east. With the U.S. pivot to the Asia-Pacific, the rise of China, and the increasing importance of both for the immediate region and of the wider Asia-Pacific to Australia's defense priorities, odds are that even more demands will be made on the ADF's amphibious capability. This is especially true in that a modern, versatile amphibious capability offers much more than just the standard roles of old-fashioned amphibious assault, raid, withdrawal, and demonstration.[53]

NOTES   1 This paper is a combination of papers presented by the authors at the 2013 McMullen Naval History Symposium, U.S. Naval Academy, Annapolis, Md. For a more detailed discussion on the logistics and strategy of amphibious operations in the Asia-Pacific see Rhys Crawley, "Sustaining Amphibious Operations in the Asia-Pacific: Logistic Lessons for Australia, 1914–2014," *Australian Defence Force Journal*, no. 193 (March/April 2014), pp. 28–39; and Peter J. Dean, "Amphibious Operations and the Evolution of Australian Defense Policy," *Naval War College Review* 67, no. 4 (Autumn 2014), pp. 20–39.

2 Jeffrey Grey, *A Military History of Australia* (Melbourne, Austral.: Cambridge Univ. Press, 2000), p. 5.

3 The major exception to this is the Pacific War in 1942, when the Japanese attacked Australian territory and posed a direct threat to the nation. See Peter J. Dean, ed., *Australia 1942: In the Shadow of War* (Melbourne, Austral.: Cambridge Univ. Press, 2013).

4 See Paul Dibb, "Is Strategic Geography Relevant to Australia's Current Defence Policy?," *Australian Journal of International Affairs* 60, no. 2 (June 2006), pp. 247–64.

5 C. E. W. Bean, *Anzac to Amiens: A Shorter History of the Australian Fighting Services in the First World War* (Canberra, ACT: Australian War Memorial, 1968), p. 31.

6 Ross Mallett, "The Preparation and Deployment of the Australian Naval and Military Expeditionary Force," in *Battles Near and Far: A Century of Overseas Deployment,* ed. Peter Dennis and Jeffrey Grey (Canberra, ACT: Army History Unit, 2005), p. 24.

7 S. S. Mackenzie, *The Official History of Australia in the War of 1914–1918,* vol. 10, *The Australians at Rabaul: The Capture and Administration of the German Possessions in the Southern Pacific* (Sydney, Austral.: Angus & Robertson, 1937), pp. 73–74.

8 Mallett, "Preparation and Deployment," pp. 24–30.

9 Mackenzie, *Australians at Rabaul,* pp. 213–15.

10 Mallett, "Preparation and Deployment," p. 32.

11 John Connor, *Anzac and Empire: George Foster Pearce and the Foundations of Australian Defence*

(Melbourne, Austral.: Cambridge Univ. Press, 2011), p. 35.

12 Russell Parkin, *A Capability of First Resort: Amphibious Operations and Australian Defence Policy 1901–2001,* Working Paper 117 (Canberra, ACT: Land Warfare Studies Centre, 2002), p. 6.

13 *Report on Combined Operations in Hobart to the Secretary of the Naval Board,* 26 April 1935, as quoted in Parkin, *Capability of First Resort,* p. 14.

14 Parkin, *Capability of First Resort,* pp. 9–13.

15 Ross Mallett, "Together Again for the First Time: The Army, the RAN and Amphibious Warfare 1942–1945," in *Sea Power Ashore and in the Air,* ed. David Stevens and John Reeve (Ultimo, Austral.: Halstead, 2007), p. 77.

16 Ibid.

17 Karl James, "'Hell Was Let Loose': Making Order from Confusion. The RAN Beach Commandos at Balikpapan, July 1945," *International Journal of Naval History* 8, no. 2 (August 2009).

18 See Peter J. Dean, "Amphibious Warfare: Lessons from the Past for the ADF's Future," *Security Challenges* 8, no. 1 (Autumn 2012), p. 71.

19 Gavin Long, *Australia in the War of 1939–1945,* vol. 7, *The Final Campaigns* (Canberra, ACT: Australian War Memorial, 1963), p. 511.

20 Gary Waters, *OBOE: Air Operations over Borneo, 1945* (Canberra, ACT: Air Power Studies Centre, 1995), p. 131.

21 Quoted in Long, *Final Campaigns,* p. 506.

22 Quoted in ibid., p. 505.

23 Mallett, "Together Again for the First Time," p. 130.

24 Long, *Final Campaigns,* p. 521.

25 Mallett, "Together Again for the First Time," p. 130.

26 James, "'Hell Was Let Loose.'"

27 See "The Strategic Position of Australia: Review by Chiefs of Staff Committee," 1947–1949, ser. A8744, item SDC233, National Archives of Australia, Canberra, ACT [hereafter NAA]; and "Defence Policy and National Security: Strategical Appreciation of a Regional Arrangement in the Pacific from the Aspect of Australian Security," Chiefs of Staff Committee minute 12/1946, 20 March 1946, ser. A5954, item 1669/6, NAA.

28 For details on the reasons why Australia led a stabilization mission to East Timor see Iain Henry, "Playing Second Fiddle on the Road to INTERFET: Australia's East Timor Policy throughout 1999," *Security Challenges* 9, no. 1 (2013), pp. 87–111, and Hugh White, "The Road to INTERFET: Reflections on Australian Strategic Decisions Concerning East Timor, December 1998–September 1999," *Security Challenges* 4, no. 1 (Autumn 2008), p. 86.

29 Quoted in David Horner, "Deploying and Sustaining INTERFET in East Timor in 1999," in *Raise, Train and Sustain: Delivering Land Combat Power,* ed. Peter Dennis and Jeffrey Grey (Canberra, ACT: Australian Military History, 2010), p. 206.

30 Ibid., p. 207.

31 Ibid., pp. 204–205.

32 Daniel Cotterill, "The New Face of Defence Logistics," *Australian Defence Magazine,* 10 January 2008.

33 Horner, "Deploying and Sustaining," pp. 207, 213.

34 Bob Breen, *Struggling for Self Reliance: Four Case Studies of Australian Regional Force Projection in the Late 1980s and the 1990s* (Canberra, ACT: Australian National Univ. Press, 2008), p. 146.

35 Susan Smith, "Logistics and Multinational Military Operations," in *Forces for Good: Cosmopolitan Militaries in the Twenty-First Century,* ed. Lorraine Elliott and Graeme Cheeseman (Manchester, U.K.: Manchester Univ. Press, 2004), p. 82.

36 Quoted in Jenny Sinclair, "Operation Chaos," *Age* (Melbourne), 19 November 2002.

37 James Cotton, "Australia's East Timor Experience: Military Lessons and Security Dilemmas" (NIDS International Symposium on Security Affairs, Tokyo, Japan, 22 January 2003), published in *Nontraditional Roles of the Military and Security in East Asia* (Tokyo: NIDS, 2003), p. 113.

38 Breen, *Struggling for Self Reliance,* p. 145.

39 David Stevens, *Strength through Diversity: The Combined Naval Role in Operation Stabilise,* Working Paper 20 (Canberra, ACT: Sea Power Centre–Australia, 2007), p. 27.

40 Cth, Parliamentary Debates, Senate, 14 August 2000, 16215 (Austl.).

41 Stevens, *Strength through Diversity,* pp. 22, 27.

42 Philip M. Mattox and William A. Guinn, "Contingency Contracting in East Timor," *Army Logistician* 32, no. 4 (July–August 2000).

43 Ibid.

44 Hollie J. Martin, "Coalition Logistics: The Way to Win the Peace, the Way to Win the War" (School of Advanced Military Studies, U.S. Army Command and General Staff College, 2007), p. 37.

45 Mattox and Guinn, "Contingency Contracting in East Timor."

46 Stevens, *Strength through Diversity,* p. 28.

47 Breen, *Struggling for Self Reliance,* pp. 157–58.

48 Commonwealth Dept. of Defence, *Defence 2000* (Canberra, ACT: 2000).

49 Commonwealth Dept. of Defence, *Defence Capability Plan 2004–2014* (Canberra, ACT: 2004).

50 David Stevens, "Operation Astute: The RAN in East Timor," Sea Power Centre–Australia *Semaphore,* no. 12 (June 2006).

51 Commonwealth Dept. of Defence, *Defending Australia in the Asia-Pacific Century: Force 2030* (Canberra, ACT: 2009), pp. 51–52, para. 6.42.

52 Commonwealth Dept. of Defence, *Defence White Paper 2013* (Canberra, ACT: 2013), p. 3, para. 3.29; p. 29, paras. 3.42–3.47; p. 62, para. 6.55.

53 For a detailed discussion of the utility of this modern ADF capability see Peter J. Dean, "Australia, Maritime Strategy and Regional Military Diplomacy," in *A Maritime School of Strategic Thought for Australia,* ed. Justin Jones (Canberra, ACT: Sea Power Centre–Australia, 2013).

XVII *Keep Watch*
The Navy League in the Interwar Period

DUNCAN REDFORD

The Navy League, as Britain's self-appointed guardian of naval affairs, had a difficult time during the interwar period. Formed in 1895 to guard against the neglect of the Royal Navy, as well as against public and political complacency about the importance of sea power to the British, the Navy League, despite financial troubles and a split in 1908 over support for Admiral Fisher, had by 1914 come to dominate the naval scene, even if its membership was as little as twelve thousand in 1901 and only a hundred thousand by 1914.[1] The league's branch structure was vital to its activities, ensuring most areas had activists preaching the navalist message, with varying degrees of success, using their own resources or speakers and materials supplied by the league's central office. At the same time, the league shared the Victorian and Edwardian enthusiasm for self-improvement—in the league's case, the improvement of urban boys through a Sea Cadet Corps that, the league believed, gave the boys discipline, character, and an education in the importance of British sea power. After the First World War, however, the Navy League had to operate in an environment where naval supremacy was not well regarded by the British, who, thinking that naval arms races had caused the war, sought to prevent a future war by embracing naval disarmament and collective security. Against such a fundamental shift away from a belief that naval supremacy was absolutely necessary for British power, security, and prestige, the Navy League was faced with real problems about how to engage the British public with its message. This paper looks at the Navy League in the interwar period and highlights some of its policies, positions, and campaigns in order to illustrate the problems it faced.

The first problem the Navy League faced was what policy to adopt concerning the eradication of the German threat to British naval supremacy and what to do about a British government that the league considered to have no naval policy.[2] The league's solution was effectively to abandon any campaign for the maintenance of British naval supremacy. Instead, the league moved toward a policy of naval arms limitations and collective security—a policy that was effectively driven by the chairman of the league's executive committee, V. Biscoe Tritton, supported by the general secretary, Rear Adm. Ronald Hopwood.

The move toward a new policy took place in September 1919, when the executive committee started formulating a memorandum outlining the league's future working policy. In his covering letter to Arnold White, a well-known naval commentator, journalist, and former chairman of the executive committee, Tritton made plain his intention to change fundamentally the league's position: "I feel deeply that the Navy League must now break new ground."[3] Tritton also suggested that the league's motto should be changed to reflect the new policy, from "Keep Watch" to "Sacrifice and Service," a change that took effect as "Sacrifice: Service" in December 1919.[4] The introduction to Tritton's 1919 memorandum outlining future policy gave warning that the new direction of the league would be very different from the past; the league would argue that the "sacrifice of pre-war custom or doctrine may be necessary, without question or hesitation."[5]

However, the policy was explained in such ambiguous and florid language in *The Navy,* the Navy League's journal, that its real meaning would have been easily hidden from the league's membership. Instead of naval supremacy, *The Navy* talked about five different areas of activity or policy: "The Memorial of Commemoration and Thanksgiving," "The Memorial of Sea Service," "The Memorial of the Ships," "The Memorial from Overseas," and "The Memorial of 'Sacrifice and Service.'"[6] The most important of these "memorials" was "Sea Service," for it was in this area that the thrust of policy was hidden; "Sea Service" subordinated, in vague language, the material strength of the navy to considerations of the spirit the navy could engender in the wider populace. To make sure the "sea-spirit" was spread throughout the population, educational activities would be paramount, especially the continued expansion of the Sea Cadet Corps.[7] In short, naval supremacy was no longer the policy of the league.

Nor did the policy changes end in September 1919. From December 1919 onward, the Navy League pressed for reductions in naval spending through arms-limitations agreements and collective-security arrangements. The executive committee even made a point of passing a memorandum—which *The Navy* stressed was a unanimous decision—congratulating the government on the 1921 Navy Estimates, a document "which endorses beyond any possible misunderstanding the views of the Navy League, as expressed in its Message of the 1st January 1921, urging the limitation of armaments by conference."[8] By July 1921 the Navy League was arguing that naval arms limitation was actually Britain and America's sea heritage and that these two nations had to lead in this matter.[9] As to the specifics of the Washington Treaty, it was argued by Tritton and the league's president, the Duke of Somerset, that "the [Navy] League cannot but believe that the Four-Power Agreement will add strength to this aim and benefit all mankind."[10]

The Navy League's official enthusiasm for the Washington Treaty should not be seen as indicating unanimous support by its membership. There was internal opposition to the league's abandonment of the principle of British naval supremacy in favor of naval limitation by agreement and of reliance on such collective-security arrangements as the League of Nations. Some members of the executive committee felt obliged to resign over the league's policies. However, until the autumn of 1921 there was no real focus for the opposition. It was then, in October 1921, that the Navy League's highly favorable reaction to the prospect of a naval conference at Washington led to the resignation from the executive committee of P. J. Hannon, its former chairman.[11] Hannon offered branches dissatisfied with the direction the league had taken since 1919 a rallying point, and by December there was open dissent over policy. The rebellion within the Navy League started with a meeting on Monday, 5 December, at the Ladies Club in London. Adm. Sir Edmund Fremantle (one of the executive committee members who had resigned in the spring of 1921) and what was described as a "representative gathering of members of the Navy League" (the chairmen or secretaries of the Chelsea, Birmingham, Cheltenham, East Dorset, Bristol, Islington, and Fulham Branches) requested the executive committee to call a special meeting—a "Grand Council"—to discuss the policy of the league.[12] Although the executive committee received support from the Isle of Man Branch and the Glasgow and South West Scotland Branch, December 1921 proved to be the start of a move by disaffected branches to call a Grand Council of the Navy League.[13] From January to June 1922 there was a major split in the league over policy, a schism that resulted in the resignation of Hopwood, Tritton, and Somerset. Eventually the league was reconstituted and in June 1922 adopted a more traditional policy in favor of naval supremacy; it also decided to use the original motto, "Keep Watch."[14]

The direct outcome of this rebellion and the resulting internal policy disputes was to distract the Navy League at the very moment the Washington Treaty discussions moved into their final stage. Indeed, such was the internal division that the league took months of meetings and arguments to adopt a policy that supported British naval power. The very fact that it took until December 1921 for any internal opposition to the policy the Navy League had been following since late 1919 to become public suggests that Tritton's policies were in alignment with general opinion outside the league's membership. Furthermore, it also suggests that within the Navy League there was sufficient support for Tritton's ideas, or apathy over the subject of naval supremacy, to allow Tritton's policies to survive until opposition was galvanized by statements made by the league after October 1921. However, it is also clear that there was vocal support for Somerset, Tritton, and Hopwood between January and April 1922.

The internal (and at times very public) dispute over policy during 1921 and 1922 left the Navy League on the back foot for the rest of the decade, during which the league contented itself with railing against further naval arms limitation and a few patronizing remarks about the ignorance of naval affairs of the Labour Party—which could not have helped it win friends and influence when

Labour took office for the first time in 1924.[15] The Navy League also—in a program that incurred the wrath of Adm. Sir Percy Scott—spent a great deal of effort, to little effect, arguing for the development of Singapore into a major fleet base and playing down the impact of airpower on the navy.[16] There was also a subtle shift in the emphasis placed on sea power. Prior to the First World War the primary concerns had been invasion and food supplies; during the middle and late 1920s the focus was on the navy's role in imperial defense.[17] However, in the 1930s the Navy League attempted two major campaigns—neither of which involved direct support for the Royal Navy.

The first campaign involved the merchant navy, and although a 1938 editorial in *The Navy* proclaimed it a success, there was little to show for it.[18] Importantly, merchant vessels, despite their unsung importance to the British economy and to its overseas earnings, were not "emblems of power like men-of-war."[19] No amount of campaigning by the Navy League was going to change this, no matter how vital an industry the merchant marine was or how romantic an image was portrayed of the archetypal tramp steamer plying its trade.

The second campaign area was that of the Navy League's Sea Cadets organization.[20] Here, the league experienced more success. In the 1920s and early 1930s membership in the Sea Cadets was static at three thousand boys.[21] By 1938 the Navy League's Sea Cadets had gone from thirty-two to sixty-six units and from three to five thousand boys as members, and *The Navy* trumpeted this success.[22] The following year a public meeting at the Free Trade Hall in Manchester was told, "Meanwhile, we can be sure that the cause for which the Navy League stands, *especially the expansion and better equipment of its Sea Cadet Corps* and the awakening of interest in the problems of our Mercantile Marine, have been made much more widely known throughout Lancashire and the North."[23] Of course, by this stage in the northwest, given the collapse of its branch network (bar one branch), the only way the Navy League had to get its message across was through the Sea Cadets. However, the message it was trying to get across was not one of sea power, of the threat of starvation or invasion, but of its own youth movement and the state of the merchant navy.

Ironically, the Navy League had almost stumbled on the root of its problems in 1929 when the chairman of the executive committee, Sir Cyril Cobb, drew attention to the formation of the new Sea Cadet unit at Dagenham during the annual Grand Council meeting of the league:

> Most of you will know that these housing estates of the London County Council are largely inhabited by people who are taken from the slum districts in the south and east of London, and they are *people who have lost all sense of the sea* and any idea of the importance of the sea to the British Empire; and to be able to found a corps in a place like Dagenham is, at any rate, a very fortunate feature of our work during the past year, and reflects great credit on those people of Dagenham who have taken up this idea and got this corps thoroughly well founded.[24]

In drawing attention to the fact that large groups of people had "lost all sense of the sea," Cobb had almost hit on the key issue—that fundamental aspects of the population's identity had changed to the point where Britain's status as an island or the importance of the fleet was irrelevant to them. A couple of years later the Navy League returned to this theme with an item in *The Navy* titled "Sea Spirit," where it was stated, "We believe, and have much evidence to prove, that although the sea spirit may now slumber and nod, it still lives and maintains its virility in every class of our inhabitants; to awaken it once more is a task which is not only honourable but greatly to our advantage and especially to that of our commerce."[25] *The Navy* made it clear to its readers that it was the "Navy League's constant endeavour to stir up this sleeping giant, to the end that we may become once more a prosperous Empire, taking pride in our sea traditions and heritage."[26] Of course, this was not necessarily a new problem. The Navy League had moaned in the pages of *The Navy* about the lack of sea sense during the 1920s, but the point was also occasionally noticed by the mainstream press: "For some time at least something seems to have been lost of a very legitimate sea-pride which centred in a service inseparable from the existence of the nation and unsurpassed in its kind anywhere in the world."[27] However, the question regarding why a community such as Dagenham, or the nation as a whole, had lost all sense of the sea—had lost its "sea spirit"—was not asked.

That the Navy League's efforts to reengage the British public with its navy were ultimately unsuccessful can be seen not only in the policies the public pursued but also in the activities, finances, and structure of the Navy League itself. The Navy League had a number of methods for getting its message to the public, but perhaps the most important of them was the branch structure of the league, around which many of its activities were based and by which funds were raised to keep both the branch and the central organization of the league going. Despite the effort put into spreading the Navy League's message by lectures, radio talks, film shows, letters to the press, and the sale of *The Navy*, the league contracted both physically and financially, as figures 1 and 2 show. The collapse in support for the Navy League in the interwar period was also recognized, as was the decrease in the political strength of the navy and in its importance to the wider public. "The estimation in which it is held is also declining, as is evidenced by the debility from which the Navy League is suffering for want of support."[28] Unfortunately, attempts by the author and naval pundit Archibald Hurd to draw attention to the plight of the Navy League in the *Fortnightly Review* do not seem to have gripped either the mainstream media or the *Review*'s readers.

In 1919 the Navy League boasted over a hundred branches across the United Kingdom; ten years later there were fewer than forty. By 1932, the lowest point of the league's fortunes during the interwar period, there were just thirty branches; in 1938, even with the rearmament and the threat of war, the total was only thirty-nine.

This was important for the league, given the activities that were organized and sponsored by local branches. In the space of twenty years the ability of the league to mobilize activists and ensure mass exposure of its message through local power bases suffered an immense blow.

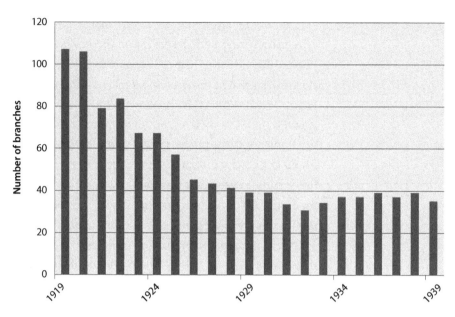

Fig. 1
Navy League home branches 1919–1939 (includes school branches)

The collapse in branch numbers also affected the league's ability to raise funds, and as a result the Navy League finances collapsed after 1919. Much of this problem may well be down to the policy followed between 1919 and 1922 and the resulting internal policy disputes. However, even after the issues were resolved in 1922, individual membership subscriptions paid to the head office never got back to their 1919 level, remaining below £100,000 (in 2008 prices) for the rest of the interwar period. Far more significant was the simultaneous collapse in donations from the branches. In 1919 this had amounted to half the income of the head office; by the mid-1920s it was vastly reduced, reflecting a major drop in the fund-raising abilities of the branch structure.

Significantly, the collapse in the Navy League's branch network meant that by the 1930s the league had no active structure to coordinate and run activities in large areas of the country. In 1920, for example, there were twenty-two branches listed for Lancashire, including Blackburn, Blackpool, Bolton, Burnley, Bury, Clitheroe, Fleetwood, Lancaster, Leyland, Lytham, Morecambe, Nelson, Oldham, Port of Manchester, Preston, Rochdale, St Helens, Southport, Ulverston, and Wigan. By 1932 only one was listed, the Port of Manchester Branch. Nor was the industrial northwest different from other industrial regions in the United Kingdom. By 1932 there were no Navy League branches in the northeast, the single branch at Newcastle upon Tyne having disappeared between 1920 and 1921 and Yorkshire having lost its Sheffield branch in 1921 and in 1931 that in Ryedale (which had only formed in 1923–24); by that time Staffordshire, Nottinghamshire, and Derbyshire as well had no active branch structure.[29] Such voids in the Navy League's network suggest a stratification of its membership along political and class grounds, despite the Navy League's frequent claims to be nonpolitical, with support concentrated in more Conservative-leaning (and rural) areas than in urban areas, where the Liberals and Labour counted the greatest support—unsurprisingly, given the Liberal/

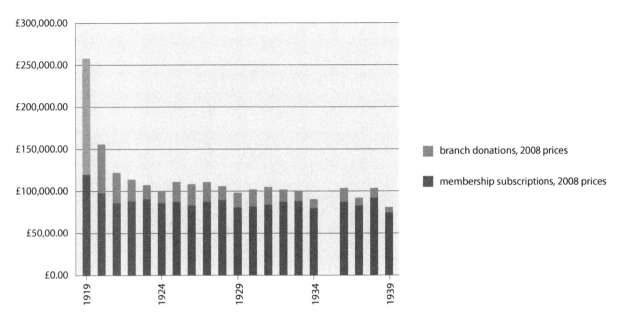

£300,000.00

£250,000.00

£200,000.00

£150,000.00

£100,000.00

£50,00.00

£0.00

1919   1924   1929   1934   1939

▪ branch donations, 2008 prices

▪ membership subscriptions, 2008 prices

Fig. 2
Navy League membership subscriptions and branch donations 1919–1939 (2008 retail price index prices)

Radical opposition to naval armaments. Yet the Navy League's ability to build up a network of twenty-two home branches in Lancashire by 1920, a staunch Liberal and Radical region, suggests that for a while at least a shared naval identity surpassed that of political and class-based identities in that region.

Given the disadvantages under which the Navy League was increasingly working as its branch structure slowly atrophied after 1923, it is remarkable how much activity it did manage to produce. In terms of spreading its message, the most important aspect was its ability to mount lectures, organized by local branches or activists using either their own resources or those lent by the head office. To support the lecture program the league had not only a wide range of slide shows but also a number of lecturers who would travel to host branches or locally organized venues. These lecturers also went on tours through particular localities, no doubt as a response to the collapse of branch and activist networks. Yet the trend of these lectures is hard to follow, with frequent fluctuations in total audiences and numbers of lectures in any given year. What is clear is that during the internal disputes and wrangles of the Washington Treaty period, a period marked by wide public uncertainty (or even disinterest) about what the Royal Navy and the Navy League were for, there was a massive fall in the total lecture attendees to under half the figure reported for 1920. In the same period, the number of lectures and film presentations also fluctuated wildly, between under two hundred to just over seven hundred, and as for total annual audience there is no discernible trend.[30] However, such patterns as there were, as shown in figures 3 and 4, do not follow the fall-off in branch numbers and finances, which suggests that the Navy League, though limited by a decreasing number of activists as a result of the collapse of local branches, was making substantial efforts to engage with the public.

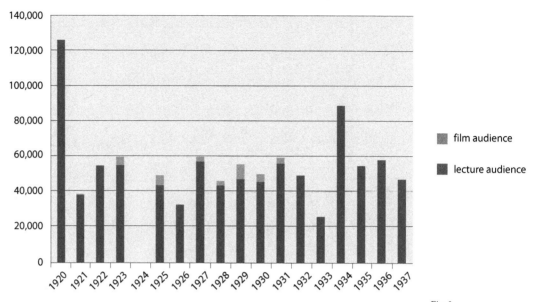

Note: Data from *The Navy*, 1920–38. The number of films shown was only recorded spasmodically in this period, and it is safe to assume that after 1932 films continued to play an increasing role in the methods available for communicating the Navy League's message.

Fig. 3
Total annual Navy League lecture and film audiences 1920–1937

Nor were public meetings and lectures its only tools. Much use was made of films and radio; a radio broadcast in Birmingham during February 1923 was credited with an audience of thirty-five thousand.[31] In addition to commercially made films about the Royal Navy, the Navy League in 1929 produced its own propaganda film, whose title mirrored the league's motto. The film *Keep Watch* was first shown in January 1929, and eight screenings were given to a total audience of 1,200 at the School Boys' Exhibition at the New Horticultural Hall.[32] At the following year's exhibition *Keep Watch* was shown fourteen times to 2,520 people.[33] Its virtues were shamelessly plugged in *The Navy*, which told its readers that

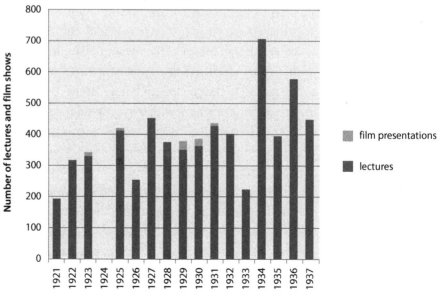

Fig. 4
Annual Navy League lectures and film shows 1921–1937

"'Keep Watch' should be seen by everyone; in the first place for its artistry, and secondly, for the facts and statistics which it contains. The enormous reduction in Britain's naval armaments since the war are clearly shown without any complicated figures. Then there are interesting snapshots of Britain's trade in far-off colonies—trades which rely solely on the Navy for protection."[34]

Notwithstanding, the medium that the league regarded as most important for getting its message out to members and nonmembers alike was its own journal, *The Navy*. However, circulation was not great, especially when it is considered that it was not only distributed to members but sold to the public. For example, between 1930 and 1932 the circulation of *The Navy* rose from 3,400 to 6,275 copies per month, which was considered worthy of note in its own pages.[35] A near doubling of circulation in two years might be considered a success, but even so the total remained depressingly small and indicates only too well the low levels of membership in the league and of resonance with the wider public. As figure 5 shows, the circulation of *The Navy* hovered between six and seven thousand during 1931–33, a time that, given the number of active branches, might be considered the nadir of the Navy League's interwar fortunes.

Yet ultimately the Navy League's efforts to stimulate widespread interest in the Royal Navy, sea power, and the merchant marine do not seem to have achieved much. In the wider contemporary press and journals there is no appreciable positive change in the interwar period. As figure 6 shows, articles on the navy in significant journals such as the *Fortnightly Review, Contemporary Review,* and the *Nineteenth Century and After* show a downward trend. Only the Washington Treaty negotiations in 1921 and 1922 produced a flurry of interest in the *Fortnightly Review* and the *Nineteenth Century and After,* while only the 1930 London Naval Treaty managed to interest all three selected journals. Even rearmament after 1933

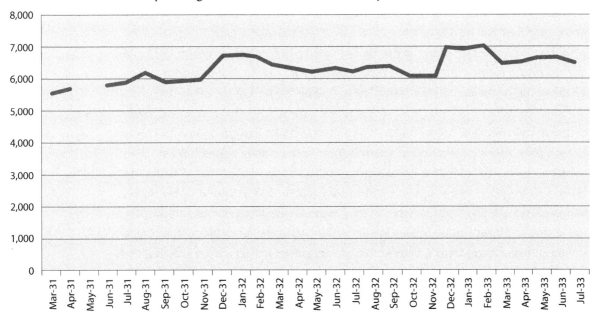

Fig. 5
Circulation of The Navy,
March 1931–July 1933

Source: MSSC, Navy League Executive Committee minute books, vol. 31, fols. 77, 82, 84, 88, 90, 95, 100, 104, 108, 111, 115, 118, 124, 127, 129, 133, 136, 140, 144, 147, 151, 153, 155.

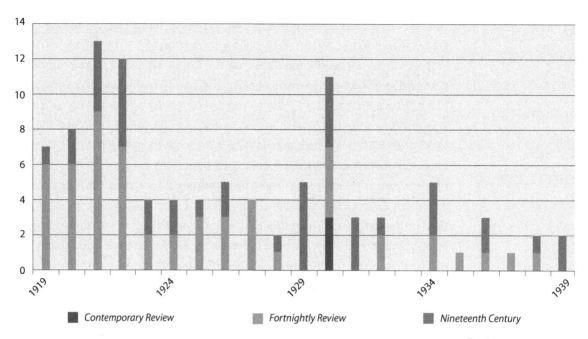

Fig. 6
Articles per year on the
Royal Navy or British sea
power 1919–1939

did not cause a significant upsurge in articles about the Royal Navy or British sea power. For all the Navy League's efforts, it had failed to place the Royal Navy back at the center of the political and public spheres.

To conclude, the Navy League suffered a significant drop in support during the interwar period. After strong growth between 1900 and 1914, it had ended the First World War with a strong central headquarters and a widespread and active local structure of 136 home and school branches. By 1939 there were only thirty-five home branches and no active school branches. The reasons for such a collapse are complex, but it is certain that the policies followed by the league between 1919 and 1922 played a significant part, undermining support for the league and its aims. The decision by the executive committee, following the lead of the chairman, Tritton, and the general secretary, Rear Admiral Hopwood, to embrace naval disarmament and collective security set off an internal revolt that prevented the Navy League from making any effective contribution to the (rather muted, in any case) debate about Britain's need for naval supremacy and its response to the Washington Naval Conference. Once the revolt had run its course, and Tritton and Hopwood had been replaced by members in favor of more-traditional policies, support for the league stabilized, but at a very low level. Furthermore, attempts by the league to mount major campaigns in support of the Singapore naval base project and the merchant marine made very little headway; only the program to increase the size of the Sea Cadet Corps met with any measure of national success.

The collapse in support for the Navy League occurred despite vigorous attempts to get its message across to the public in print, by film, and on the radio. The collapse of the local branch structure in the early 1920s likely undercut the effectiveness of the campaigns, as it left wide areas with no league representation around which interest could coalesce. Further, the loss of branches hit the north of England hardest, ensuring that despite all its protests of political impartiality, the Navy League ceased to be a truly national organization. Instead it became associated with mainly Conservative areas and had little or no visibility in areas dominated by the Labour movement or Liberals.

In many ways the collapse of support for the Navy League in the interwar period parallels wider British attitudes to defense and security measures. New weapons and new modes of fighting made warfare more terrifying and threatened to end Britain's reliance on its position as an island nation and on its navy to insulate it from the realities of modern combat. Against such a background, any belief in the importance of or need for naval superiority was going to be hard to nurture. The Navy League was out of step with the very thing that it needed in order to succeed —the British public and its perceptions of maritime security.

NOTES I should like to thank the Leverhulme Trust for its support, without which the research that went into this paper would have been impossible.

1 Frans Coetzee, *For Party or Country: Nationalism and the Dilemmas of Popular Conservatism in Edwardian England* (Oxford, U.K.: Oxford Univ. Press, 1990), p. 23; W. Mark Hamilton, "The Nation and the Navy: Methods and Organization of British Navalist Propaganda, 1889–1914" (PhD thesis, University of London, 1977), p. 124.

2 *Navy* 25 (1920), p. 45.

3 Biscoe Tritton to Arnold White, 4 September 1919, WHI 136, National Maritime Museum, London.

4 "Sacrifice: Service," *Navy* 24 (1919), p. 145.

5 Tritton to White, 4 September 1919, enclosure "The Navy League."

6 "Navy League. Future Policy," *Navy* 24 (1919), p. 118.

7 Ibid.

8 *Navy* (April 1921), p. 98.

9 *Times,* 5 July 1921.

10 *Times,* 31 December 1921.

11 Marine Society & Sea Cadets [hereafter MSSC], *Navy League Minute Book,* vol. 22, minutes of Special Meeting of Executive Committee, 11 October 1921, Executive Committee, 3 November 1921.

12 *Times,* 7 December 1921, p. 12.

13 MSSC, *Navy League Minute Book,* vol. 22, minutes of Special Meeting of Executive Committee, 1 December 1921, Executive Committee, 21 December 1921.

14 *Navy* 27 (1922), pp. 79, 103, 113, 127–30, 177, 189–90; "Notes and Comments," *Naval and Military Record* 40 (1922), p. 225; "Leader: Keeping Watch," *Naval and Military Record* 40 (1922), p. 392.

15 *Times,* 1 January 1924, p. 7.

16 *Times,* 15 March 1924, p. 15, and 18 March 1924, p. 10.

17 Examples include *Times,* 21 October 1924, p. 15, and 3 March 1926, p. 12.

18 "Editor's Notes," *Navy* 43 (1938), p. 363.

19 A. Hurd, "The World's Shipping: The Balance of Power," *Fortnightly Review* 108 (1920), p. 586.

20 "Editor's Notes: The Great Idea," *Navy* 42 (1937), p. 61; "The Sea Cadet Campaign," *Navy* 42 (1937), pp. 91–92; "The Navy League Sea Cadet Corps: Great Campaign for Expansion Launched at the Mansion House," *Navy* 42 (1937), pp. 102–103, 106–107; "Editor's Notes," *Navy* 43 (1938), p. 1; "The Affairs of the Sea Cadet Corps," *Navy* 43 (1938), pp. 59–60; "Editor's Notes: The Grand Council," *Navy* 43 (1938), p. 193.

21 "The Work of the Navy League To-day," *Navy* 25 (1920), p. 28; "Editor's Notes," *Navy* 43 (1938), p. 363.

22 "Editor's Notes," *Navy* 43 (1938), p. 363.

23 "Editor's Notes: Navy League Consciousness," *Navy* 44 (1939), p. 2 [my emphasis].

24 "Grand Council Meeting," *Navy* 34 (1929), p. 166 [my emphasis].

25 H.M.D., "Sea Spirit," *Navy* 36 (1931), p. 155.

26 Ibid.

27 "A Salute to the Navy," *Observer,* 27 July 1924, p. 10.

28 A. Hurd, "The Decline of British Naval Power," *Fortnightly Review* 115 (1924), p. 555.

29 MSSC, *Navy League Annual Reports* (1919–39).

30 The figures recorded by the Navy League for 1921 and 1933 are incomplete, and no figures were given for 1924.

31 *Navy* 28 (1923), p. 116.

32 "Head Office Notes," *Navy* 34 (1929), p. 90.

33 "Head Office Notes," *Navy* 35 (1930), p. 90.

34 "Navy League Film," *Navy* 34 (1929), p. 79.

35 "Grand Council Meeting," *Navy* 38 (1932), p. 173.

XVIII *Delivering the Goods*
The U.S. Merchant Marine in the Second World War

SALVATORE R. MERCOGLIANO

The day before the German invasion of Poland, a large group of dignitaries, including Mrs. Eleanor Roosevelt, assembled at the Newport News Shipbuilding Yard to celebrate the launching of hull number 1 in the Maritime Commission shipbuilding program. Although other ships had already been built, the liner SS *America* was meant to symbolize the American merchant marine's resurrection. Its keel had been laid almost a year previously as the future new flagship of the United States Lines. It was 723 feet long and displaced over thirty-five thousand tons. Two sets of steam turbines could propel it at a service speed of twenty knots, although it hit over twenty-four during its initial trials. Accommodations were provided for 1,202 passengers and a crew of 643. It was fitted with two king posts, fore and aft, and its two large, angled stacks, adorned with the colors of the United States Lines—red, white, and blue—were easily visible to the thirty thousand spectators who attended its launching on 31 August 1939. By the time it was ready to carry passengers the following year, the Battle of the Atlantic precluded it from operating on the New York to Southampton run; instead, it cruised to the West Indies, transporting American tourists and military personnel to new bases acquired in exchange for fifty obsolete destroyers given to the British. In the spring of 1941, the Navy requisitioned the ship and designated it USS *West Point* (AP 23). In September 1942, it was formally commissioned; its naval crew consisted largely of the merchant mariners who had previously sailed the ship.[1] The role that *America* played in the war is symbolic of how the merchant marine performed in the Second World War. The building program proved a key linchpin, along with the ships and men of the American merchant marine, in the United Nations' defeat of the Axis.

The Second World War was the most destructive conflict in the annals of history, but it also witnessed the emergence of the United States as a superpower. American materiel or forces were present in every theater of the war, and equally important, American supplies were funneled to all the major Allies, under the auspices of Lend-Lease. From ports throughout the nation, American merchant ships delivered 75 percent of all the munitions, supplies, and fuel shipped by sea to support the Soviet Union, the British Commonwealth, the Free French, the Chinese, and

American armies in the war. Between 7 December 1941 and 15 August 1945, the U.S. merchant marine transported 203,522,000 long tons of cargo and 64,730,000 long tons of petroleum.[2]

In the First World War, the nation had found itself unprepared to meet the daunting sealift demands it faced at the conflict's outset. To meet the challenge, the nation established three organizations: the U.S. Shipping Board (USSB), created under the Shipping Act of 1916; the Cruiser and Transport Force (CTF), in 1917, to supervise the movement of the American Expeditionary Force to Europe; and in the following year, the Naval Overseas Transportation Service (NOTS), which coordinated the movement of supplies and materiel. The United States had in that conflict merely to focus on carrying forces to Western Europe, assisted by the Allies, principally the British. The Second World War required a far more extensive transportation network, and it called on three organizations to meet the demands of the American and Allied militaries—the U.S. Maritime Commission, the U.S. Maritime Service (USMS), and the War Shipping Administration (WSA).

The U.S. Maritime Commission: A Fleet for the Arsenal of Democracy

The Maritime Commission, originally headed by Joseph Kennedy (who was replaced by Rear Adm. Emory S. "Jerry" Land, USN [Ret.], on 16 April 1937), set out to build a fleet of five hundred ships over a ten-year period.[3] Except for *America,* all the vessels would be freighters and tankers, intended to convey the nation's commerce across the world's oceans. It is significant that neither Franklin D. Roosevelt nor the Maritime Commission provided for any substantial passenger-ship construction, even after the lessons of the First World War. *America* was solely a symbolic gesture, built to replace the aged *Leviathan,* which, before its scrapping in 1938, had symbolized the nation's merchant marine in the interwar years.[4] This failure to anticipate the need to transport large numbers of troops overseas reinforces the perception that Roosevelt intended the United States to serve as the "Arsenal of Democracy" for the nations of Western Europe. Only after the fall of France did this situation change radically and force an alteration to the country's sealift policy.[5]

The ships built by the Maritime Commission proved highly successful, with not only commercial industry but also the military. Instead of constructing ships for individual companies or trade routes, the commission decided to build four standardized classes. This was a marked difference from the policy adopted in the First World War by the U.S. Shipping Board, which had awarded contracts to shipyards and allowed them to build ships to their own designs. The Maritime Commission ships included freighters of three sizes and a group of tankers. The first fifty ships authorized under section 701 of the Merchant Marine Act of 1936 were *America,* twelve "T-3" tankers, twenty "C-2" freighters, and seventeen larger "C-3" freighters.

The T-3s were larger than most commercially built tankers and included notable national-defense features. Prior to their construction, representatives of the U.S. Navy had met with the Maritime Commission to propose that these ships be built to a standard that would easily allow conversion into Navy oilers—ships capable of refueling other naval vessels while under way and therefore requiring higher speed and large-capacity cargo pumps. An agreement was reached with the Standard Oil Company of New Jersey by which the company would operate the vessels (and would not object to their turnover in time of emergency) and the Navy would underwrite their higher operating costs. Four shipyards were selected—Bethlehem, Federal, Newport News, and Sun—and each was assigned three ships. The tankers were 553 feet long, with a deadweight capacity of 18,300 tons. They had four steam turbines driving two shafts, capable of propelling them at speeds up to eighteen knots, although Standard operated them at a much slower pace to conserve fuel and reduce operating expenses. These twelve tankers had short commercial careers; the Navy purchased three prior to completion and the remaining nine soon afterward. Four subsequently underwent extensive conversion and emerged as the successful *Sangamon* class of escort carriers.[6]

The C classes of freighters all conformed to a standard configuration, although differing in overall size, engine horsepower, and passenger and cargo capacities. They all possessed the same hold arrangement, with three holds forward of the superstructure and engine spaces—each containing three decks below the main hatch—and two aft, containing only two decks. The ships introduced the use of pontoon hatches, consisting of a series of large covers that could be lifted off and stacked by the ship's booms. This arrangement was a major improvement over the older plank hatches, which required several people to remove each section, a difficult and time-consuming task. Additionally, the boards frequently twisted and warped from the motion of the ship, making it necessary to remember the order in which they had been removed to ensure a tight seal when replaced.[7]

Many of the ships also featured oversize hatches that facilitated the transportation of such unusual items as locomotives, aircraft, artillery pieces, engineering equipment, and military vehicles. Also, large-capacity booms were fitted, allowing the ships to work independently of shoreside crane support and making them ideal for use in forward or war-torn areas. The C-1s were intended as replacements for ships engaged in coastal operations or in the tramp trade. The C-2 emerged as the standard-size freighter, designed to replace the First World War–era fleet built by the USSB. The final class, the C-3, was an enlarged version of the C-2, with greater passenger capacity, making it an ideal candidate for conversion into an attack transport.[8]

However, this rebirth of the commercial merchant fleet was short-lived: the military took possession of thirty-seven of the first fifty vessels built under the Maritime Commission program. On a larger scale, the evidence is clear that the Merchant Marine Act of 1936, while providing relief to the ailing shipbuilding industry and replacing worn-out ships of the commercial marine, actually served as a means to hasten the rearmament of the United States. All told, the Maritime Commission built 5,777 ships. Many maritime and naval historians laud this as the greatest shipbuilding feat in history.[9] While that is true, the ships built proved a mixed bag and a questionable investment in the postwar years as a consequence of their impact on the commercial industry and the nation's military sealift effort. Of the ships, 682 were constructed specifically for naval use, of types ranging from troop transports and tenders, to landing ships and frigates. Many smaller vessels, including coasters, barges, tugs, and ore carriers, a total of 727, were included in the grand total. Of the four major types of vessels originally promulgated by the Maritime Commission, only 160 C-1, 229 C-2, one hundred C-3, and thirty-five T-3 tankers were built, and many of these were taken over by the military. The largest number of ships built were in a category termed "emergency construction," designed for rapid fabrication, most notably some 2,708 Liberty ships, 414 cargo Victory ships, and 523 T-2 tankers. Of these, all but the tankers had places in the postwar commercial fleet, and only the Victories possessed some military utility.[10]

Instead of being a charter for a revived commercial industry, the Merchant Marine Act of 1936 served as a precursor for the Two-Ocean Navy Act of 1940 and provided most of the auxiliaries used by the Navy, as well as the cargo ships needed to sustain the Army, Army Air Forces, and Marines in their campaigns.[11] The military's need for merchant ships proved insatiable, and its response in many ways reflected the practice that led to the War of 1812—impressment. The government resorted to wholesale chartering, requisitioning, and commandeering of ships to support the military, at the expense of the commercial sector, in a manner similar to the efforts of the Union during the Civil War. In the 1942 invasions of Guadalcanal (August) and Morocco (November), all the transports and cargo ships were ex–merchant ships requisitioned by the Navy.[12] In later campaigns, such as Normandy (June) and the Marianas (June) in 1944 and Okinawa (April) in 1945, ex–merchant ships were reinforced by Maritime Commission vessels either converted or purpose-built as attack transports or cargo ships, not to mention tankers and support vessels providing logistical support to the fleet, including civilian-manned merchant ships.

The U.S. Maritime Service: Training the Mariners

When enacted in 1936, the Merchant Marine Act stated as one of its goals, "It is necessary for the national defense and development of its foreign and domestic commerce that the United States shall have a merchant marine . . . (b) capable of serving as a naval and military auxiliary in time of war and national emergency."[13] Title VII of the act led to the government building program overseen by the Maritime Commission, but with the addition of five hundred ships to the 1,340 vessels already in service on the eve of American entry into the war, along with initially hundreds, and later thousands, of emergency-construction Liberty- and Victory-class freighters and T-2 tankers. The fifty-five thousand mariners employed by the merchant marine were insufficient to crew and staff this new "Victory Fleet."

To oversee the growth of the civilian workforce, which eventually increased fivefold to a peak of 250,000, an amendment to the Merchant Marine Act of 1936—section 216, passed in 1938—included a provision for a new uniformed service under the Department of Commerce. This new organization was tasked with the mission

> to establish and maintain a voluntary organization for the training of citizens of the United States to serve on Merchant Marine vessels of the United States to be known as the United States Maritime Service. . . . The ranks, grades, and ratings for personnel of the United States Maritime Service shall be the same as for the personnel of the United States Coast Guard.[14]

Initially, the USMS resided under the Maritime Commission. However, with the declaration of war in December 1941, supervision shifted to the U.S. Coast Guard, since it administered the testing for credentials. But with the transfer of the Coast Guard to the Navy in November of that year, the Coast Guard's wartime mission took precedence over the training of noncombatant mariners. On 11 July 1942 the USMS finally found a home, with the new War Shipping Administration, under the oversight of the Deputy Administrator for Labor Relations, Manning, Training, and Recruitment, Capt. Edward Macauley, USN (Ret.).

A total of thirty-seven recruitment offices were established around the nation to look for men from seventeen and a half years old (later lowered to sixteen) all the way to fifty. Unlike the majority of the armed services in the war, the USMS was racially integrated, allowing African Americans to serve in rolls alongside existing crews and in some cases to command merchant vessels. Once joined, new USMS members were sent to basic and advanced schools. One of the largest training centers was at Sheepshead Bay, New York. At this site on the northern shore of Long Island, not far from the home of the new U.S. Merchant Marine Cadet Corps at the Chrysler Mansion in Kings Point—the site of the modern U.S. Merchant Marine Academy—cadets received four weeks of preliminary training in twenty subjects, ranging from swimming and physical training to knots, firefighting, and gunnery practice. Following their preliminary training, cadets proceeded to one of six advanced sections—Deck, Engine, Cooks and Bakers, Pursers, Hospital Corps, or Chief Steward Courses. This stage involved a total of thirteen weeks of training for deck and engine officers and corpsmen, and six weeks for the others. Upon completion, they received their ranks in the USMS, sailing credentials, and assignments to ships.

In addition to the U.S. Maritime Service, there were the traditional sources of personnel, the maritime schools (the five state maritime academies [Maine, Massachusetts, New York, Pennsylvania, and California]) or union and vocational training facilities around the country. One of the largest sources, however, comprised a hundred thousand ex-mariners who were encouraged to return to the sea and resume their previous careers. The final source was the new U.S. Merchant Marine Cadet Corps at Kings Point. Its midshipmen received training both on shore and at sea. Unlike cadets and midshipmen at the U.S. Military Academy or Naval Academy, merchant marine students went to sea on ships in the war zones; a total of 142 cadets paid the ultimate sacrifice during the war and, of these, eight received the Distinguished Service Medal for heroism beyond the call of duty.

The War Shipping Administration: Delivering the Goods

For the U.S. Navy, the Second World War has become the epitome of Alfred Thayer Mahan's prophecy of the power of the main battle fleet, while emphasizing the assertion of Sir Julian Corbett that wars are won on land.[15] The naval combatants served the concurrent roles of protecting and supporting amphibious assaults and drives across the Pacific and Atlantic. After all, the fleets of the United States and Japan did not meet haphazardly to do battle. Instead, every major fleet engagement took place in connection with key strategic locations ashore: Port Moresby, Midway, Guadalcanal, Saipan, the Philippines. The U.S. Navy failed to acknowledge this fact, and as a consequence strategic sealift was once again relegated to secondary priority during and following the war. The same, of course, had happened a generation earlier, and despite the vaunted battle fleet's inactivity during the First World War and the centrality of NOTS and CTF to the American war effort, professional myopia was just as pronounced as it would be later. The merchant marine, the Naval Transportation Service (NTS), and the Army Transport Service (ATS) in the Second World War ordinarily receive scant attention, even though they were instrumental to Allied success.

One of the reasons for this inattention may be the rather haphazard way in which the military initially handled sealift. The ATS proved better organized for the outbreak of the Second World War than did the NTS. The former chartered ships to supplement its fleet, competing against commercial interests and other government agencies, particularly after Lend-Lease took effect. In May 1941 the Navy, seeking to build up its auxiliary fleet, requested five ships being built by the Maritime Commission. Admiral Land, seeing his task as rebuilding the commercial industry, refused; the vessels were earmarked for commercial operators in the Lend-Lease trade.[16] Additionally, as the Navy sought additional ships, the ATS faced a serious manpower shortage, many of its civilian civil-service crews leaving for more-profitable work on board the newly built Maritime Commission ships.

To alleviate this problem the Army proposed to transfer its fleet to the Navy, just as it had done in the Great War. As early as 1935, both services had agreed that the Navy would operate all ships traversing potential war zones, much as NOTS and CTF had done. On 5 May 1941, the Secretaries of War and the Navy signed a memorandum that directed the transfer of the ATS to the NTS for the duration of the emergency.[17] The ATS prepared to deliver twenty-six ships to the Navy, along with a host of contract-operated ships under short-term charters. However, like the ATS, the Navy faced severe personnel shortfalls, and it placed a higher priority on manning its warships than it did on crewing auxiliary ships for the support of the Army. The planned transfer accordingly collapsed; the result was the creation of a civilian organization, outside the military chain, to control and operate the vast merchant fleet being constructed by the Maritime Commission, a fleet that would be needed by both services to supplement their own sealift forces.[18]

Initially the Navy attempted to utilize the NTS to coordinate the use of merchant shipping, but that agency's limitations became readily apparent in a little-known operation code-named Operation BOBCAT. While this mission paled in comparison to a D-Day-style landing, it aptly demonstrated the unpreparedness of the Navy for its sealift mission. With a pressing need to provide a secure supply line between the West Coast and Allied forces in Australia, on 30 December 1941 the outgoing Chief of Naval Operations, Adm. Harold R. Stark, recommended the establishment of a fueling base at Bora-Bora in the South Pacific, along the convoy route. Elements of an Army National Guard regiment and the 1st Naval Construction Battalion were assigned to construct a 270,000-barrel fueling depot there. While the Army prepared the troops, the Navy scurried for six ships to transport them and their supplies. Only three commercial vessels—SS *President Fillmore, President Tyler,* and *Irene Dupont*—could be found, and the Navy had to request an additional three—USS *Alchiba, Hamul,* and *Mercury*—from the Maritime Commission. As a consequence of this scramble, delays in the arrival of cargo at the ports of embarkation, and the failure of the NTS to coordinate the undertaking properly, Convoy BC-100 did not sail until 27 January 1942, thirty-two days after the plan's conception. When the ships arrived at the Pacific paradise, troubles they had experienced in the United States reappeared. It was found that vital gear needed to off-load the ships had been stowed first, deep within the holds of the vessels, where it was inaccessible. In the words of one historian, it was a "classic Catch-22": "the ships could not be unloaded without the floating equipment and the floating equipment could not be assembled without unloading."[19] The six ships were eventually off-loaded, but the fifty-two days it took was an ominous sign of what lay ahead for sealift in the Second World War.[20]

Immediately following the attack on Pearl Harbor, both the Army and Navy began to solicit commercial industry for ships to supplement their sealift organizations. This solicitation, however, defied a 1939 agreement by which both services had agreed to allow the Maritime Commission to handle such negotiations. As all three parties attempted to charter ships, a situation similar to that at the beginning of the Spanish-American War arose, many operators raising their rates and allowing the services to bid against each other. President Roosevelt hoped to avoid this outcome with the creation of the Strategic Shipping Board on 23 December 1941, but much like many of his other wartime creations it proved cumbersome and was hamstrung by having too many high officials assigned to it.[21]

To correct these deficiencies, Roosevelt created the civilian-led War Shipping Administration, under the supervision of Admiral Land, on 7 February 1942. Unlike the Emergency Fleet Corporation of the First World War, the WSA was charged with the control of all U.S.-flagged shipping except combatant, auxiliary, and transport vessels of the armed services. This step relieved the services of the responsibility for operating and managing merchant ships, but it also took these vital assets out of their direct control. What the armed forces did not comprehend was that the WSA operated as an executive agency directly under the president and therefore had great operational latitude. Indeed, Roosevelt assigned it five distinct and diverse missions, of which only two involved the sustainment of the Army and Navy overseas. The other three encompassed the transportation of Lend-Lease materials to the United Nations, ensuring that the "Arsenal of Democracy" received enough raw materials to produce both war and consumer goods, and supporting the State Department's Foreign Economic Administration shipments to Latin American and other neutral nations (to prevent them from siding with the Axis, an initiative similar to the Marshall Plan during the Cold War). Since Admiral Land was appointed to head the WSA, USMS, and the Maritime Commission concurrently, the WSA's deputy administrator, Lewis W. Douglas, became the point man in dealing with the military, until replaced by Granville Conway in February 1944.[22]

The need for ships led the administration to issue on 18 April 1942 a directive that allocated all commercial American shipping subject to requisition. In addition to the vessels, 107 American steamship companies were designated as agents for the operation of Maritime Commission–built vessels and those acquired from the commercial industry. This move alleviated the administrative burden of organizing an operations branch and utilized the expertise inherent in the seafaring-business community. In addition, by eliminating competition, the WSA could establish uniform charter rates and prevent shipping firms from charging different rates to different services. The major bone of contention that erupted during the war concerned the control of ships dispatched to theater and service commands.

The military viewed the ships as its own assets when they arrived in theater and retained many of them for inordinate amounts of time. The WSA, on the other hand, attempted to keep ships in nearly perpetual motion to improve the logistical flow to the commands and also to utilize returning ships for the delivery of raw materials when practical.[23]

With the Navy backing out of its May 1941 agreement to incorporate the ATS, the comedy of errors at Bora-Bora, and the war's global scope, a separate agency was clearly required to handle merchant shipping. Unlike the First World War, where the focus had been on the western front, the Second World War saw fighting on nearly every continent, and America took on a role as the supplier for most of the United Nations. Land thus found himself in the uncomfortable position of fielding competing demands from the Navy's commander in chief / Chief of Naval Operations (CNO), Adm. Ernest J. King; the Army Chief of Staff, Gen. George C. Marshall; and theater commanders, industry leaders at home, and representatives of Allied nations. On top of these demands, the merchant marine also had to contend with enemy action.

In Peace and War

The war had a significant effect on the military's perception of the merchant marine. A generally antagonistic view emerged, one that was to plague relations between the two entities during the postwar years. The dean of American naval history in the Second World War, Samuel Eliot Morison, for instance, is among the harshest critics of the merchant service. His fifteen-volume *History of United States Naval Operations in World War II* remains the most comprehensive work on the subject. In it Morison frequently stresses the supposed attitudinal differences between the Navy and the merchant marine. In particular, he cites the problem that emerged when naval armed-guard detachments were placed on board the civilian ships, a move deeply resented by merchant mariners.

> Relations between the Navy and the merchant marine have always been somewhat delicate, and the presence of the Naval Armed Guards on merchant vessels created a new point of friction. . . . At the beginning of the war, trouble or friction with merchant seamen on board was reported by about 30 percent of the Naval Armed Guard officers. Naturally the presence on board ship of military personnel who were neither under union control nor interested in pay, bonuses and overtime was galling to many of the seamen and their union officials. . . . In the merchant marine there is a sturdy independence which in time of war becomes a fault; certain masters and mates were resentful of gold braid.[24]

The source of this resentment stemmed from the federal takeover of merchant shipping during the First World War and their merging into the U.S. Naval Auxiliary Reserve and the Naval Overseas Transportation Service. Many of the mariners of the early 1940s doubtless saw the naval armed guards as a prelude to nationalizing the service again or to shutting the merchant marine out of the war.

Most damning is Morison's allegation of differing attitudes motivating naval seamen and merchant sailors: "The trouble between naval seamen and merchant seamen had its root in totally different attitudes. Any ship in which a bluejacket serves is his ship, his country's ship, to be defended with his life if need be. But to the union-indoctrinated merchant seaman the ship is the owner's ship, his class enemies' ship, to whom he owes nothing, and from which he is morally entitled to squeeze all he can."[25]

On the basis of his research, Morison uncharitably concludes that "the merchant marine should either be absorbed by the Navy or made an auxiliary service under military discipline, like the Naval Construction Battalions, the famous Seabees."[26] In his 1963 single-volume synopsis, *The Two-Ocean War,* he attempted to soften some of his earlier strictures and paid an overdue tribute to the mariners he had routinely maligned or ignored. The penultimate paragraph of his survey praises the merchant marine for its service and adds, "We must never forget that . . . it [the Navy] can never function properly without a strong and efficient merchant marine, or without the know-how of master mariners and seamen."[27] This remark, written at a time when the merchant marine was in decline but the nation seemed on the brink of a conflict with the Soviet Union over Cuba, Berlin, and Southeast Asia, aptly highlights the role of the merchant marine in national defense. Since the merchant marine lacks an official history on the scale of Morison's work, the role it played in World War II has remained both controversial and clouded by accusations and suppositions.

Yet, in their two-volume *Global Logistics and Strategy,* Robert Coakley and Richard Leighton examine the U.S. Army's view of supply in the war and convincingly conclude that merchant shipping, above all else, proved to be the most limiting factor faced by the Allies in the war, a view echoed by Richard Overy in *Why the Allies Won* (1995).[28] Not all historians have perceived the intricacies of the Allies' sealift strategy. Clay Blair has argued that the German U-boat offensive failed to interdict in any appreciable measure the flow of supplies from the United States across the Atlantic to Europe.[29] However, this argument overlooks all the limitations that the Allies faced in delivering the men, materiel, and supplies needed to defeat the Axis during the Second World War. German submarine operations represented but one, and arguably not the most serious, of the obstacles faced by the Allies.

In the early part of 1942, when U-boats launched attacks against American shipping off the East Coast, merchant mariners continued to sail without adequate naval escort and suffered six agonizing months of attacks with little assistance from the American military.[30] Much has been written on the Battle of the Atlantic, and there is little doubt that the U-boat was a real and critical threat to the Allies. Had not this menace been contained, the buildup of the American army in England would have been impossible.[31] However, a further bottleneck appeared with the acceleration of offensives in both Europe and the Pacific. While many historians have viewed Allied merchant shipping strategy in terms akin to Russell Weigley's view of the American military, fighting like an industrial steamroller—that is, producing more ships than the enemy could sink—the truth is that the United States suffered an acute shortage of the right types of vessels throughout the conflict.[32] Such a common misunderstanding is illustrated by the love affair of maritime and military historians with the Liberty ships. Admiral Land detested these vessels and did not want the Maritime Commission to become involved with them in any large measure. Instead, he favored accelerating construction of C-class standard freighters, but with the Navy taking them over as fast as they could be built, he endorsed the larger, faster, and more efficient emergency Victory-class design. For 1944, he proposed curtailing Liberty-ship production and switching shipyards to the newer design. The chairman of the Joint Chiefs, Adm. William D. Leahy, concurred, but a critical shortage of steel and of steam turbines, along with an acceleration of the Pacific War, impelled the continuation of the smaller Liberty ship, to the detriment of the Victory and C-type freighter programs.[33]

Yet ships were only one cog in the network of logistical support. Ports of debarkation, storehouses, and inland transportation networks were essential to the continuous flow of ocean cargo. In late 1942, during the Guadalcanal offensive, New Caledonia's port of Nouméa served as the forward base to support Operation WATCHTOWER. The South Pacific island lacked the necessary infrastructure and host-nation support —it was a French colony, with which the Allies had bad relations, due to their opposition to the Vichy government—to sustain a large military presence. It was furthermore a poor choice on grounds of proximity, being four hundred miles from Guadalcanal. The overall commander, Vice Adm. Robert Ghormley (later replaced by Vice Adm. William Halsey), clamored for supplies, and the WSA attempted to meet his demands by dispatching ships to Nouméa, but the port proved to be a "black hole." On 23 September 1942, eighty-six merchant vessels lay at anchor, effectively taken out of the war by logistical constraints.[34] The port lacked suitable pier space, warehouses, and stevedores to handle the influx of ships, so only high-priority cargo was off-loaded, and other vessels remained in the roadstead as floating warehouses—a poor use for scarce hulls when commanders everywhere were crying out for ships and supplies. Halsey eventually alleviated this situation by assigning a general officer to oversee the port, but as the war progressed across the Pacific new ports and bases had to be developed, particularly given the dual advances of the Southwest Pacific offensive under Gen. Douglas MacArthur and the Central Pacific campaign under Adm. Chester W. Nimitz. In Europe, while ports and infrastructure existed, developing the capacity necessary to handle several million troops, with their associated logistical tail, and provide for newly liberated civilian populations required similar solutions.[35]

The competition for shipping resources led to the establishment in May 1943 of the Joint Military Traffic Committee, under the Joint Chiefs of Staff. This was initially an attempt to usurp control of civilian shipping from the WSA, but failing to do this, the committee eventually became a venue of cooperation and mutual discussion of logistical matters.[36] At the same time, the services utilized their own shipping agencies to meet their specific needs. The NTS played only a very minor role throughout the war. To handle the shipment of bulk petroleum products, Admiral King established the Navy Allocated Tanker Service under the Assistant CNO, Material; this organization supplemented the service forces with leased WSA tankers.[37]

Far more significant was the rise of the ATS. On 31 July 1942, the Army officially established the Transportation Corps and transferred the water division of the Quartermaster Corps to this organization. The ATS created a clear working agreement to provide shipping and to ensure that the loading and off-loading of these ships were coherently organized. The Army expanded its control of ports in the United States and overseas to provide a smooth transition for cargo, something that the NTS failed to accomplish until very late in the war. Most remarkable was the growth of the ATS fleet. In *U.S. Army Ships and Watercraft of World War II*, David H. Grover details the vast enlargement of the Army's fleet during the war. Including many ships under charter, the force under ATS control outstripped that of the U.S. Navy—111,006 Army vessels to 74,708 naval ships.[38] Most revealing are the figures for ships over one thousand gross tons. Of these, the ATS controlled 261 troop transports and hospital ships and 1,445 freighters, for a total deadweight tonnage of sixteen million. This total exceeded the prewar capacity of the entire American commercial merchant marine. The overall success of the United Nations required the United States to erect a "bridge of ships" across all the world's oceans. While no one element can be singled out, merchant shipping must rank as one of the most decisive elements for the Allied victory.

Following the war, Admiral Land had the WSA issue a report on its role in the conflict, a report that, while only eighty-one pages in length, admirably sums up the service's accomplishments. The U.S. merchant marine lost 733 ships of over a thousand gross tons, up to V-J Day. Another twenty-five were lost owing to mines in subsequent days. A total of 5,638 merchant mariners died or were listed as missing in action, and another 581 became prisoners of war.[39] While these losses do not rival the casualties suffered by the armed services, proportionally the merchant marine suffered significant losses. Indeed, as a corrective to Morison and others, it should be borne in mind that the merchant marine was the only civilian profession in America to put itself on the front line during World War II.[40]

The defeat of the Axis left the United States in a position similar to that it had encountered after the First World War. It possessed a large merchant marine and a dominant economic base. The United States had many troops deployed overseas, but it now faced a new quandary: whether to retreat back toward the Western Hemisphere or retain its place on the world stage. The result of this decision and the experiences during the first half of the twentieth century were to affect how the military and the commercial shipping industry met the challenge of the Cold War and to influence the creation of the nation's maritime sealift strategy.

NOTES   1 L. A. Sawyer and W. H. Mitchell, *From America to United States: History of the Long-Range Merchant Shipbuilding Programme of the United States Maritime Commission* (Kendal, U.K.: World Ship Society, 1979), vol. 1, pp. 23–24; Felix Riesenberg, Jr., *Sea War: The Story of the U.S. Merchant Marine in World War II* (New York: Rinehart, 1956), pp. 51–52. The executive officer of *West Point,* Lt. Cdr. Giles C. Steadman, had been its merchant captain, but his Naval Reserve rank did not allow him to command the ship when commissioned. On the transport *Wakefield,* formerly the liner SS *Manhattan,* its ex-captain, Harry Manning, was relegated to serving as navigator. By the end of the war both of these men had achieved flag rank.

2 War Shipping Administration, *The United States Merchant Marine at War* (Washington, D.C.: 1946), p. 9.

3 Kennedy presided over a historic report on the status of the merchant marine. *The Economic Survey of the American Merchant Marine* (Washington, D.C.: 1937) examined five important questions: "1. Should the United States attempt to compete in the international carrying trade? 2. What are the requirements of the United States? 3. What is the present status of the subsidized merchant marine? 4. What should be the policy of the United States? 5. What will it cost to maintain an adequate merchant marine in foreign trade?" The commission determined that the United States needed to be represented in some twenty

major trade areas; however, since commercial firms lacked the funds to replace their old USSB-built ships, it argued, the Maritime Commission should aid in the replacement of these vessels; further, it found, a government-sponsored shipbuilding program would be more economical than subsidies to operators.

4 John Maxtone-Graham, *The Only Way to Cross: The Golden Era of the Great Atlantic Express Liners— from the* Mauretania *to the* France *and the* Queen Elizabeth 2 (New York: Barnes & Noble, 1997), p. 350.

5 René de la Pedraja, *A Historical Dictionary of the U.S. Merchant Marine and Shipping Industry: Since the Introduction of Steam* (Westport, Conn.: Greenwood, 1994), pp. 19–20; Sawyer and Mitchell, *From America to United States,* pp. 23–24.

6 L. A. Sawyer and W. H. Mitchell, *Victory Ships and Tankers: The History of the "Victory" Type Cargo Ships and of the Tankers Built in the United States of America during World War II* (Cambridge, Md.: Cornell Maritime Press, 1974), pp. 88–91; Thomas Wildenberg, "The Origins and Development of the T2 Tanker," *American Neptune* (Summer 1992), pp. 158–60. Of the twelve vessels, USS *Neosho* was lost during the war; the rest remained in the Navy, except for the carrier *Sangamon,* which was heavily damaged by kamikazes and instead of being repaired was returned to its original configuration and operated by a commercial steamship company until 1960.

7 Sawyer and Mitchell, *From America to United States,* pp. 15–16; William B. Hayler, *American Merchant Seaman's Manual, for Seamen by Seamen,* 6th ed. (Centreville, Md.: Cornell Maritime Press / Tidewater Publishers, 1981), pp. 5-9 to 5-10.

8 Gerald J. Fischer, *A Statistical Summary of Shipbuilding under the U.S. Maritime Commission during World War II* (Washington, D.C.: U.S. Maritime Commission, 1949), p. 24.

9 George W. Baer, *One Hundred Years of Sea Power: The U.S. Navy, 1890–1990* (Stanford, Calif.: Stanford Univ. Press, 1994), p. 200; Samuel Eliot Morison, *History of United States Naval Operations in World War II,* vol. 1, *The Battle of the Atlantic, September 1939–May 1943* (Boston: Little, Brown, 1947), pp. 290–96; Allan Nevins, *Sail On: The Story of the American Merchant Marine* (New York: United States Lines, 1946), pp. 94–95.

10 U.S. Maritime Commission, *A Statistical Summary of Shipbuilding,* Report No. 2 (Washington, D.C.: 1949), pp. B-3, 24.

11 Joel R. Davidson, *The Unsinkable Fleet: The Politics of U.S. Navy Expansion in World War II* (Annapolis, Md.: Naval Institute Press, 1996).

12 Samuel Eliot Morison, *History of United States Naval Operations in World War II,* vol. 4, *Coral Sea, Midway and Submarine Actions, May 1942–August 1942* (Boston: Little, Brown, 1949), pp. 270–75; Morison, *History of United States Naval Operations in World War II,* vol. 2, *Operations in North African Waters* (Boston: Little, Brown, 1947), pp. 36–40.

13 Public Law 835, 74th Congress, 2nd sess. (1936), sec. 101.

14 Ibid., sec. 1306.

15 Julian S. Corbett, *Some Principles of Maritime Strategy* (London: Longmans, Green, 1911): "Since men live upon the land and not upon the sea, great issues between nations at war have always been decided— except in the rarest cases—either by what your army can do against your enemy's territory and national life, or else by the fear of what the fleet makes it possible for your army to do" (p. 14).

16 Bureau of Naval Personnel, *Military Sea Transportation Service,* NAVPERS 10829-B (Washington, D.C.: U.S. Government Printing Office, 1962), p. 46.

17 Bureau of Naval Personnel, *Military Sea Transportation and Shipping Control,* NAVPERS 10829-A (Washington, D.C.: U.S. Navy Dept., 1954), p. 64. On 7 May 1941 the Secretaries of War and the Navy agreed "that the increasing burden being imposed upon the Army Transport Service, and the inability of the service [Army] to accomplish satisfactorily, with union-controlled civilian crews the tasks now assigned and to be assigned, makes it desirable for the Army to surrender operation of its transport service for the term of the present emergency. Immediate transfer of this service to the Navy . . . will enable the Navy to be prepared to meet more promptly the Navy task . . . for the overseas movement of Army forces against naval opposition."

18 Bureau of Naval Personnel, *Military Sea Transportation,* pp. 62–65. In his analysis of the Navy in the Second World War, Robert Love blames the CNO, Harold Stark, for allowing the Army to assume this mission. This is a common misconception—Love and others have failed to acknowledge the larger picture.

19 Charles R. Shrader, "Rapid Deployment in 1942," in *United States Army Logistics, 1775–1992: An Anthology,* ed. Charles R. Shrader (Washington, D.C.: Center of Military History, 1992), vol. 3, pp. 707–18.

20 Robert W. Coakley and Richard M. Leighton, *Global Logistics and Strategy, 1943–1945* (Washington, D.C.: U.S. Army Dept., Chief of Military History, 1968), pp. 179–85; Bureau of Naval Personnel, *Military Sea Transportation,* pp. 71–72.

21 The members of the Strategic Shipping Board were Admiral Land, the Army Chief of Staff (Gen. George C. Marshall), the CNO (Admiral Stark), and the president's personal adviser, Harry L. Hopkins. See William L. O'Neill, *A Democracy at War: America's Fight at Home and Abroad in World War II* (Cambridge, Mass.: Harvard Univ. Press, 1993), pp. 75–103, for a discussion of President Franklin Roosevelt's attempts to organize the government for war.

22 Coakley and Leighton, *Global Logistics and Strategy, 1943–1945,* pp. 57–89.

23 Pedraja, *Historical Dictionary of the U.S. Merchant Marine and Shipping Industry,* pp. 647–50; Richard M. Leighton and Robert W. Coakley, *Global Logistics and Strategy, 1940–1943* (Washington, D.C.: U.S. Army Dept., Center of Military History, 1955), pp. 398–404, 455–70.

24 Morison, *Battle of the Atlantic,* pp. 298–99.

25 Ibid., p. 300.

26 Ibid.

27 Samuel Eliot Morison, *The Two-Ocean War: A Short History of the United States Navy in the Second World War* (Boston: Little, Brown, 1963), p. 586.

28 Coakley and Leighton, *Global Logistics and Strategy, 1943–1945:* "World War II was the first war fought by the United States on a truly global scale. The American war effort involved establishment and support of many fighting fronts stretched around the globe and of allies, great and small, engaged in a common struggle against the Axis Powers. Both the fighting fronts and the Allies had to be supported over long sea lines of communications. Sea transport, in all its varied forms, became the most important single element in logistics. . . . In the first stage of the war scarcities of both materiel and shipping hamstrung Allied planners at every turn. In the last phase almost every article in the catalogue was in plentiful supply for a one-front war, but the timing of the final blow was still controlled by the logistical processes involved in moving selected portions of the military machine into place. . . . First it was merchant shipping, then assault shipping: and in the final stage it was military manpower and reception and clearance capacity within overseas theaters" (pp. 795, 819); Richard Overy, *Why the Allies Won* (New York: W. W. Norton, 1995), pp. 26–27, 44–48, 60–62, 193–94.

29 Clay Blair, *Hitler's U-boat War,* vol. 2, *The Hunted, 1942–1945* (New York: Random House, 1998), pp. 706–11.

30 Michael Gannon, *Operation Drumbeat: The Dramatic True Story of Germany's First U-boat Attacks along the American Coast in World War II* (New York: Harper and Row, 1990), pp. 191–213. Not until 1988 were merchant mariners who served in the Second World War entitled to veterans' benefits and that only after a prolonged legal fight with the government. For the vexed status of merchant mariners in wartime, see Charles Gibson, *Merchantman: Or Ship of War—A Synopsis of Laws, U.S. State Department Positions, and Practices Which Alter the Peaceful Character of the U.S. Merchant* (Camden, Maine: Ensign, 1986).

31 Coakley and Leighton, *Global Logistics and Strategy, 1943–1945,* pp. 351–68.

32 Clay Blair, *Hitler's U-boat War,* vol. 1, *The Hunters, 1939–1942* (New York: Random House, 1996): "A mindless theory had taken deep root in Washington—fostered by Jerry Land at the U.S. Maritime Commission and others—that one way to defeat the U-boat was simply to produce merchant ships at a much faster rate that U-boats could sink them" (p. 451). This quotation demonstrates Blair's failure to grasp the immensity of the sealift effort in the Second World War and is typical of a myopic view of one theater that fails to take into account global implications.

33 Coakley and Leighton, *Global Logistics and Strategy, 1943–1945,* pp. 246–70. Leahy wrote to Douglas Wilson of the WSA: "The JCS believe . . . that shipping . . . will not continue to be the bottleneck of our war effort overseas, that limitations in production of war products other than merchant shipping will govern. The urgent necessity to produce the greatest possible number of ships in a given time, met by mass production of Liberty ships, therefore becomes less compelling. . . . This experience leads to the conviction that our strategic needs in 1944 will best be met by the maximum number of fast ships" (p. 250).

34 Ibid., pp. 398–404.

35 Although once the Allies had landed in Normandy, their logistics were deeply and insolubly confounded by stubborn defense of some ports and by the systematic destruction of infrastructure and scuttling of ships by the Germans in ports they could not hold.

36 Bureau of Naval Personnel, *Military Sea Transportation,* p. 70.

37 Duncan S. Ballentine, *U.S. Naval Logistics in the Second World War* (Princeton, N.J.: Princeton Univ. Press, 1947); Worrall Reed Carter and Elmer Ellsworth Duvall, *Ships, Salvage, and Sinews of War: The Story of Fleet Logistics Afloat in Atlantic and Mediterranean Waters during World War II* (Washington, D.C.: U.S. Navy Dept., 1954); Worrall Reed Carter, *Beans, Bullets, and Black Oil: The Story of Fleet Logistics Afloat in the Pacific during World War II* (Washington, D.C.: U.S. Government Printing Office, 1953).

38 David H. Grover, *U.S. Army Ships and Watercraft of World War II* (Annapolis, Md.: Naval Institute Press, 1987), pp. ix–x.

39 War Shipping Administration, *United States Merchant Marine at War,* pp. 6–7. The number of merchant mariners killed has come under criticism as being too low. The two best sources for the losses during the Second World War are Robert M. Browning, Jr., *U.S. Merchant Vessel War Casualties of World War II* (Annapolis, Md.: Naval Institute Press, 1996), and Arthur R. Moore, *"A Careless Word—a Needless Sinking": A History of the Staggering Losses Suffered by the U.S. Merchant Marine, Both in Ships and Personnel during World War II* (Kings Point, N.Y.: American Merchant Marine Museum, 1988).

	Number Serving	Battle Deaths (no.)	Battle Deaths (%)
Merchant marine	215,000	8,380	3.898
Marine Corps	669,100	19,733	2.949
Army	11,260,000	234,874	2.086
Navy	4,183,466	36,950	0.883
Coast Guard	241,093	574	0.238

40 Bruce L. Felknor, ed., *The U.S. Merchant Marine at War, 1775–1945* (Annapolis, Md.: Naval Institute Press, 1998), p. 331.

XIX The Battle of Quemoy
The Amphibious Assault That Held the Postwar Military Balance in the Taiwan Strait

MAOCHUN MILES YU

In the annals of the communist world, the month of October enjoys supreme sanctity. The Red October of 1917 ushered in the first socialist government, which would eventually become the Soviet Union. In the People's Republic of China (PRC), October is indelibly enshrined as the anniversary month of the founding of the communist state, observed with a multiday national celebration.

But each year, amid glorious celebratory glow marking the inauguration of the PRC, the memory of a forbidden and inglorious episode surfaces—inevitably, albeit surreptitiously and furtively—within China's educated and political elite. The event took place a little over three weeks after Mao Zedong triumphantly announced at Tiananmen Square, on 1 October 1949, the establishment of the People's Republic. It is the subject of a substantial and nagging controversy that is antithetical to the overall academic and political discouragement of real historical debate, especially concerning any stain on the exalted victories of the People's Liberation Army (PLA). To most inside China who know and care about the episode, it was an ignominious defeat that undercuts the familiar and mandatory political culture of triumph and glory.

The episode was the battle of Quemoy, known in Taiwan as the battle of Guning-tou Beach, which raged for three days, 25 to 27 October 1949. The outcome was the total annihilation of three PLA regiments, totaling over nine thousand soldiers, at the hands of a beat-up and retreating Nationalist contingent. But what has made the battle of Quemoy so significant in the military history of the PRC, what has shaped its enduring legacy and impact, is not just the lopsided defeat of the PLA troops but how it was fought, its inauspicious timing, and the exposure of the PLA's inability to conduct naval and amphibious warfare.

This paper seeks to analyze the key contentious issues related to the PLA's Quemoy fiasco, mainly from documents and sources published in mainland China and recently made available to the public. Though not grand or ambitious in scope, the paper endeavors to look at how and why the battle of Quemoy was fought and to dispel a few prevailing but mistaken notions based on faulty logic and the changing historical narratives emerging from China's highly mutable political climate.

Finally, it addresses, first, the pivotal role the battle played in setting the pattern of confrontation that has produced a six-decade political and military separation between Nationalist Taiwan and Communist China and, second, how the battle affected the United States in its Cold War strategy.

The Battle

Quemoy, variously also called Jinmen, Chin-men, or Kinmen, is a tiny, barren archipelago consisting mainly of Greater Quemoy and Lesser Quemoy, totaling a mere fifty-nine square miles. In October 1949 there were only about forty thousand residents on the islands.[1] The most striking feature of Quemoy lies not in its size but in its extreme geographical proximity to the PRC mainland—only six miles away from the metropolis of Xiamen (Amoy), which was in 1949 the second-largest city in Fujian Province and had a population of over two hundred thousand. It is important to point out that Xiamen Island (now connected to the mainland, on which part of the city stands) is merely one mile from the Chinese mainland and would be the primary spot to assemble troops and amphibious vessels for any attempt to invade Taiwan.

But Quemoy controls the sea access in and out of Xiamen and the adjacent coastal areas (see the map). For the Nationalist (Kuomintang, or KMT) government, which was in rapid strategic retreat to Taiwan, Quemoy assumed supreme strategic importance to its own survival, because it could effectively frustrate the PLA's vowed intention to invade and take Taiwan.[2]

By the summer of 1949, the Chinese Civil War between the Nationalists and the Communists had been raging for over three years and the Nationalists were near total defeat all across China. By late July it was beyond any doubt that the escape destination for the Nationalist government would be Taiwan. As a result, massive transportation of assets and government functions from the mainland to Taiwan began in full. Also that month the KMT's leader, Chiang Kai-shek, started to prepare for a pivotal battle to hold Quemoy, which was not even fortified at the time. Although nearby Xiamen Island was much more important in a political and psychological sense, Quemoy would be more crucial militarily, because it could control all maritime assets in and access to the area, including Xiamen. So from the beginning Chiang Kai-shek was prepared to lose Xiamen but determined to keep Quemoy at any cost. He deployed the KMT's 22nd Army to garrison Quemoy, with about twenty thousand troops, in addition to a tank battalion with twenty-one American-made M5A1 Stuart tanks, each of which had a rapid-fire 47 mm gun. The Stuart tanks would play a pivotal role.

For three days, between 25 and 27 October, a battle for Quemoy raged. Invading PLA troops were greatly outnumbered, and the fighting was desperate on both sides. In the end, however, the PLA suffered a devastating defeat, one that shocked its high command. The entire three PLA regiments committed—9,086 men in all,

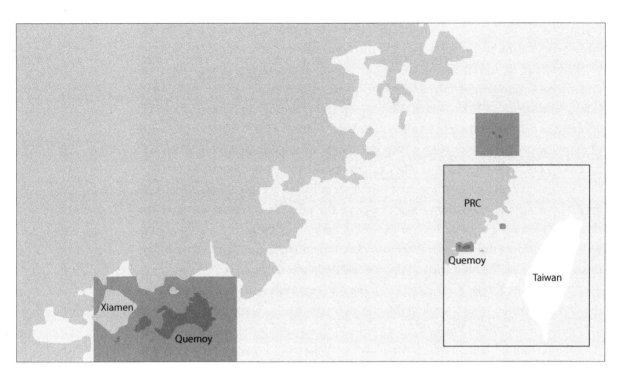

including 350 local fishermen conscripted as captains of transport craft—were annihilated. About five thousand were killed, and the rest were captured as prisoners
of war.[3]

Was the Shortage of Transport Ships Responsible for the Fiasco?

There is no doubt that a severe shortage of troop transports was a key factor in
deciding the outcome of the battle of Quemoy. But the problem was not just a lack
of vessels but poor planning and hostility from local residents.

The transport shortage had much to do with faulty planning by the PLA commanders. From the beginning, an attack on Xiamen had outweighed all other offensives along the Fujian coast, greatly diminishing any meaningful preparation for
the planned assault on Quemoy. The mission of taking Xiamen and Quemoy was
handed to the PLA 3rd Field Army's 10th Army, under the command of a battle-
hardened general, Ye Fei. He divided his three corps into two task forces. The 29th
and 31st Corps would take on Xiamen. These corps were more offensively oriented
and much better equipped than the smaller and weaker 28th Corps, which would
take on Quemoy, then considered less important than Xiamen. The original plan
was that the two task forces would launch simultaneous assaults on the KMT defenders of both Xiamen and Quemoy.

But doing so would require the two task forces to commandeer a large number
of fishing vessels from local villages as troop transports. The commanding general
of the 10th Army, General Ye, believed that many fishing vessels in the region were

being systematically destroyed by KMT planes to avoid their being used by the advancing Communist troops.[4] But Ye's memoir does not provide any evidence of such bombing or instances when it occurred. On the contrary, most damage to and losses of commandeered fishing vessels were caused by storms during a minor island offensive prior to the attacks on Xiamen and Quemoy.[5] In his memoir Ye Fei contradicts himself, stating that in the island battles immediately prior to the battle of Quemoy not a single transport ship was lost to enemy planes and that this was taken as a welcome sign that the KMT might not use planes at Quemoy either.[6]

The primary reason for the lack of fishing vessels was that local fishermen were generally hostile to the Communist troops in the area. The biggest sector of the economy in the region was fishing, and the most important asset for a fisherman was his boat. Most fishermen resisted the PLA demand to surrender their vessels as troop transports. They hid their vessels or scuttled them to avoid their being taken over by the PLA troops.[7] Gen. Xiao Feng, the on-scene, operational commander in the Quemoy battle, would recall in his own memoir that "fishermen in this coastal area either abandoned their fishing vessels and fled from us, or took their vessels with them and hid them; others even deliberately destroyed their fishing vessels to avoid being commandeered by us. We could not find the vessels when we found the fishermen; or we could not find the fishermen to operate these vessels when we found the vessels."[8]

Because of the shortage of transport ships, the original plan to attack Xiamen and Quemoy simultaneously was abandoned. The new plan was to attack Xiamen first, concentrating all the ships and boats already commandeered by the 10th Army, and to postpone the campaign against Quemoy until the Xiamen campaign was over and the ships and boats used in it could be released.

The battle for Xiamen started on 15 October and lasted two full days. The battle had something expected and something unexpected. The "expected" was the outcome, a smashing victory over demoralized defenders, who did not put up a real fight. Some twenty-seven thousand KMT soldiers were either killed or captured, the majority of the originally stationed defenders having fled on ships to either Taiwan or other outlying islands still under KMT control. The unexpected result of the Xiamen campaign was devastating losses of transport vessels. After the Xiamen campaign, what remained for the 28th Corps to use in its upcoming Quemoy assault was fewer than three hundred small fishing boats, none motorized.

The battle plan for Quemoy was to land twenty thousand PLA troops on the island's beaches. But with fewer than three hundred small boats available, the task force would have to be transported in two groups. The first would be three PLA regiments, or about 8,700 troops, in addition to the 350 fishermen, most of them unwilling to serve the PLA but having no choice. The plan contemplated that once the first landing group reached the beachhead, the vessels would return to the PLA positions to take the second landing group, which would consist of four regiments, another eleven thousand troops. PLA intelligence estimated that there were about twenty thousand KMT defenders on Quemoy at the time and that the combined invasion force, twenty thousand PLA soldiers, would reach parity in strength, one to one. Given the PLA's superior morale and fighting spirit, victory over the defeatist and demoralized KMT defenders on Quemoy would be inevitable.[9]

But the plan went badly. After the first three regiments were delivered to the beachhead—in the middle of the night, apparently undetected by the defenders—the tide went out, and all the ships grounded in the shoals, where they were mercilessly destroyed by the KMT defenders by shore, sea, and air. Not a single ship or boat was able to return to pick up the reinforcing second landing group. Although grave miscalculation of ocean tides was later blamed by most participants and PRC historians as the chief culprit for the transport debacle, it was not the most decisive factor in the failure of the transport vessels to return for the second group.

Ignoring advice from local fishermen, the PLA commanders on board the vessels had ordered the vessels to approach the shore as closely as possible so that the invasion troops would have an easier walk to the beach. The vessels arrived at high tide, between 0130 and 0200 (1:30 and 2:00 AM), passing over underwater antiship obstacles and ship-snatching barbed wire. When the tide began to recede, some vessels became entangled with the newly exposed obstacles. PLA commanders realized the danger and ordered the swift return of the vessels to deeper water before the tide got too low. But it was too late; all of them became stuck on a long stretch of beach in a scene of total chaos.[10] When a land mine near the landing beach was accidentally ignited by a KMT patrol, the explosion triggered feverish searchlight sweeps by the coastal defenses, which discovered the shambles of landing vessels stuck on and near the beach.[11] Gunfire and bombing erupted and lasted for more than two hours. Dawn, when it arrived, allowed KMT B-25 bombers and warships to shell the hapless landing forces, destroying all of them. Not a single vessel escaped.[12] The entire Quemoy battle plan, which hinged critically on the ability of the transport vessels to return to pick up eleven thousand more PLA troops, had turned into a complete fiasco.

Was the PLA's Lack of Naval Power and Airpower Responsible for the Fiasco?

In his memoir, Ye Fei, the officer in overall charge of the battle of Quemoy, blames the PLA's lack of naval power and airpower during the battle for the defeat. "The most important and most salient lesson [for the defeat at Quemoy] was that at the time, the Chiang Kai-shek army had a navy and an air force, which remained basically intact during the War of National Liberation [the Civil War, 1946–49]; while our army did not have a navy and an air force, which forced us to cross the sea to fight by way of sailboats, without air cover, without naval support from the sea."[13] So states Ye Fei, and his argument seems reasonable on the surface. However, a careful scrutiny will reveal that his summary of the reasons for the defeat is without merit.

During the battle of Quemoy, the KMT had at its disposal twenty-five B-25 light bombers and about fifty FB-26 fighter-bombers.[14] The PLA had a squadron of P-51 Mustangs, captured from the KMT, but these pursuit planes had been used in the ceremonial extravaganza in Beijing marking the founding of the People's Republic of China in early October. They were still in North China.[15] On the naval side, the KMT had a total of nine ships, mostly small patrol vessels and light frigates.

During the battle, the PLA command was fully aware of these KMT naval and air assets and took measures to deny their usefulness. The most important decision made by Ye Fei, in this connection, and his subordinate Xiao Feng—and it was a correct one—was to conduct the amphibious assault at night, because the KMT air force did not have a nighttime capability. Also, with the cover of night the PLA troops could avoid being detected by the KMT warships and so launch a surprise attack. On both accounts the PLA command was right, and the invasion troops did successfully avoid attack by KMT air or naval assets during the entire trip to the beaches on the first night of the battle. In addition, the PLA mounted a battery of eighty pieces of artillery on nearby Dadeng Island.[16] Though not overwhelming, these guns could silence the KMT's small patrol boats during the landing phase.

Ye Fei's argument is even less plausible if one considers the many amphibious battles the PLA launched against even more dominant KMT sea and air superiority, notably at Hainan Island some six months later. In virtually all these other instances, despite overwhelming KMT naval and air superiority, the PLA island assaults prevailed.

What General Ye neglected to point out in his memoir is another key reason for the Quemoy defeat—the fatefully delayed departure of the invasion forces. It was less than six miles from the PLA embarkation points to the Quemoy beaches. Under the weather conditions at the time, a favorably robust northeast breeze, it would take less than one hour to reach the destination. The invasion forces were accordingly ordered to board the vessels around 1900 (seven o'clock) on the evening of 24 October. But indecision on the part of Ye Fei and Xiao Feng and command ambiguity between them, in addition to utterly chaotic boarding and loading procedures, delayed the departure by several hours, greatly shortening the period of darkness, the window during which the KMT air and sea forces could not attack. Most of the vessels did not sail until after midnight.[17]

The armada itself was also disorganized. The three regiments set sail from three different spots. Once entering open water, their vessels were to rendezvous at a designated area and then proceed together. This order wasted about an hour. Worse, because of radio silence to avoid enemy detection, the vessels had no communications with each other. As a result, the rendezvous was never really completed; the vessels swarmed to Quemoy without any coordination or unified command, arriving intermittently between 0130 and 0200, far later than originally planned, with only three or four hours left within which to land their troops.

Given that delay, even if all three hundred transport vessels had returned to the rear echelon and picked up the eleven thousand men of the second group, they would most likely have been annihilated. The most important element of a victory —that is, inability of the KMT forces to attack by air or sea—would have been lost with the advent of daylight on 25 October.

We can then safely conclude that Ye Fei's theory about the primary reason for the Quemoy fiasco is incorrect.

Was Intelligence Failure Crucial for the Fiasco?

Before the assault was launched on 24 October, the PLA commanders gathered a substantial amount of intelligence on the enemy and the target area. Reports poured into the command headquarters of General Ye, the overall commander, and of Xiao Feng, the operational commander. These reports were generally classified as either political or operational intelligence. In both categories the PLA commanders fundamentally misjudged the intelligence in front of them and made seriously flawed decisions that doomed the entire invasion.

Political intelligence had been the PLA's forte, as it dealt with timely and accurate assessment of the enemy's will to fight. Yet both commanders erred gravely in the Quemoy assault. Their overall assessments of the Quemoy defenders were more romantic than professional. They believed deeply that the KMT's 22nd Army on Quemoy was morbidly defeatist and incompetent, ready to flee at the sight of the PLA invaders. "Landing on the beach of Quemoy is victory itself" was the watchword given to many PLA units in the operation.[18] So pervasive was the assumption of the enemy's lack of will to fight that the transports carrying the primary assault regiment contained large amounts of cash in several heavy chests for the use of celebrating the "liberation of Quemoy" in an extravaganza planned for the next day. Several other larger ships were loaded with live pigs and with office furniture to be used by the new local government to be run by communist cadres.[19]

To be fair, this was not the problem of only PLA commanders in Fujian Province at the time. Rao Shushi, the political commissar of the PLA's 3rd Field Army, which was in charge of the entire East China region, was hopelessly contemptuous, on the eve of the battle, of the KMT troops' will to fight. "Rao Shushi developed a 'mentality of underestimating the enemy,'" later recalled Marshal Chen Yi, who commanded the 3rd Field Army. "He believed that once our troops landed on the beach, enemies on Quemoy would surrender without fighting. All we needed was to send in one or two divisions to attack, the Quemoy problem would be solved."[20]

But the PLA commanders' estimate of the enemy's will to fight was wrong. Admittedly, the KMT troops were indeed a ragtag bunch. The 22nd Army, then stationed at Quemoy, was under the command of a general named Li Liangrong. Li and his troops were not Chiang Kai-shek's favorites, and they were generally underequipped and undertrained. But General Li made these troops into a formidable fighting force that displayed tenacity and ruthlessness in the three-day battle.

First of all, Li was given substantial reinforcement at the crucial time. Chiang Kai-shek realized Li's inadequacy in troop strength and redeployed, swiftly and sub rosa, one of his best units, the 18th Army, totaling twenty thousand troops, to Quemoy. Arriving before and during the battle, these troops greatly boosted the morale of General Li's men. The determination of this ragtag but spirited army, however, was already extraordinarily high, in part because of an utter hatred of the communists.

A recent popular writing in mainland China by a high-level PLA general tells a revealing story, one that explains the abject hatred of General Li's men for PLA soldiers and the ruthlessness of Quemoy's defenders. It relates to the battle of Xiamen, fought several miles away immediately prior to the battle for Quemoy. The PLA won that battle, during which many KMT soldiers took off their uniforms and hid as civilians in residential neighborhoods. The PLA commander in Xiamen ordered cars to broadcast via loudspeakers promises of leniency and safe repatriation to Taiwan if they came out and surrendered. Within hours, hundreds of KMT officers and soldiers answered the propaganda and emerged from hiding. They were rounded up by PLA troops at the harbor. After dusk, they were machine-gunned, execution-style.[21] Fear and outrage generated by incidents like this permeated the 22nd Army on Quemoy, and General Li adroitly used such psychology to instill in his troops despair and ruthlessness—the very essence of a formidable enemy.[22]

If PLA political intelligence was inaccurate, tactical and operational intelligence was not much better. Gen. Ye Fei was never clear about exactly how many defenders there were on Quemoy. He believed there were no more than twenty thousand; further, he estimated at the time, "Li Liangrong's 22nd Army was nothing but maimed soldiers and defeated generals [残兵败将]." He was completely fooled by a KMT deception plan. Chiang meant to hold on to Quemoy at any cost, and as noted, he had reinforced it with his crack force, the 18th Army, under the able Hu Lian. But even more important, Chiang ordered the armada carrying General Hu's troops to land secretly on the rocky south side of Quemoy Island, opposite the anticipated PLA landing strips on the north and northwest sides. Unbeknownst to Ye Fei, by 24 October, when the PLA launched the assault, half of Hu's twenty thousand troops were already on the island. The other half was struggling to land safely through heavy waves; they succeeded after the battle started.

This intelligence would have been crucial. Had General Ye known of it, he would never have ordered the attack. The PLA force would have been greatly outnumbered, in a ratio of less than one to two, even if all his planned troops had been able to land at once, which would not be the case. In the end, the actual PLA/KMT troop ratio during the battle was one to five.[23] Faulty intelligence led General Ye to believe that he could reach troop parity on Quemoy if he could land close to twenty thousand soldiers. Ye's landing plan was to be utterly invalidated and disastrous, but in the meantime he was so confident in this parity that he refused to consider any alternatives even when newly acquired evidence pointed to the strong possibility that the enemy had already been reinforced by the entire twenty-thousand-man 18th Army.

On 14 October, ten days before the order was given to invade Quemoy, General Xiao, the PLA operational commander of the battle of Quemoy, received a shocking piece of intelligence. Two KMT officers belonging to Hu Lian's 18th Army, captured in an unrelated skirmish, had revealed that the whole 11th Division of that army had landed on Quemoy five days earlier.[24] General Xiao immediately reported this crucial piece of intelligence to his superior, General Ye, who dismissed it as bunk.[25] Frustrated by Ye's intransigence, Xiao did something daring—he managed to report his concern to Ye's superior, Gen. Su Yu, the deputy commander for operations for the 3rd Field Army. General Su had been designated by Mao Zedong as the overall planner for a quick invasion of Taiwan, fulfilling Mao's vow "to carry the Revolution to the ultimate end."

Alarmed by the Quemoy situation, Su issued an instruction, now famous in the Chinese military, known as the "three conditions for calling off the Quemoy campaign." That is, the attack on Quemoy should be called off if one of the following three conditions existed: first, if the enemy augmented the island defending force by more than one regiment; second, if there were not enough transports to carry six regiments at one time; or third, if there were not at least six thousand pro-Communist, politically reliable boat handlers available from the old "Liberated Area" of northern Jiangsu and Shandong, nearly a thousand miles north of Fujian.[26]

But General Ye did not heed Su's instructions and bullheadedly went on with his attack plan. Nevertheless, Ye sensed General Xiao's lack of enthusiasm in light of the mounting difficulties of attacking Quemoy. On 18 October, six days before the battle began, he spent nearly three hours with General Xiao and Xiao's commissar, Gen. Li Mancun, trying to dispel their doubts and eventually ordering them to launch the earliest possible attack.[27]

But Xiao and Li Mancun were still not persuaded. "I raised the issue to my superior of the 10th Army," Xiao recounted in his memoir, "that . . . we did not know how many enemy reinforcements had arrived at Quemoy, which made the preparation for the invasion of Quemoy inadequate and it would be difficult to launch an early assault on Quemoy."[28] But General Ye and his headquarters staff would have none of this. "My superiors at the 10th Army all replied to me by saying that the 28th Corps should resolutely implement the 10th Army headquarters' order to seize the battlefield advantage to launch an earliest possible invasion to liberate Quemoy," Xiao Feng would bitterly recall.[29] As to what exactly the "battlefield advantage" was, General Ye declared with relish, "The enemies defending Quemoy have already become frightened by us, like birds scared by the mere twang of a bowstring [惊弓之鸟]."

On 20 October, four days before the battle began, General Xiao, still spooked by uncertainty about enemy troop strength on Quemoy, again requested General Ye to postpone the operation.[30] Ye was not amused by the new request and denied it with alacrity. However, two days later, on 22 October, new intelligence reports came to General Xiao that another division of Hu Lian's 18th Army had just appeared in waters off Quemoy. General Xiao immediately reported to Ye, hoping that a delay of action would be approved.[31]

Incredibly, General Ye interpreted the intelligence the wrong way. He picked up the phone and personally told Xiao that the intention of the KMT force near Quemoy was not clear and that the PLA attack should be hurried, before General Hu's troops could land.[32] We now know that General Ye was completely out of the picture with regard to Hu's reinforcements. Not only had one of Hu's divisions landed on Quemoy days earlier, but the division reported to be on the sea was just waiting for the choppy seas to calm in order to land, which happened within hours.

General Xiao, still unwilling to take the risk of attacking, stated that he could not possibly proceed with the operation the next day as ordered and requested a one-day delay, until 24 October. Ye Fei finally agreed, and the operation was thus set for the 24th. Incredibly, though, in granting the delay, Ye told Xiao that "according to various intelligence reports, there had been no reinforcement of enemy's troops in Quemoy, which was only at 12,000 troops strong."[33] In fact, at the time, there were more than thirty thousand KMT troops on Quemoy.

The departure for the invasion was set at night, to avoid naval and air raids. Three regiments from General Xiao's 28th Corps boarded the nearly three hundred small fishing boats being used as transports between 6 and 7 PM, ready to set sail to attack Quemoy. Around 8 PM, however, Xiao received a revised intelligence report from 10th Army headquarters in Xiamen that the KMT 18th Army had just landed a regiment on the south side of Quemoy. However, 10th Army directed that General Ye's order to attack Quemoy that evening was not to be changed—instead, Xiao's troops were to race to reach Quemoy ahead of the rest of Hu Lian's force.

But General Xiao, shocked by the new report, immediately ordered all three of his regiments, on board and ready to set sail, to stand fast. He placed an urgent call to the 10th Army headquarters in Xiamen and requested that the entire attack plan be called off until more intelligence on enemy troop strength could be ascertained and more transports could be commandeered. But General Ye was nowhere to be found. Answering General Xiao's urgent call was Liu Peishan, Ye's deputy commissar and political director, who rejected Xiao's request. General Xiao later recalled, "I clearly stated to Liu on the phone that we [should] halt the attack plan, wait for clarification on the true situations of the enemy, obtain more transport ships before we take action. Hearing that, Director Liu only said, 'Proceed according to the original plan, the decision shall not be changed.' Then he hung up the phone."[34]

Around midnight, the invading armada set sail for Quemoy. It arrived an hour and a half later, and the epic battle began.

Was Command Chaos Responsible for the Fiasco?

In the aftermath of the disastrous defeat, Xiao Feng went to his superior, Ye Fei, and asked to be punished for the defeat. Ye replied that it was he himself who should be punished for the infamy at Quemoy. General Ye promptly drafted a lengthy cable to his superior, Gen. Su Yu at the 3rd Field Army, asking for punishment. Su, however, rejected Ye's request and instead cabled Mao Zedong directly asking that he, Su, be punished, for his failure to ensure victory. Mao, the supreme leader of the Communist forces in China, rejected General Su's request, saying essentially that nobody should be punished. "The loss at Quemoy is not a matter of punishment," Mao declared. "Instead, it's a matter of learning a lesson from it."[35]

All this is telling, because it reflects the kind of command chaos that existed before and during the battle of Quemoy. No one was responsible for command integrity or organizational coordination.

The 10th Army commander, Gen. Ye Fei, had been born in the Philippines of Chinese parents from the Fujian area. Ye, who had joined the communists seventeen years earlier as a young man of no social or political distinction, had returned to his hometown as a glorious conqueror and wartime leader of over 120,000 troops.[36] When Ye captured the picturesque metropolis of Xiamen, he promptly moved his headquarters to the city, immersing himself in urban life and acting more like a mayor than a military commander with battles still raging in his area.[37] In fact, the moment Ye moved into Xiamen he sent for his mother, who had been living in rural Fujian, moving her into his headquarters to share the euphoria and glory.[38]

For the remaining, and militarily more daunting, task of taking Quemoy, General Ye designated the weakest of his three corps, the 28th Corps. However, in late August 1949 the 28th Corps's longtime commander, Gen. Zhu Shaoqing, had suffered a stomach illness and was now in Shanghai, newly captured from the KMT, for medical treatment. The political commissar of the 28th Corps, Gen. Chen Meizao, was in a hospital in Fuzhou, the capital of Fujian Province, enjoying the ease of urban life. In addition, the 28th Corps's longtime chief of staff, Wu Shu, had been reassigned without replacement. General Ye then appointed Zhu Shaoqing's deputy commander, a staff general named Xiao Feng, to command the 28th Corps, without a deputy commander or a chief of staff.[39]

The first invasion group was to consist of three regiments. However, as General Ye ordered, only two would come from the 28th Corps; the third would come from another corps, the 29th, also under Ye's command. This was done mainly so that the 29th Corps could share the anticipated glory of victory at Quemoy. But mixing troops from competing units confused the organic command structure of the 28th Corps.[40] Also, there was some rivalry between the 28th Corps and 29th Corps, and there had been ill feeling in the competition to commandeer local fishing vessels.[41]

General Ye realized the potential for rivalry among the three hurriedly mixed regiments, but his response, rather inexplicably, was that there should be no overall commander for the entire invasion force. The three regimental commanders were to act with equal command authority, with individual battle plans; Xiao Feng was to stay in the rear echelon listening to their radio reports once the battle started.[42] To achieve the element of surprise, however, as we have seen, radio silence was ordered while the armada of wooden sailing vessels was on its way. So there was absolutely no communication among vessels during the entire landing process, which further aggravated the command problem.

In the event, the most deadly weapons used by the KMT defenders against the invading PLA troops and vessels were the twenty-one M5A1 Stuart tanks. The PLA command had known about the tanks beforehand and had prepared antitank rockets to deal with them. But the antitank rockets came in three parts, which needed to be assembled before launch. General Xiao ordered the parts carried by separate ships. When the force attempted to land and came under fierce and devastating tank fire, none of the antitank rockets could be assembled.[43]

Was the Battle of Quemoy a "Turning Point" in History?

Mao Zedong admitted that the battle of Quemoy was the biggest loss to the PLA during the Chinese Civil War.[44] Three regiments of PLA troops were completely wiped out by the KMT, in utter contrast to the military zeitgeist of the time, when the Nationalist army as a whole was in an avalanche of retreat and defeat. In the annals of the Nationalists' military history, the triumph at Quemoy, known in Taiwan as the battle of Guningtou Beach, marked a turning point, the final halting of the momentum of the PLA assault against Taiwan. It was the battle that saved the Republic of China; it was Chiang Kai-shek's battle of Midway, turning the tide of history and sealing for the future the general pattern of the Cold War confrontation in Asia.

The KMT claim is not entirely without merit. The battle of Quemoy did indeed end the PLA's amphibious attempts to capture the offshore islands. But far more importantly, Quemoy has since become a focal point and symbol of the epic struggle between communist and noncommunist forces in Asia. Metaphorically and realistically, the battle made the tiny island of Quemoy, just a few miles from Communist China, Asia's West Berlin, triggering decades of military confrontations in and around it. In 1954 and 1958 the PLA launched major artillery bombardments almost bringing on a nuclear Armageddon by involving the United States and possibly the Soviet Union. Intermittent artillery bombardment on Quemoy, with real shells or pamphlets, would last for many years. They would not stop until 1 January 1979, when the United States abandoned its diplomatic recognition of Taipei and switched to Beijing as the legitimate government of "China."

However, the PLA historian Xu Yan disputes the idea that the battle of Quemoy was really a turning point of anything:[45] "The defeat at Quemoy at the hands of the KMT forces was only a small episode at the last stage of the PLA's strategic pursuit against the collapsing KMT regime[;] . . . it did not affect the strategic outcome of the war a bit" (p. 93). It is hard to disagree with Mr. Xu Yan. However, it should also be noted that the battle of Quemoy had an unintended strategic consequence that few could have realized at the time. That is, the utter shambles at Quemoy may have saved the PLA from an even bigger catastrophe known as the battle of Taiwan, which had been actively contemplated by the PLA high command, from Mao Zedong on down.

After the fiasco, Mao ordered the 3rd Field Army to prepare for an even larger invasion of Taiwan. The task fell on the shoulders of Gen. Su Yu, the deputy commander for operations of the 3rd Field Army and the realist who had cautioned about the three conditions that should have invalidated any attack on Quemoy. Three weeks later, General Su, now the chairman of the Liberating Taiwan Working Committee, proceeded with specific planning for an invasion of Taiwan. On 20 November 1949 he laid out his plan to senior PLA commanders.[46]

The Quemoy lessons loomed large in Su Yu's plan. By mid-December he had become the leading voice of reason and calm, realistically assessing the difficulties of an amphibious invasion of Taiwan. He reported to Mao Zedong several times his concerns and cautions. That might not have gained him favor from the triumphalist chairman, then getting ready to travel to Moscow to meet Joseph Stalin and take charge of "making revolutions" in Asia while the Soviet Union occupied itself with Western and Eastern Europe. Nevertheless, on 17 December Su Yu officially postponed the date for invading Taiwan.[47]

Gen. Ye Fei may have left the best summary of this point. "In the early 1950s, when our navy and air force were still inferior to the enemy, if we proceeded with wooden sailboats to liberate Taiwan by crossing the Taiwan Strait, we would have had an even bigger fiasco than the battle of Quemoy. After the defeat at Quemoy, we learned our lesson; our head became more clear and lucid. Perhaps the real significance of learning from the lessons and experience of our Quemoy operation lies exactly here."[48]

Yet the real significance of the battle of Quemoy goes beyond even this. The battle may be most important not in itself but in spite of itself. Its importance has something to do with what else was going on in the much larger international arena.

At the time, the Harry Truman administration in the United States had all but given up supporting the Chiang Kai-shek government. Two months before the battle of Quemoy, the White House approved a China white paper that largely blamed Chiang Kai-shek and his government for the loss of China to the Communists. Washington expected the defeat of the KMT army to be thorough and inevitable, including the loss of the island of Taiwan, although it had been heavily built up by Chiang for the impending transfer of his government. The Nationalist general Sun Liren, the garrison commander of Taiwan and a favorite of the U.S. administration, reported to Washington by a separate channel in September 1949, a few weeks before Quemoy, that the PLA was capable of assembling an invading armada of a thousand vessels carrying two hundred thousand troops who would take over Taiwan within twenty-four hours.[49] The newly established Central Intelligence Agency too was thoroughly convinced that the PLA would take over Taiwan militarily by the end of 1950.[50]

But the battle of Quemoy changed all that. One week after the Nationalist victory at Quemoy and most likely in response to it, the Truman administration initiated contact with Chiang for the first time since 1948. The American consul general in Taipei officially informed Chiang on 3 November that the U.S. government would support his efforts toward reform and democracy in Taiwan.[51] This was an enormous morale boost for Chiang and his defeated government. He now for the first time had Washington's support for using Taiwan as a base from which he might stage a comeback to the mainland. It also marked the beginning of official American recognition of the Republic of China in Taiwan, which lasted until the 1970s.

Further, after the battle of Quemoy the U.S. Joint Chiefs of Staff adjusted, albeit with a certain subtlety, its military posture toward Chiang in Taiwan. The Joint Chiefs now suggested to the White House that limited military assistance be provided to the KMT troops in Taiwan, though it ruled out direct military involvement in Taiwan.[52] The momentum of readjustment by the United States in favor of the KMT government in Taiwan created by the battle of Quemoy, however nuanced and limited, would be given robust boosts by two other major international events: the outbreak of the Korean War less than eight months later and the loss of the U.S. monopoly on atomic bombs at the same time.

In this sense, the battle of Quemoy was not only a turning point for the Civil War that still remains unresolved across the Taiwan Strait but also the beginning of a chain of events that shaped the Cold War throughout Asia and the Pacific region for decades to come.

NOTES   The author's research and writing for this article were made possible by a McMullen Seapower Fellowship through the U.S. Naval Academy Foundation.

1 Xu Yan, *The Battle of Quemoy* [徐焰, 金门之战, 中国广播电视出版社, 北京] (1992), pp. 47–48.

2 Ibid., p. 48.

3 Dangdai zhongguo de junshi gongzuo [当代中国的军事工作, 中国社会科学院出版社] (1989), p. 237; Xiao Feng, "My Recollection of the Battle of Quemoy," in *Recollections of the Amphibious Battle of Quemoy,* ed. Xiao Feng et al. [回顾金门之战, 载于萧锋, 李曼村等, 回顾金门登陆战, 人民出版社] (1994), p. 40; Xu, *Battle of Quemoy,* p. 82; Liu Yazhou, *Examination of the Campaign of Quemoy* [金门战役检讨, 载于中国报道周刊] (20 April 2004), p. 12. There is little disagreement among mainland historians on the numbers of PLA soldiers who were killed. On the prisoner-of-war (POW) number, Xu Yan believes it should be around three thousand, while Liu Yazhou's number is four thousand. It is likely that Xu confuses the actual number, which should be around four thousand, with the number of PLA POWs returned to mainland China between 1950 and 1956, which was around three thousand; see Liu, *Examination of the Campaign of Quemoy,* p. 12. The returned PLA POWs all became "nonpersons" in China and would suffer harsh treatments ranging from dishonorable discharge to prison terms—even outright execution—for being "traitors." See Liu, *Examination of the Campaign of Quemoy,* p. 12, and Feizi Longxiang, "The Fate of Returned POWs Captured from the Battle of Quemoy" [飞子龙翔: 金門之戰回歸戰俘的命运], *Feizi Longxiang's Blog,* zxy0808.bokee.com/.

4 Ye Fei, *Ye Fei Memoir* [叶飞回忆录, 解放军出版社] (1988), p. 601.

5 Ibid., pp. 598–601.

6 Ibid., p. 599.

7 Xiao, "My Recollection of the Battle of Quemoy," p. 23.

8 Ibid.

9 Xu, *Battle of Quemoy*, pp. 44–47.

10 Ibid., p. 66.

11 Ibid., p. 64.

12 Ye, *Ye Fei Memoir*, p. 604; Xiao, "My Recollection of the Battle of Quemoy," p. 33; Xu, *Battle of Quemoy*, p. 66.

13 Ye, *Ye Fei Memoir*, p. 606.

14 Xu, *Battle of Quemoy*, p. 61.

15 Ibid., p. 45.

16 Ibid., p. 61.

17 Ibid., p. 64.

18 Liu, *Examination of the Campaign of Quemoy*, p. 3.

19 Ibid.

20 Ibid.

21 Ibid., p. 6.

22 Ibid.

23 Xu, *Battle of Quemoy*, pp. 61–62.

24 Xiao, "My Recollection of the Battle of Quemoy," p. 23.

25 Ibid.

26 Su Yu was ensnared in a major political purge in 1958 and as the PLA's Chief of Staff was a main target of a relentless "antidogmatism in military affairs" campaign engineered by his immediate superior, Marshal Peng Dehuai, Mao's defense minister for much of the 1950s. A year later, in July 1959, Peng was purged in turn by Mao for opposing the chairman's disastrous "Great Leap Forward" movement. In the 1980s, after Mao's death, Peng was politically rehabilitated. But one cannot rehabilitate a victim of a rehabilitated PLA marshal; also, the chief henchman who carried out Peng's "Struggling against Su Yu" campaign in 1958 was Deng Xiaoping, who essentially ruled China from 1978 until his death in 1997. As a result, positive spin in recent decades on Su Yu's salient caution about the Quemoy battle, in the form of the "three conditions for calling off the Quemoy campaign," generates intense, politically motivated internal debate among factions of the PLA. For such positive spin on Su Yu, see Xiao Feng, "Unforgettable Instructions," in *The General of Our Generation: Remembering Comrade Su Yu* [萧锋,难忘的教诲,载于"一代名将: 回忆粟裕同志," 上海人民出版社] (1986), p. 299; Xu, *Battle of Quemoy*, pp. 89–90; and Liu, *Examination of the Campaign of Quemoy*, p. 4. For a negative view see Hong Xiaoxia, "Doubting and Investigating 'The Three Conditions for Calling off the Quemoy Campaign'—and Assessing the Value of Memoirs as Historical Evidence," *Journal of Modern History Studies* 3 (2002) [洪小夏《金门战斗"三不打"的质疑与考证—兼论回忆录的史料价值及其考辨》,《近代史研究》, 2002年第3期], and Wang Hongguang, "An Inquiry into the 'Three Conditions for Calling off the Quemoy Campaign,'" *Journal of Military History*

(November 2012) [王洪光,对金门战役"三不打"的考证《军事历史》2012/11].

27 Ye, *Ye Fei Memoir*, pp. 600–601; Xiao, "My Recollection of the Battle of Quemoy," p. 24.

28 Xiao, "My Recollection of the Battle of Quemoy," p. 24.

29 Ibid.

30 Ibid., p. 25.

31 Ibid.

32 Ibid.

33 Ibid., p. 26.

34 Ibid., pp. 28–29.

35 Xu, *Battle of Quemoy*, p. 91; Ye, *Ye Fei Memoir*, p. 606.

36 Liu, *Examination of the Campaign of Quemoy*, pp. 2–3.

37 Xu, *Battle of Quemoy*, pp. 597–98.

38 Liu, *Examination of the Campaign of Quemoy*, pp. 2–3.

39 Xiao, "My Recollection of the Battle of Quemoy," p. 16.

40 Liu, *Examination of the Campaign of Quemoy*, pp. 3–4.

41 Ye, *Ye Fei Memoir*, p. 600.

42 Xiao Feng was originally designated the overall commander and told to accompany the invasion troops, but hours before the departure of the armada General Ye's headquarters ordered him to stay behind; Xiao, "My Recollection of the Battle of Quemoy," p. 29. Xiao also recalls in his memoir that he designated a division commander, Zhong Xianwen, to be the overall commander of the three regiments and asked him to go to Quemoy with the first invasion group. But, according to Xiao, Zhong's flagship was commandeered by one of the three regiment commanders as a troop transport (p. 33). This is quite implausible, because a regiment commander could not possibly commandeer a division commander's flagship. If this did indeed happen, it further testifies to the miserable command chaos suffered by the 28th Corps in the hands of an incompetent, understaffed, and weak corps commander.

43 Liu, *Examination of the Campaign of Quemoy*, p. 8.

44 Mao Zedong to key PLA field army commanders, 29 October 1949, in Xiao, "My Recollection of the Battle of Quemoy," p. 42.

45 Xu, *Battle of Quemoy*, pp. 92–93.

46 *The Chronicle of Su Yu's Life* [粟裕年谱] (Jiangsu Party History Work Office, Contemporary China, 2006), pp. 487–89.

47 Ibid.

48 Ye, *Ye Fei Memoir*, p. 608.

49 Jay Taylor, *The Generalissimo's Son: Chiang Ching-kuo and the Revolutions in China and Taiwan*, Chinese ed. (Beijing: Huawen, 2010), p. 156.

50 Ibid., p. 160.

51 Ibid., p. 157.

52 Ibid., pp. 159–60.

XX The PLA at Sea
China's Search for a Naval Strategy

PETER LORGE

Naval strategy and amphibious operations "occupy" curious places in the long and detailed intellectual history of Chinese military thought—they do not exist. What makes that odd is that neither aspect of naval warfare was ever subjected to theorization despite the importance of both in Chinese history. Consequently, when the People's Liberation Army (PLA) looks for a theory of naval strategy it ends up with Alfred Thayer Mahan (1840–1914) and his *Influence of Sea Power upon History, 1660–1783* and his subsequent publications or, when it comes to amphibious warfare, other foreign writings. Whereas the PLA can draw on a mature and highly developed tradition of thought for land warfare and overall strategy, it is really at sea when it comes to naval theory. There is a history of naval warfare in China but not a theory of naval warfare.

All of this would be academic were it not for the PLA's current program of shipbuilding. Experts in a number of fields are asked to explain or predict the PLA's intentions. Should we be guided by history or theory? Both have their limitations as guides to the future, as do abstract theories of power and international relations. My goal here is to describe an important intellectual break between China's past and present with respect to naval warfare and to provide some of the reasons for that. As with so many issues concerning a very old civilization, even a significant break with the past is only partial. The legitimacy of the past and its marker of position in identity formation keep tradition in the mainstream for all but the most radical people.

I will first provide some historical explanation for the background of naval warfare in China, including the reasons for its lack of theorization. I will then discuss the PLA Navy's reason for embracing Mahan and its discussions of amphibious warfare. Finally, I will discuss why purely abstract theories alone will not explain Chinese intentions.

Naval Warfare in Chinese History
The main tradition of Chinese military thought grew from texts written or compiled in the Warring States period, with the addition of a few more from the early Han dynasty. It was only in the third century CE that Cao Cao (155–220) began

the commentarial tradition on Sunzi's *Art of War*. The commentarial tradition was paralleled by the tradition of intellectuals reading and arguing about the various texts of military thought. That intellectual tradition developed over the succeeding centuries until the creation of the specific canon of Chinese military thought, *The Seven Military Classics,* in 1083. The intellectual history of military thought was based upon early texts whose importance was based on their ancient origin. There was no early text devoted to naval warfare, a fact that placed any future consideration of naval warfare and strategy at a disadvantage.

We know very little about Chinese seafaring in the Warring States, Qin, and Han periods, but river crossings and battles on rivers happened regularly.[1] Chinese armies needed to cross rivers on their campaigns, commerce followed and crossed rivers, and canals were built to facilitate war and commerce. Before the Qin conquest and unification of China in 221 BCE, the creation of a Chinese government, in the sense of a single temporal authority spanning all of "China," did not require crossing major rivers. A unified Chinese government, however, required such crossings. One could not conquer all of China without spanning the Yellow, Huai, and Yangzi Rivers.

Innumerable battles were fought on the rivers of China over the two thousand years of imperial Chinese history. Why didn't anyone attempt a broader strategic discussion of naval warfare? Since the point of the naval battles was to facilitate or prevent armies crossing rivers or to lay siege to or raise the siege of a city, the naval aspects fell well within the existing, nonnaval strategic framework. There was nothing really to say beyond the obvious point that control over a waterway controlled access across it.

There are three exceptions to this orientation: the Mongol invasion of Japan, coastal piracy, and Zheng He's voyages. The Mongol invasions of Japan in 1274 and 1281 were operationally consistent with Mongol practice. A force would attack, get as far as it could, and then fall back; subsequent, similar attacks would follow. Because the Mongols attacked in the same place in 1281 as they had in 1274, the Japanese were better prepared the second time and beat back the attack again. The attacks on Japan ended less because of failure than through the lack of interest of later rulers. They were mainly aimed at the extension of Mongol power, as it happened, across Eurasia.

Coastal piracy, a particular problem during the Ming dynasty, was dealt with by moving the population back from the coast and strengthening defenses. By contrast, the Koreans had actually raided pirate bases and destroyed them to reduce piracy. Later in the Ming, when the Japanese invaded Korea, Ming and Korean ships attacked Japanese shipping to cut off the Japanese army in Korea. These were all defensive measures, however, that left overseas commerce to the merchants and coastal defense to the military.

Zheng He's voyage was explicitly military.[2] It projected Ming power beyond China's shores, and then it stopped. Zheng He's Treasure Fleet followed the preexisting trade routes; it did not create them. Moreover, it neither facilitated trade nor brought in revenue. The lack of theorizing about the navy is clearest with Zheng He. Without a larger rationale or even a clear explanation for an oceangoing government navy, the endeavor ended. Chinese historians have been wont to agonize over the failure to continue Zheng He's voyages, assuming that had they continued imperial China would have "discovered" Europe rather than the other way around.[3] Perhaps an exploration-oriented China would have taken over and benefited from world trade.

These what-ifs conveniently focus on the benefits to Europe of global trade and skip over the fact that Europe had nothing of benefit to China in the fifteenth century. European states valued external trade because it expanded their economic opportunities outside of western Eurasia to much wealthier parts of the world. Without New World bullion, Europeans would have been initially hard-pressed to afford Chinese goods. Only the vast increase in bullion allowed the vast increase in trade that preceded the European substitution of opium for Chinese goods. Zheng He's voyages found no similar sources of great wealth, and his trips were effective only in promoting imperial prestige. Unfortunately, prestige was expensive, and the returns on promoting it in distant lands were limited.

The PLA and Mahan

The entries under "naval strategy" and "theory of sea power" in the military-thought volume of the *Encyclopedia of Chinese Military Affairs* lead us immediately to Mahan and, curiously, Philip Howard Colomb (1831–99).[4] The latter entry asserts that sea power originated in ancient Greece of the sixth to fifth centuries BCE and then jumps to capitalist countries, like America and England, in the nineteenth century. It is worth noting that after a brief moment in ancient Greece, neither in the West nor in China did anyone seriously write about sea power before the nineteenth century. I will resist generalizing about the rest of the world beyond stating that I am not personally aware of anyone writing about sea power anywhere else in the world before that time. It is therefore not surprising that the Chinese did not write about sea power, since it was scarcely a topic anywhere else. The ancient Greeks were concerned about sea power, because they were primarily oriented to the sea. The ancient Chinese were primarily oriented to the land.

Even in the West, no one wrote about sea power for over two thousand years. And just like the Westerners, the Chinese turned to Mahan to provide the intellectual framework to support the building of the navy they wanted to build. Only Mahan (and Colomb) could be used to make the case for the creation of a blue-water navy. At the same time, the only clearly delineated goal of their navy is the capture of Taiwan. Beyond Taiwan and possibly the Diaoyu/Senkaku Islands, the PLA has some trouble reconciling a powerful navy with a "peaceful rise." From the Chinese perspective, the support by the PLA Navy (PLAN) of Chinese drilling and exploration in waters of Southeast Asia, including seizing and maintaining positions on some islands, is not part of an external naval strategy, since they claim preexisting ownership of them.

As the PLA embraces Mahan, it is important to see how selective is its choice of theorists. Corbett is nowhere to be found, nor any of the *guerre de course* theorists. As others have also recognized, the PLA adoption of Mahan is frighteningly similar to the Prussian and Japanese adoption of Mahan in the early twentieth century. Lacking a history of Chinese theorists to engage, the PLA has been free to choose among Western theorists. Yet in many ways its choice of theorists is at odds with the untheorized but actual use of naval force in Chinese history.

Amphibious Warfare

The PLA and PLAN are similarly at sea with respect to amphibious warfare.[5] Virtually all of their amphibious-warfare experience came shortly after the founding of the People's Republic of China, was limited in scope and effectiveness, and ended in 1955. Since that time, the PLA has not engaged in any significant naval combat or amphibious warfare with a comparable opponent, though it has bullied Vietnam and several other small Southeast Asian states at sea. As with naval warfare theory, in the absence of experience on which to draw the PLA has turned to the history of other nations to inform its planning.

Since I do not have access to classified documents or intelligence, my perspective will be drawn from contemporary Chinese encyclopedias, particularly ones published by the PLA, available to the general public. This is, of course, a very particular perspective, and one that cannot claim to reveal the inner workings or direct thoughts of the PLA leadership.[6] On the other hand, this widely disseminated information likely encompasses not simply a shadow or reflection of PLA thinking on this issue but also some autocommunication between parts of the PLA. This is to say that publicly available information is an attempt to set out beliefs that those producing it would like others to absorb.

In examining those beliefs we must be aware of not only what is said but also what is not said. The U.S. military, for example, has long held an aversion to "counterinsurgency" and after the Vietnam War almost erased it from its vocabulary, or at least its training manuals.[7] Consequently, when we look at Chinese military encyclopedias we must be aware of which amphibious operations are discussed and which are not discussed, as well as what is actually said about them. A further caveat, of course, is that there have been very few large-scale amphibious operations in history. Contested landings are rare, because they are so difficult to execute successfully.

When the communists came to power in China in 1949 and the Nationalist regime fled to Taiwan, it seemed inevitable that the communist government would try to destroy the last vestiges of its main political and military opponent. Nationalist forces were driven out of some islands close to China's coast, but not all of them. Of course, the United States played a critical role in these military events, but many practical military problems also played roles in preventing the PLA from conquering or liberating Taiwan. It is actually quite difficult to cross the Taiwan Strait from the continent, with the distance ranging from 180 kilometers (110 miles) to 130 kilometers (81 miles), difficult currents, and often challenging weather. While the PLA just barely had the sealift capability and ships necessary to attack the nearby islands, Taiwan itself was probably impossible in the 1950s. The PLA was certainly unlikely to have been able to land successfully against opposition.

While the Chinese communist government and the PLA continued to be interested in capturing Taiwan, an amphibious assault was inconceivable as long as the United States dominated the Taiwan Strait and chose to defend Taiwanese independence. Even today U.S. air and naval dominance remains one of the most critical factors maintaining Taiwanese independence. These military realities did not change when mainland China took over the seat held by Taiwan at the United Nations, though the political realities became more complicated.

China maintains that Taiwan is part of China and that accordingly any move on its part to take actual control over the island is an internal matter. To back up that claim and to keep Taiwan from declaring independence, China must maintain a credible threat of force. This threat runs the full gamut from actual military capabilities to plans, statements, and scholarship. To this point these threats have prevented Taiwan from declaring independence and testing its actual capabilities.

It is safe to assume that the PLA has a variety of plans for a military conquest of Taiwan. Here we are concerned with the amphibious option. Chinese encyclopedias on military history duly cover amphibious operations in general.[8] Both the Normandy and Inchon landings warrant their own entries, but Gallipoli does not.[9] This is both curious and noteworthy, since the authors of these Chinese encyclopedias include a simply astonishing variety and breadth of battles and wars of world military history. Moreover, Gallipoli is mentioned in the general discussion of World War I; still, it does not get its own entry.[10]

The Normandy landings, the encyclopedia notes, showed the need for strong coordination between the sea, air, and ground forces. Inchon showed the importance of control of the sea and air, as well as of deception, and that a landing can succeed despite unfavorable terrain. The Inchon entry also points out how unprepared the North Korean forces were. Gallipoli, by contrast, is covered by a passing comment that it failed because of tenacious Turkish resistance.

Taken together, we see five distinct and obvious historical lessons that are more or less welcome to a PLA considering amphibious landings on Taiwan. First, sea, air, and land forces must be carefully coordinated. Second, the attacking force needs control of the sea and air. Third, deception and attack on unfavorable terrain can work. Fourth, an unprepared force can be defeated. And, fifth, tenacious resistance can defeat an assault. Not surprisingly, this last point is distinctly downplayed overall.

Turning to what this reading of encyclopedias tells us, we should be aware that these entries are not simple items of information. The editors and authors of these works were not private individuals working for private publishers. When a PLA publishing house puts together a work on history, the result is as much a "performative utterance," to insert J. L. Austin's concept, as a description. In the U.S. military, arguments over historical analysis are critical for determining and supporting particular training regimes, as part of a "lessons learned" approach. The meaning of an event leads naturally to certain policy conclusions. Hence the fight over policy regresses to a fight over not just the meaning of events but which events are actually significant.

We could read these entries naïvely as just information, but that would ignore their real context. Most obviously, these are Chinese reference works written in Chinese for a Chinese audience. They are not secret documents transmitting information among the upper leadership but public statements setting out the interpretation of past events. The Chinese military is not a monolithic group with a unified understanding of the world. There is debate and disagreement, some of which is played out in public or partially public forums.

Like the U.S. military, the PLA has to make strategic and operational arguments to justify its expenditures. Sometimes procurement decisions flow from operational needs, and sometimes what the leadership wants to purchase is provided with an operational justification. Sometimes larger political needs simply require the acquisition of capabilities similar to those of other powers, whether justified operationally or not. Ultimately, though, if the PLA is truly intent on acquiring the ability to launch an amphibious assault on Taiwan, it has only previous foreign operations to study. It must use those operations to plan its own training and acquisitions. Those operations can also be used to argue against certain kinds of training and acquisitions.

Chinese encyclopedia entries are fundamentally about autocommunication within the PLA and Chinese government. Hence when their compilers choose to examine two successful amphibious operations in detail and proportionately to slight an unsuccessful one, they are implicitly arguing that these operations have been done successfully and so can be done successfully again. A famous unsuccessful operation cannot completely be ignored, since that would impugn the knowledge of the researchers and appear glaringly biased. The lesson learned, however, is that amphibious operations are eminently doable.

At the same time, those operations require a highly coordinated military with a sophisticated navy and air force able to control the sea and air. This becomes an argument for developing those capabilities, a message to the PLA's army-dominated leadership (though slightly less so recently) that an amphibious operation requires significant investment in the air force and navy. To the extent that this requirement dovetails with the larger goal of modernizing the PLA and extending its reach, it is hard to distinguish preparation for an amphibious operation from general improvement of the navy and air force.

Deception and attack against an unprepared enemy collectively seem like a much more attractive tactical approach, but modern satellite reconnaissance makes it highly unlikely that a surprise amphibious assault of significant size could be launched. Of course, given that the Taiwanese military currently has its beach obstacles stored in a warehouse rather than deployed on the only usable beaches, surprise might have uses. Landing in unexpected places would be very challenging in Taiwan, because of the terrain. As for a tenacious defense, the PLA cannot really be sure about that. It might hope for an early Taiwanese surrender, but any significant resistance could easily doom an amphibious operation in its early stages.

Power

I would like to mention briefly one final perspective on China's desire for or use of naval power. Scholars of political science and international studies have long debated whether culture affects strategy. In the China field, Alistair Iain Johnston argues for the influence of culture and Yuan-Kang Wang against it.[11] This is a great oversimplification of a complex and ongoing debate, and everyone understands that the reality of decision making is much sloppier than theory would have us believe.

What appears to be really going on is that the PLA moves between these two positions in its actions. Unlike the British, who had a clear strategic need to control the English Channel, a need from which all other decisions flowed, the Chinese do not, in fact, have a clear strategic naval need. Of course, this is true on land as well, because China is not externally threatened. Without clear interests beyond a vague notion of becoming stronger and more modern, it is hard for the PLA to make strategic plans.

Of course, scholars arguing for one position or the other do not admit the possibility of actions outside of an overall theory. A functional theory must accurately explain all actions. But I think what we see is a situation in which the PLA and the Chinese government are not only aware of these theories but subject to them. They are navigating, perhaps unsuccessfully, through theories of power and theories of naval war. And this does not even address the dramatic shift that interest in naval theories requires of a mainly land-based military. It is not just that China was focused on the land in premodern times but that it has been focused on the land until today. Even for the army, an outward orientation is more attractive than being configured for maintaining internal stability.

If we are to accept this self-awareness, we must recognize that the PLA explicitly understands Mahan's theories as part of Western imperialism. Mahan's theories are somewhat tainted, and it is hard to argue for a "peaceful rise" when you build an imperialist navy. Perhaps the best China might aim for is an intermediate goal of being the regional hegemon, bullying smaller states with its amphibious forces. Under that strategy Taiwan only needs to be intimidated, not invaded. We cannot expect that if such a strategy existed it would be discussed in an openly available encyclopedia; obviously, much more could be done in thinking through these possibilities.

Conclusion

Understanding and explaining the PLA's naval strategy are extremely challenging, because China has a very limited history of military engagement with the sea. A blue-water navy serves no obvious strategic interest consistent with China's history. Even an invasion of Taiwan could be better approached with a cheaper and more modest navy. But that is not the navy that the PLAN or the government wants to build. The government's interest seems close to that of Zheng He's Ming-dynasty fleet, an intimidating force designed to project power.

Like the Prussian kaiser, the Chinese want a first-class navy even if they can't really find a strategic justification for it. And like the kaiser, they have turned to Mahan without really considering whether he was right. One wonders whether they too would end up pursuing *guerre de course* with their submarines in the event of a war. PLA modernization has stimulated a low-level arms race in Asia, undermined Chinese diplomatic efforts, and increased instability. These might have significant economic consequences for China; a war certainly would, calling into question the strategy it is pursuing. In the end it seems most likely that the PLA is a military in search of a naval strategy. It has not found one yet.

NOTES 1 See Peter Lorge, "Water Forces and Naval Operations," in *A Military History of China,* ed. David Graff and Robin Higham, updated ed. (Lexington: Univ. of Kentucky Press, 2012).

2 The best work on Zheng He and his voyages is Edward L. Dreyer, *Zheng He: China and the Oceans in the Early Ming Dynasty, 1405–1433* (Upper Saddle River, N.J.: Pearson, 2006).

3 Setting aside here any discussion of the utter nonsense of Gavin Menzies's *1421* and his claims that the Chinese discovered America before Columbus.

4 Song Shilun and Xiao Ke, eds., *Zhongguo Junshi Baike Quanshu* (Beijing: Junshi Kexue Chubanshe, 1997), vol. 1, s.vv. "Haijun Zhanlue," "Haiquan Lun," respectively, pp. 84–86. A new edition of this encyclopedia is in production, but I have not had access to it.

5 For some earlier treatments on Chinese amphibious warfare see Bradley Hahn, "The Chinese Marine Corps," U.S. Naval Institute *Proceedings* (March 1984), pp. 121–27; Hahn, "China: Big Amphibious Strides," *Pacific Defense Reporter* 14 (April 1988), pp. 28–29; and G. Jacobs, "China's Amphibious Navy," *Asian Defense Journal* (June 1985), pp. 34–43. My thanks to Mike Yared for pointing these out to me.

6 It is worth noting in this context that Deng Xiaoping did the calligraphy for the title page of the *Zhongguo Junshi Baike Quanshu.*

7 See David Fitzgerald, *Learning to Forget* (Stanford, Calif.: Stanford Univ. Press, 2013).

8 Song and Xiao, *Zhongguo Junshi Baike Quanshu,* vol. 2, s.vv. "Denglu Zhandou" [Amphibious Landing Combat], "Denglu Zhanyi" [Amphibious Landing Campaign], and "Denglu Zuozhan" [Amphibious Landing Operation], pp. 44–48.

9 Ibid., vol. 8, s.vv. "Nuomandi Denglu Zhanyi" [Normandy Landings], "Renchuan Denglu Zhanyi" [Inchon Landings], pp. 878–80, 954, respectively.

10 Ibid., vol. 7, p. 239.

11 Alastair Iain Johnston, *Cultural Realism: Strategic Culture and Grand Strategy in Chinese History* (Princeton, N.J.: Princeton Univ. Press, 1995); Yuankang Wang, *Harmony and War: Confucian Culture and Chinese Power Politics* (New York: Columbia Univ. Press, 2011). For completeness I also include Huiyun Feng, *Chinese Strategic Culture and Foreign Policy Decision-Making: Confucianism, Leadership, and War* (London: Routledge, 2007). Feng's work is deeply problematic and in no way intellectually comparable to Johnston's or Wang's; it is best ignored, or used as a paradigmatic example of a particular delusional Chinese view of the past held by conservative ideologues.

XXI *From Pearl Harbor to Vietnam*
Chairman of the Joint Chiefs of Staff Adm. Arthur Radford and U.S. Foreign Policy in East Asia

ZACHARY M. MATUSHESKI

At the end of 1952, President-elect Dwight D. Eisenhower had every reason to view Adm. Arthur Radford, a candidate for the position of chairman of the Joint Chiefs of Staff (JCS), with suspicion. In the years immediately following World War II Radford had resisted defense unification, an objective Eisenhower believed critical to the security of the country. During the 1952 Republican convention Radford supported Senator Robert Taft over Eisenhower.[1] Yet after the election the president-elect knew that Radford could play a critical role in the success of his policy in East Asia. Radford served as Commander in Chief Pacific (CINCPAC) from 1949 to 1953. He traveled widely and knew many of the leaders of American-allied governments in East Asia. Eisenhower saw how savvy a political operator Radford was over these years. Putting aside a skewed view of the admiral helped the president, as Radford invested great effort to further the president's security policy.

Indeed, of all the members of the JCS who served in Eisenhower's two terms, Radford proved the most loyal to the president's broad foreign-policy vision and the White House's goals in East Asia. In the first term, Radford pushed forward the president's policy in Indochina and the Taiwan Strait. With the president's support, he pursued a more robust U.S. role in the French-Indochina War. The outcome of Radford's policy advocacy in Eisenhower's first term shaped defense policy for years to come. For these reasons, understanding the first years of Radford's tenure as chairman of the JCS is a critical objective in grasping the history of the JCS as an institution and, more broadly, of U.S. Cold War security policy.

Despite Radford's importance to this period of strategic history, little is known about the admiral. No book-length biography of him exists. Many scholars simplify his importance by portraying him as the embodiment of the missteps in American foreign policy in the 1950s, especially those related to Vietnam.[2] Indeed, the admiral predicted that he might be criticized in these ways and so decided to focus much of his memoir, *From Pearl Harbor to Vietnam,* on explaining why he took the positions he did. Any measure of Radford's tenure as chairman of the JCS must take into account events in East Asia, but it must go farther than blame. It must reach toward explaining why he took the positions he did and to what degree those positions furthered the desires of his civilian masters. An entire book could be centered on Radford and East Asia in the 1950s; this paper will focus on Radford and the crisis at Dien Bien Phu, as his contribution during that moment deepened American involvement in the post–World War II wars in Southeast Asia.

No historical rendering of any chairman of the JCS can be understood outside the context of the White House for which he works. Great controversy typified the Eisenhower White House when Radford arrived. Eisenhower attempted to reform Cold War defense strategy. His reforms, known as the "New Look," accepted key facets of containment policy, like support of multilateral institutions and military aid programs for countries on the containment border. But the president worried that continuing Harry Truman's spending policies would bankrupt the country. The victorious general turned president believed that big defense budgets jeopardized American freedoms.[3] In his perception of the nature of the Cold War, economic failure was disastrous. U.S. survival in the Cold War, he postulated, required a strong, self-sustaining economy. Eisenhower did not believe that war with the Soviet Union was imminent or inevitable. He rejected the "year of maximum danger" thesis, which suggested that once Soviet power reached parity with the United States the communist bloc would launch World War III. Eisenhower thought that the Soviet Union and other communist powers valued self-preservation. He believed that the Soviets and the Chinese fomented instability to keep the United States on the defensive. Chinese intervention in the Korean War served as an example of this strategy. While limiting military spending, Eisenhower wanted the United States to be able to choose the time, place, and circumstances of conflict in the Cold War. Nuclear deterrence provided a possible path to this goal. During the Korean War, Eisenhower turned to nuclear strikes as a possible solution to end the war, deter the communist powers, and gain the initiative during the Cold War.

Radford's predecessor, U.S. Army general Omar Bradley, had disagreed with the president's thinking on both the Korean War and defense spending. Eisenhower's suggestion of launching atomic strikes in the former accelerated Bradley's efforts to find peace. At the same time as Bradley was seeking peace, Eisenhower searched for savings. Bradley resisted the president's moves. In a letter to Secretary of Defense Charles Wilson the JCS supported the idea that war with the Soviet Union was inevitable. A majority of the JCS characterized an increase in conventional forces as a "vital need."[4] The JCS that Eisenhower inherited called for more spending.

Eisenhower knew that the next chairman of the JCS would have to be in accord with his views if he was to achieve his budgetary goals. Eisenhower found such a chairman in Adm. Arthur Radford. Eisenhower had witnessed Radford's political savvy during the admiral's campaign in the years following World War II against defense unification, a program Eisenhower supported. On the recommendation of the Chief of Naval Operations, William Fechteler, Eisenhower met with Radford, then serving as CINCPAC, on his way to Korea in December 1952. He now took another measure of his former opponent, asking the admiral about his views on pertinent security issues in Asia. Under this line of questioning, Radford showed, in the estimation of his flag secretary, Cdr. Means Johnson, that he "knew his Pacific well and it was obvious that General Eisenhower was impressed."[5] Indeed, Eisenhower recalled later that after the meeting he thought that Radford "could be extremely useful in Washington. He was, as it turned out, that rare combination—a man of tough conviction who would refuse to remain set in his ways."[6] Eisenhower's formal nomination of the admiral during the summer of 1953 was a bet that Radford would be more loyal to the president's program than Bradley had been.

Radford matched Eisenhower's vision in two ways. First, Radford believed in the superiority of U.S. airpower, a way of war on which Eisenhower planned to rely to cut the defense budget. Radford had built his career promoting naval airpower. He passionately supported naval aviation. He took pride in the growth of naval aviation during World War II. Radford remembered feeling that in 1944 successful naval air strikes at Truk in the Carolines had "redeemed" the Navy's honor after the surprise attack at Pearl Harbor.[7] The strength of the U.S. Navy in 1945 was a point of pride. Radford wrote that when he looked at the Navy's carriers in 1945 he saw "the immense advances made by U.S. naval aviation" since Pearl Harbor that had allowed the United States to "strike repeatedly against the heart of Japan, which all of us felt would contribute greatly to victory by the end of 1945."[8] For Radford, naval airpower was a major war-winning weapon.

Radford confirmed his commitment to airpower and to his service during the 1949 "Revolt of the Admirals." Defense unification battles of the late 1940s pitted the Air Force's strategic-bombing doctrine against the Navy's carrier aviation program.[9] Naval elites perceived the Air Force as a threat to the survival of the Navy's airpower capabilities. At issue was proving that naval forces could not only control the seas but also project power on land to defeat an enemy.[10] Radford doubted that reliance on atomic bombs produced security. Ironically, the positions he held in the unification crisis were directly opposed to those that he would promote as chairman of the JCS. In the late 1940s, Radford slammed defense cuts and reliance on atomic deterrence; during his term as chairman he championed these ideas. This switch in viewpoints underscores how unsettled the Navy's postwar future was in the late 1940s and how transformative the Korean War was. Radford needed to rally to the Navy's cause, because he thought that those promoting unification aimed to destroy his service. At the same time, Radford perceived the divisiveness and defense cuts wrought by the unification debates as encouraging the Soviets to, in his words, "unleash the Koreans."[11] In a post–Korean War world, Radford held, the country could no longer afford a divisive public conversation on defense. Peace required unity of purpose on defense issues.

Radford's familiarity with issues in East Asia represented the second reason that Eisenhower found Radford an attractive candidate for chairman of the JCS. During the Korean armistice negotiations, Radford stayed in contact with the American negotiation team. Over this time, Radford thought, as Eisenhower had, that the Korean War and other offensives were Soviet and Communist Chinese wars of choice. As Radford put it later, the Korean War was "the right war in the right place to the Russians and Chinese."[12] While monitoring the Korean War, Radford also worked with the French in Indochina.

Toward the end of pushing the president's security policy forward, Radford secured some concessions from the incoming Army Chief of Staff, Matthew Ridgway, and the Chief of Naval Operations, now Robert Carney, after two days on board the presidential yacht, USS *Sequoia.* During the cruise both agreed to a security policy that put nuclear weapons at the center to save money. But the statement of approval included critiques that would guide Ridgway's and Carney's resistance to the New Look. Ridgway claimed that the United States should not reduce its ground forces in NATO or shrink the number of soldiers elsewhere, as to do so would risk the security of the continental United States. Without claiming that the United States was in danger, Carney agreed. He feared that relying solely on elements in the Air Force and Navy that delivered nuclear weapons "could never constitute an effective deterrent to enemy ground forces."[13] Nonnuclear means of deterrence would be necessary to keep the peace.

Once back on dry land, Ridgway broke his pledge to support a defense policy having nuclear weapons at the center, as he was not yet Chief of Staff of the Army and did not have access to his staff. The *Sequoia* agreement, however, was more than a story of a cruise rife with arguments. It provided Radford with a glimpse of how hard Ridgway would argue for ground forces. Because divisions would continue between members of the JCS during the Indochina crisis, the *Sequoia* episode served as a microcosm of the ideas that Radford and the other chiefs contested.

While the administration finalized the policy statement instituting the New Look, the president also sought an approach to the French war in Indochina. France waged war in Southeast Asia to retake its colonial possession, Indochina, after World War II. Eisenhower supported the war. In his inaugural address he equated the French fighting in Indochina with American sacrifices in Korea. He stated that the idea of the Cold War as a conflict of freedom versus tyranny "confers a common dignity upon the French soldier who dies in Indo-China, the British soldier killed in Malaya, the American life given in Korea."[14] The French war in Indochina was, in Eisenhower's view, a part of a larger Cold War.

Eisenhower's approval of the French war was more than a rhetorical flourish. Before the armistice breakthrough in Korea in late 1953, Eisenhower and Secretary of State John Foster Dulles agreed that the war in Indochina was "more important than Korea," because "a loss there could not be localized, but would spread throughout Asia and Europe."[15] Eisenhower and Dulles worried that a French loss in Southeast Asia would lower French commitments to the European anticommunist alliance. They both thought that the United States needed to relieve some of France's war burden.

Radford passionately supported the French cause in Indochina. On 4 September 1953, Radford championed giving money to the French to support their mission in Indochina, as he thought that if the French lost the war there it "would so clearly mean the end of France as a great power."[16] He believed that the United States had either to support French Indochina or risk losing an ally on which the United States depended in maintaining the containment border in Europe and Asia. Ridgway disagreed. As the Supreme Allied Commander Europe before becoming Chief of Staff of the Army, Ridgway knew many of the French leaders asking for U.S. aid in Indochina. He did not believe that the French had much "offensive spirit" or will to win.[17] Radford agreed that France moved too slowly in prosecuting the war, but he reasoned that sending an American adviser could solve this problem. The French offensive drive mattered to the New Look, because the policy depended, in part, on allies sharing the burden of maintaining the containment border. If foreign-policy crises such as the war in Indochina showed that allies could not be trusted to bear bigger parts of the defense burden, New Look policies would have to be redesigned.

Radford and Ridgway sparred over the implications that policy failure in Indochina would have on American credibility. Ridgway worried that the French could dump their war on the United States. Giving funds was one step farther toward getting the Americans into the war. If the United States refused to intervene or did so and lost, its reputation as defender of the noncommunist world would be tarnished. Radford discounted this possibility, declaring that there was "nothing to keep us from backing down on our part" or de-escalating.[18] Radford gambled that the money would stop France from blackmailing the United States into intervention by claiming that the United States had not done enough to stave off defeat of its Cold War ally in Indochina. Radford did not realize that answering such requests so quickly could chain the United States to the war in Indochina as an American investment. In the end, Eisenhower approved the U.S. plan to assist the French with $385 million. Radford and Ridgway's disagreements over this loan marked the first of many they were to have on the administration's policy toward Asia.

The multimillion-dollar aid package at the end of 1953 did not mark the end of France's lobbying for help in Indochina nor did it mean the end of Radford's advocacy of its cause. The French requested more air support. They wanted to use planes to make their forces in Indochina more mobile, hoping that greater airlift capabilities would give them more control of the war on the ground. Their request cut straight to Radford's experience as CINCPAC. In that position he had loaned C-119 "Flying Boxcars" to protect the United States from accusations of not doing enough to help the French. By the winter of 1953 the question of loaning more planes to the French was not without controversy. The Air Force's Military Assistance and Advisory Group (MAAG) and Air Force attachés in Indochina sent a report to the Chief of Staff of the Air Force, CINCPAC, and Far Eastern Air Force Tokyo describing deep weaknesses in the French air force's efforts in Indochina. MAAG and the attachés estimated that the total number of planes that the French would be able to maintain was less than what the French already had. MAAG reported that members of the French air force had "confided" that more could be done if there were fewer planes to maintain.[19]

The air attachés and MAAG used their critiques to reach larger problems in the French war effort. Asking for more planes was, in their view, part of "a long line of excuses for not winning."[20] The analysts described the French as behaving like "a neurotic woman with too many dresses who when faced with a decision of going out complains she cannot go because she has no new dress."[21] Loaning planes would not win the war. Instead, it would become a distraction. Despite his knowledge of these critiques, Radford recommended that the loans go forward. Even though he agreed that the French lacked "proper facilities" to accommodate the increase in planes, Radford advised that loaning them would show that the United States supported the French cause.[22]

In short order, the French would advocate more than symbolic gestures. By the start of 1954 the Viet Minh, as the group resisting France in Indochina was known, trapped French forces near the village of Dien Bien Phu. The Viet Minh set up artillery pieces in the hills around the area and bombarded the French. Eisenhower's reaction to the crisis was mixed. He said in a meeting on 8 January 1954 that a U.S. ground war in Indochina would "absorb our troops by divisions!"[23] At the same time, he was not against a training mission conducted by American soldiers. He asked Radford whether he believed that the French would allow the United States to "take over a considerable number of their training camps, with perhaps several hundred U.S. officers instead of two."[24] When cabinet members pointed out the risks of larger intervention, Radford responded that the monetary support the United States provided meant the United States was committed to the French cause in "a big way."[25] He did not think that the United States should back down. Eisenhower agreed. He ordered that more planes be sent and that a group of Central Intelligence Agency pilots be made available to the French. Radford's advocacy pushed intervention forward.

Ten days later, the president appointed Radford to a special committee tasked with exploring how the United States should approach Indochina. Stacked with advocates of various shades of intervention, the committee discussed U.S. involvement, not how to avoid war. Eisenhower wanted an "action plan" for Indochina.[26] The advisory group's parameters, set by the president, reflected Eisenhower's views on the war. His words at the meeting that commissioned the group affirmed the concept that defeat in Indochina could be a "prelude" to "real disaster" in Southeast Asia.[27] To underscore the war's importance, Eisenhower ordered that the country spend up to $800 million in 1954 and 1955. Indochina was excluded from the cost cutting that the administration adopted in most other areas. At the same meeting the group came to the consensus that no amount of money, planes, hardware, or French valor could win the war unless local people were invested. Eisenhower pushed the group to consider how to improve the training program. Remarking that U.S. foreign policy "suffered from a certain amount of scatteration and lack of coordinated *area* planning," Eisenhower wanted the group to think about the Indochina challenge from the perspective of the American position in the region.[28] In this way, what Radford and the rest of the group would produce on Indochina was potentially an addendum to the New Look, a strategy for dealing with crises in Southeast Asia that the nuclear threat could not solve.

Radford and the committee crafted a solution that expanded the number of American boots on the ground. In a 29 January meeting, Radford lent support to a proposal of Under Secretary of State Walter Bedell Smith to send two hundred mechanics from the U.S. armed forces. When some in the committee suggested that this was too risky, Radford warned the group not to be "too restrictive" in thinking about American combat forces.[29] Eisenhower eventually approved the proposal, agreeing with Radford that the United States had to deepen its efforts to stave off French defeat.

For his part, Ridgway, on the basis of some of the reports of Army officers in Indochina and drawing on his experiences before rising to the position of Chief of Staff, dissented. He launched his campaign against American intervention at a dinner party held in April 1954 for Radford's French counterpart, Paul Ely.[30] In conversation at the reception, Ridgway interrupted Radford as he was summarizing the thrust of the French request for help. On the basis of his memories of the Korean War, a conflict in which the United States had had air superiority, Ridgway did not believe "that some additional air power was going to bring decisive results on the ground."[31] Ridgway's views stood directly in line with his private ruminations on the problems of the New Look. As the policy promised more reliance on air strikes, it limited the variety of military responses to a crisis. More importantly, Ridgway believed, territory could not be held solely by air superiority or by threat of annihilation. Military forces had to be mixed. Ridgway worked to convince those with whom he spoke that airpower would not be enough.

Ridgway's arguments with Ely during his visit to the United States speak to his criticism of Radford's leadership style as well. Radford used many moments during Ely's trip to reassure the French general of U.S. support.[32] Ely would later recall that Radford reminded him of the president's support "on several occasions."[33] Radford wanted to make clear to Ely that the president "did not want to be in the position of denying any aid critically needed in Indochina."[34] When Dulles expressed frustration with French requests for more help, Ely recalled that Radford had given him the "personal impression" that the U.S. "position might be a little different from that of the Secretary of State."[35] While Dulles tried to communicate to the French visitor the limits of American intervention, Radford reminded him of the American commitment to help the French win the war.

Ridgway labeled Radford's behavior during the Indochina crisis as inappropriate political lobbying. Ridgway railed against Radford's performance during the trip and the chairman's later characterization of his own view as the unified JCS position. Ridgway thought that the JCS "must not advocate any such course."[36] When Radford tried to bring the chiefs together on a policy of intervention on 31 March 1954, each chief dissented against deeper involvement in Indochina. A few days later Ridgway bemoaned Radford's attempt as "outside the scope of authority" accorded to the chairman of the JCS.[37] He claimed that the JCS was "not charged with formulating foreign policy nor advocating it" unless the president or Defense Secretary sought JCS guidance.[38] Ridgway did not believe that it was appropriate for any member of the Joint Chiefs to think beyond the military implications of a problem. For Ridgway, the military and political dimensions of security issues could be separated. It was civilian leadership's prerogative to consider the political. The JCS's job was to give objective advice.

Radford's behavior during Ely's visit and the days that followed, however, needs a different interpretation. The conclusion that Radford was a policy advocate is too simple. While Radford used nearly every opportunity during Ely's trip to support the French mission, he also invited a major dissenter among the chiefs, Ridgway, to be a part of the tour. He did not do so to isolate Ridgway, as many within and outside the military disagreed with the idea of larger intervention. Instead, it suggests that Radford was confident in his position and believed even dissenting members of the JCS had a right to air their views. This approach links with the larger discussion of the New Look, as at no point during those discussions did Radford ever block a request from Ridgway to meet with the president or make his case to the administration. In fact, on more than one occasion Radford objectively summarized the case against the New Look to the president. In the end, Radford's policy advocacy during Ely's stay reflected his efforts to further the president's chosen policy rather than an attempt to ensure the victory of his own views.

Radford's belief that his advocacy was in line with the president's position proved right. In a National Security Council meeting the day following the chiefs' unified dissent, Eisenhower brushed that dissent aside. The president declared that nearly unanimous JCS disagreement was no reason to stop exploring intervention, as such a matter was for "statesmen" to decide, not military authorities.[39] In spite of strong military dissent, the president wanted to discuss intervention.

In the weeks that followed, the French effort in Indochina collapsed. When approached by Dulles and Radford, leading senators refused to support wider intervention. British leaders echoed the Senate in their rejection of an allied response, removing the chance for the unified political and allied support Eisenhower wanted. The United States did not intervene at Dien Bien Phu, but damage was done to the larger U.S. strategy in Southeast Asia, as the crisis caused the United States to invest more deeply in the anticommunist war in Indochina, a commitment that eventually turned into a large American war.

Radford's legacy as chairman, then, is mixed. He obeyed the president without forcing consensus. In this way, he stands out as a chairman from those who came after who were willing to paper over differences among the services to further what they perceived as the president's goals. Radford's willingness to tolerate policy fights destroyed any danger that the president would not be informed of all sides on the question of intervention.

At the same time, Radford's relationship with the other chiefs and to the president's policy in East Asia is emblematic of contested ideas about security in the 1950s. In the Navy, Radford was part of the group that pushed airpower as a central war-fighting tool. His faith in this way of using force enabled him to serve the president's vision for cutting the defense budget. Those who like Ridgway resisted this plan represented the counterargument to this view that airpower could be a cure-all. In this way, understanding Radford and Ridgway's arguments over Indochina makes it easier to appreciate how controversial airpower and Eisenhower's New Look were in the 1950s.

Radford's contribution to Eisenhower's Indochina policy explains in part why the great tragedy of the Vietnam War took place. Both the president and Radford believed that keeping Indochina in French hands was important. They thought that to lose the country to the communist bloc would put the United States on the strategic defensive, a position that would raise defense spending and risk the militarization of American society. In seeking to send messages of resolve, Radford and Eisenhower began a pattern that Presidents John Kennedy, Lyndon Johnson, and Richard Nixon would repeat when they decided to make Vietnam the place where they would make a stand against the communist bloc and "save" East Asia from communism.

NOTES   1 Jeffrey G. Barlow, *From Hot War to Cold: The U.S. Navy and National Security Affairs, 1945–1955* (Stanford, Calif.: Stanford Univ. Press, 2009), p. 367.

2 See Richard Immerman and George C. Herring, "The Day We Didn't Go to War: Revisited," *Journal of American History* 71, no. 2 (September 1982), pp. 343–63. See also Evan Thomas, *Ike's Bluff: President Eisenhower's Secret Battle to Save the World* (New York: Little, Brown, 2012).

3 For more on the background of this philosophy and Eisenhower's thoughts, see Aaron L. Friedberg, *In the Shadow of the Garrison State: America's Anti-statism and Its Cold War Strategy* (Princeton, N.J.: Princeton Univ. Press, 2000), pp. 127–30. See also Robert Bowie and Richard Immerman, *Waging Peace: How Eisenhower Shaped an Enduring Cold War Strategy* (New York: Oxford Univ. Press, 1998), pp. 41–83, 96–108. Bowie headed the equivalent of the Policy Planning staff. He corralled the different opinions of the State Department and Department of Defense to write a basic national security policy that matched the president's views.

4 Bowie and Immerman, *Waging Peace,* p. 99.

5 Barlow, *From Hot War to Cold,* p. 366.

6 Dwight D. Eisenhower, *Mandate for Change: 1953–1956* (Garden City, N.Y.: Doubleday, 1963), p. 96.

7 Arthur Radford, *From Pearl Harbor to Vietnam: The Memoirs of Arthur W. Radford,* ed. Stephen Jurika, Jr. (Stanford, Calif.: Hoover Institution Press, 1980), p. 25.

8 Ibid., p. 62.

9 Jeffrey G. Barlow, *Revolt of the Admirals: The Fight for Naval Aviation 1945–1950* (Washington, D.C.: Naval Historical Center, 1994), pp. 2–3.

10 Ibid., pp. 253, 268.

11 Radford, *From Pearl Harbor to Vietnam,* p. 142.

12 Ibid., p. 266.

13 S. Everett Gleason, "Memorandum of Discussion at the 160th Meeting of the National Security Council," 27 August 1953, in *Foreign Relations of the United States, 1952–1954,* vol. 2, *National Security Affairs Part 1,* ed. William Z. Slany (Washington, D.C.: U.S. Government Printing Office [hereafter GPO], 1984), p. 445.

14 Dwight D. Eisenhower, "Inaugural Address," 20 January 1953, *American Presidency Project Online,* www.presidency.ucsb.edu/.

15 John Foster Dulles, "Memorandum of Conversation," 24 March 1953, in *Foreign Relations of the United States, 1952–1954,* vol. 13, *Indochina Part 1,* ed. John P. Glennon (Washington, D.C.: GPO, 1982) [hereafter *FRUS, 1952–1954: Indochina Part 1*], p. 419.

16 "Substance of Discussions of State–Joint Chiefs of Staff Meeting," 4 September 1953, in *FRUS, 1952–1954: Indochina Part 1,* p. 754.

17 Ibid., p. 756.

18 Ibid., p. 757.

19 USAIRA Saigon Indochina to CSAF Wash DC, CINCPAC Pearl Harbor, FEAF Tokyo, 22 November 1953, p. 1, Record Group [RG] 218, Records of the Joint Chiefs of Staff, "Chairman's Files," box

10, National Archives and Records Administration, College Park, Md. [hereafter NARA II].

20 Ibid.

21 Ibid.

22 James C. H. Bonbright, Jr., "Memorandum by the Deputy Assistant Secretary of State for European Affairs," 23 November 1953, in *FRUS, 1952–1954: Indochina Part 1,* p. 883.

23 S. Everett Gleason, "Memorandum of Discussion at the 179th Meeting of the National Security Council," 8 January 1954, in *FRUS, 1952–1954: Indochina Part 1,* p. 949.

24 Ibid., p. 950.

25 Ibid., p. 951.

26 C. D. Jackson, "Indochina and Southeast Asia," 18 January 1954, p. 1, RG 218, Records of the Joint Chiefs of Staff, "Chairman's Files," box 10, NARA II.

27 Ibid.

28 Ibid., p. 2 [emphasis original].

29 Brig. Gen. Charles H. Bonesteel III, "Memorandum of the President's Special Committee on Indochina," 29 January 1954, in *FRUS, 1952–1954: Indochina Part 1,* p. 1005.

30 See Ronald Spector, *U.S. Army in Vietnam: Advise and Support—the Early Years, 1941–1960* (Washington, D.C.: U.S. Army Center for Military History, 1983), p. 187. An oral history conducted with Gen. William Rosson offers another perspective of the Army's work in Vietnam. Rosson arrived in Indochina in late February 1954 to work as MAAG's campaign planner, but when he reported, Navarre refused to allow him to execute those orders. Instead, Rosson went on an inspection tour of the country. He recalls in his oral history that the tour gave "little cause for optimism with respect to victory." See Gen. William Rosson, interview by Lt. Col. Douglas R. Burges, Senior Officers Oral History Program (1981), p. 211, U.S. Army Military History Institute, Carlisle, Pa. [hereafter USAMHI].

31 Matthew Ridgway, "Memorandum of Conversation at the Home of Admiral Radford," 22 March, p. 2, Ridgway Papers, series 3, Official Papers, Army Chief of Staff Historical Record July 1953–June 1955, box 78, USAMHI.

32 Paul Ely, *Mémoires: L'Indochine dans la Tourmente* (Paris: Plon, 1964), p. 28; Radford, *From Pearl Harbor to Vietnam,* p. 391.

33 Ely, *L'Indochine dans la Tourmente,* p. 28.

34 Radford, *From Pearl Harbor to Vietnam,* p. 391.

35 Ely, *L'Indochine dans la Tourmente,* p. 30.

36 Matthew Ridgway, "Memorandum for the Record," 29 March 1954, p. 1, Ridgway Papers, series 3, Official Papers, Army Chief of Staff Historical Record July 1953–June 1955, box 78, USAMHI.

37 "Memorandum of the Chief of Staff, United States Army," 2 April 1954, in *FRUS, 1952–1954: Indochina Part 1,* p. 1220.

38 Ibid.

39 S. Everett Gleason, "Memorandum of Discussion at the 191st Meeting of the National Security Council," 1 April 1954, in *FRUS, 1952–1954: Indochina Part 1,* p. 1201.

XXII Repairing the Wreckage of Vietnam
The Marine Corps's Great Personnel Campaign, 1975–1979

NATHAN R. PACKARD

The U.S. Marine Corps was paralyzed by internal disorder in the aftermath of the Vietnam War. In the early 1970s its rates of indiscipline were at record highs, and quality indicators were at all-time lows. The percentage of Marines incarcerated, absent without leave, or court-martialed was far greater than the corresponding percentages in the other services. In certain categories—desertion, for example—the Marine Corps's rate exceeded those of all the other services combined.[1] Nearly half of all Marines used illegal drugs, and many reported being high on duty.[2] Barely 50 percent of new recruits had high school diplomas, and 75 percent scored at or below average on the Armed Forces Qualification Test. Statistics such as these called into question the service's reputation as an elite fighting force.

In response, leaders implemented a series of reforms known as the "Great Personnel Campaign." By the early 1980s the Marine Corps had the lowest rates of indiscipline in its history. Ultimately, the service overcame the personnel challenges of the post-Vietnam era through prudent policies and innovative leadership. This paper offers an account of this pivotal period in Marine Corps history. It begins by describing the manpower crisis, as well as its underlying causes. Next, it discusses and analyzes the corrective measures taken. Because most of the policies remain in effect, the paper concludes with the enduring legacies of these reforms.

Peacetime administrative matters are not typically the preserve of military historians; however, in this case personnel reform laid the foundation for modernization in other areas. Most studies of the U.S. military in the decades after Vietnam have focused on the technological dimension of warfare. But technological sophistication would have mattered little in the absence of good order and discipline. In the words of Gen. Louis H. Wilson, Commandant from 1975 to 1979, "the most modern, well-equipped armed services in the world are never any better than the people who serve in them."[3] Simply put, the Marine Corps needed disciplined and competent individuals to accomplish its mission.

The Marine Corps's manpower crisis resulted from three interrelated causes: the Vietnam War, shifting norms in American society, and a series of missteps on the part of Headquarters Marine Corps. The Vietnam War was a disaster for the service in terms of personnel management. Sgt. Maj. Edgar Huff, the senior enlisted Marine in Vietnam during two separate tours, commented, "If I were asked to sum up the 'Marine Experience' in Vietnam, I would say that the Corps grew far too fast and that this growth had a devastating impact on our leadership, training, and combat effectiveness."[4] From its prewar end strength (that is, congressionally authorized manpower) of 180,000 the Corps expanded to a peak of 320,000 in 1968.[5] In addition, it committed a larger percentage of its manpower to the war than did the other services. In 1968, eight of its twelve infantry regiments, representing 30 percent of the total force, were in Vietnam. By comparison, the Army devoted 20 percent of its manpower to the war and the Navy and Air Force less than 7 percent.[6]

To support the war effort, the service implemented a series of misguided manpower policies, which included lowering enlistment standards; shortening recruit training, "boot camp," by one-third; and eliminating a requirement for three months of on-the-job training prior to deployment overseas. In addition, in 1965 the service adopted the Army's individual-rotation policy. From that point forward units experienced nearly constant turnover. The number of draftees and of two-year enlistees also increased steadily. The result, according to Capt. David Dawson, an expert on Vietnam-era manpower issues, was that "the Marine Corps changed from a stable, long service organization to one marked by high turnover and constant personnel turbulence."[7] The net effect of these policies was that by 1969 unit cohesion and combat effectiveness were at record lows.

Changes in American society were an additional source of strain. In the areas of racial strife and substance abuse, the Marine Corps's problems mirrored those plaguing the country as a whole. Spiraling rates of crime and divorce, decreased civic involvement, and a general mistrust of authority caught Headquarters Marine Corps off guard.[8] Many senior Marines were convinced that American society was coming apart at the seams. According to Brig. Gen. Bernard Trainor, at roughly the same time that the public had turned against the Vietnam War "a social upheaval had taken place in the United States, which was particularly manifest among the youth of the land. Its most negative aspects were marked by a drug culture, a climate of permissiveness, racial discord, a rejection of authority and established values, cynicism and a philosophical commitment to rights without responsibilities."[9] Similar sentiments were echoed by a number of other officers and were officially endorsed by Headquarters Marine Corps in a study known as the Haynes Board Manpower Report, completed in 1975.[10]

In addition, and more than Vietnam or changing societal norms, Headquarters Marine Corps itself was responsible for the manpower crisis. As outlined above, decisions made to meet wartime manpower requirements weakened the service. In 1970 the Commandant, Gen. Leonard F. Chapman, told Marines that Vietnam represented "the most difficult circumstances we have ever experienced," yet he predicted it would only take a year to return to a high state of readiness; he was off by more than a decade.[11] The transition took ten times longer than predicted because for the next five years senior leaders failed to take the actions necessary to ensure a smooth postwar transition.

General Chapman's inaction is surprising considering his determined efforts to address racial discord. Following a series of race riots on Marine installations in 1969, Headquarters Marine Corps implemented a series of sweeping changes. Chapman's equal-opportunity initiatives were embraced by his successor, Gen. Robert Cushman, Commandant from 1971 to 1975, who likewise made race relations a top priority. As a result, by 1972 Marine-on-Marine racial violence had been reduced to manageable levels. Unfortunately, both Chapman and Cushman failed to act in other areas, owing to a series of bad assumptions.

Initially, it was assumed that problems would end once the service withdrew from Vietnam. In 1970, General Chapman told a reporter that he did not think the service had a discipline problem. Once the postwar downsizing was complete, the Marine Corps would once again be an elite, highly disciplined fighting force.[12] Exactly one year later, in June 1971, there were only five hundred Marines in Vietnam, down from a high of eighty-five thousand in 1969, but the rates of misconduct continued to rise.

The most disastrous decision was to preserve end strength at all costs. In both World War II and the Korean War the Marine Corps had lowered entrance standards to meet wartime needs. Unlike in those conflicts, however, standards were kept low long after the Vietnam War ended. At the direction of General Cushman, the service prioritized quantity over quality. Between 1969 and 1971 end strength dropped from 317,000 to 204,000 Marines. Cushman feared that if the latter number could not be maintained Congress would make additional cuts.[13] Although the Commandant may have been correct, many of his fellow generals thought it preferable to have a smaller, more professional force.[14] Ultimately, General Cushman's decision perpetuated the crisis and did untold damage to the service's public image.

In the area of recruiting, Headquarters Marine Corps operated under the false assumption that boot camp could turn anyone into a Marine. In a process that began during the Vietnam War, it repeatedly relaxed entrance requirements. At the highest levels, the Marine Corps mistakenly focused on mental test scores rather than possession of high school diplomas as the best indicators of potential recruits' future success. Not surprisingly, the number of Marines with high school diplomas dropped precipitously. By 1973 roughly half of all recruits were high school dropouts, and 75 percent scored at or below average on the Armed Forces Qualification Test.[15] In 1975, 2nd Lt. Kent Ellis, surveying his infantry company, was shocked to discover that only 14 percent of his men had high school diplomas.[16]

In addition, Headquarters Marine Corps erred in taking a "business as usual" approach to the end of the draft on 1 July 1973.[17] Despite years to prepare, almost nothing had been done. Marines were under the assumption that they would have little trouble getting volunteers. What they failed to realize was the degree to which volunteers prior to 1973 had been draft motivated; a significant percentage of recruits had volunteered for the Marines simply to avoid getting forced into the Army. Without the draft, enlistees proved hard to find. The new recruiting environment called for recruiters who could sell the Corps in a competitive marketplace, yet insufficient resources were devoted to the project.[18] The Marine Corps's effort to bolster its recruiting force paled in comparison to the Army's—cause for concern, since both services were going after the same demographic. Prior to the end of the draft, the Army increased its recruiting force by 71 percent and reprogrammed forty million dollars for enlistment bonuses. The equivalent numbers for the Marine Corps were 18 percent and a paltry fifteen thousand dollars, respectively.[19] Rather than devote personnel and resources to the challenge, headquarters placed its faith in the service's elite image to attract applicants. At the time, however, that image was in doubt.

Also, leaders blamed forces beyond their control. Such views were best expressed by Maj. Gen. Edwin B. Wheeler, at the 1972 General Officers' Symposium. Wheeler, the Marine Corps's top manpower official, blamed Congress and society for the service's woes. If Congress granted the service the end strength it desired and American youth were more patriotic, there would be no problem. Wheeler accurately described the spiraling rates of indiscipline, but when it came to solutions he remarked, "We have no pat answer."[20]

Senior Marines, to include Generals Chapman and Cushman, specifically blamed Project 100,000. The standard argument at the time, and one that has persisted, was that Secretary of Defense Robert McNamara came up with a misguided program that allowed underqualified black militants into the Marine Corps, where they caused a great deal of trouble. In reality, the argument was simply a way to blame civilian politicians and black militants for the organization's troubles. The Marine Corps's manpower crisis peaked around 1974, long after most Project 100,000 men had been discharged. In addition, too few men entered under the program to be credited with all the recorded cases of misconduct. The fact that the majority of Marines convicted at courts-martial in the early 1970s were Caucasian dispels the black-militant portion of the myth.[21]

On the ground, the focus on preserving end strength led to widespread recruiter malpractice. To meet quotas recruiters ignored criminal records, falsified test scores, and signed up the physically and mentally unfit. What was known as "recruiting out of the back of the courthouse" was commonplace. There are no data on the total number of recruits previously charged with or convicted of a felony. However, it was not unheard of for officers to learn that some of their Marines had been involved in serious crimes, such as murder or rape, prior to joining the Corps.[22] In the opinion of future Commandant Robert Barrow, "recruiting malpractice was rampant. . . . The worst was that there was an attitude of just get anybody."[23]

Recruiters cast a wide net, under the assumption that drill instructors could turn wayward youths into Marines. The problems carried over into recruit training. In the Marine Corps, boot camp is viewed as a transformative, even spiritual, experience. The two recruit depots—at Parris Island, South Carolina, and San Diego, California—not only harden the bodies and minds of young enlistees but instill an esprit de corps that is central to the service's ethos. The process is intended to be a rite of passage.[24] As evidenced by battlefield victories dating back to World War I, the boot camp experience has proved remarkably effective at preparing young Americans to fight for their country. But there is a fine line between discipline and brutality. Such initiation rites open the door to hazing and abuse if not carefully regulated. Beginning in the late 1960s, overworked drill instructors repeatedly resorted to unauthorized measures.

In the 1971 book *See Parris and Die: Brutality in the U.S. Marines,* investigative reporters H. Paul Jeffers and Dick Levitan offered a thorough accounting of all the incidents that had taken place prior to the book's release. The investigation had been spawned by the deaths of two recruits only days after they arrived at Parris Island in 1969. Letters from concerned parents, elected officials, and veterans groups were reprinted verbatim. The overall picture was of drill instructors resorting to extreme forms of physical and mental abuse, to include using racial slurs and making recruits drink urine. Perhaps most damning were comments by the medical staff. According to psychologist Waldo Lyon, who had worked at Parris Island for more than a decade, "brutality and other maltreatment are so ingrained in the Marines that the Corps could serve as a laboratory for the study of institutionalized violence." In his opinion, recruit abuse was a fact of life and had become central to the process. It was officially prohibited but was subtly condoned at the highest levels.[25]

Jeffers and Levitan's findings were backed up by a number of Marines. Drill instructors were deliberately and knowingly violating *Recruit Training: Standard Operating Procedure,* the manual that defined the parameters of recruit training. One Marine referred to the regulations as "a lot of bullshit."[26] While inspecting the Parris Island medical facilities in 1972, one general was shocked to learn that over the course of the year twenty-three recruits had been treated for broken jaws. He concluded that abuse "was just in the system" and the situation was "very bad" and "very wrong."[27] Another general officer was surprised at how many "very stupid things" were being done at the depots.[28]

As with recruiting, standards existed, but Headquarters Marine Corps did not press for rigorous enforcement. Here again the focus on end strength was to blame.

Headquarters refused to allow the depots to wash out more than 10 percent of recruits. Recruiters were bringing in people who had no business being in the Marine Corps, and drill instructors had to ensure the vast majority of them completed training. Both recruiters and drill instructors viewed failure to meet quotas as more likely than misconduct to end their careers. Jeffers and Levitan urged Headquarters Marine Corps to take action. In their opinion, barring strict enforcement of regulations it was only a matter of time before a disaster occurred similar to the Ribbon Creek incident of 1956.[29]

Enforcement was not forthcoming, and the predicted disaster came to pass in late 1975, quickly followed by more. In early December a recruit died of heat-related injuries only two days after arriving at Parris Island. He had been allowed to enlist despite being overweight and had not been given a physical exam upon arriving at boot camp. Two days later, at Recruit Depot San Diego, recruit Lynn McClure was beaten unconscious during pugil stick training. An investigation revealed that he was a high school dropout with a criminal record. McClure never regained consciousness and eventually died. Less than a month later, on 3 January 1976, a recruit was shot in the hand by his drill instructor at Parris Island. Each incident was reported extensively by the media.

In May 1976, Congress held hearings to examine Marine Corps recruiting and recruit training. Several congressmen had received what they considered an alarming number of complaints. Testimony given by recruiters, drill instructors, and medical personnel painted a picture of widespread abuse and systemic misconduct. None of the problems described by Jeffers and Levitan five years earlier had been addressed. Witnesses described a system marked by reckless disregard for the physical and mental well-being of the young people in its charge. One congressman concluded, "Congress finds totally unacceptable any repetition of the kinds of abuses that have befallen my constituents. . . . This problem can and must be solved."[30] Some congressmen contemplated placing restrictions on Marine Corps training and possibly closing the depots.

Misconduct was not confined to the drill field. Absenteeism, substance abuse, and indiscipline were rampant in the operating forces. Apologists claimed that such high rates of misconduct were due to force structure. The Marine Corps was the youngest of the services; 55 percent of Marines were under age twenty-two, compared with 34 percent for all the services; and it was the most heavily male.[31] While aggressive young males are an asset on the battlefield, they constitute a demographic prone to misconduct. However, pair this tendency with the Marine Corps's strict disciplinary standards, so the argument went, and the statistics were not so alarming. There was a degree of truth in this line of reasoning; historically, the service's force structure had led to higher rates of indiscipline. Nevertheless, in the early 1970s something was amiss. Rates were significantly higher than at any other point in the service's history. Furthermore, in certain categories—desertion, for example—rates did not just exceed those of the Army, as had historically been the case, but were three or four times greater.

Of all categories of misconduct, absenteeism was the most troubling. In 1970, more Marines were deserting than ever before. Headquarters believed the numbers would decrease as the service withdrew from Vietnam. Instead, surprisingly, the numbers rose over the next five years. By 1975, for every hundred Marines there were thirty instances of absenteeism, eleven of which involved absences for more than thirty days, resulting in a desertion rate of more than 10 percent. The percentage of Marines in a deserter status exceeded the peak rates in World War II, Korea, and Vietnam. Research showed that absenteeism was costing the Marine Corps more than two million man-days of service per year. Conservative estimates placed the dollar cost of these losses in the hundreds of millions.[32] Absenteeism stood in direct contradiction to the service's claim to be a force in readiness.[33]

The number of Marines using illegal drugs also increased significantly. Prior to Vietnam, instances of drug abuse had been so rare that headquarters had seen no need to track them. However, ready access to cheap marijuana and heroin in Vietnam coincided with rising substance abuse in American society to bring about major changes. By 1971 survey data indicated that 48 percent of Marines had used illegal drugs.[34] That same year, Secretary of the Navy John H. Chafee described drug abuse in the Navy and Marine Corps as "out of control."[35] As with absenteeism, leaders thought drug use would subside with the end of the war, but it continued to rise.[36]

Indiscipline sullied relations with local communities. In Oceanside, California, near Camp Pendleton, the Marine Corps's main West Coast base, city leaders requested $1.2 million from the federal government in 1974 to deal with a crime surge they attributed to the "misfits, social and educational dropouts, and hostile malcontents" of the Marine Corps. Of the ten murders that took place in Oceanside in 1973, Marines were involved in seven. From October of 1973 through May of 1974 more than eight hundred Marines were arrested in the city. They were responsible for 40 percent of all crimes, including murders, rapes, and assaults. According to the police chief, himself a former Marine, his force spent much of its time protecting residents from Marines. Similar situations were reported near other Marine installations.[37]

Junior officers highlighted the negative impact that misconduct was having on readiness. First Lt. David Kelly, writing in 1974, argued that the Marine Corps was no longer capable of rapid deployment. Kelly, who had recently completed a tour on Okinawa, told readers, "When one of the Regiments on Okinawa is preparing to deploy one of its Infantry Battalions, the remaining two Battalions must be cannibalized for equipment and personnel." His claims that the Marine Corps would be hard-pressed to field one combat-ready division from the three that existed on paper were reprinted in the *Washington Post*.[38]

Similar sentiments were expressed in a thirteen-page collection of short articles in the June 1975 issue of the *Marine Corps Gazette,* the service's professional journal. The authors, ranging in rank from gunnery sergeant to lieutenant colonel, offered examples based on their own experiences to illustrate the extent of the problem. According to Capt. Arthur Weber, "without a doubt . . . the Battalion Landing Teams that go afloat are not adequately prepared for combat." One gunnery sergeant outlined his daily schedule to show that on average nearly half his working hours were spent on disciplinary issues. Another captain related that sixteen men in his last company had had extensive police records. The common theme was that the Corps had major internal problems and was not ready for combat.[39]

Reform required change at the top. In the summer of 1975, General Cushman's career came to a premature end. Earlier, he had been connected tangentially to the Watergate scandal by his long-standing relationship with President Richard Nixon. In a separate incident, subordinates accused Cushman of using coded letters and undue influence to secure the appointment of one of his favorites as his successor.[40] Although investigators found the allegations "unprovable," Cushman opted for early retirement.[41]

To replace him, Secretary of the Navy J. William Middendorf II and Secretary of Defense James R. Schlesinger recommended Gen. Louis H. Wilson, an adaptable and innovative leader who had close personal ties to a number of influential senators and congressmen, among them Senator John C. Stennis, chair of the Armed Services Committee. Wilson, a Congressional Medal of Honor recipient in World War II, was a hero to his fellow Marines. Middendorf and Schlesinger believed he had the qualities and connections needed to pull the service out of its post-Vietnam doldrums. President Gerald Ford approved the nomination, and Wilson assumed the commandantcy on 1 July 1975.

As previously mentioned, in the mid-1970s Congress was considering mandating changes to recruiting and recruit training, as well as reducing the size of the service to restore its elite reputation. Wilson was determined not to let any of that happen. He welcomed outside advice, but Headquarters Marine Corps would drive the reform process. The Commandant made his intentions clear during his change of command. He ordered all Marines "to get in step, and to do it smartly."[42] From the outset, his top priority was personnel reform. In this quest Wilson was assisted by Lt. Gen. Robert Barrow, himself a decorated combat veteran, who served as deputy chief of staff for manpower. Barrow was to succeed Wilson as Commandant, ensuring the durability of what came to be known as the Wilson-Barrow reforms.

To begin, Wilson stopped blaming external factors. He took full responsibility and acknowledged that Headquarters Marine Corps's mistakes and bad planning assumptions lay at the root of the problem. He expected junior leaders to do the same, telling them, "The Marine Corps and its leaders are responsible for everything that is done or left undone in the Corps."[43] For years junior officers had been saying much the same thing in the pages of the *Gazette*. Many felt inspired by Wilson, who shared their values, encouraged their participation, and responded to the concerns they raised. The attitude of Headquarters Marine Corps went from defensive and reactive to receptive and proactive.

Personal leadership and adherence to standards lay at the center of Wilson's program. In 1921 the Commandant, Maj. Gen. John A. Lejeune, wrote that the relationship between leaders and led should be like that between a teacher and student or a father and son. Leaders who set good examples and were personally involved in the lives of their Marines achieved better results than those who took a more bureaucratic approach.[44] In 1975, Headquarters Marine Corps reaffirmed the service's tradition of personal leadership. Wilson stressed that young Marines were "the single most vital resource of the Marine Corps[;] . . . there is no substitute for personal involvement and concern for the individual Marine."[45] The rationale was straightforward—if leaders were more involved, there would be far fewer disciplinary issues. Along these same lines, General Barrow insisted that leaders act like "surrogate parents" to the young people in their charge.[46]

The emphasis on personal relationships extended beyond the Marine Corps to Congress, the media, and the American public. At the highest levels, Wilson used his connections in Congress and the Department of Defense to gain support for Marine Corps policies and programs. It should be noted, however, that Wilson's network was not limited to those at the top. He made skillful use of the Congressional Marines, a bipartisan group made up of anyone who worked on Capitol Hill who had an interest in the Corps. The group included senators and congressmen, as well as interns, janitors, and security guards.[47] Wilson and other key leaders made a habit of informally presenting initiatives at Congressional Marine breakfasts to foster support. The Commandant also cultivated personal relationships through speaking engagements, visits, and correspondence. As much of a politician as anyone in Washington, Wilson used the trappings of his office to build relationships.

The same could be said of the Commandant's relationship with the media. Most of the articles written on the Marine Corps in the early 1970s were not flattering. Nevertheless, Wilson encouraged subordinates to stop being defensive and to view the media as a tool for communicating with the American public. Reporters, he urged, should not be faulted for reporting the truth. In fact, journalists served as a second set of eyes and ears for a commander. As with its approach to Congress, headquarters changed how it dealt with the media. Leaders at all levels were expected to foster positive ties in the local community, whether with the city council or the police department, and to make sure positive stories appeared in local papers.

Vietnam and the ensuing manpower crisis had done immeasurable damage to the service's public image. In the late 1970s, reconnecting with the American people became a top priority.[48]

Although Generals Wilson and Barrow deserve the preponderance of the credit for developing sound policies, implementation depended on a cadre of motivated junior officers. The typical junior enlisted Marine seldom came into contact with a general officer. However, enlisted Marines interacted with their lieutenants and captains on a regular basis. Thus, if policies were determined in Washington, junior officers served as their conduits. Accordingly, Commandant Wilson made a habit of communicating with officers and noncommissioned officers in the operating forces, and their perspectives influenced policy. According to General Barrow, the junior officers who weathered the storm in the late 1960s and early 1970s were the true heroes. In his opinion, "they had their baptism of fire . . . in the personnel business" and "merit special commendation." Ultimately, empowered junior leaders were critical to the reform process.[49]

Along with the principles of personal leadership and empowering subordinates, General Wilson emphasized quality over quantity. He was willing to make drastic cuts in manpower if that was what it would take to return the service to its previously high standards. Unlike his predecessor, he was not preoccupied with meeting congressionally authorized end strength. His primary focus was that the force be capable and well disciplined. At one point he remarked that he would rather have a Marine Corps that was small enough to fit in a phone booth than one that was poorly trained and undisciplined.[50] General Wilson's mind-set represented a sea change from the Cushman era and goes far in explaining the success of the Great Personnel Campaign.

In his first service-wide announcement, General Wilson declared that immediate corrective action was required in key areas.[51] Recruiting was the most pressing. The assumption that anyone could be turned into a Marine was false and lay at the root of the service's personnel problems. According to the Haynes Board Manpower Report, everything from desertion to drug abuse stemmed "almost entirely from past acceptance of excessive numbers of substandard applicants."[52] The Marine Corps had to be more selective. Wilson announced that by fiscal year 1977, 75 percent of enlistees would be high school graduates. As the Commandant put it, "This is a requirement to the recruiting service, not a goal, and we're going to get this or we're going down in strength."[53] This policy was a far cry from when only two years earlier headquarters had petitioned Congress for relief from mandatory quality standards.

The importance of focusing on high school diplomas rather than test scores cannot be overstated. From as early as 1960 manpower analysts had argued that graduation from high school was the single best indicator of whether a Marine would successfully complete the first enlistment. A diploma increased a recruit's chances of success by 20–40 percent, depending on other variables. Graduating from high school demonstrated what one researcher termed a "stick-to-it-iveness" that carried over into other areas.[54] Beginning in 1975, headquarters focused on using both educational levels and mental test scores, the goal being a majority of recruits in the "high quality" category. "High quality" was defined as possession of a high school diploma and an above-average score on aptitude tests.

Headquarters Marine Corps introduced corrective procedures and took disciplinary action as well. In June 1976, operational control of recruiting shifted from headquarters to the commanding generals of the two recruit depots. Prior to the realignment, recruiting and screening had been the responsibility of six different Marine Corps district directors, each responsible to the Commandant. The reorganized chain of command gave recruiters personal stakes in whom they shipped to boot camp. According to General Barrow, it was a fairly easy fix: "If the guy responsible for training recruits also was responsible for recruiting him, he is not going to send himself someone he can't work with, in the simplest terms. Or in other terms, some recruiter is not going to send his boss a misfit."[55]

In addition, a recruiter's Social Security number would be recorded in the permanent record of each recruit he brought into the Corps. Recruiters' fitness reports would be based on the number of their recruits who completed boot camp rather than the number who started, as had previously been the case.[56] Finally, computers were used to track recruiter performance, identify trends, and provide feedback. Two senior officers, one at each depot, served as assistant chiefs of staff for recruiting and oversaw the effort. In fiscal year 1975 alone, 252 recruiters were relieved for failure to comply with the new standards. From 1975 onward, the system of incentives rewarded recruiters on the basis of the types of individuals they recruited, not just the total numbers.

Marine recruiters, however, had to have something worth selling. In the early 1970s the Marine Corps had unveiled a new slogan: "The Marines are looking for a few good men." The campaign was premised on exclusivity, selectivity, and aggressive masculinity. The other services had adapted to the end of the draft by highlighting skills training, exotic travel, and monetary incentives. They also appealed to individualism and materialism, as evidenced by campaigns centered on "Today's Army wants to join you" and "Find yourself in the Air Force." The Marine Corps, on the other hand, offered a sense of community based on shared hardship. The intent was to go after a niche market of young men looking to prove their manhood.

The Corps's public image in the early 1970s, however, did not lend itself to an advertising campaign based on selectivity. Talk of duty, honor, and high standards fell flat in light of Marine misconduct reported by the media. With recruiters enlisting high school dropouts and criminals, prospective enlistees and their parents doubted the Corps's claims that it was an elite outfit. Once headquarters raised the entry standards, however, the "few good men" campaign began to resonate. In time, it proved to be the most effective advertising campaign in Marine Corps history and an asset to Marine recruiters.

In addition to recruiting, Headquarters Marine Corps reformed recruit training. The McClure incident was a shocking example of where the combination of recruiting malpractice and recruit abuse could lead. Recruiters had long promised that Americans would return home better off for having joined the Corps. To survive in the all-volunteer environment, Headquarters Marine Corps had to make good on this promise. In a *Gazette* article, Wilson told Marines that as he traveled the country, he "must be able to look every parent right in the eye and say, 'If your son or daughter joins the Corps, he will have a good life in a healthy environment.'"[57]

Making this promise a reality required fundamentally altering the recruit / drill instructor relationship. Recruits would be tested, but they would be treated with dignity and respect in the process.[58] The underlying principle was to reaffirm the notion of "teacher to student, father to son." Training would be challenging, not demeaning.[59] Under the new system, wrote one officer, "training was to remain personally demanding, but it was to be conducted with firmness, fairness and dignity and, when necessary, with compassion." Wilson and Barrow were willing to take on the drill instructor community to see that their changes were carried out. The Commandant made it clear that he was the senior drill instructor in the Marine Corps and that anyone who did not like it could leave—an implied threat carried out by the depot commanders, who relieved, transferred, or retired "old-timers" who would not get with the program.[60]

Changes in philosophy were paired with reforms to standard operating procedures. Limits on attrition were lifted. Rates rose from 10 percent to 25 percent in some cases.[61] Motivation Platoon, a holding unit for recalcitrant recruits and a hotbed of abuse, was likewise abolished. The option to separate substandard performers substantially reduced cases of abuse. As had been the case with recruiters, the process of screening and training drill instructors was made more rigorous. A number of measures were introduced to reduce stress: the number of recruits per platoon dropped from ninety to seventy-five, sixty-eight hours were cut from the program of instruction, and recruits were given an hour of free time each evening. For quality-control purposes, headquarters assigned eighty-four additional officers, forty-two at each depot, to serve as assistant series commanders, concerned with supervision and safety. As much as drill instructors may have resented it, increased officer supervision was arguably the single most important factor in ensuring the proper treatment of recruits.[62]

Finally, a degree of transparency was achieved by opening the entire process to public scrutiny. Parents, local officials, and the general public were encouraged to visit the recruit depots to see for themselves how the Corps turned the youth of America into proud men and women. In an interview with *People Weekly,* General Wilson told readers, "I'd like to say that the recruit depots are open to anyone, anytime. Visitors can walk in and watch training or look up any individual they know."[63] In this way, the Marine Corps met the challenges posed by the All-Volunteer Force by returning to its roots—high standards and demanding training—and then selling what it had done to the American people.

The focus on discipline and standards extended to the operating forces. On 6 August 1975, Headquarters Marine Corps suspended all non-EAS (that is, non–end of active service) attrition rate goals. The category included all Marines who left the service prior to the end of their terms of enlistment, typically for disciplinary or physical reasons. Under General Cushman, commanders were expected to maintain artificially low rates to preserve end strength. In extreme cases, commanders had to delay prosecuting offenders lest they garner unwanted attention from headquarters. By suspending the goals, General Wilson freed commanders to discharge poor performers as they deemed necessary. To ease the process, in November 1975 General Wilson announced an Expeditious Discharge Program. Two years earlier, the House Appropriations Committee, alarmed by rising rates of military misconduct, had mandated that all services streamline administrative discharge procedures. At the time, Headquarters Marine Corps had refused to comply. The service was actually in the habit of delaying discharges to preserve end strength; by 1975 the Marine Corps was the only service without expeditious discharge procedures.[64]

As outlined in *Marine Corps Bulletin 1900,* the Expeditious Discharge Program eliminated the complex legal proceedings that had previously surrounded punitive discharges. If a Marine and his commander agreed, a voluntary, early separation was allowed; the one stipulation was that the Marine could never reenlist. The program pushed separation authority down to the battalion level and dramatically reduced the time associated with the process. Prior to implementation it had taken weeks and sometimes months to separate someone; afterward it took days.[65] During the first three months of the program, approximately two thousand Marines were separated for failing to meet standards. By late 1976 the total had exceeded ten thousand.[66]

As a result of the reforms outlined above, by 1978 the Marine Corps had dramatically improved quality standards and brought incidents of indiscipline down to manageable levels. Between fiscal years 1975 and 1978 the percentage of enlistees who were high school graduates increased from roughly 50 percent to 76.8 percent, desertion rates dropped 60 percent, the confined population rate dropped 54 percent, and special courts-martial were down 60 percent.[67] By 1978, the turnaround was so complete that one general was led to proclaim victory in the personnel campaign.[68] The situation had so improved that a number of correctional facilities were closed. The positive trends continued into the 1980s. On 15 October 1982, the

Marine Corps announced that it had met its recruiting goals for 1982 and that 90 percent of recruits were high school graduates. By the end of the decade over 98 percent of Marines were high school graduates, and no recruits were in Mental Group IV. Only fifteen years earlier, 50 percent of Marines had been dropouts and upward of 40 percent had been Mental Group IVs.[69] Due to bold and innovative leadership on the part of Headquarters Marine Corps, the service's military readiness was no longer in question.[70]

Substance abuse was one area, however, where headquarters failed to take meaningful action in the late 1970s. In 1970 the service had adopted a no-tolerance policy. A year later, under pressure from the Department of Defense, the focus shifted to rehabilitation. The emphasis on rehabilitation remained in effect under Commandant Cushman. Both Wilson and Barrow mistakenly believed that drug use would decline as other reforms took effect and that it was not a top priority. They held to this assumption even after a manpower study conducted in 1975 found that the Marine Corps had the highest per capita rate of drug use of all the services.[71]

Substance abuse did not receive the attention it deserved until late 1981. Following a drug-related mishap, a flight-deck crash, on board the aircraft carrier USS *Nimitz* that took the lives of fourteen sailors, surveys were conducted to determine the extent of drug abuse in the military. General Barrow later described being shocked to learn that 47 percent of Marines had used drugs in the previous year. The statistics were almost exactly what they had been back in 1971. The Commandant announced a new no-tolerance policy and declared himself the service's chief drug-control officer.[72] Although abuse rates steadily declined with the introduction of rigorous urinalysis testing, the Marine Corps's reputation for being the hardest partying of the services endured into the twenty-first century.[73] General Barrow was to consider the lateness with which he addressed substance abuse one of his major regrets.[74]

Other downsides to the reforms became evident over time as well. While commanders applauded the Expeditious Discharge Program, what General Barrow referred to as "[throwing Marines] out right and left" had its drawbacks.[75] It ran counter to the motto of "Once a Marine, always a Marine." It could be argued that the Marine Corps was breaking faith with some of its members, some of whom may have been suffering from the aftereffects of serving in Vietnam. Second, it was a solution that could only be implemented during peacetime; leaders who were quick to separate underperformers would be ill prepared should war break out. Would they know how to motivate subordinates when separation was not an option? Finally, critics argued, the program introduced a "zero-defects Corps" in which the primary goal was to keep one's record clean at all costs. They claimed that over time young Marines would become more and more risk averse and the service would be less innovative as a result.[76]

Furthermore, to recruit effectively in an all-volunteer environment, the Marine Corps presented itself as a distinct culture. It set itself apart from, perhaps even above, civilian society, as a sort of warrior class. Although the service had long considered itself an elite organization, the Wilson–Barrow years represent a departure in this regard. Efforts to differentiate the Corps from the other services proved successful in meeting manpower needs; however, research done in the 1990s indicated that it was becoming increasingly disconnected from society in the process. In the mid-1990s, Thomas Ricks, who at the time was the *Washington Post*'s Pentagon correspondent, followed a group of Marines through the initial stages of their careers. He explored how they adapted to the service as well as how they were perceived by their civilian friends and family members. Ultimately, Ricks concluded that most Americans respected, and even loved, their Marine Corps but believed it was different from the rest of America. As much as they liked Marines, most people could not imagine themselves actually being one, or wanting their child to be one, for that matter.

For their part, Marines had gone from "thinking of themselves as a better version of American society to a kind of dissenting critique of it."[77] Ricks discovered that the officer corps was becoming increasingly isolated and politicized. A 1995 survey of officers attending Marine Corps University in Quantico, Virginia, found that the majority self-identified as conservative and that less than half believed it was important to have people with different views in their organization. According to an officer who conducted the survey, "Instead of viewing themselves as the representatives of society, the participating officers believe they are a unique element within society."[78] The danger of politicization is that if officers are viewed as political actors, civilian officials will no longer trust them to provide sound military advice.

Although these drawbacks are cause for concern, the personnel reforms implemented during the Wilson–Barrow years were remarkably successful. Through innovative leadership and a focus on quality over quantity, the Marine Corps overcame the disastrous consequences of the Vietnam War and regained the confidence of the American public. The process took far longer than expected, but over time Headquarters Marine Corps learned from its mistakes and crafted effective policies in all major areas. By the late 1980s, rates of indiscipline were at historical lows and the service had successfully adapted to the All-Volunteer Force. Indiscipline no longer defined the Marine Corps's public image or impeded its military readiness. As General Barrow put it, "In any institution or undertaking, the importance of people transcends all else."[79] Had the Marine Corps not first focused itself internally, it would have been impossible to pursue initiatives in other areas. Americans would not have enlisted, nor would Congress have funded an organization in disarray. Also, the reforms have stood the test of time. Four decades later most of the policies remain in effect, and the Marine Corps's reputation as an elite organization is no longer in question.

NOTES 1 As a case in point, in 1974 there were 71.6 courts-martial per thousand enlisted Marines. The number was more than twice that of the Army, three times that of the Navy, and seventeen times that of the Air Force. In fact, it exceeded the combined total for all the other services, which stood at fifty-three per thousand that year. Numbers for the other services were as follows: Army 29.9, Navy 19.1, and Air Force 4.0. Data for the years 1971, 1972, 1973, and 1975 follow the same pattern; see Martin Binkin and Jeffrey Record, *Where Does the Marine Corps Go from Here?* (Washington, D.C.: Brookings Institution, 1976), pp. 62–63, table 6-4. Binkin and Record used data provided by the Department of Defense, Office of the Assistant Secretary for Manpower and Reserve Affairs, November 1975.

2 Lieutenant General Jones, "Attitudinal Survey in Human Affairs," Studies and Reports, Conferences, General Officers Symposium, October 1972, Marine Corps Archives and Special Collections, Quantico, Va. [hereafter MCASC].

3 Gen. Louis H. Wilson, "Remarks to the Mississippi State Legislature," Jackson, Miss., 25 March 1976, Wilson Biographical File, Marine Corps History and Museums Division, Quantico, Va. [hereafter MCHMD].

4 Graham A. Cosmas and Lt. Col. Terrence R. Murray, USMC, *U.S. Marines in Vietnam: Vietnamization and Redeployment, 1970–1971* (Washington, D.C.: Headquarters U.S. Marine Corps, History and Museums Division, 1986), p. 344; Henry I. Shaw and Ralph Donnelly, *Blacks in the Marine Corps* (Washington, D.C.: Headquarters U.S. Marine Corps, History and Museums Division, 1975), pp. 79–80.

5 Allan R. Millett, *Semper Fidelis: The History of the United States Marine Corps* (New York: Macmillan, 1991), p. 577.

6 Capt. David A. Dawson, USMC, *The Impact of Project 100,000 on the Marine Corps* (Washington, D.C.: Headquarters Marine Corps, History and Museums Division, 1995), p. 93.

7 Ibid., p. 94.

8 James T. Patterson, *Restless Giant: The United States from Watergate to Bush v. Gore* (Oxford, U.K.: Oxford Univ. Press, 2005), pp. 43–70, provides a detailed account of American society during the 1970s.

9 Brig. Gen. Bernard E. Trainor, "The Personnel Campaign Issue Is No Longer in Doubt," *Marine Corps Gazette* (January 1978), p. 22.

10 Dawson, *Impact of Project 100,000 on the Marine Corps*, pp. 158–59.

11 Gen. Leonard F. Chapman, Jr., "A Letter from the CMC," *Marine Corps Gazette* (June 1970), p. 16.

12 Gen. Leonard F. Chapman, Jr., "Remarks at Luncheon Meeting of National Press Club, Washington, D.C.," 23 June 1970, Papers of Leonard F. Chapman, Jr., "Public Statements CMC, 1970," 2001–3171, MCASC.

13 Gen. Robert E. Cushman, Jr., interview by Benis M. Frank, USMC (Ret.), Oral History Transcript, History and Museums Division, Headquarters, U.S. Marine Corps, Washington, D.C., 1984 [hereafter Cushman Oral History], pp. 359–63. Asked about his approach to manpower, Cushman described himself as having fought a rearguard action in Congress based on "the fear that if we simply refused to recruit enough people to come fairly close to filling up our authorized strength, that the Congress would soon cut the Corps to whatever we were able to maintain with our recruiting" (p. 362). He described himself as having been somewhat surprised when "we all of a sudden had the bottom fall out" (p. 359). He attributed Commandant Wilson's ability to preserve end strength and improve quality to Wilson's close ties with Congress (p. 363).

14 Lt. Gen. Leo J. Dulacki, USMC (Ret.), interview by Benis M. Frank and Dr. Graham A. Cosmas, Oral History Transcript, History and Museums Division, Headquarters, U.S. Marine Corps, Washington, D.C., 1988 [hereafter Dulacki Oral History], p. 314. General Dulacki, who had been deputy chief of staff for manpower May–December 1973, commented: "I know I tried on more than one occasion to develop a plan—as a matter of fact we developed a plan—to gradually raise the standards—education, the mental group categories and all—and develop statistics to show that certain improvements in the standards would not have the adverse effect on the numbers. But I was never able to convince the Commandant that that should be done. For some reason we were so preoccupied with numbers at that time. My own feeling, my own philosophy was that it would have been better to have 150,000 good men than 190,000 men, 40,000 of whom were trouble-makers and just went through the Marine Corps like a turnstile; come in and get in trouble and go out."

15 Jeffrey Record, "Where Does the Corps Go . . . Now?," U.S. Naval Institute *Proceedings* (May 1995), pp. 91–94.

16 Kent D. Ellis, "Quality, Quantity Recruiting," *Marine Corps Gazette* (January 1976). The Corps's inability to find qualified applicants got to the point that it petitioned Congress for relief from legislation stipulating that no more than 45 percent of new recruits could be non–high school graduates; Bernard Rostker, *I Want You! The Evolution of the All-Volunteer Force* (Santa Monica, Calif.: RAND, 2006), pp. 272–73. See also Dawson, *Impact of Project 100,000 on the Marine Corps*, pp. 166–68. Dawson's research shows that between 1963 and 1966 roughly 60 percent of Marines scored in Mental Groups III and IV, the two lowest groupings, and that by 1972 the proportion was more than 75 percent. The number of enlistees with high school educations dropped from around 75 percent in the early 1960s to 50 percent in the early 1970s. For more information on declining quality indicators see Record, "Where Does the Corps Go . . . Now?," p. 91; Binkin and Record, *Where Does the Marine Corps Go from Here?*, p. 60; Trainor, "The Personnel Campaign Issue Is No Longer in Doubt"; and Millett, *Semper Fidelis*, pp. 597–98.

17 Rostker, *I Want You!*, p. 146.

18 Office of the Assistant Secretary of Defense, ASD(M&RA), "Fact Sheet: Project Volunteer Organization within the Military Service," Washington, D.C., 12 November 1970. Document available in the electronic document collection that accompanies Rostker, *I Want You!*

19 Rostker, *I Want You!*, pp. 160–61.

20 Maj. Gen. Edwin B. Wheeler, "A Report on the State of Marine Corps Manpower," Studies and Reports, Conferences, General Officers Symposium, October 1972, MCASC.

21 Dawson, *Impact of Project 100,000 on the Marine Corps*, pp. 4–5, 141–45, 200.

22 Charles Jones, *Boys of '67: From Vietnam to Iraq, the Extraordinary Story of a Few Good Men* (Mechanicsburg, Pa.: Stackpole Books, 2006), p. 154. For detailed descriptions, many from the recruiters themselves, of falsifying test scores, doctoring documents, and providing faulty background checks, see *Hearings on Marine Corps' Recruit Training and Recruiting Programs, before the Subcommittee on Military Personnel of the Committee on Armed Services, House of Representatives,* 94th Cong., 2nd sess. (Washington, D.C.: U.S. Government Printing Office, 1976); and "Too Few Men: Some Marine Recruiters Will Sign Up Almost Anyone," *Time,* 23 October 1978.

23 Gen. Robert H. Barrow, interview by Brig. Gen. Edwin H. Simmons, USMC (Ret.), session 11, Oral History Transcript, History and Museums Division, Headquarters, U.S. Marine Corps, Washington, D.C., 1978–94 [hereafter Barrow Oral History].

24 Commandant Gen. James F. Amos touched on the spiritual nature of entry-level training in a 2010 planning document: "The spirit of our Corps, embodied in the eagle, globe and anchor, lives within the soul of every Marine. This spirit is born through arduous rites of passage at boot camp and officer training, after which a young man or woman is called

a 'United States Marine' for the first time. . . . What happens on the parade decks at Parris Island and San Diego, or in the hills of Quantico, is what *makes us* Marines—it is the hardening of body and mind, the infusion of discipline and the casting of an indelible *esprit de corps* forged in the cauldron of 'things endured and things accomplished, such as regiments hand down forever.' It is almost spiritual!" Gen. James F. Amos, *35th Commandant's Planning Guidance* (Washington, D.C.: Headquarters Marine Corps, 2010).

25 H. Paul Jeffers and Dick Levitan, *See Parris and Die: Brutality in the U.S. Marines* (New York: Hawthorn Books, 1971), pp. 9, 68–69.

26 Ibid., p. 79.

27 Barrow Oral History, session 10.

28 Bernard Weinraub, "Marine Corps Is Softening the Role of the Hard-Boiled Drill Instructor," *New York Times,* 11 May 1977.

29 Jeffers and Levitan, *See Parris and Die,* p. 200. The Ribbon Creek incident occurred in April 1956. It involved an allegedly intoxicated drill instructor marching his platoon into a creek, resulting in the deaths of six recruits.

30 *Hearings on Marine Recruit Training and Recruiting Programs,* House Armed Services Committee (Washington, D.C.: U.S. Government Printing Office, 1976), testimony of Lt. Gen. Robert H. Barrow, p. 20.

31 "Haynes Board Manpower Report," Studies and Reports, Force Structure Studies, 1971–1975, MCASC.

32 D. J. Jenkins, "Unauthorized Absenteeism in the United States Marine Corps" (Department of Operations Research and Administrative Sciences, Naval Postgraduate School, Monterey, Calif., June 1975), pp. 24–25.

33 "Marine Corps Desertions Triple Rate Recorded during Vietnam War," *Baltimore Sun,* 22 March 1976; Binkin and Record, *Where Does the Marine Corps Go from Here?,* pp. 62–63.

34 Jones, "Attitudinal Survey in Human Affairs."

35 Col. Robert D. Heinl, Jr., "The Collapse of the Armed Forces," *Armed Forces Journal,* 7 June 1977, pp. 30–38.

36 Dulacki Oral History, pp. 322–23.

37 Everett R. Holless, "Crime Rate in Coast City Is Linked to Marine Base: Different Type of Recruit Help from the Corps," *New York Times,* 22 May 1974.

38 David E. Kelly, "Must the Marine Corps Shrink or Die?," *Armed Forces Journal,* October 1974, p. 18. See also Michael Getler, "Marine Officer Hits Corps: Combat Unreadiness, Morale Problems Cited," *Washington Post,* 7 November 1974. Allan Millett, the leading historian of the Marine Corps and a serving officer at the time, concurred. In Allan Millett, "The U.S. Marine Corps: Adaptation in the Post-Vietnam Era," *Armed Forces and Society* 9, no. 3 (Spring 1983), p. 378, he argued, "As defined by the Department of Defense—and as accepted by Congress—the Marine Corps was an organization of doubtful readiness because of the indiscipline of its enlisted men."

39 "Commentaries on the Corps: Leadership and Quality," *Marine Corps Gazette* (June 1975), pp. 41–54, esp., for the specific cases mentioned, Capt. Arthur S. Weber, Jr., "Unsolved Problem Areas," p. 41, and GySgt. John H. Lofland, "High Cost of AWOLs," p. 45.

40 Cushman Oral History, pp. 410–11.

41 Seymour Hersh, "Marine Corps Head Linked to C.I.A.'s Authorization for Ellsberg Burglary," *Washington Post,* 7 May 1973; Cushman Oral History, pp. 410–11. That Cushman was implicated in both events led some critics to refer to the latter as the "Marine Corps Watergate."

42 Allan Millett and Jack Shulimson, eds., *Commandants of the Marine Corps* (Annapolis, Md.: Naval Institute Press, 2004), p. 429.

43 Wilson before the San Diego, Calif., Navy League on 6 October 1976, Wilson Papers, "Excerpts from Statements, Speeches, and Published Articles," box 68, folder 10, MCASC.

44 Headquarters U.S. Marine Corps, *Marine Corps Manual* (Washington, D.C.: U.S. Government Printing Office, 1922), available at archive.org/.

45 Gen. Louis H. Wilson, "CMC Reports on Meeting the Challenges of Future Battlefields," *Marine Corps Gazette* (April 1978), pp. 21–23.

46 General Barrow's notes, Studies and Reports, Conferences, General Officers Symposium, General Simmon's Notes, 1981, MCASC.

47 Gen. Louis H. Wilson, USMC (Ret.), interview by Brig. Gen. Edwin H. Simmons, Oral History Transcript, History and Museums Division, Headquarters, U.S. Marine Corps, Washington, D.C., 1988, p. 93.

48 In 1980, General Barrow expressed his views on the subject in a letter to all commanders: "We do owe the American people a full explanation of what we do as well as what we may fail to do on occasion[;] . . . our approach must be one of candor, truthfulness, and timeliness. . . . [C]ommanders are encouraged to provide members of the local community with opportunities for firsthand observation of Marines. . . . I urge commanders to take every opportunity to tell the Marine Corps story to a wide range of audiences—civilian as well as military—through personal contact and public appearances"; White Letter No. 2-80, Public Affairs, 6 February 1980, Robert H. Barrow Collection, "Speeches and Letters, 1981–1983," MCASC.

49 Barrow Oral History, sessions 10 and 11. For more on this core group of junior officers, see Jones, *Boys of '67;* and James Kitfield, *Prodigal Soldiers: How the Generation of Officers Born of Vietnam Revolutionized the American Style of War* (New York: Simon & Schuster, 1995). By the 1990s, many, such as Anthony Zinni and James Jones, were serving at the highest levels of the U.S. military. In a speech given at the U.S. Naval Institute in 2000, General Zinni described his and his peers' commitment: "For me, joining the Marines was the closest thing to becoming a priest. One way or another, all of us were programmed to believe what we were doing was not a job; not even a profession; but a calling." Quoted in Jones, *Boys of '67,* p. 10. To a man, these

officers consider Generals Wilson and Barrow the key figures in post-Vietnam personnel reforms.

50 Kitfield, *Prodigal Soldiers,* p. 254.

51 Louis H. Wilson, "A Message from the Commandant," *Leatherneck,* 16 July 1975. See also "Haynes Board Manpower Report."

52 "Haynes Board Manpower Report."

53 "Today's Marines: A Conversation with the Commandant," *Sea Power,* November 1975, pp. 15–21, esp. 15–16. In Trainor, "The Personnel Campaign Issue Is No Longer in Doubt," pp. 26–27, the author recalled that "the Commandant made it clear to all involved in the recruiting business that quotas were to be considered goals but that quality was a requirement."

54 Anne Hoiberg and Newell H. Berry, "There's No Doubt about It, a Diploma Goes a Long Way for Combat Efficiency," *Marine Corps Gazette* (September 1977). See also Robert Alan Packard, Jr., "Premature Attrition in the U.S. Marine Corps" (master's thesis, Naval Postgraduate School, Monterey, Calif., December 1976).

55 Barrow Oral History, session 11.

56 Trainor, "The Personnel Campaign Issue Is No Longer in Doubt," p. 28.

57 Louis H. Wilson, "The Third Hundred Years," *Marine Corps Gazette* (November 1975), p. 21.

58 In an interview, Wilson explained his approach: "We must be dedicated to the concept of being tough but fair, demanding but humane, firm but understanding. Abuse of the system or of any Marine in any environment will not be tolerated. Dignity of treatment to all Marines must be foremost in our minds. When you think about it, mutual respect for each other as human beings goes a long way toward improving quality within our ranks, increasing combat readiness, enhancing training, and bettering our standards." Wilson on Hotline, November 1976, Wilson Papers, "Excerpts from Statements, Speeches, and Published Articles," box 68, folder 10, MCASC.

59 Trainor, "The Personnel Campaign Issue Is No Longer in Doubt," pp. 30–31.

60 Weinraub, "Marine Corps Is Softening the Role of the Hard-Boiled Drill Instructor."

61 Barrow Oral History, session 10.

62 Trainor, "The Personnel Campaign Issue Is No Longer in Doubt," p. 31.

63 Clare Crawford, "In His Own Words: Boot Camp Should Be Tough, but Never Brutal; Gen. Wilson Tells That to the Marines—Interview with Louis Wilson," *People Weekly,* 13 September 1978, p. 63.

64 Maj. Ronald R. Borowicz, USMC, "Evolution of the Marine Corps Expeditious Discharge Program" (Independent Research Project, Marine Corps Command and Staff College, 31 March 1976), Student Papers and Reports, MCASC.

65 Headquarters U.S. Marine Corps, *Marine Corps Bulletin 1900* (Washington, D.C.: 12 November 1975).

66 Borowicz, "Evolution of the Marine Corps Expeditious Discharge Program," p. 38.

67 M. Brice, "Overview: The Wilson Years," U.S. Marine Corps press release, 30 June 1979, Wilson Bio File, MCHMD. For more-specific numbers see Green Letter No. 1-78, Report from the General Officers Conference, 12 January 1978, Wilson Papers, "Green Letter, Back-Up File, 1979," MCASC. Special courts-martial, the most serious kind, were reduced from 8,318 in fiscal year (FY) 1975 to 4,385 in FY 1977; incidence of unauthorized absence had dropped more than 50 percent, from 52,200 in FY 1975 to 24,600 in FY 1977; non-EAS attrition was down from a high of 34,100 in FY 1976 to a projected 21,200 for FY 1978.

68 Trainor, "The Personnel Campaign Issue Is No Longer in Doubt," p. 22. Of the personnel campaign, Trainor wrote, "Few campaigns in Marine Corps history have been as difficult and critical. Few campaigns have been so dramatically marked by defeats and victories. In no other campaign was the future of our Corps so threatened."

69 Aline D. Quester, *Marine Corps Recruits: A Historical Look at Accessions and Boot Camp Performance* (Arlington, Va.: Center for Naval Analyses, September 2010); Packard, "Premature Attrition in the U.S. Marine Corps," p. 8.

70 According to defense analyst Jeffrey Record, who in the mid-1970s as a congressional staffer had been one of the service's harshest critics, "By the end of the 1980s, the Corps boasted the highest manpower quality and lowest rates of indiscipline in its history." See Record, "Where Does the Corps Go . . . Now?," p. 92.

71 "Haynes Board Manpower Report."

72 See Barrow Oral History, session 11; and Green Letter No. 5-81, Marine Corps Drug Abuse Policy, 1 December 1981, Robert H. Barrow Collection, "Speeches and Letters, 1981–1983," MCASC. At the same time, Barrow released a "white letter" on the topic that was disseminated Marine Corps–wide. See also Peter H. Stoloff and Renee K. Barnow, *Alcohol and Drug Use in the Marine Corps in 1983* (Alexandria, Va.: Center for Naval Analyses, 1984), pp. 1-2, 1-5, and table 5-6.

73 According to the most recent data available from the Department of Defense, less than 2 percent of Marines were using illegal substances in 2011. At the same time, the Marine Corps continues to have by far the greatest rates of binge drinking (48.6 percent, compared with an all-services average of 33.1 percent); U.S. Defense Dept., *2011 Health Related Behaviors Survey of Active Duty Military Personnel* (Washington, D.C.: February 2013), available at tricare.mil/.

74 Barrow Oral History, session 19.

75 Ibid., session 11.

76 Lt. Col. Richard S. Alvarez, "The Spirit of Marines," *Marine Corps Gazette* (February 1987), pp. 40–41.

77 Thomas E. Ricks, *Making the Corps* (New York: Scribner's, 1997), pp. 22–23.

78 Thomas E. Ricks, "The Widening Gap between Military and Society," *Atlantic* (July 1997).

79 Quoted in Brig. Gen. Edwin H. Simmons, USMC (Ret.), "Robert Hilliard Barrow," in *Commandants of the Marine Corps,* ed. Millett and Shulimson, p. 456.

ABOUT THE AUTHORS

Alan M. Anderson received his PhD in war studies from King's College London. His research focused on the laws of war and naval strategy in Great Britain and the United States from 1899 to 1909. He received the Rear Admiral John D. Hayes Pre-doctoral Fellowship from the U.S. Naval History and Heritage Command for 2013–14.

R. M. Barlow is an assistant editor of the Adams Papers at the Massachusetts Historical Society in Boston. She has a PhD from the University of Virginia, where her dissertation was on John Adams's foreign policy.

Lori Lyn Bogle is a professor of American social/cultural military history at the U.S. Naval Academy. Her first book, *The Pentagon's Battle for the American Mind,* looks at the historical role of the military in shaping the national character; her current research is on Theodore Roosevelt's public relations efforts. She served as director of the 2013 McMullen Naval History Symposium.

Samantha A. Cavell is the Visiting Assistant Professor in Military History at Southeastern Louisiana University. She received her PhD in naval and maritime history from the University of Exeter in the United Kingdom, where she received the Exeter Research Fellowship. Recent publications include *Midshipmen and Quarterdeck Boys in the British Navy, 1771–1831* and contributions to *The Battle of New Orleans Reconsidered.*

Cori Convertito is curator at the Key West Art & Historical Society in Key West, Florida, and an adjunct instructor at Florida Keys Community College. She holds a PhD from the University of Exeter, where her dissertation was "The Health of British Seamen in the West Indies, 1770–1806."

Rhys Crawley is a historian at the Australian War Memorial, a visiting fellow at the Strategic and Defence Studies Centre, Australian National University, and an adjunct lecturer at the University of New South Wales, Canberra. He is currently writing the official history of Australian operations in Afghanistan, 2005–10. His previous books include *Climax at Gallipoli: The Failure of the August Offensive* (2014) and, with John Blaxland, *The Secret Cold War: The Official History of ASIO 1975–1983* (2016).

J. Ross Dancy is an assistant professor of military history at Sam Houston State University in Texas. He received his DPhil from the University of Oxford, where his research examined British naval manning at the end of the eighteenth century; his *Myth of the Press Gang* was published in 2015. He is a coeditor of and contributed an article to a 2016 collection, *Strategy and the Sea,* in honor of John B. Hattendorf. He served as a U.S. Marine for four years, deploying throughout the western Pacific and the Indian Ocean.

Laura June Davis is an assistant professor of history at Southern Utah University, where she teaches courses in history, women's studies, and social studies education. She received her PhD from the University of Georgia in 2016 and is currently working on a manuscript based on her dissertation about pro-Confederate boat burners operating along the Mississippi River.

Peter J. Dean is a senior fellow at the Strategic and Defence Studies Centre, Australian National University. He is a former Fulbright Scholar in Australia–United States alliance studies, and is the author of *Architect of Victory: Lieutenant General Sir Frank Horton Berryman,* the editor of *Australia 1942: In the Shadow of War* and *Australia 1943: The Liberation of New Guinea,* and a coeditor of *Australia's Defence: Towards a New Era.* He is a former managing editor of *Security Challenges* and a current editorial board member of *Global War Studies.*

Andrew J. Forney received his PhD in 2017 from Texas Christian University with a dissertation entitled "The Federalist Empire: Insecurity and Expansion in the Revolutionary Atlantic, 1793–1800." His scholarship focuses on civil-military relations, race, and the political economy of force. As an active-duty Army officer, Andrew has taught at the U.S. Military Academy and served in several cavalry units, and is preparing to serve as a strategist at the Army Capabilities Integration Center.

Darrell J. Glaser, who received his PhD in economics from the University of Wisconsin–Madison, specializes in the economics of human capital and intrafirm personnel decisions. His most recent research has dealt with career decisions of military personnel. He is an associate professor at the U.S. Naval Academy.

Robert Gudmestad is an associate professor of history at Colorado State University and author of *A Troublesome Commerce: The Transformation of the Interstate Slave Trade* and of *Steamboats and the Rise of the Cotton Kingdom*. He is currently writing a history of naval warfare on western waters during the Civil War.

Carl Cavanagh Hodge is a professor of political science at the University of British Columbia–Okanagan. He is the author or editor of nine books and numerous articles on European and American politics and history, including *The Age of Imperialism, 1800–1914* (2008) and *U.S. Presidents and Foreign Policy, from 1789 to the Present* (2007).

Debra Jackson, an independent scholar, has produced articles and reviews for *African American National Biography, New York History,* and the *Virginia Magazine of History and Biography*. Her current research explores how the inland waterway systems of the southern United States supported slavery in the Louisiana sugar belt. She was an administrator at the Metropolitan Museum of Art in New York and is currently working in academic affairs at Columbia Graduate School of Journalism.

Peter Lorge is an assistant professor of Chinese and military history at Vanderbilt University, specializing in the tenth and eleventh centuries. He is the author, most recently, of *The Reunification of China: Peace through War under the Song Dynasty* and *Chinese Martial Arts: From Antiquity to the Twenty-First Century*. He served as editor of *The Five Dynasties and Ten Kingdoms* and *Debating War in Chinese History*. He also edits the Routledge book series Asian States and Empires and is coeditor of *Chinese and Indian Warfare: From Classical Times until 1870*.

Zachary M. Matusheski is a postdoctoral fellow in the Ohio State University History Department. In 2015, he completed his dissertation at Brandeis University on the history of American foreign policy in the 1950s. His project, entitled "To the Brink of War: East Asian Crises and Dwight D. Eisenhower's New Look," examined the ways the Korean War and other conflicts in East Asia in the 1950s shaped foreign policy reform.

Salvatore R. Mercogliano, an associate professor of history at Campbell University, earned his PhD in military and naval history at the University of Alabama. His articles and reviews have appeared in *Sea History, Parameters, Nautical Research Journal, Northern Mariner,* and *Journal of Military History*. In 2006 he taught at the U.S. Military Academy.

Nathan R. Packard holds a PhD in history from Georgetown University and is an assistant professor at Marine Corps University. His research focuses on military reform, with an emphasis on post-Vietnam reform in the U.S. Marine Corps. He also has taught courses on various aspects of military history for the U.S. Naval War College, the U.S. Naval Academy, and Georgetown University.

Madeleine (Peckham) Shakotko earned a master's degree in history at the University of Saskatchewan in 2015. Her thesis focused on Admiral Edward Vernon and British national identity, 1730–45. Other interests include the participation of Royal Navy personnel in eighteenth-century exploration and imperial expansion. She works for the Order of Malta Federal Association, a Catholic lay religious order in Washington, D.C.

Ahmed S. Rahman received his PhD in economics from the University of California–Davis and is currently an associate professor at the U.S. Naval Academy. His research focuses on the long-run causes and consequences of economic growth and on the historical and contemporary relationships between economic and military power. He has published numerous papers in leading economics journals.

Duncan Redford is Head of Research and Senior Research Fellow, Modern Naval History, at the National Museum of the Royal Navy and Honorary Senior Research Fellow in Modern Naval History at the University of Portsmouth. His doctoral research resulted in *Submarine: A Cultural History from the Great War to Nuclear Combat* (2010). He is the general editor of a series on the history of the Royal Navy, to which he is contributing, as author or coauthor, three volumes. He is a former Royal Navy officer, serving in submarines.

James C. Rentfrow, a designated naval flight officer, is a member of the U.S. Navy's permanent military professor program. Captain Rentfrow earned a doctoral degree at the University of Maryland and currently teaches history at the U.S. Naval Academy. His first book is *Home Squadron: The U.S. Navy on the North Atlantic Station* (2014). He was director of the 2015 McMullen Naval History Symposium.

Dennis Ringle earned master's degrees from Central Michigan University and Eastern Michigan University. Retired from the U.S. Navy in 1997, he taught at Henry Ford College and is the author of *Life in Mr. Lincoln's Navy.*

Richard A. Ruth, who teaches in the Department of History at the U.S. Naval Academy, is a historian of modern Southeast Asian history, specializing in Thailand and Vietnam in the twentieth century. He is the author of *In Buddha's Company: Thai Soldiers in the Vietnam War* (2011). Before earning his PhD in history at Cornell University, he worked as a field agent for American nongovernmental aid organizations in Vietnam, Thailand, and Cambodia. He is the current department chair of the History Department, U.S. Naval Academy.

Gene Allen Smith, a PhD graduate of Auburn University, is currently a professor of history at Texas Christian University (TCU), having served during 2013–14 as the Class of 1957 Distinguished Chair in Naval Heritage at the U.S. Naval Academy. He is author or editor of eight books—including, most recently, *The Slaves' Gamble: Choosing Sides in the War of 1812*—and of numerous articles and reviews. He is the director of the Center for Texas Studies at TCU.

Evan Wilson is associate director of international security studies and lecturer in the History Department at Yale University. He received his DPhil from the University of Oxford, and his first monograph, *A Social History of British Naval Officers, 1775–1815,* recently was published. He contributed to and helped edit the Festschrift for John Hattendorf, *Strategy and the Sea.* His research focuses on the relationship between European militaries and societies in the eighteenth and nineteenth centuries.

Jorit Wintjes, Dr. phil. habil. (Julius-Maximilians-Universität Würzburg, 2003 and 2013), is currently a senior lecturer in ancient history at the Julius-Maximilians-Universität Würzburg. His main research interests include ancient and nineteenth-century naval history.

Maochun Miles Yu is a professor of East Asian military and naval history at the U.S. Naval Academy. His books include *OSS in China: Prelude to Cold War* (1997) and *The Dragon's War: Allied Operations and the Fate of China, 1937–1947* (2006). He received a doctorate in history from the University of California, Berkeley; a master's degree from Swarthmore College; and a bachelor's degree from Nankai University.

NAVAL WAR COLLEGE HISTORICAL MONOGRAPH SERIES

1. *The Writings of Stephen B. Luce,* edited by John D. Hayes and John B. Hattendorf (1975).

3. *Professors of War: The Naval War College and the Development of the Naval Profession,* Ronald Spector (1977).

4. *The Blue Sword: The Naval War College and the American Mission, 1919–1941,* Michael Vlahos (1980).

5. *On His Majesty's Service: Observations of the British Home Fleet from the Diary, Reports, and Letters of Joseph H. Wellings, Assistant U.S. Naval Attaché, London, 1940–1941,* edited by John B. Hattendorf (1983).

7. *A Bibliography of the Works of Alfred Thayer Mahan,* compiled by John B. Hattendorf and Lynn C. Hattendorf (1986).

8. *The Fraternity of the Blue Uniform: Admiral Richard G. Colbert, U.S. Navy and Allied Naval Cooperation,* Joel J. Sokolsky (1991).

9. *The Influence of History on Mahan: The Proceedings of a Conference Marking the Centenary of Alfred Thayer Mahan's* The Influence of Sea Power upon History, 1660–1783, edited by John B. Hattendorf (1991).

10. *Mahan Is Not Enough: The Proceedings of a Conference on the Works of Sir Julian Corbett and Admiral Sir Herbert Richmond,* edited by James Goldrick and John B. Hattendorf (1993).

11. *Ubi Sumus? The State of Naval and Maritime History,* edited by John B. Hattendorf (1994).

12. *The Queenstown Patrol, 1917: The Diary of Commander Joseph Knefler Taussig, U.S. Navy,* edited by William N. Still, Jr. (1996).

13. *Doing Naval History: Essays toward Improvement,* edited by John B. Hattendorf (1995).

14. *An Admiral's Yarn*, edited by Mark R. Shulman (1999).

15. *The Memoirs of Admiral H. Kent Hewitt*, edited by Evelyn Cherpak (2004).

16. *Three Splendid Little Wars: The Diary of Joseph K. Taussig, 1898–1901*, edited by Evelyn Cherpak (2009).

17. *Digesting History: The U.S. Naval War College, the Lessons of World War Two, and Future Naval Warfare, 1945–1947*, Hal M. Friedman (2010).

18. *To Train the Fleet for War: The U.S. Navy Fleet Problems, 1923–1940*, Albert A. Nofi (2010).

19. *Talking about Naval History: A Collection of Essays*, John B. Hattendorf (2011).

20. *New Interpretations in Naval History: Selected Papers from the Sixteenth Naval History Symposium Held at the United States Naval Academy 10–11 September 2009*, edited by Craig C. Felker and Marcus O. Jones (2012).

21. *Blue versus Orange: The U.S. Naval War College, Japan, and the Old Enemy in the Pacific, 1945–1946*, Hal M. Friedman (2013).

22. *Major Fleet-versus-Fleet Operations in the Pacific War, 1941–1945*, Milan Vego (2014).

23. *New Interpretations in Naval History: Selected Papers from the Seventeenth McMullen Naval History Symposium Held at the United States Naval Academy 15–16 September 2011*, edited by Marcus O. Jones (2016).

24. *Blue versus Purple: The U.S. Naval War College, the Soviet Union, and the New Enemy in the Pacific, 1946*, Hal M. Friedman (2017).